PLAYFAIR
CRICKET ANNUAL
1989

42nd edition

EDITED BY ~~~

All statistics ~~~

PLAYFAIR CRICKET COMPETITION 1989
ENGLAND v AUSTRALIA CRICKET QUIZ
£1500 TO BE WON

PLUS NATWEST FINAL TICKETS AND HOSPITALITY
PLUS 25 CONSOLATION PRIZES

First Prize   £500 + overnight accommodation (B & B) at the Westmoreland Hotel (opposite Lord's) on 1 and 2 September + TWO tickets to the 1989 NatWest Trophy Final + NatWest hospitality

Second Prize   £400 + TWO tickets to the 1989 NatWest Trophy Final

Third Prize   £300 + TWO tickets to the 1989 NatWest Trophy Final

Fourth Prize   £200
Fifth Prize   £100

Consolation prizes

Senders of the next 25 correct entries will each receive a copy of HOMES OF CRICKET – THE FIRST-CLASS GROUNDS OF ENGLAND AND WALES by George Plumptre and published by Queen Anne Press at £14.95

Closing date for entries is 12.00 noon on 2 August 1989

Winning entries will be drawn by the Man of the Match Adjudicator at one of the NatWest semi-finals played on Wednesday 16 August

PLAYFAIR CRICKET COMPETITION 1989

TEST CRICKET QUIZ

ENTRY FORM

Please PRINT your answers in the spaces provided and answer every question.

1 Who took the first wicket and held the catch in Test cricket? ....

2 On which ground did three brothers play in a Test match between England and Australia? ....

3 Who made his England debut in the first Test ever staged at Trent Bridge? ....

4 How long did Trevor Bailey take to reach the slowest 50 in first-class cricket? ....

5 Who took only 28 minutes to score 50 in a Test that aroused Queen Victoria's interest? ....

6 How many wickets did Hedley Verity take on 25 June 1934? ....

7 Who is the only Middlesex batsman to score a Test century against Australia at Lord's? ....

8 What is the most runs scored by an England batsman before lunch on the first day? ....

9 Who was the first wicket-keeper to score two fifties in a Test match? ....

10 What exact age was reached by the longest-lived man to play for England v Australia? ....

Your name and address:

....

....

....

Your daytime telephone number: ....

Post to: PLAYFAIR CRICKET COMPETITION, Corporate Affairs, National Westminster Bank PLC, 8th Floor, Finsbury Court, 101/117 Finsbury Pavement, London EC2A 1EH.

Entries must be received before noon on 2 August 1989. All-correct entries will go into the prize-winning draw on 16 August and all winners will be notified individually.

Rules All entries must be on this official form. Proof of posting is not proof of entry. The decision of the editor regarding the answers to this quiz shall be final and binding; no correspondence may be entered into.

1988 PLAYFAIR CRICKET COMPETITION

TEST CRICKET QUIZ ANSWERS

1	Whom did Richard Hadlee dismiss to become the joint leading wicket-taker in Tests?	TONY DODEMAIDE
2	What was Len Hutton's score at close of play on the second day at The Oval in 1938?	300 NOT OUT
3	On which ground did Sunil Gavaskar score his 10,000th run in Test matches?	AHMEDABAD
4	A round-arm off-break bowler, he was the first Test cricketer to die. Who was he?	JAMES SOUTHERTON
5	Who was the first batsman to score 1,000 runs in Test cricket?	ARTHUR SHREWSBURY
6	How many runs did Donald Bradman score on 1 July 1930?	309
7	Who, at the age of 50 years 320 days, was the oldest Test captain?	W.G.GRACE
8	In which year did 27 wickets fall in a day of Test cricket?	1888
9	Who took 16 wickets for 136 runs in his very first Test match?	NARENDRA HIRWANI
10	What is the highest number of runs conceded by a bowler in one Test innings?	298

There were 170 sets of correct answers out of a total of 646 entries. The winners were drawn by Jim Parks (Sussex, Somerset and England) and Glen Emanuel (Campaign Manager, Promotions at NatWest Bank) after the 1988 NatWest Trophy semi-final between Surrey and Middlesex at The Oval.

First Prize:	£500 + two nights accommodation + two tickets and hospitality at the 1988 NatWest Trophy Final	D.H.KNOWLES (Morpeth)
Second Prize:	£400 + two tickets to the 1988 NatWest Trophy Final	M.J.DONALDSON (Berkhamsted)
Third Prize:	£300 + two tickets to the 1988 NatWest Trophy Final	T.C.GREEN (South Ockendon)
Fourth Prize:	£200	R.WALLBRIDGE (Halstead)
Fifth Prize:	£100	M.POPE (Mexborough)

25 Runners-up: each received a copy of *The Wisden Book of Obituaries*.

Mrs E.E.Addiscott (Eastbourne)
M.Barber (Grimsby)
S.C.Batra (New Delhi, India)
M.Berry (Rawtenstall)
B.M.Bond (Glossop)
G.Cotter (Lancaster)
N.Davies (Kirkby-in-Ashfield)
J.B.Duggan (Fernhill Heath, Worcs)
D.G.Edney (Chelmsford)
G.Gibb (Monkseaton)
A.T.Guthrie (Sunderland)
T.M.Hayes (Eastcote)
P.J.Lane (St Thomas, Exeter)

D.Lewis (Chepstow)
N.Mann (Wootton Bassett)
C.O'Rourke (Raunds)
S.J.O'Rourke (Higham Ferrers)
T.Saint (Hertford Heath)
N.S.Smith (Luton)
D.Speers (Cockfosters)
T.J.L.Stokes (Woolacombe)
P.Sumner (Dorchester)
T.P.Synge (Lee, London SE21)
A.Wainwright (Walsgrave, Coventry)
A Waterall (Mapperly, Notts)

EDITORIAL PREFACE

This 42nd edition of 'Playfair' chronicles a period which has added little to cricket's heritage and detracted in some measure from its image as a civilised sport. Amid almost unremitting gloom, the batting performances and modest politeness of Graeme Hick have provided a beacon of hope in a wasteland of dissent and mediocrity. That Test cricket should be deprived of such massive talent until 1991 is, however, to some extent his own fault. Had he chosen to throw in his lot with his native Zimbabwe their chance of swift promotion to Test status must have been considerably enhanced. Much as it desperately needs a player of his class, the England team is in great danger of losing its identity.

This year has already brought about the most vital legislation in the history of the International Cricket Conference and no praise can be too high for the tireless efforts and determination of the TCCB's chairman, Raman Subba Row, to negotiate a set of ground rules to cover players' contact with South Africa which were acceptable to all ICC members. It may not have pleased Mr McWhirter's freedom fighters or the embattled SACU in its bid to coach young cricketers of every hue but it should save Test cricket from further expedient meddling from politicians.

Some might question whether Test cricket in its present form is worth saving. With its high physical risk against the sort of 'rollerball' attack Douglas Jardine must have dreamt of commanding, batting against the current West Indies team has little association with sport. It has virtually become a form of jousting but it is hard to see what measures could be introduced to compel teams to field balanced attacks. Perhaps the Sydney curator had the perfect answer: slow turning pitches.

This is a vital summer for English cricket with an enthralling Ashes series in prospect. England with the visionary 'Lord Ted' at the helm are unlikely to underestimate the potential of an Australian team which includes the immense talent of Steve Waugh and has as captain that most indomitable and durable of the current national skippers, Allan Border.

My thanks again go to NatWest and particularly to Glen Emanuel, their Campaign Manager, for their sponsorship and for funding and administering our annual competition with its generous prizes of NatWest Final tickets, accommodation and hospitality.

Other debts of gratitude are due to Richard Beswick of Queen Anne Press for his calm control of production and publication, to Geoffrey Saulez and Vic Isaacs for their familiar contributions, and to Debbie Brown for cheerfully attacking the chore of proof-checking.

BILL FRINDALL

AUSTRALIA v ENGLAND (Bicentenary Test)

Played at Sydney Cricket Ground on 29, 30, 31 January and 1, 2 February 1988
Toss: England. Result: match drawn
Debuts: nil

ENGLAND

B.C. Broad b Waugh	139
M.D. Moxon b Sleep	40
R.T. Robinson c Veletta b Dodemaide	43
*M.W. Gatting c Dyer b Waugh	13
C.W.J. Athey c and b Taylor	37
D.J. Capel c Sleep b Taylor	21
J.E. Emburey st Dyer b Sleep	23
†B.N. French st Dyer b Taylor	47
N.A. Foster c Border b Taylor	19
E.E. Hemmings not out	8
G.R. Dilley b Waugh	13
Extras (B4, LB9, W1, NB8)	22
Total	**425**

AUSTRALIA

D.C. Boon c French b Foster	12	not out	184
G.R. Marsh c French b Capel	5	c Athey b Emburey	56
D.M. Jones c Emburey b Hemmings	56	c Moxon b Capel	24
*A.R. Border c Broad b Capel	2	not out	48
M.R.J. Veletta c Emburey b Hemmings	22		
S.R. Waugh c French b Dilley	27		
P.R. Sleep c Athey b Foster	41		
†G.C. Dyer lbw b Dilley	0		
P.L. Taylor c French b Hemmings	20		
A.I.C. Dodemaide not out	12		
C.J. McDermott c Foster b Dilley	1		
Extras (LB10, W1, NB5)	16	(B3, LB7, NB6)	16
Total	**214**	**(2 wickets)**	**328**

AUSTRALIA	O	M	R	W	O	M	R	W	FALL OF WICKETS			
										E	A	A
McDermott	35	8	65	0					Wkt	1st	1st	2nd
Dodemaide	36	10	98	1					1st	93	18	162
Taylor	34	10	84	4					2nd	192	25	218
Waugh	22.5	5	51	3					3rd	245	34	—
Sleep	45	8	114	2					4th	262	82	—
ENGLAND									5th	313	116	—
Dilley	19.1	4	54	3	13	1	48	0	6th	314	147	—
Foster	19	6	27	2	15	6	27	0	7th	346	153	—
Emburey	30	10	57	0	38	5	98	1	8th	387	183	—
Capel	6	3	13	2	17	4	38	1	9th	410	209	—
Hemmings	22	3	53	3	52	15	107	0	10th	425	214	—

Umpires: A.R. Crafter and P.J. McConnell
M.R.J. Veletta kept wicket briefly at the end of England's innings after G.C. Dyer had been injured.

Test No. 1090/263

NEW ZEALAND v ENGLAND (1st Test)

Played at Lancaster Park, Christchurch, on 12, 13, 14, 16, 17 February 1988
Toss: New Zealand. Result: match drawn
Debuts: England – P.W. Jarvis
‡(M.J. Greatbatch)

ENGLAND

B.C. Broad c Smith b Sneddon	114	c sub‡ b Chatfield	20
M.D. Moxon c Jones b Morrison	1	c Jones b Chatfield	27
R.T. Robinson c Smith b Morrison	70	c Wright b Chatfield	2
R.T. Robinson c Smith b Morrison	70	c Wright b Chatfield	2
*M.W. Gatting c sub‡ b Morrison	8	b Snedden	23
C.W.J. Athey c sub‡ b Morrison	22	c Smith b Snedden	19
D.J. Capel c Bracewell b Chatfield	42	c M.D. Crowe b Chatfield	19
J.E. Emburey c Jones b Morrison	7	run out	0
†B.N. French c Smith b Chatfield	7	c J.J. Crowe b Sneddon	3
P.A.J. DeFreitas c Morrison b Chatfield	4	lbw b Snedden	16
P.W. Jarvis c Smith b Chatfield	14	not out	10
G.R. Dilley not out	7	c Jones b Morrison	2
Extras (LB11, W1, NB7)	19	(LB7, NB4)	11
Total	**319**		**152**

NEW ZEALAND

J.G. Wright c Moxon b Dilley	10	lbw b Dilley	23
T.J. Franklin c Athey b Dilley	10	lbw b Dilley	12
A.H. Jones c French	8	not out	54
M.D. Crowe c Moxon b Dilley	5	c French b Harvis	6
*J.J. Crowe c French b DeFreitas	28	lbw d DeFreitas	0
J.G. Bracewell c French b Dilley	31	not out	20
R.J. Hadlee c French b Dilley	37		
†I.D.S. Smith c Capel b Jarvis	13		
M.C. Snedden lbw b DeFreitas	0		
D.K. Morrison b Jarvis	0		
E.J. Chatfield not out	0	(B6, LB4, NB5)	15
Extras (B2, LB12, NB12)	26		
Total	**168**	**(4 wickets)**	**130**

NEW ZEALAND	O	M	R	W	O	M	R	W
Hadlee	18	3	50	0	21.1	4	64	1
Morrison	21.1	3	69	5	30	13	36	4
Chatfield	42	13	87	4	23	8	45	4
Snedden	33	9	86	1				
Bracewell	6	1	16	0				
ENGLAND								
DeFreitas	22	6	39	2	19	6	26	1
Dilley	24.5	9	38	6	18	5	32	2
Capel	10	2	32	0	13	5	16	0
Jarvis	21	8	43	2	17	7	30	1
Emburey	4	3	2	0	10	4	16	0

FALL OF WICKETS

	E	NZ	E	NZ
Wkt	1st	1st	2nd	2nd
1st	7	20	32	37
2nd	175	25	38	43
3rd	187	32	55	61
4th	219	40	95	78
5th	237	96	96	—
6th	241	131	99	—
7th	248	151	118	—
8th	260	155	125	—
9th	285	156	147	—
10th	319	168	152	—

Umpires: B.L. Aldrige and S.J. Woodward

Test No. 1091/64

NEW ZEALAND v ENGLAND (2nd Test)

Played at Eden Park, Auckland, on 25, 26, 27, 28, 29 February 1988
Toss: England. Result: match drawn
Debuts: New Zealand – M.J.G. Greatbatch

NEW ZEALAND

J.G. Wright c French b Dilley	103		c French b Radford	49
T.J. Franklin b Jarvis	27		b Dilley	62
*J.J. Crowe c Capel b Dilley	11		lbw b Dilley	1
M.D. Crowe c Capel b Emburey	36		lbw b Jarvis	26
M.J. Greatbatch c French b Dilley	11		not out	107
K.R. Rutherford b Capel	29		b Emburey	2
J.G. Bracewell c Moxon b Dilley	9	(8)	lbw b Gatting	38
†I.D.S. Smith c French b Jarvis	23	(9)	not out	23
M.C. Snedden c Moxon b Dilley	14	(7)	c French b Capel	20
D.K. Morrison not out	14			
E.J. Chatfield c French b Capel	10			
Extras (B1, LB2, W2, NB9)	14		(B8, LB8, NB6)	22
Total	**301**		**(7 wickets declared)**	**350**

ENGLAND

B.C. Broad c M.D. Crowe b Bracewell	9
M.D. Moxon c J.J. Crowe b Chatfield	99
R.T. Robinson c Morrison b Bracewell	54
*M.W. Gatting c Smith b Morrison	42
N.H. Fairbrother c Smith b Chatfield	1
D.J. Capel c Bracewell b Morrison	5
J.E. Emburey c Smith b Chatfield	45
†B.N. French c Franklin b Bracewell	13
P.W. Jarvis c Smith b Sneddon	10
N.V. Radford b Chatfield	8
G.R. Dilley not out	8
Extras (B12, LB12, NB5)	29
Total	**323**

ENGLAND	O	M	R	W	O	M	R	W	FALL OF WICKETS			
										NZ	E	NZ
Dilley	28	9	60	5	23	9	44	2	Wkt	1st	1st	2nd
Jarvis	33	9	74	2	27	7	54	1	1st	77	27	117
Radford	30	4	79	0	20	4	53	1	2nd	98	135	119
Capel	26.2	4	57	2	21	4	40	1	3rd	169	211	119
Emburey	17	7	28	1	57	24	91	1	4th	191	220	150
Gatting					17	4	40	1	5th	207	222	153
Fairbrother					2	0	9	0	6th	219	234	232
Moxon					2	0	3	0	7th	254	267	296
NEW ZEALAND									8th	262	282	—
Morrison	32	7	95	2					9th	279	308	—
Chatfield	31.1	15	37	4					10th	301	323	—
Bracewell	39	8	88	3								
Snedden	34	14	71	1								
Rutherford	5	1	8	0								

Umpires: F.R. Goodall and R.L. McHarg

Test No. 1092/65

NEW ZEALAND v ENGLAND (3rd Test)

Played at Basin Reserve, Wellington, on 3, 4, 5, 6‡, 7 March 1988
Toss: New Zealnd. Result: match drawn
Debuts: New Zealand – R.H. Vance   ‡(no play)

NEW ZEALAND

*J.G. Wright c Fairbrother b Capel		36
T.J. Franklin lbw b DeFreitas		14
R.H. Vance run out		47
M.D. Crowe lbw b Gatting		143
M.J. Greatbatch c DSeFreitas b Emburey		68
K.R. Rutherford not out		107
J.G. Bracewell c Fairbrother b Capel		54
†I.D.S. Smith not out		33
S.J. Boock		
D.K. Morrison } did not bat		
E.J. Chatfield		
Extras (LB10)		10
Total (6 wickets declared)		512

ENGLAND

B.C. Broad b Boock		61
M.D. Moxon not out		81
R.T. Robinson c Smith b Chatfield		0
*M.W. Gatting not out		33
N.H. Fairbrother		
D.J. Capel		
J.E. Emburey		
†B.N. French } did not bat		
P.A.J. DeFreitas		
E.E. Hemmings		
G.R. Dilley		
Extras (LB6, NB2)		8
Total (2 wickets)		183

ENGLAND	O	M	R	W
Dilley	11	1	36	0
Defreitas	50.1	21	110	1
Capel	39	7	129	2
Emburey	45.5	10	99	1
Hemmings	45	15	107	0
Gatting	6	1	21	1
NEW ZEALAND				
Morrison	6	0	41	0
Chatfield	23	10	38	1
Bracewell	23	9	44	0
Boock	26	9	53	1
Rutherford	1	0	1	0

FALL OF WICKETS

	NZ	E		
Wkt	1st	1st	2nd	2nd
1st	33	129		
2nd	79	132		
3rd	132	—		
4th	287	—		
5th	336	—		
6th	470	—		
7th	—	—		
8th	—	—		
9th	—	—		
10th	—	—		

Umpires: B.L. Aldrige and S.J. Woodward

Test No. 1093/66

9

NEW ZEALAND v ENGLAND AVERAGES

NEW ZEALAND – BATTING AND FIELDING

	M	I	NO	HS	Runs	Avge	100	50	Ct/St
M.J. Greatbatch	2	3	1	107*	186	93.00	1	1	—
K.R. Rutherford	2	3	1	107*	138	69.00	1	—	—
I.D.S. Smith	3	4	2	33*	92	46.00	—	—	10
J.G. Wright	3	5	0	103	221	44.20	1	—	1
M.D. Crowe	3	5	0	143	216	43.20	1	—	2
J.G. Bracewell	3	5	1	54	152	38.00	—	1	2
T.J. Franklin	3	5	0	62	125	25.00	—	1	1
D.K. Morrison	3	2	1	14*	14	14.00	—	—	2
M.C. Snedden	2	3	0	20	34	11.33	—	—	—
J.J. Crowe	2	4	0	28	40	10.00	—	—	2
E.J. Chatfield	3	2	1	10	10	10.00	—	—	—

Played in one Test: S.L. Boock did not bat; R.J. Hadlee 37; A.H. Jones 8, 54* (4 ct); R.H. Vance 47.

NEW ZEALAND – BOWLING

	Overs	Mdns	Runs	Wkts	Avge	Best	5 wI	10 wM
E.J. Chatfield	126.1	51	198	13	15.23	4-36	—	—
D.K. Morrison	80.2	14	269	8	33.62	5-69	1	—
M.C. Snedden	90	31	202	6	33.66	4-45	—	—

Also bowled: S.L. Boock 26-9-53-1; J.G. Bracewell 68-18-148-3; R.J. Hadlee 18-3-50-0; K.R. Rutherford 6-1-9-0.

ENGLAND – BATTING AND FIELDING

	M	I	NO	HS	Runs	Avge	100	50	Ct/St
M.D. Moxon	3	4	1	99	208	69.33	—	2	4
B.C. Broad	3	4	0	114	204	51.00	1	1	—
J.E. Emburey	3	3	0	45	106	35.33	—	—	—
M.W. Gatting	3	4	1	42	106	35.33	—	—	—
R.T. Robinson	3	4	0	70	126	31.50	—	2	—
P.W. Jarvis	2	3	1	14	34	17.00	—	—	—
G.R. Dilley	3	3	2	8*	17	17.00	—	—	1
P.A.J. DeFreitas	2	2	0	16	20	10.00	—	—	1
B.N. French	3	3	0	13	23	7.66	—	—	11
D.J. Capel	3	3	0	11	16	5.33	—	—	3
N.H. Fairbrother	2	1	0	1	1	1.00	—	—	3

Played in one Test: C.W.J. Athey 22, 19 (1 ct); E.E. Hemmings did not bat; N.V. Radford 8.

ENGLAND – BOWLING

	Overs	Mdns	Runs	Wkts	Avge	Best	5 wI	10 wM
G.R. Dilley	104.5	33	210	15	14.00	6-38	2	—
P.W. Jarvis	98	31	201	6	33.50	2-43	—	—
P.A.J. DeFreitas	91.1	33	175	4	43.75	2-39	—	—
D.J. Capel	109.2	22	274	5	54.80	2-57	—	—

Also bowled: J.E. Emburey 133.5-48-236-3; N.H. Fairbrother 2-0-9-0; M.W. Gatting 23-5-61-2; E.E. Hemmings 45-15-107-0; M.D. Moxon 2-0-3-0; N.V. Radford 50-8-132-1.

AUSTRALIA v SRI LANKA (Only Test)

Played at W.A.C.A. Ground, Perth, on 12, 13, 14, 15 February 1988
Toss: Australia. Result: Australia won by an innings and 108 runs
Debuts: Sri Lanka – C.P. Ramanayake

AUSTRALIA

G.R. Marsh b Labrooy	53
D.C. Boon b Ratnayeke	64
D.M. Jones lbw b Labrooy	102
*A.R. Border b Ratnayeke	88
M.R.J. Veletta c de Alwis b Ratnayeke	21
S.R. Waugh c Labrooy b Amalean	20
†G.C. Dyer c Ramanayake b Amalean	38
P.L. Taylor c Amalean b Ratnayeke	18
A.I.C. Dodemaide not out	16
C.J. McDermott c de Alwis b Amalean	4
M.G. Hughes b Amalean	8
Extras (LB12, W5, NB6)	23
Total	**455**

SRI LANKA

R.S. Mahanama c Dyer b Dodemaide	41	run out	28
D.S.B.P. Kuruppu c Marsh b McDermott	19	c Dyer b Dodemaide	3
S.M.S. Kaluperuma lbw b McDermott	0	c and b Hughes	6
P.A. De Silva lbw b Waugh	6	lbw b Dodemaide	7
A. Ranatunga c and b Waugh	55	lbw b Dodemaide	45
*R.S. madugalle c Border b Dodemaide	6	c Waugh b Hughes	7
J.R. Rathnayeke c Marsh b McDermott	24	c Dyer b Dodemaide	38
†R.G. de Alwis c Dyer b Waugh	0	c Waugh b Hughes	8
C.P.H. Ramanayake c Dyer b Waugh	9	c Veletta b Hughes	0
G.F. Labrooy c Dyer b Dodemaide	4	b Hughes	4
K.N. Amalean not out	7	not out 0	
Extras (B1, LB6, W2, NB14)	23	(LB6, NB1)	7
Total	**194**		**153**

SRI LANKA	O	M	R	W	O	M	R	W	FALL OF WICKETS			
										A	SL	SL
Ratnayeke	40	6	98	4					Wkt	1st	1st	2nd
Labrooy	36	5	108	2					1st	120	51	36
Ramanayake	17	2	58	0					2nd	133	51	42
Amalean	22.2	1	97	4					3rd	289	60	42
Kaluperuma	13	0	62	0					4th	346	93	66
Ranatunga	8	2	18	0					5th	346	107	83
De Silva	1	0	3	0					6th	380	147	111
AUSTRALIA									7th	418	148	130
McDermott	20	3	50	3	4	2	8	0	8th	434	181	131
Hughes	18	2	61	0	21	7	67	5	9th	443	182	153
Dodemaide	22.3	6	40	2	19.1	7	58	4	10th	455	194	153
Waugh	20	7	33	4	8	4	14	0				
Taylor	2	1	3	0								

Umpires: R.C. Bailhache and P.J. McConnell

Test No. 1094/2

WEST INDIES v PAKISTAN (1st Test)

Played at Bourda, Georgetown, on 2, 3, 4, 6 April 1988
Toss: West Indies. Result: Pakistan won by 9 wickets
Debuts: West Indies – C.E.L. Ambrose

WEST INDIES

D.L. Haynes c Salim Yousuf b Imran	1	b Ijaz Faqih	5
P.V. Simmons b Ijaz Faqih	16	b Qadir	11
R.B. Richardson c Shoaib b Imran	75	c Salim Yousuf b Qadir	16
*C.G. Greenidge c Salim Malik b Wasim	17	b Imran	43
A.L. Logie lbw b Qadir	80	c Salim Yousuf b Imran	24
C.L. Hooper c Wasim b Imran	33	c Salim Malik b Qadir	30
†P.J.L. Dujon lbw b Imran	15	c Imran b Shoaib	11
W.K.M. Benjamin lbw b Imran	2	c Miandad b Shoaib	0
C.A. Walsh b Imran	7	c Salim Yousuf b Imran	14
C.E.L. Ambrose not out	25	not out	1
B.P. Patterson b Imran	10	b Imran	0
Extras (B2, LB3, W2, NB6)	11	(B4, LB8, NB5)	17
Total	**292**		**172**

PAKISTAN

Mudassar Nazar b Ambrose	29	lbw b Paterson	0
Ramiz Raja c Haynes b Patterson	5	not out	18
Shoaib Mohammad c Greenidge b Walsh	46	not out	13
Javed Miandad b Patterson	114		
Salim Malik c Greenidge b Patterson	27		
Ijaz Ahmed c Haynes b Ambrose	31		
*Imran Khan c Simmons b Benjamin	24		
†Salim Yousuf lbw b Walsh	62		
Ijaz Faqih b Hooper	5		
Abdul Qadir b Walsh	19		
Wasim Akram not out	2		
Extras (B21, LB8, W4, NB38)	71	(NB1)	1
Total	**435**	(1 wicket)	**32**

PAKISTAN	O	M	R	W	O	M	R	W	FALL OF WICKETS				
Imran	22.4	2	80	7	14.4	0	41	4		WI	P	WI	P
Wasim	14	5	41	1	6	1	7	0	Wkt	1st	1st	2nd	2nd
Ijaz Faqih	14	0	60	1	15	4	38	1	1st	7	20	18	0
Qadir	24	2	91	1	25	5	66	3	2nd	41	57	34	—
Mudassar	5	2	9	0					3rd	95	127	44	—
Salim Malik	1	0	6	0					4th	144	217	109	—
WEST INDIES									5th	220	297	120	—
Patterson	24	1	82	3	2	0	19	1	6th	244	300	145	—
Ambrose	28	5	108	2	1.3	0	13	0	7th	248	364	145	—
Walsh	27	4	80	3					8th	249	383	166	—
Benjamin	31	3	99	1					9th	258	423	172	—
Hooper	12	0	37	1					10th	292	435	172	—

Umpires: D.M. Archer and L.H. Baker

Test No. 1095/23

WEST INDIES v PAKISTAN (2nd Test)

Played at Queen's Park Oval, Port-of-Spain, on 14, 15, 16, 17, 19 April 1988
Toss: Pakistan. Result: match drawn
Debuts: nil ‡(Naved Anjum)

WEST INDIES

C.G. Greenidge c Ijaz Ahmed b Imran	1	c sub‡ b Imran	29
D.L. Haynes lbw b Wasim	17	c Ijaz Ahmed b Imran	0
R.B. Richardson c Qadir b Wasim	42	c Salim Yousuf b Imran	40
A.L. Logie c Miandad b Qadir	18	b Imran	1
*I.V.A. Richards c Miandad b Qadir	49	lbw b Wasim	123
C.L. Hooper c Salim Yousuf b Qadir	0	c Ijaz Ahmed b Qadir	26
†P.J.L. Dujon c Salim Yousuf b Imran	24	not out	106
M.D. Marshall not out	10	b Qadir	2
C.E.L. Ambrose lbw b Imran	4	lbw b Qadir	9
W.K.M. Benjamin b Qadir	0	lbw b Qadir	16
C.A. Walsh b Imran	5	st Salim Yousuf b Qadir	12
Extras (LB2, NB2)	4	(B9, LB44, NB4)	27
Total	**174**		**391**

PAKISTAN

Mudassar Nazar c Haynes b Marshall	14		c Dujon b Benjamin	13
Ramiz Raja c Richardson b Marshall	1		c Richardson b Marshall	44
Shoaib Mohammad c Richards b Ambrose	14		b Benjamin	0
Javed Miandad b Benjamin	18		c Richards b Ambrose	102
Ijaz Faqih c Richards b Benjamin	0	(10)	not out	10
Salim Malik c Logie b Hooper	66	(5)	lbw b Walsh	30
Ijaz Ahmed c Logie b Benjamin	3		st Dujon b Richards	43
*Imran Khan c Logie b Marshall	4	(6)	c Dujon b Benjamin	1
†Salim Yousuf c Dujon b Marshall	39	(8)	lbw b Richards	35
Wasim Akram run out	7	(9)	c Hooper b Marshall	2
Abdul Qadir not out	17		not out	0
Extras (B1, LB4, NB8)	13		(B17, LB17, W2, NB25)	61
Total	**194**		**(9 wickets)**	**341**

PAKISTAN	O	M	R	W	O	M	R	W		FALL OF WICKETS			
Imran	16.3	2	38	4	45	9	115	5			WI	P	WI	P
Wasim	14	4	35	2	25	4	75	1		Wkt	1st	1st	2nd	2nd
Ijaz faqih	3	0	13	0	4	0	22	0		1st	2	3	1	60
Mudassar	1	0	3	0						2nd	25	25	55	62
Qadir	19	2	83	4	47.4	6	148	4		3rd	80	46	66	67
WEST INDIES										4th	89	49	81	153
Marshall	20	4	55	4	30	4	85	2		5th	89	50	175	169
Ambrose	14	3	44	1	30	7	62	1		6th	147	62	272	282
Walsh	8	1	23	0	29	8	52	1		7th	157	68	284	288
Benjamin	8	0	32	3	32	9	73	3		8th	166	162	301	311
Hooper	9.1	1	35	1	4	1	18	0		9th	167	170	357	341
Richards					4	1	17	2		10th	174	194	391	—

Umpires: L.H. Barker and C.E. Cumberbatch Test No. 1096/24

13

WEST INDIES v PAKISTAN (3rd Test)

Played at Kensington Oval, Bridgetown, on 22, 23, 24, 26, 27 April 1988
Toss: West Indies. Result: West Indies won by 2 wickets
Debuts: nil

PAKISTAN

Mudassar Nazar b Ambrose	18		c Greenidge b Hooper	41
Ramiz Raja c Greenidge b Benjamin	54		c Logie b Marshall	4
Shoaib Mohammad c Greenidge b Ambrose	54		c and b Richards	64
Javed Miandad c Richardson b Marshall	14		c Dujon b Marshall	34
Salim Malik b Hooper	15		lbw b Benjamin	9
Aamer Malik c Hooper b Benjamin	32		c Logie b Marshall	2
*Imran Khan c Dujon b Benjamin	18		not out	43
†Salim Yousuf retired hurt	32	(9)	c Richards b Benjamin	28
Wasim Akram c Benjamin b Marshall	38	(8)	lbw b Marshall	0
Abdul Qadir c Walsh b Marshall	17		c Greenidge b Marshall	2
Salim Jaffer not out	1		b Ambrose	4
Extras (LB7, NB9)	16		(B3, LB14, NB14)	31
Total	**309**			**262**

WEST INDIES

C.G. Greenidge lbw b Imran	10		c Shoaib b Salim Jaffer	35
D.L. Haynes c Aamer b Mudassar	48		c Salim Malik b Wasim	4
R.B. Richardson c Aamer b Wasim	3		st Aamer b Qadir	64
C.L. Hooper b Wasim	54		run out	13
*I.V.A. Richards c Mudassar b Wasim	67		b Wasim	30
A.L. Logie c Miandad b Mudassar	0		b Qadir	3
†P.J.L. Dujon run out	0	(8)	not out	29
M.D. Marshall c Aamer b Imran	48	(9)	lbw b Wasim	15
E.L.C. Ambrose lbw b Imran	7	(7)	c Salim Jaffer b Wasim	1
W.K.M. Benjamin run out	31		not out	40
C.A. Walsh not out	14			
Extras (B5, LB11, NB8)	24		(B9, LB6, NB10)	25
Total	**306**		**(8 wickets)**	**268**

WEST INDIES	O	M	R	W	O	M	R	W		FALL OF WICKETS			
Marshall	18.4	3	79	4	23	3	65	5			P	WI	P	WI
Ambrose	14	0	64	2	26.5	3	74	1	Wkt	1st	1st	2nd	2nd
Benjamin	14	3	52	3	15	1	37	2	1st	46	18	6	21
Walsh	10	1	53	0	12	1	22	0	2nd	99	21	100	78
Richards	6	0	19	0	7	3	8	1	3rd	128	100	153	118
Hooper	12	3	35	0	10	1	39	1	4th	155	198	165	128
PAKISTAN									5th	186	198	167	150
Imran	25	3	108	3	6	0	34	0	6th	215	199	169	159
Wasim	27	1	88	3	31	7	73	5	7th	218	201	182	180
Qadir	15	1	35	0	32	5	115	2	8th	297	225	234	207
Salim Jaffer	7	1	35	0	5	0	25	1	9th	309	283	245	—
Mudassar	10	4	24	2					10th	—	306	262	—
Shoaib					3	1	6	0					

Umpires: D.M. Archer and L.H. Barker

Test No. 1097/25

In Pakistan's first innings, Salim Yousuf retired at 285-7. Aamer Malik kept wicket in both innings of the West Indies.

14

WEST INDIES v PAKISTAN AVERAGES

WEST INDIES – BATTING AND FIELDING

	M	I	NO	HS	Runs	Avge	100	50	Ct/St
I.V.A. Richards	2	4	0	123	278	69.50	1	1	6
P.J.L. Dujon	3	6	2	106*	185	46.25	1	—	5/1
R.B. Richardson	3	6	0	75	240	40.00	—	2	2
C.L. Hooper	3	6	0	54	156	26.00	—	1	2
M.D. Marshall	2	4	1	48	75	25.00	—	—	—
C.G. Greenidge	3	6	0	43	135	22.50	—	—	6
A.L. Logie	3	6	0	80	126	21.00	—	1	5
W.K.M. Benjamin	3	6	1	40*	89	17.80	—	—	1
C.A. Walsh	3	5	1	14*	52	13.00	—	—	1
D.L. Haynes	3	6	0	48	75	12.50	—	—	3
C.E.L. Ambrose	3	6	2	25*	47	11.75	—	—	—

Played in one Test: B.P. Patterson 10, 0; P.V. Simmons 16,11 (1 ct).

WEST INDIES – BOWLING

	Overs	Mdns	Runs	Wkts	Avge	Best	5 wI	10 wM
M.D. Marshall	91.4	14	284	15	18.93	5-65	1	—
W.K.M. Benjamin	100	16	293	12	24.41	3-32	—	—
B.P. Patterson	26	1	101	4	25.25	3-82	—	—
C.E.L. Ambrose	114.2	18	365	7	52.14	2-64	—	—
C.A. Walsh	86	15	230	4	57.50	3-80	—	—

Also bowled: C.L. Hooper 47.1-6-164-3; I.V.A. Richards 17-4-44-3.

PAKISTAN – BATTING AND FIELDING

	M	I	NO	HS	Runs	Avge	100	50	Ct/St
Javed Miandad	3	5	0	114	282	56.40	2	—	4
Salim Yousuf	3	5	1	62	196	49.00	—	1	7/1
Shoaib Mohammad	3	6	1	64	189	37.80	—	2	2
Salim Malik	3	5	0	66	147	29.40	—	1	3
Ijaz Ahmed	2	3	0	43	77	25.66	—	—	3
Ramiz Raja	3	6	1	54	126	25.20	—	1	—
Imran Khan	3	5	1	43*	90	22.50	—	—	1
Mudassar Nazar	3	6	0	41	115	19.16	—	—	1
Abdul Qadir	3	5	2	19	55	18.33	—	—	1
Wasim Akram	3	5	1	38	49	12.25	—	—	1
Ijaz Faqih	2	3	1	10*	15	7.50	—	—	—

Played in one Test: Aamer Malik 32, 2 (3 ct, 1 st). Salim Jaffer 1*, 4 (1 ct).

PAKISTAN – BOWLING

	Overs	Mdns	Runs	Wkts	Avge	Best	5 wI	10 wM
Imran Khan	129.5	16	416	23	18.08	7-80	2	1
Wasim Akram	117	22	319	11	29.00	4-73	—	—
Abdul Qadir	162.4	21	538	14	38.42	4-83	—	—

Also bowled: Ijaz Faqih 36-4-133-2; Mudassar Nazar 16-6-36-2; Salim Jaffer 12-1-60-1; Salim Malik 1-0-6-0; Shoaib Mohammad 8-1-22-2.

ENGLAND v WEST INDIES (1st Test)

Played at Trent Bridge, Nottingham, on 2, 3, 4, 6, 7 June 1988
Toss: England. Result: match drawn
Debuts: nil

ENGLAND

G.A. Gooch	b Marshall	73	c Dujon b Patterson	146
B.C. Broad	b Marshall	54	c Dujon b Ambrose	16
*M.W. Gatting	c Logie b Marshall	5	b Marshall	29
D.I. Gower	c Dujon b Ambrose	18	not out	88
A.J. Lamb	lbw b Marshall	0	not out	6
D.R. Pringle	b Marshall	39		
†P.R. Downton	not out	16		
J.E. Emburey	c Dujon b Marshall	0		
P.A.J. DeFreitas	b Ambrose	3		
P.W. Jarvis	b Ambrose	6		
G.R. Dilley	b Ambrose	2		
Extras	(LB13, W5, NB11)	29	(LB10, NB6)	167
Total		**245**	(3 wickets)	**301**

WEST INDIES

C.G. Greenidge	c Downton b Jarvis	25
D.L. Haynes	c Downton b Jarvis	60
R.B. Richardson	c Gatting b Emburey	17
*I.V.A. Richards	c Gooch b DeFreitas	80
C.L. Hooper	c Downton b DeFreitas	84
A.L. Logie	c Gooch b Pringle	20
†P.J.L. Dujon	c and b Dilley	16
M.D. Marshall	b Emburey	72
C.E.L. Ambrose	run out (Gooch)	43
C.A. Walsh	not out	3
B.P. Patterson	did not bat	
Extras	(B6, LB8, NB14)	28
Total (9 wickets declared)		**448**

WEST INDIES	O	M	R	W	O	M	R	W	FALL OF WICKETS			
										E	WI	E
Marshall	30	4	69	6	13	4	23	1				
Patterson	16	2	49	0	24	6	69	1	*Wkt*	*1st*	*1st*	*2nd*
Ambrose	26	10	53	4	23	4	56	1	1st	125	54	39
Walsh	20	4	39	0	25	5	84	0	2nd	141	84	116
Hooper	8	1	20	0	14	1	33	0	3rd	161	159	277
Richards	1	0	2	0	9	1	26	0	4th	161	231	—
ENGLAND									5th	186	271	—
Dilley	34	5	101	1					6th	223	309	—
DeFreitas	27	5	93	2					7th	223	334	—
Jarvis	18.1	1	63	2					8th	235	425	—
Pringle	34	11	82	1					9th	243	448	—
Emburey	16	4	95	2					10th	245	—	—

Umpires: H.D. Bird and J. Birkenshaw

Test No. 1098/91

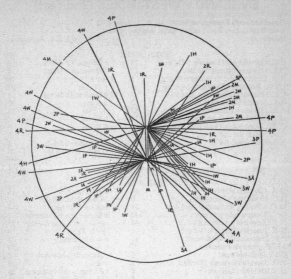

BOWLER	SYMBOL	BALLS	RUNS ·				TOTAL
			1	2	3	4	
AMBROSE	A	48	5	1	2	1	17
HOOPER	H	41	13	·	·	1	17
MARSHALL	M	64	3	5	·	1	17
PATTERSON	P	72	8	3	2	4	36
RICHARDS	R	26	7	1	·	2	17
WALSH	W	52	5	2	3	6	42
TOTALS		303	41	12	7	15	146

GRAHAM GOOCH
at Trent Bridge

146 RUNS
303 BALLS
410 MINUTES

© BILL FRINDALL 1988

17

ENGLAND v WEST INDIES (2nd Test)

Played at Lord's London, on 16, 17, 18, 20, 21 June1 1988
Toss: West Indies. Result: West Indies won by 134 runs
Debuts: nil

‡(K.L.T. Arthurton)

WEST INDIES

C.G. Greenidge	c Downton b Dilley	27	c Emburey b Dilley	103
D.L. Haynes	c Moxon b Dilley	12	c Downton b Dilley	5
R.B. Richardson	c Emburey b Dilley	5	lbw b Pringle	26
*I.V.A. Richards	c Downton b Dilley	6	b Pringle	72
C.L. Hooper	c Downton b Small	3	c Downton b Jarvis	11
A.L. Logie	c Emburey b Small	81	not out	95
†P.J.L. Dujon	b Emburey	53	b Jarvis	52
M.D. Marshall	c Gooch b Dilley	11	b Jarvis	6
C.E.L. Ambrose	c Gower b Small	0	b Dilley	0
C.A. Walsh	not out	9	b Dilley	0
B.P. Patterson	b Small	0	c Downton b Jarvis	2
Extras	(LB6, NB1)	7	(LB19, W1, NB5)	25
Total		**209**		**397**

ENGLAND

G.A. Gooch	b Marshall	44	lbw b Marshall	16
B.C. Broad	lbw b Marshall	0	c Dujon b Marshall	1
M.D. Moxon	c Richards b Ambrose	26	run out (Patterson)	1
D.I. Gower	c sub‡ b Walsh	46	c Richardson b Patterson	1
A.J. Lamb	lbw b Marshall	10	run out (Hooper/Walsh)	113
D.R. Pringle	c Dujon b Walsh	1	lbw b Walsh	0
†P.R. Downton	lbw b Marshall	11	lbw b Marshall	27
*J.E. Emburey	b Patterson	7	b Ambrose	30
G.C. Small	not out	5	c Richards b Marshall	7
P.W. Jarvis	c Haynes b Marshall	7	not out	29
G.R. Dilley	b Marshall	0	c Richardson b Patterson	28
Extras	(LB6, NB2)	8	(B5, LB20, W2, NB14)	41
Total		**165**		**307**

ENGLAND	O	M	R	W	O	M	R	W	FALL OF WICKETS				
Dilley	23	6	55	5	27	6	73	4		WI	E	WI	E
Jarvis	13	2	47	0	26	3	107	4	Wkt	1st	1st	2nd	2nd
Small	18.5	5	64	4	19	1	76	0	1st	21	13	32	27
Pringle	7	3	20	0	21	4	60	2	2nd	40	58	115	29
Emburey	6	2	17	1	15	1	62	0	3rd	47	112	198	31
WEST INDIES									4th	50	129	226	104
Marshall	18	5	32	6	25	5	60	4	5th	54	134	240	105
Patterson	13	3	52	1	21.5	2	100	2	6th	184	140	371	161
Ambrose	12	1	39	1	20	4	47	1	7th	199	153	379	212
Walsh	16	6	36	2	20	1	75	1	8th	199	157	380	232
									9th	199	165	384	254
									10th	209	165	397	307

Umpires: K.E. Palmer and D.R. Shepherd

Test No. 1099/892

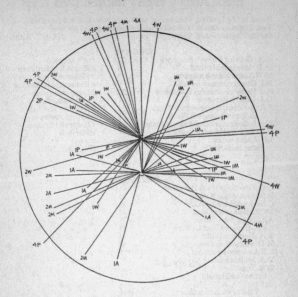

PAVILION END

BOWLER	SYMBOL	BALLS	RUNS				TOTAL
			1	2	3	4	
AMBROSE	A	40	8	1	-	1	14
MARSHALL	M	59	9	5	-	2	27
PATTERSON	P	52	6	1	-	7	36
WALSH	W	62	9	2	1	5	36
TOTALS		213	32	9	1	15	113

ALLAN LAMB
at Lord's

113 RUNS
213 BALLS
338 MINUTES

© BILL FRINDALL 1988

19

ENGLAND v WEST INDIES (3rd Test)

Played at Old Trafford, Manchester, on 30 June June, 1, 2, 4, 5 July 1988
Toss: England. Result: West Indies won by an innings and 156 runs
Debuts: England – J.H. Childs

‡(K.L.T. Arthurton)

ENGLAND

G.A. Gooch c Dujon b Benjamin		27	lbw b Marshall		1
M.D. Moxon b Marshall		0	c Richards b Benjamin		15
M.W. Gatting lbw b Marshall		0	c Richardson b Marshall		4
D.I. Gower c Harper b Walsh		9	c Richardson b Marshall		34
A.J. Lamb c Greenidge b Ambrose		33	c Logie b Ambrose		9
D.J. Capel b Benjamin		1	c sub‡ b Marshall		0
†P.R. Downton c Greenidge b Walsh		24	c Harper b Marshall		6
*J.E. Emburey c Dujon b Walsh		1	c Logie b Ambrose		8
P.A.J. DeFreitas c Greenidge b Ambrose		15	c Harper b Marshall		0
G.R. Dilley b Walsh		14	b Marshall		4
J.H. Childs not out		2	not out		0
Extras (LB4, NB5)		9	(B1, LB10, NB1)		12
Total		**135**			**93**

WEST INDIES

C.G. Greenidge lbw b DeFreitas		45
R.B. Richardson b Dilley		23
C.L. Hooper lbw b Childs		15
*I.V.A. Richards c Capel		47
A.L. Logie lbw b Dilley		39
†P.J.L. Dujon c Capel b Dilley		67
R.A. Harper b Dilley		74
M.D. Marshall not out		43
C.E.L. Ambrose not out		7
W.K.M. Benjamin } did not bat		
C.A. Walsh		
Extras (LB21, NB3)		24
Total (7 wickets declared)		**384**

WEST INDIES	O	M	R	W	O	M	R	W	FALL OF WICKETS			
Marshall	12	5	19	2	15.4	5	22	7		E	WI	E
Ambrose	17	5	35	2	16	4	36	2	Wkt	1st	1st	2nd
	14	0	64	2	26.5	3	74	1	1st	12	35	6
Walsh	18.2	4	46	4	4	1	10	0	2nd	14	77	22
Benjamin	13	4	31	2	4	1	6	1	3rd	33	101	36
Harper					2	1	4	0	4th	55	175	73
Hooper					1	0	4	0	5th	61	187	73
ENGLAND									6th	94	281	73
Dilley	28.1	4	99	4					7th	98	373	87
Emburey	25	7	54	0					8th	113	—	87
DeFreitas	35	5	81	1					9th	123	—	93
Capel	12	2	38	1					10th	135	—	93
Childs	40	12	91	1								

Umpires: D.J. Constant and N.T. Plews

Test No. 1100/93

ENGLAND v WEST INDIES (4th Test)

Played at Headingley, Leeds, on 21, 22, 23, 25, 26 July 1988
Toss: West Indies. Result: West Indies won by 10 wickets
Debuts: England – T.S. Curtis, R.A. Smith; West Indies – K.L.T. Arthurton

ENGLAND

T.S. Curtis lbw b Benjamin	12		b Ambrose	12
C.W.J. Athey lbw b Ambrose	16		c Dujon b Walsh	11
D.I. Gower c Dujon b Benjamin	13		c Dujon b Marshall	2
A.J. Lamb c Dujon b Ambrose	64	(8)	c Dujon b Amrose	19
R.A. Smith c Dujon b Ambrose	38	(5)	lbw b Marshall	11
*C.S. Cowdrey lbw b Marshall	0	(6)	b Walsh	5
†C.J. Richards b Ambrose	2	(7)	b Ambrose	8
D.R. Pringle c Dujon b Marshall	0		b Benjamin	3
N.A. Foster not out	8		c Hooper b Benjamin	0
G.R. Dilley c Hooper b Ambrose	8		not out	2
Extras (LB1, LB18, W6, NB6)	31		(B3, LB8, NB4)	15
Total	**201**			**138**

WEST INDIES

D.L. Haynes lbw b Pringle	54	not out	25
†P.J.L. Dujon c Smith b Dilley	13	not out	40
C.L. Hooper lbw b Foster	19		
*I.V.A. Richards c Curtis b Foster	18		
A.L. Logie c Foster b Pringle	44		
K.L.T. Arthurton c Richards b Pringle	27		
R.A. Harper c Gower b Foster	56		
M.D. Marshall c Gooch b Pringle	3		
C.E.L. Ambrose lbw b Pringle	8		
W.K.M. Benjamin run out (sub)	9		
C.A. Walsh not out	9		
Extras (LB15)	15	(LB2)	2
Total	**275**	**(0 wicket)**	**67**

WEST INDIES	O	M	R	W	O	M	R	W	FALL OF WICKETS				
										E	WI	E	WI
Marshall	23	8	55	3	17	4	47	2		1st	1st	2nd	2nd
Ambrose	25.1	8	58	4	19.5	4	40	3	Wkt	1st	1st	2nd	2nd
Benjamin	9	2	27	2	5	4	2	2	1st	14	15	56	—
Walsh	12	4	42	0	20	9	38	3	2nd	43	61	80	—
ENGLAND									3rd	58	97	85	—
Dilley	20	5	59	12	4	0	16	0	4th	80	137	85	—
Foster	32.2	6	98	3	7	1	36	0	5th	183	156	105	—
Pringle	27	7	95	5					6th	183	194	105	—
Cowdrey	2	0	8	0	3.3	0	13	0	7th	185	210	127	—
									8th	185	222	132	—
									9th	201	245	132	—
									10th	—	275	138	—

Umpires: H.D. Bird and D.R. Shepherd
A.J. Lamb retired hurt at 183-4

Test No. 1101/94

21

ENGLAND v WEST INDIES (5th Test)

Played at Kennington Oval, London, on 4, 5, 6, 8 August 1988
Toss: England. Result: West Indies won by 8 wickets
Debuts: England – R.J. Bailey, M.P. Maynard   ‡(K.L.T. Arthurton)

ENGLAND

*G.A. Gooch c Logie b Ambrose	9		c Greenidge b Ambrose	84
T.S. Curtis c Dujon b Benjamin	30		lbw b Marshall	15
R.J. Bailey c Dujon b Ambrose	43		b Benjamin	3
R.A. Smith c Harper b Marshall	57		lbw b Benjamin	0
M.P. Maynard c Dujon b Ambrose	16	(6)	c and b Benjamin	10
D.J. Capel c Marshall b Harper	16	(7)	lbw b Walsh	12
†C.J. Richards c Logie b Harper	0	(8)	c Dujon b Walsh	3
D.R. Pringle c Dujon b Marshall	1	(9)	b Harper	8
P.A.J. DeFreitas c Haynes b Harper	18	(10)	c Haynes b Harper	0
N.A. Foster c sub‡ b Marshall	7	(5)	c Logie b Benjamin	34
J.H. Childs not out	0		not out	0
Extras (LB6, NB15)	21		(B3, LB15, NB15)	33
Total	**205**			**202**

WEST INDIES

C.G. Greenidge c DeFreitas b Foster	10	c Richards b Childs	77
D.L. Haynes c Richards b Foster	2	not out	77
C.L. Hooper c Gooch b Foster	11	b Foster	23
*I.V.A. Richards c Curtis b Foster	0	(4) not out	38
†P.J.L. Dujon lbw b Pringle	64		
R.A. Harper run out (Foster/Capel/Pringle)	17		
M.D. Marshall c and b Childs	0		
C.E.L. Ambrose not out	17		
W.K.M. Benjamin b Pringle	0		
C.A. Walsh c DeFreitas b Pringle	5		
Extras (LB7, W1, NB2)	10	(B2, LB3, NB6)	11
Total	**183**	(2 wickets)	**11**

WEST INDIES	O	M	R	W	O	M	R	W	FALL OF WICKETS				
Marshall	24.3	3	64	3	25	6	52	1		*E*	*WI*	*E*	*WI*
Ambrose	20	6	31	3	24.1	10	50	1	*Wkt*	*1st*	*1st*	*2nd*	*2nd*
Walsh	10	1	21	0	12	5	21	2	1st	12	9	50	131
Benjamin	14	2	33	1	22	4	52	4	2nd	77	16	55	162
Harper	21	7	50	3	6	3	39	2	3rd	116	16	55	—
Hooper	1	1	0	0					4th	121	57	108	—
ENGLAND									5th	160	126	125	—
Foster	16	2	64	5	18	3	52	1	6th	160	155	139	—
DeFreitas	13	4	33	0	17	2	46	0	7th	165	156	157	—
Pringle	17	4	45	3	13	4	24	0	8th	167	167	175	—
Capel	7	0	21	)	3	0	20	0	9th	198	168	177	—
Childs	6	1	13	1	40	16	79	1	10th	205	183	202	—

Umpires: H.D. Bird and K.E. Palmer   Test No. 1102/95

ENGLAND v WEST INDIES AVERAGES

ENGLAND – BATTING AND FIELDING

	M	I	NO	HS	Runs	Avge	100	50	Ct/St
G.A.Gooch	5	10	0	146	459	45.90	1	3	6
A.J.Lamb	4	8	2	113	254	42.33	1	1	—
D.I.Gower	4	8	1	88*	211	30.14	—	1	2
R.A.Smith	2	4	0	57	106	26.50	—	1	1
P.R.Downton	3	5	1	27	84	21.00	—	—	9
P.W.Jarvis	2	3	1	29*	42	21.00	—	—	1
B.C.Broad	2	4	0	54	71	17.75	—	1	—
T.S.Curtis	2	4	0	30	69	17.25	—	—	2
N.A.Foster	2	4	1	34	49	16.33	—	—	1
M.D.Moxon	2	4	0	26	55	13.75	—	—	1
G.R.Dilley	4	7	1	28	58	9.66	—	—	1
M.W.Gatting	2	4	0	29	38	9.50	—	—	1
J.E.Emburey	3	5	0	30	46	9.20	—	—	3
D.R.Pringle	4	7	0	39	52	7.42	—	—	1
D.J.Capel	2	4	0	16	29	7.25	—	—	1
P.A.J.DeFreitas	3	5	0	18	36	7.20	—	—	2
C.J.Richards	2	4	0	8	13	3.25	—	—	3
J.H.Childs	2	4	4	2*	2	—	—	—	1

Played in one Test: C.W.J.Athey 16, 11; R.J.Bailey 43, 3; C.S.Cowdrey 0, 5;
M.P.Maynard 3. 10; G.C.Small 5*, 7.

ENGLAND – BOWLING

	Overs	Mdns	Runs	Wkts	Avge	Best	5 wI	10 wM
G.R.Dilley	136.1	26	403	15	26.86	5-55	1	—
N.A.Foster	73.2	12	250	9	27.77	5-64	1	—
D.R.Pringle	119	33	326	11	29.63	5-95	1	—
G.C.Small	37.5	6	140	4	35.00	4-64	—	—
P.W.Jarvis	57.1	6	217	6	36.16	4-107	—	—

Also bowled: D.J.Capel 22-2-79-1; J.H.Childs 86-29-183-3; C.S.Cowdrey 5.3-0-
21-0; P.A.J.DeFreitas 92-16-253-3; J.E.Emburey 62-14-228-3.

WEST INDIES – BATTING AND FIELDING

	M	I	NO	HS	Runs	Avge	100	50	Ct/St
A.L.Logie	5	7	2	95*	364	72.80	—	2	6
P.J.L.Dujon	5	7	1	67	305	50.83	—	4	20
R.A.Harper	3	3	0	74	147	49.00	—	2	5
C.G.Greenidge	4	6	0	103	282	47.00	1	1	4
D.L.Haynes	4	7	2	77*	235	47.00	—	3	3
I.V.A.Richards	5	6	0	80	223	37.16	—	2	3
M.D.Marshall	5	6	1	72	135	27.00	—	1	1
C.L.Hooper	5	7	0	84	166	23.71	—	1	3
C.E.L.Ambrose	5	6	2	43	75	18.75	—	—	1
R.B.Richardson	3	4	0	26	71	17.75	—	—	4
C.A.Walsh	5	5	3	9*	26	13.00	—	—	1
W.K.M.Benjamin	3	2	0	9	9	4.50	—	—	1
B.P.Patterson	2	2	0	2	2	1.00	—	—	—

Played in one Test: K.L.T.Arthurton 27.

WEST INDIES – BOWLING

	Overs	Mdns	Runs	Wkts	Avge	Best	5 wI	10 wM
W.K.M.Benjamin	67	17	151	12	12.58	4-52	—	—
R.A.Harper	29	11	63	5	12.60	3-50	—	—
M.D.Marshall	203.1	49	443	35	12.65	7-22	3	1
C.E.L.Ambrose	203.1	56	445	22	20.22	4-53	—	—
C.A.Walsh	157.2	40	412	12	34.33	4-46	—	—
B.P.Patterson	74.5	13	270	4	67.50	2-100	—	—

Also bowled: C.L.Hooper 24-3-5-0; I.V.A.Richards 10-1-28-0.

ENGLAND v SRI LANKA (Only Test)

Played at Lord's, London, on 25, 26, 27, 29, 30 August 1988
Toss: England. Result: England won by 7 wickets
Debuts: Sri Lanka – A.W.R. Madurasinghe, M.A.R. Samarasekera

SRI LANKA

Batsman	1st innings		2nd innings	
D.S.B.P. Kuruppu	c Gooch b Newport	46	c Barnett b Foster	25
†S.A.R. Silva	c Russell b Foster	1	c Russell b Newport	16
M.A.R. Samarasekera	c Russell b Foster	0	lbw b Emburey	57
P.A. de Silva	c Gooch b Newport	3	lbw b Lawrence	18
*R.S. Madugalle	lbw b Foster	3	b Foster	20
A. Ranatunga	lbw b Newport	5	b Newport	78
L.R.D. Mendis	c Smith b Lawrence	21	lbw b Pringle	56
A.W.R. Madurasinghe	not out	59	c Lamb b Lawrence	32
A.W.R. Madurasinghe	run out (Lawrence)	4	b Newport	2
C.P.H. Ramanayake	lbw b Pringle	0	(11) c Gooch b Newport	2
G.F. Labrooy	lbw b Pringle	42	(10) not out	9
Extras	(B1, LB7, NB2)	10	(LB8, NB8)	18
Total		**194**		**331**

ENGLAND

Batsman	1st innings		2nd innings	
*G.A. Gooch	lbw b Ratnayeke	75	c Silva b Samarasekera	36
R.T. Robinson	c Samarasekera b Ratnayeke	19	not out	34
†R.C. Russell	c Samarasekera b Labrooy	94		
K.J. Barnett	c Ranatunga b Labrooy	66	(3) c Silva b Samarasekera	0
A.J. Lamb	b Labrooy	63	(4) c De Silva b Ranatunga	8
R.A. Smith	b Ranatunga	31	(5) not out	8
D.R. Pringle	c Silva b Labrooy	14		
J.E. Emburey	c De Silva b Samarasekera	0		
P.J. Newport	c De Silva b Samarasekera	26		
N.A. Foster	not out	14		
D.V. Lawrence	c Mendis b Ramanayake	4		
Extras	(B1, LB3, W2, NB17)	23	(LB8, W2, NB4)	14
Total		**429**	(3 wickets)	**100**

ENGLAND	O	M	R	W	O	M	R	W
Foster	21	5	51	3	33	10	98	2
Lawrence	15	4	37	1	21	5	74	2
Newport	21	4	77	3	26.3	7	87	4
Pringle	6.5	1	17	2	11	2	30	1
Emburey	2	1	4	0	18	9	34	1
SRI LANKA								
Ratnayeke	32	3	107	2	7	1	16	0
Labrooy	40	7	119	4	9	0	24	0
Ramanayake	27.2	3	86	2				
Madurasinghe	16	4	41	0				
Samarasekera	22	5	66	1	10	0	38	2
Ranatunga	6	3	6	1	8.4	4	14	1

FALL OF WICKETS

Wkt	SL 1st	E 1st	SL 2nd	E 2nd
1st	7	40	43	73
2nd	44	171	51	73
3rd	52	233	96	82
4th	53	320	145	—
5th	61	358	147	—
6th	63	373	251	—
7th	122	378	309	—
8th	127	383	311	—
9th	130	420	323	—
10th	194	429	331	—

Umpires: D.J. Constant and J.W. Holder   Test No. 1103/3

PAKISTAN v AUSTRALIA (1st Test)

Played at National Stadium, Karachi, on 15, 16, 17, 19, 20 September 1988
Toss: Pakistan. Result: Pakistan won by an innings and 188 runs
Debuts: Australia – I.A. Healy

PAKISTAN

Mudassar Nazar b Reid	0
Ramiz Raja c Healy b Reid	9
Shoaib Mohammad b Waugh	94
*Javed Miandad c Boon b Reid	211
Tausif Ahmed c Boon b May	35
Salim Malik c Boon b May	45
Ijaz Ahmed c Boon b Reid	12
Aamer Malik not out	17
†Salim Yousuf c Wood b May	5
Abdul Qadir c Marsh b May	8
Iqbal Qasim did not bat	
Extras (B16, LB12, NB7)	33
Total (9 wickets declared)	**469**

AUSTRALIA

G.R. Marsh b Qasim	8		lbw b Tausif	17
D.C. Boon b Qadir	14	(3)	b Qasim	4
D.M. Jones lbw b Qasim	3	(4)	c Ijaz b Qadir	4
G.M. Wood b Qasim b Tausif	23	(5)	lbw b Qasim	15
*A.R. Border c Aamer Malik b Qasim	4	(6)	b Qasim	18
S.R. Waugh lbw b Qasim	0	(7)	st Yousuf b Qasim	13
P.L. Taylor not out	54	(2)	c Ijaz b Aamer Malik	2
†I.A. Healy c Iajaz b Mudassar	26		c Shoaib b Qadir	21
A.I.C. Dodemaide c Ijaz b Salim Malik	8		st Yousuf b Tausif	2
T.B.A. May c Yousuf b Qadir	6		lbw b Qadir	0
B.A. Reid lbw b Qasim	0		not out	8
Extras (B12, LB7)	19		(B6, LB6)	12
Total	**165**			**116**

AUSTRALIA	O	M	R	W	O	M	R	W	FALL OF WICKETS		
Reid	41	10	109	4						*P*	*A*	*A*
Dodemaide	29	13	35	0					*Wkt*	*1st*	*1st*	*2nd*
Waugh	26	3	94	1					1st	0	19	4
May	40.5	10	97	4					2nd	21	23	10
Taylor	16	2	73	0					3rd	217	40	15
Border	17	7	33	0					4th	284	48	46
PAKISTAN									5th	398	54	50
Mudassar	10	3	15	1	3	0	5	0	6th	428	64	80
Aamer Malik	2	0	6	0	2	2	0	1	7th	444	106	93
Qasim	39	24	35	5	25	14	49	4	8th	457	139	104
Qadir	37	16	54	2	13	4	34	3	9th	469	162	104
Tausif	26	15	28	1	21.4	13	16	2	10th	—	165	116
Shoaib	2	1	1	0								
Salim Malik	6	4	7	1								

Umpires: Khizar Hayat and Mahboob Shah

Test No. 1104/29

25

PAKISTAN v AUSTRALIA (2nd Test)

Played at Iqbal Stadium, Faisalabad, on 23, 24, 25, 27, 28 September 1988
Toss: Pakistan. Result: match drawn
Debuts: nil

PAKISTAN

Mudassar Nazar c Marsh b Reid	9	c Border b May	27
Ramiz Raja lbw b Dodemaide	0	c Boon b Waugh	32
Shoaib Mohammad b Dodemaide	11	st Healy b May	74
*Javed Miandad c Boon b May	43	lbw b Reid	107
Salim Malik b Dodemaide	0	c Border b Reid	10
Ijaz Ahmed b Reid	122	c Healy b Reid	0
†Salim Yousuf c Boon b Dodemaide	62	not out	66
Abdul Qadir b Reid	6	(10) c Reid b May	13
Tausif Ahmed not out	35	(8) c Waugh b Dodemaide	2
Iqbal Qasim c and b Sleep	16	(9) lbw b Reid	28
Salim Jaffer lbw b Sleep	0		
Extras (B2, LB6, NB4)	12	(LB6, NB13)	19
Total	**316**	**(9 wickets declared)**	**378**

AUSTRALIA

D.C. Boon b Mudsaar	13	(2) c Mudassar b Tausif	15
G.R. Marsh b Tausif	51	(1) b Qadir	9
D.M. Jones lbw b Qasir	16	not out	21
G.M. Wood lbw b Jaffer	32	(5) not out	2
A.I.C. Dodemaide c Ijaz b Mudassar	19		
*A.R. Border not out	113		
S.R. Waugh st Yousuf b Tausif	1	(4) c and b Shoaib	19
P.R. Sleep b Tausif	12		
†I.A. Healy c Qasim b Jaffer	27		
T.B.A. May c sub (Moin-ul-Atiq) b Qadir	14		
B.A. Reid c Yousuf b Qasim	1		
Extras (B4, LB15, W1, NB2)	22	(B1)	1
Total	**321**	**(3 wickets)**	**67**

AUSTRALIA	O	M	R	W	O	M	R	W
Reid	31	8	92	3	30	6	100	4
Dodemaide	34	6	87	4	20	4	48	1
Waugh	11	3	36	0	18	6	44	1
Sleep	5.5	1	24	2	13	4	51	0
May	19	3	58	1	34.4	7	126	3
Border	6	1	11	0	4	3	0	
PAKISTAN								
Jaffer	29	7	69	2	2	0	8	0
Mudassar	17	4	39	2	2	0	5	0
Qadir	34	5	84	2	10	1	34	1
Tausif	35	10	73	3	11	4	17	1
Qasim	14.5	4	37	1				
Shoaib					1	0	2	1

FALL OF WICKETS

	P	A	P	A
Wkt	1st	1st	2nd	2nd
1st	4	24	64	18
2nd	20	65	64	30
3rd	24	122	236	65
4th	25	122	264	—
5th	144	167	265	—
6th	255	170	269	—
7th	255	204	274	—
8th	267	256	344	—
9th	316	318	378	—
10th	316	321	—	—

Umpires: Mahboob Shah and Tariq Ata   Test No. 1105/30

PAKISTAN v AUSTRALIA (3rd Test)

Played at Gaddafi Stadium, Lahore, on 7, 8, 9, 10, 11 October 1988
Toss: Australia. Result: match drawn
Debuts: nil

AUSTRALIA

D.C. Boon c Shoaib b Jaffer	43	(2)	c Miandad b Jaffer	28
G.R. Marsh st Yousuf b Qasim	64	(1)	not out	84
D.M. Jones lbw b Tausif	0		lbw b Jaffer	0
*A.R. Border c Yousuf b Tausif	75		c Yousuf b Tausif	20
G.M. Wood lbw b Mudassar	15			
P.L. Taylor st Yousuf b Qadir	29	(5)	not out	25
S.R Waugh c Ijaz b Qasim	59			
†I.A. Healy lbw b Qadir	0			
A.I.C. Dodemaide c Qasim b Qadir	14			
T.B.A. May not out	13			
B.A. Reid c Mudassar b Tausif	8			
Extras (B4, LB12, NB4)	20		(LB4)	4
Total	340		(3 wickets declared)	161

PAKISTAN

Mudassar Nazar c Boon b May	27		c Border b Taylor	49
Ramiz Raja b Healy b Reid	64		c Boon b May	21
Shoaib Mohammad run out (Waugh)	13		lbw b May	3
*Javed Miandad c Healy b by Reid	74		c Border b May	24
Salim Malik c and b Dodemaide	26		c Healy b Taylor	13
Ijaz Ahmed lbw b Dodemaide	23		c Taylor b Dodemaide	15
†Salim Yousuf c Healy b Reid	1		c Waugh b Taylor	2
Abdul Qadir lbw b Dodemaide	18		st Healy b Taylor	6
Iqbal Qasim b May	14		not out	10
Tausif Ahmed c Boon b May	3		not out	1
Salim Jaffer not out	0			
Extras (LB6 NB11)	17		(B6, LB1, NB2)	9
Total	233		(8 wickets)	153

PAKISTAN	O	M	R	W	O	M	R	W	FALL OF WICKETS				
Jaffer	33	9	82	1	14	2	60	2		A	P	A	P
Mudassar	15	6	23	1	3	0	8	0	Wkt	1st	1st	2nd	2nd
Qadir	37	10	88	3	4	1	26	0	1st	87	80	71	36
Tausif	50	20	85	3	17	2	48	1	2nd	88	104	71	48
Qasim	22	6	42	2	3	0	15	0	3rd	155	118	108	86
Shoaib	1	0	4	0					4th	200	172	—	107
AUSTRALIA									5th	231	172	—	123
Reid	23	3	53	3					6th	241	173	—	125
Waugh	18	4	34	0	5	1	8	0	7th	241	206	—	131
Dodemaide	26	6	56	3	12	5	20	1	8th	294	228	—	147
May	27.2	6	73	3	35	20	39	3	9th	331	232	—	—
Taylor	4	2	11	0	28	9	78	4	10th	340	233	—	—
Border					4	3	1	0					

Umpires: Khizar Hayat and Salim Badar

Test No. 1106/31

PAKISTAN v AUSTRALIA AVERAGES

PAKISTAN – BATTING AND FIELDING

	M	I	NO	HS	Runs	Avge	100	50	Ct/St
Javed Miandad	3	5	0	211	412	82.40	2	—	1
Shoaib Mohammad	3	5	0	94	195	39.00	—	2	3
Ijaz Ahmed	3	5	0	122	172	34.40	1	—	6
Salim Yousuf	3	5	1	66*	136	34.00	—	2	4/5
Tausif Ahmed	3	5	2	35*	76	25.33	—	—	—
Ramiz Raja	3	5	0	64	126	25.20	—	1	—
Iqbal Qasim	3	4	1	28	68	22.66	—	—	3
Mudassar Nazar	3	5	0	49	112	22.40	—	—	2
Salim Malik	3	5	0	45	94	18.80	—	—	—
Abdul Qadir	3	5	0	18	51	10.20	—	—	—
Salim Jaffer	2	2	1	0*	0	0.00	—	—	—

Played in one Test: Aamer Malik 17* (1 ct).

PAKISTAN – BOWLING

	Overs	Mdns	Runs	Wkts	Avge	Best	5 wI	10 wM
Iqbal Qasim	103.5	48	178	12	14.83	5-35	1	—
Mudassar Nazar	50	13	95	4	23.75	2-39	—	—
Tausif Ahmed	160.4	64	267	11	24.27	3-73	—	—
Abdul Qadir	135	37	320	11	29.09	3-34	—	—
Salim Jaffer	78	18	219	5	43.80	2-60	—	—

Also bowled: Aamer Malik 4-2-6-1; Salim Malik 6-4-7-1; Shoaib Mohammad 4-1-7-1.

AUSTRALIA – BATTING AND FIELDING

	M	I	NO	HS	Runs	Avge	100	50	Ct/St
A.R. Border	3	5	1	113*	230	57.50	1	1	4
P.L. Taylor	2	4	2	54*	110	55.00	—	1	1
G.R. Marsh	3	6	1	84*	233	46.60	—	3	2
G.M. Wood	3	5	1	32	87	21.75	—	—	1
D.C. Boon	3	6	0	43	117	19.50	—	—	10
I.A. Healy	3	4	0	27	74	18.50	—	—	6/2
S.R. Waugh	3	5	0	59	92	18.40	—	1	2
T.B.A. May	3	4	1	14	33	11.00	—	—	—
A.I.C. Dodemaide	3	4	0	19	43	10.75	—	—	1
D.M. Jones	3	6	1	21*	44	8.80	—	—	—
B.A. Reid	3	4	1	8*	17	5.66	—	—	1

Played in one Test: P.R. Sleep 12 (1 ct).

AUSTRALIA – BOWLING

	Overs	Mdns	Runs	Wkts	Avge	Best	5 wI	10 wM
B.A. Reid	125	27	354	14	25.28	4-100	—	—
A.I.C. Dodemaide	121	34	246	9	27.33	4-87	—	—
T.B.A. May	156.5	46	393	14	28.07	4-97	—	—
P.L. Taylor	48	13	162	4	40.50	4-78	—	—

Also bowled: A.R. Border 28-11-48-0; P.R. Sleep 18.5-5-75-2; S.R. Waugh 78-17-216-2.

INDIA v NEW ZEALAND (1st Test)

Played at Chinnaswamy Stadium, Bangalore, on 12, 13, 14, 16, 17 November 1988
Toss: India. Result: India won by 172 runs
Debuts: New Zealand – C.M. Kuggeleijn

In India's first innings, D.B. Vengsarkar (73) retired hurt at 186-2 and resumed at
244-4. In New Zealand's first innings, R.J. Hadlee (1) retired ill at 145-6 and
resumed at 183-9.

INDIA

K. Srikkanth	b Hadlee	1	not out	58
Arun Lal	c Kuggeleijn b Hadlee	6	c and b Gray	33
N.S. Sidhu	c Jones b Gray	116	not out	43
*D.B. Vengsarkar	b Hadlee	75		
M. Azharuddin	c Smith b Hadlee	42		
W.V. Raman	b Hadlee	3		
R.J. Shastri	c Rutherford b Gray	54		
Kapil Dev	c Jones b Chatfield	24		
†K.S. More	lbw b Kuggeleijn	46		
Arshad Ayub	not out	2		
N.D. Hirwani	not out	0		
Extras	(B4, LB4, NB7)	15	(B5, LB2)	7
Total	(9 wickets declared)	**384**	(1 wicket declared)	**141**

NEW ZEALAND

T.J. Franklin	c Azharuddin b Ayub	28		b Hirwani	16
*J.G. Wright	c Arun Lal b Ayub	22		lbw b Hirwani	58
A.H. Jones	c Srikkanth b Ayub	45		lbw b Hirwani	17
M.J. Greatbatch	c Srikkanth b Raman	14		c Kapil Dev b Ayub	10
K.R. Rutherford	c Arun Lal b Hirwani	14	(6)	lbw b Hirwani	0
E.J. Gray	lbw b Hirwani	1	(5)	c Srikkanth b Hirwani	2
R.J. Hadlee	b Gray	5	(8)	not out	13
J.G. Bracewell	c More b Ayub	3	(3)	c Arun Lal b Ayub	11
†I.D.S. Smith	lbw b Kapil Dev	30		lbw b Hirwani	25
E.J. Chatfield	not out	4	(11)	c Vengsarkar b Ayub	0
C.M. Kuggeleijn	lbw b Kapil Dev	0	(7)	c More b Ayub	0
Extras	(B6, LB8, NB9)	23		(B10, NB2)	12
Total		**189**			**164**

NEW ZEALAND	O	M	R	W	O	M	R	W	FALL OF WICKETS			
										I	*NZ*	*I*	*NZ*
Hadlee	30	10	65	5					*Wkt*	*1st*	*1st*	*2nd*	*2nd*
Chatfield	30	12	53	1	14	0	61	0	1st	9	58	64	77
Kuggeleijn	13	2	50	1					2nd	10	62	—	92
Gray	45	8	128	2	6	0	39	1	3rd	236	118	—	107
Bracewell	24	1	80	0	8	0	34	0	4th	244	128	—	113
INDIA									5th	254	135	—	113
Kapil Dev	9.3	4	24	3	4	0	16	0	6th	258	140	—	113
Ayub	48	21	51	4	35.4	12	53	4	7th	294	149	—	113
Hirwani	31	12	62	2	30	10	59	6	8th	378	183	—	143
Shastri	14	8	11	0	7	1	21	0	9th	384	183	—	164
Raman	17	8	26	1	2	0	5	0	10th	—	189	—	164
Srikkanth	3	2	1	0									

Umpires: S.K. Ghosh and P.D. Reporter

Test No. 1107/26

INDIA v NEW ZEALAND (2nd Test)

Played at Wankhede Stadium, Bombay, on 24, 25, 26, 27, 29 November 1988
Toss: New Zealand. Result: New Zealand won by 136 runs
Debuts: India – R. Patel

NEW ZEALAND

T.J. Franklin st More b Ayub	18		c More b Kapil Dev	2
*J.G. Wright c More b Hirwani	33		lbw b Hirwani	36
A.H. Jones lbw b Kapil Dev	3		lbw b Ayub	78
M.J. Greatbatch lbw b Shastri	46		b Hirwani	31
K.R. Rutherford c Srikkanth b Hirwani	6		c Arun Lal b Ayub	17
T.E. Blain c Kapil Dev b Shastri	16		lbw b Ayub	5
R.J. Hadlee c Patel b Hirwani	10		c Vengsarkar b Hirwani	1
†I.D.S. Smith b Shastri	13		c Vengsarkar b Ayub	54
J.G. Bracewell c More b Shastri	52	(1)	c and b Ayub	32
D.K. Morrison not out	27	(9)	c More b Hirwani	0
E.J. Chatfield b Kapil Dev	0		not out	2
Extras (LB5, NB7)	12		(B4, LB8, W1, NB8)	21
Total	**236**			**279**

INDIA

K. Srikkanth c Franklin b Hadlee	94		lbw b Hadlee	0
Arun Lal lbw b Hadlee	9		c Greatbatch b Hadlee	47
N.S. Sidhu lbw b Chatfield	6		b Bracewell	14
*D.B. Vengsarkar c Blain b Bracewell	25		b Bracewell	0
M. Azharuddin c Greatbatch b Bracewell	9		c Rutherford b Bracewell	21
R.J. Shastri b Chatfield	32		c Smith b Hadlee	6
Kapil Dev b Hadlee	7		c Wright b Bracewell	36
†K.S. More b Hadlee	28		b Bracewell	2
Arshad Ayub c Bracewell b Hadlee	10		not out	4
R. Patel c Rutherford b Hadlee	0		c Smith b Hadlee	0
N.D. Hirwani not out	3		c Chatfield b Bracewell	3
Extras (LB5, NB7)	12		(B5, LB4, NB3)	12
Total	**234**			**145**

INDIA	O	M	R	W	O	M	R	W	FALL OF WICKETS			
									NZ	I	NZ	I
Kapil Dev	15.3	4	48	2	24	5	52	1	Wkt	1st	1st	2nd	2nd
Patel	4	0	14	0	10	0	37	0				
Ayub	25	10	42	1	33	11	50	5	1st	36	26	2	0
Hirwani	31	6	82	3	38	7	93	4	2nd	43	34	73	48
Shastri	18	1	45	4	10	1	35	0	3rd	67	134	147	54
NEW ZEALAND									4th	83	150	163	89
Hadlee	20.5	5	49	6	16	3	39	4	5th	110	150	169	89
Morrison	16	1	58	0	6	1	27	0	6th	121	170	176	134
Chatfield	18	6	41	2	10	1	19	0	7th	141	209	176	134
Bracewell	21	6	81	2	17.4	3	51	6	8th	158	224	181	141
									9th	234	229	250	142
									10th	236	234	279	145

Umpires: R.B. Gupta and V.K. Ramaswamy

Test No. 1108/27

INDIA v NEW ZEALAND (3rd Test)

Played at Lal Bahadur Stadium, Hyderabad, on 2, 3, 4, 6 December 1988
Toss: New Zealand. Result: India won by 10 wickets
Debuts: India – S.K. Sharma

NEW ZEALAND

T.J. Franklin c Arun Lal b Ayub	7	c Kapil Dev b Hirwani	15
*J.G. Wright c and b Ayub	17	c and b Shastri	62
A.H. Jones c Kapil Dev b Ayub	8	c Vengsarkar b Ayub	5
M.J. Greatbatch not out	90	(5) lbw b Hirwani	5
T.E. Blain b Hirwani	15	(6) c Arun Lal b Hirwani	0
C.M. Kuggeleijn c Vengsarkar b Hirwani	7	(7) c Sharma b Ayub	0
R.J. Hadlee c Azharuddin b Ayub	1	(8) c More b Kapil Dev	31
†I.D.S. Smith c Srikkanth b Kapil Dev	79	(9) b Kapil Dev	0
J.G. Bracewell c Vengsarkar b Sharma	3	lbw b Kapil Dev	0
M.C. Snedden lbw b Sharma	0	(4) lbw b Ayub	0
E.J. Chatfield c Srikkanth b Sharma	0	not out	0
Extras (B8, LB11, W1, NB7)	27	(LB1, W5)	6
Total	**254**		**124**

INDIA

K. Srikkanth c Bracewell b Snedden	69	not out	18
Arun Lal c Greatbatch b Hadlee	8	not out	0
N.S. Sidhu c Franklin b Snedden	19		
*D.B. Vengsarkar c Hadlee b Chatfield	32		
R.J. Shastri c Franklin b Chatfield	42		
M. Azharuddin c Smith b Chatfield	81		
Kapil Dev c Wright b Hadlee	40		
†K.S. More c Bracewell b Snedden	0		
Arshad Ayub c Smith b Hadlee	19		
S.K. Sharma not out	18		
N.D. Hirwani c and b Snedden	17		
Extras (LB9, NB4)	13	(NB4)	4
Total	**358**	(0 wicket)	**22**

INDIA	O	M	R	W	O	M	R	W	FALL OF WICKETS				
Kapil Dev	26	6	71	1	10	3	21	3		*NZ*	*I*	*NZ*	*I*
Sharma	17	4	37	3	4	0	13	0	*Wkt*	*1st*	*1st*	*2nd*	*2nd*
Ayub	30	9	55	4	25	12	36	3	1st	25	17	49	—
Shastri	6	2	15	0	3.3	1	10	1	2nd	33	48	58	—
Hirwani	15	2	51	2	23	10	43	3	3rd	38	116	60	—
Srikkanth	1	0	6	0					4th	82	150	71	—
NEW ZEALAND									5th	90	217	75	—
Hadlee	34	7	9	3					6th	91	279	80	—
Chatfield	33	6	82	3	1	0	5	0	7th	230	281	118	—
Snedden	18.3	3	69	4	1	0	13	0	8th	246	310	118	—
Bracewell	18	1	86	0					9th	248	322	124	—
Kuggeleijn	3	0	13	0	0.1	0	4	0	10th	254	358	124	—

Umpires: S.K. Ghosh and R.B. Gupta

Test No. 1109/28

INDIA v NEW ZEALAND AVERAGES

INDIA – BATTING AND FIELDING

	M	I	NO	HS	Runs	Avge	100	50	Ct/St
K. Srikkanth	3	6	2	94	240	60.00	—	3	6
N.S. Sidhu	3	5	1	116	198	49.50	1	—	4
M. Azharuddin	3	4	0	81	153	38.25	—	1	2
R.J. Shastri	3	4	0	54	134	33.50	—	1	1
D.B. Vengsarkar	3	4	0	75	132	33.00	—	1	6
Kapil Dev	3	4	0	40	107	26.75	—	—	4
Arun Lal	3	6	1	47	103	20.60	—	—	6
K.S. More	3	4	0	46	76	19.00	—	—	7/1
Arshad Ayub	3	4	2	19	35	17.50	—	—	2
N.D. Hirwani	3	4	2	17	22	11.00	—	—	—

Played in one Test: R. Patel 0, 0 (1 ct); W.V. Raman 3; S.K. Sharma 18* (1 ct).

INDIA – BOWLING

	Overs	Mdns	Runs	Wkts	Avge	Best	5 wI	10 wM
Arshad Ayub	196.4	75	287	21	13.66	5-50	1	—
N.D. Hirwani	168	47	390	20	19.50	6-59	1	—
Kapil Dev	89	22	232	10	23.20	3-21	—	—
R.J. Shastri	58.3	14	137	5	27.40	4-45	—	—

Also bowled: R. Patel 14-0-51-0; W.V. Raman 19-8-31-1; S.K. Sharma 21-4-50-3; K. Srikkanth 4-2-7-0.

NEW ZEALAND – BATTING AND FIELDING

	M	I	NO	HS	Runs	Avge	100	50	Ct/St
M.J. Greatbatch	3	6	1	90*	196	39.20	—	1	3
J.G. Wright	3	6	0	62	228	38.00	—	2	2
I.D.S. Smith	3	6	0	79	201	33.50	—	2	5
A.H. Jones	3	6	0	78	156	26.00	—	1	2
J.G. Bracewell	3	6	0	52	101	16.83	—	1	3
T.J. Franklin	3	6	0	28	86	14.33	—	—	3
R.J. Hadlee	3	6	1	31	61	12.20	—	—	1
K.R. Rutherford	2	4	0	17	37	9.25	—	—	3
T.E. Blain	2	4	0	16	36	9.00	—	—	1
E.J. Chatfield	3	6	3	4*	6	2.00	—	—	1
C.M. Kuggeleijn	2	4	0	7	7	1.75	—	—	1

Played in one Test: E.J. Gray 1, 2 (1 ct); D.K. Morrison 27*, 0; M.C. Snedden 0, 0 (1 ct).

NEW ZEALAND – BOWLING

	Overs	Mdns	Runs	Wkts	Avge	Best	5 wI	10 wM
R.J. Hadlee	100.5	25	252	18	14.00	6-49	2	1
M.C. Snedden	19.3	3	82	4	20.50	4-69	—	—
J.G. Bracewell	88.4	11	332	8	41.50	6-51	1	—
E.J. Chatfield	106	25	261	6	43.50	3-83	—	—

Also bowled: E.J. Gray 51-8-167-3; C.M. Kuggeleijn 16.1-2-67-1; D.K. Morrison 22-2-85-0.

AUSTRALIA v WEST INDIES (1st Test)

Played at Woolloongabba, Brisbane on 18, 19, 20, 21 November 1988
Toss: Australia. Result: West Indies won by 9 wickets
Debuts: nil

†(K.L.T. Arthurton)

AUSTRALIA

G.R. Marsh c Logie b Ambrose	27		lbw b Ambrose		2
D.C. Boon lbw b Marshall	10		c Dujon b Marshall		12
M.R.J. Veletta b Hooper	37		c Hooper b Walsh		10
G.M. Wood c Greenidge b Ambrose	6	(5)	lbw b Walsh		0
*A.R. Border c Dujon b Ambrose	4	(6)	c Haynes b Anbrose		41
S.R. Waugh lbw b Marshall	4	(4)	c Haynes b Marshall		90
†I.A. Healy c Logie b Walsh	27		c mbrose b Marshall		28
A.I.C. Dodemaide v Richards b Walsh	22		c Richards b Marshall		7
C.J. Mc Dermott c Logie b Walsh	2		not out		32
C.D. Matthews c Dujon b Walsh	1		c sub† b Walsh		32
T.B.A. May not out	4		c Hooper b A.,brose		5
Extras (B1, LB5, W1, NB16)	23		(B3, LB5, NB21)		30
	—				—
Total	**167**				**289**

WEST INDIES

C.G. Greenidge b May	80		c Healy b Dodemaide		16
D.L. Haynes c Healy b Waugh	40		not out		30
R.B. Richardson lbw b Dodemaide	81		not out		7
C.L. Hooper c Border b Waugh	1				
*I.V.A. Richards c McDermott b May	68				
A.L. Logie c Border b May	19				
†P.J.L. Dujon c May b McDermott	27				
M.D. Marshall c Border b McDermott	11				
C.E.L. Ambrose not out	19				
C.A. Walsh lbw b McDermott	0				
B.P. Patterson lbw d Dodemaide	0				
Extras (B5, LB9, W6, NB28)	48		(LB4, W3, NB3)		10
	—				—
Total	**394**		(1 wicket)		**63**

WEST INDIES	O	M	R	W	O	M	R	W	FALL OF WICKETS				
Marshall	18	3	39	2	26	2	92	4		A	WI	A	WI
Patterson	3.1	1	5	0					Wkt	1st	1st	2nd	2nd
Ambrose	16.5	5	30	3	26.1	5	78	3	1st	19	135	14	43
Walsh	18.3	3	62	4	19	3	61	3	2nd	52	156	16	
Hooper	12	2	24	1	4	0	23	0	3rd	64	162	65	
Richards	1	0	1	0	11	4	26	0	4th	76	270	65	
AUSTRALIA									5th	86	307	157	
McDermott	28	3	99	3	4	0	12	0	6th	126	359	199	
Matthews	21	3	62	0	3.5	1	18	0	7th	138	361	212	
Dodemaide	16.4	2	60	2	5.2	1	15	1	8th	140	389	212	
May	29	6	90	3	6	0	14	0	9th	150	393	270	
Waugh	18	2	61	2					10th	167	394	289	
Border	1	0	8	0									

Umpires: A.R. Crafter and P.J. McConnell

Test No. 1110/63

AUSTRALIA v WEST INDIES (2nd Test)

Played at W.A.C.A. Ground, Perth on 2, 3, 4, 5, 6 December 1988
Toss: Australia. Result: West Indies won by 169 runs
Debuts: nil

WEST INDIES

C.G. Greenidge b Lawson	40	lbw b Hughes		0
D.L. Haynes lbw b Hughes	11	c Healy b Hughes		100
R.B. Richardson c Boon b Hughes	66	c Healy b Hughes		48
C.L. Hooper c Boon b Lawson	26	c Dodemaide b Hughes		64
*I.V.A. Richards c Dodemaide b Lawson	146	lbw b Hughes		5
A.L. Logie c Waugh b May	93	b Hughes		30
†P.J.L. Dujon c Veletta b May	32	c Dodemaide b Hughes		9
N.D. Marshall c Veletta b Hughes	4	c Healy b Dodemaide		23
C.E.L. Ambrose c Healy b Hughes	8	c Wood b Hughes		15
C.A. Walsh not out	0	not out		17
B.P. Patterson c Dodemaide b Hughes	1	not out		6
Extras (B1, LB12, NB9)	22	(B14, LB9, NB9)		32
Total	**449**	**(9 wickets declared)**		**349**

AUSTRALIA

G.R. Marsh c Richardson b Walsh	30	c Logie b Marshall		6
D.C. Boon c Logie b Ambrose	80	b Patterson		4
M.R.J. Veletta run out	11	c Dujon b Marshall		13
G.M. Wood c Richardson b Ambrose	111	c Greenidge b Walsh		43
*A.R. Border c Dujon b Ambrose	6	b Hooper		26
S.R. Waugh c Dujon b Ambrose	91	c Hooper b Patterson		26
I.A. Healy lbw b Marshall	8	c Logie b Ambrose		52
A.I.C. Dodemaide not out	7	lbw b Ambrose		11
T.B.A. May c Richards b Ambrose	2	not out		8
G.F. Lawson retired hurt	0	absent hurt		
M.G. Hughes did not bat		(10) c Logie b Ambrose		0
Extras (B5, LB9, NB35)	49	(B5, LB4, NB37)		46
Total (8 wickets declared)	**395**			**234**

AUSTRALIA	O	M	R	W	O	M	R	W	FALL OF WICKETS			
										WI	A	WI	A
Lawson	32	7	97	3					Wkt	1st	1st	2nd	2nd
Hughes	36.1	7	130	5	37	9	87	8	1st	16	83	0	14
Dodemaide	17	1	79	0	24		2	101	1	2nd	82	139	103	14
Waugh	28	3	90	0	23	1	70	0	3rd	126	152	216	36
May	10	3	40	2	14	1	69	0	4th	180	167	236	93
WEST INDIES									5th	343	367	246	138
Marshall	23	3	84	1	12	0	50	2	6th	421	374	259	140
Patterson	16	1	95	0	14	2	58	2	7th	426	388	300	190
Walsh	19	3	58	1	15	1	46	1	8th	440	395	310	232
Ambrose	23.3	3	72	5	17	1	66	3	9th	448	—	341	234
Richards	14	0	43	0					10th	449	—	—	—
Hooper	5	0	29	0	5	2	5	1					

Umpires: R.C. Bailhache and T.A. Prue   Test No. 1111/64

AUSTRALIA v WEST INDIES (3rd Test)

Played at Melbourne Cricket Ground on 24, 26, 27, 28, 29 December 1988
Toss: Australia. Result: West Indies won by 285 runs
Debuts: nil

†(K.L.T. Arthurton)   ‡R.A. Harper

WEST INDIES

C.G. Greenidge	c Healy b Alderman	49	not out	36
D.L. Haynes	c Boon b McDermott	17	lbw b Alderman	23
R.B. Richardson	c Taylor b Alderman	26	c and b Waugh	122
C.L. Hooper	c Border b McDermott	38	lbw b Alderman	4
*I.V.A. Richards	c Border b Waugh	12	(6) lbw b Waugh	63
A.L. Logie	lbw b Alderman	10	(1) c Border b Waugh	17
†P.J.L. Dujon	c Healy b Waugh	26	(5) c Wood b Alderman	46
M.D. Marshall	c Jones b Waugh	7	(7) c Alderman b Waugh	19
C.E.L. Ambrose	lbw b McDermott	44	(8) c Marsh b McDermott	5
C.A. Walsh	not out	30	(9) c Marsh b Waugh	6
B.P. Patterson	lbw d Alderman	13	not out	3
Extras	(B1, LB4, NB3)	8	(LB1, NB16)	17
Total		**280**	**(9 wickets declared)**	**361**

AUSTRALIA

D.C. Boon	run out	23	lbw b Marshall	20
G.R. Marsh	b Patterson	36	b Patterson	1
D.M. Jones	b Ambrose	28	c sub‡ b Ambrose	18
G.M. Wood	c Haynes b Patterson	12	c Ambrose b Walsh	7
*A.R. Border	b Ambrose	0	c Haynes b Patterson	20
S.R. Waugh	c Greenidge b Ambrose	42	c sub‡ b Ambrose	3
†I.A. Healy	lbw b Patterson	4	c Hooper b Walsh	8
P.L. Taylor	c Greenidge b Ambrose	14	not out	18
C.J. McDermott	c Marshall b Patterson	28	c sub‡ b Patterson	0
M.G. Hughes	not out	21	c Dujon b Patterson	4
T.M. Alderman	b Walsh	3	c Dujon b Patterson	0
Extras	(B2, LB14, NB15)	31	(B4, LB5, NB6)	15
Total		**242**		**114**

AUSTRALIA	O	M	R	W	O	M	R	W	FALL OF WICKETS			
Hughes	14	3	52	0	24	8	71	0		WI	A	WI	A
Alderman	14	3	52	0	24	8	71	0	Wkt	1st	1st	2nd	2nd
McDermott	19	3	62	3	26	3	78	1	1st	68	40	38	7
Waugh	21	3	77	3	24	5	92	5	2nd	68	103	92	30
WEST INDIES									3rd	114	117	191	56
Marshall	30	8	68	0	9	12	1		4th	137	117	284	58
Ambrose	27	7	60	4	13	5	21	2	5th	147	155	317	64
Walsh	17.3	3	49	1	16	7	21	2	6th	166	161	324	75
Patterson	20	2	49	4	15.1	3	39	5	7th	185	186	324	104
Richards					4	1	12	0	8th	199	190	335	104
									9th	256	234	356	114
									10th	280	242	—	114

Umpires: A.R. Crafter and P.J. McConnell   Test No. 1112/65
In West Indies' second innings, C.G. Greenidge (25) retired hurt at 69-1 and resumed at 335-8.

AUSTRALIA v WEST INDIES (4th Test)

Played at Sydney Cricket Ground on 26, 27, 28, 29, 30 January 1989
Toss: West Indies. Result: Australia won by 7 wickets
Debuts: Australia – T.V. Hohns, M.A. Taylor

WEST INDIES

C.G. Greenidge c Waugh b P.L. Taylor	56	c and b Hughes	4
D.L. Haynes c Boon b Hohns	75	c M.A. Taylor b Border	143
R.B. Richardson c P.L. Taylor b Border	28	c Hughes b P.L. Taylor	22
C.L. Hooper c Marsh b Border	0	c Jones b Hohns	35
*I.V.A. Richards c Boon b Border	11	c Jones b Hohns	4
A.L. Logie b Border	0	c P.L. Taylor b Hohns	6
†P.J.L. Dujon c Hughes b Border	18	run out	9
R.A. Harper c P.L. Taylor b Border	17	lbw b Border	12
M.D. Marshall c Marsh b Border	9	c P.L. Taylor b Border	3
C.E.L. Ambrose c Jones b P.L. Taylor	1	c Boon b Border	5
C.A. Walsh not out	4	not out	7
Extras (B1, W1, NB3)	5	(B1, W1, NB4)	6
Total	**224**		**256**

AUSTRALIA

G.R. Marsh c Dujon b Marshall	2	b Richards	23
M.A. Taylor b Ambrose	25	c Haynes b Ambrose	3
D.C. Boon c Dujon b Walsh	149	c Harper b Marshall	10
D.M. Jones b Richards	29	not out	24
*A.R. Border b Marshall	75	not out	16
S.R. Waugh not out	55		
†I.A. Healy c Logie b Marshall	11		
P.L. Taylor lbw b Marshall	0		
T.V. Hohns b Marshall	0		
M.G. Hughes c Dujon b Walsh	12		
T.M. Alderman run out	9		
Extras (B6, LB14, NB14)	34	(B3, LB1, NB2)	6
Total	**401**		**82**

AUSTRALIA	O	M	R	W	O	M	R	W		FALL OF WICKETS			
											WI	A	WI	A
Alderman	10	2	17	0	2	0	6	0	Wkt	1st	1st	2nd	2nd
Hughes	10	3	28	0	18	6	29	1	1st	90	14	17	3
P.L. Taylor	25.2	8	65	2	29	4	91	1	2nd	144	43	56	16
Hohns	24	8	49	1	34	11	69	3	3rd	156	114	167	55
Border	26	10	46	7	18.4	3	50	4	4th	174	284	188	—
Waugh	4	0	18	0	3	0	10	0	5th	174	335	198	—
WEST INDIES									6th	174	355	225	—
Marshall	31	16	29	5	8	2	17	1	7th	199	357	232	—
Ambrose	33	5	78	1	7	1	16	1	8th	213	357	244	—
Harper	37	9	86	0					9th	220	388	247	—
Walsh	22.5	5	48	2	3	0	9	0	10th	224	401	256	—
Hooper	37	10	72	0	10.3	2	24	0					
Richards	31	1	68	1	7	2	12	1					

Umpires: L.J. King and T.A. Prue

Test No. 1113/66

AUSTRALIA v WEST INDIES (5th Test)

Played at Adelaide Oval on 3, 4, 5, 6, 7 February 1989
Toss: Australia. Result: match drawn
Debuts: nil

AUSTRALIA

G.R. Marsh c Dujon b Ambrose	21		c Dujon b Ambrose	79
M.A. Taylor run out	3		run out	36
D.C. Boon c Richardson b Ambrose	34		not out	55
D.M. Jones run out	216		lbw b Richards	6
*A.R. Border b Marshall	64	(6)	not out	6
S.R. Waugh c Dujon b Walsh	12	(5)	run out	8
†I.A. Healy lbw b Walsh	0			
T.V. Hohns c Hooper b Walsh	9			
T.B.A. May c Richardson b Ambrose	24			
M.G. Hughes not out	72			
M.R. Whitney c Dujon b Patterson	2			
Extras (LB18, NB40)	58		(B11, LB13, NB10)	34
Total	**515**		**(4 wickets declared)**	**224**

WEST INDIES

C.G. Greenidge b Whitney	12		c Boon b May	104
D.L. Haynes run out	83		c Healy b Whitney	15
R.B. Richardson c Jones b Whitney	106		c Border b Whitney	22
C.L. Hooper c Healy b Whitney	2		b May	0
*I.V.A. Richards c Boon b Witney	69		not out	68
A.L. Logie c Healy b Hohns	21		run out	2
†P.J.L. Dujon b Hohns	28			
M.D. Marshall c Marsh b Whitney	0			
C.E.L. Ambrose c Boon b Whitney	9			
C.A. Walsh c Healy b Whitney	4			
B.P. Patterson not out	9			
Extras (B6, LB10, NB10)	26		(B3, LB7, W1, NB11)	22
Total	**369**		**(4 wickets)**	**233**

WEST INDIES	O	M	R	W	O	M	R	W	FALL OF WICKETS				
										A	WI	A	WI
Marshall	23	3	67	1	12	2	30	0	*Wkt*	*1st*	*1st*	*2nd*	*2nd*
Patterson	30.5	1	130	1	8	1	29	0	1st	7	19	98	21
Ambrose	26	4	93	3	15	2	44	1	2nd	64	186	176	87
Walsh	33	5	120	3	13	2	26	0	3rd	75	190	187	89
Hooper	3	0	14	0	3	1	7	0	4th	289	231	213	212
Richards	25	1	73	0	24	3	64	1	5th	311	293	—	—
AUSTRALIA									6th	311	315	—	—
Hughes	15	0	86	0	9	5	20	0	7th	333	315	—	—
Whitney	30	6	89	7	20	4	60	2	8th	383	331	—	—
May	16	6	42	0	23	2	60	2	9th	497	346	—	—
Waugh	3	0	17	0	9	3	23	0	10th	515	369	—	—
Hohns	47.4	9	106	2	15	3	56	0					
Border	10	2	13	0	5	3	4	0					

Umpires: R.J. Evans and P.J. McConnell   **Test No. 1114/67**

AUSTRALIA v WEST INDIES AVERAGES

AUSTRALIA – BATTING AND FIELDING

	M	I	NO	HS	Runs	Avge	100	50	Ct/St
D.M. Jones	3	6	1	216	321	64.20	1	—	5
D.C. Boon	5	10	1	149	397	44.11	1	2	9
S.R. Waugh	5	9	1	91	331	41.37	—	3	3
M.G. Hughes	4	5	2	72*	109	36.33	—	1	3
A.R. Border	5	10	2	75	258	32.25	—	2	7
G.M. Wood	3	6	0	111	178	29.66	1	—	5
G.R. Marsh	5	10	0	79	227	22.70	—	1	2
C.J. McDermott	2	4	1	32*	62	20.66	—	—	1
M.R.J. Veletta	2	4	0	37	71	17.75	—	—	1
I.A. Healy	5	8	0	52	138	17.25	—	1	12
M.A. Taylor	2	4	0	36	67	16.75	—	—	1
P.L. Taylor	2	3	1	18*	32	16.00	—	—	1
A.I.C. Dodemaide	2	4	1	22	47	15.66	—	—	4
T.B.A. May	3	5	2	24	43	14.33	—	—	1
T.V. Hohns	2	2	0	9	9	4.50	—	—	—
T.M. Alderman	2	3	0	9	12	4.00	—	—	1

Played in one Test: G.F. Lawson 0*; C.D. Matthews 1, 32; M.R. Whitney 2.

AUSTRALIA – BOWLING

	Overs	Mdns	Runs	Wkts	Avge	Best	5 wI	10 wM
A.R. Border	61.4	19	121	11	11.00	7-46	1	—
M.R. Whitney	50	10	149	9	16.55	7-89	1	—
T.M. Alderman	80.1	23	169	7	24.14	4-68	—	—
C.J. McDermott	77	9	251	7	35.85	3-62	—	—
M.G. Hughes	163.1	41	503	14	35.92	8-87	2	1
T.B.A. May	98	18	314	7	44.85	3-90	—	—
S.R. Waugh	133	17	458	10	45.80	5-92	1	—
T.V. Hohns	120.4	31	280	6	46.66	3-69	—	—
A.I.C. Dodemaide	63	6	255	4	63.75	2-60	—	—

Also bowled: G.F. Lawson 32-7-97-3; C.D. Matthews 24.5-4-80-0; P.L. Taylor 70.2-16-213-3.

WEST INDIES – BATTING AND FIELDING

	M	I	NO	HS	Runs	Avge	100	50	Ct/St
D.L. Haynes	5	10	1	143	537	59.66	2	2	5
R.B. Richardson	5	10	1	122	528	58.66	2	2	4
I.V.A. Richards	5	9	1	146	446	55.75	1	4	3
C.G. Greenidge	5	10	1	104	397	44.11	1	2	4
A.L. Logie	5	9	1	93	198	24.75	—	1	8
P.J.L. Dujon	5	8	0	46	195	24.37	—	—	15
C.A. Walsh	5	8	5	30*	68	22.66	—	—	—
C.L. Hooper	5	9	0	64	170	18.88	—	1	5
C.E.L. Ambrose	5	8	1	44	106	15.14	—	—	2
B.P. Patterson	4	6	3	13	32	10.66	—	—	—
M.D. Marshall	5	8	0	23	76	9.50	—	—	1

Played in one Test: R.A. Harper 17, 12 (1 ct).

WEST INDIES – BOWLING

	Overs	Mdns	Runs	Wkts	Avge	Best	5 wI	10 wM
C.E.L. Ambrose	204.3	38	558	26	21.46	5-72	1	—
M.D. Marshall	192	44	488	17	28.70	5-29	1	—
C.A. Walsh	176.5	32	500	17	29.41	4-62	—	—
B.P. Patterson	107.1	11	405	12	33.75	5-39	1	—

Also bowled: R.A. Harper 37-9-86-0; C.L. Hooper 79.3-17-198-2; I.V.A. Richards 117-12-299-3.

Happily, this year, the community is over £10,000,000 better off.

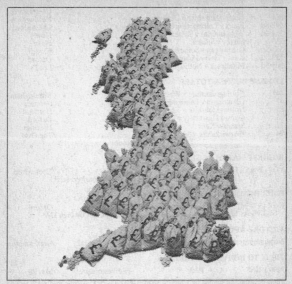

This year, NatWest have already committed over £10,000,000 to help with the running of hundreds of environmental, social, arts and sporting projects all over the country.

♻ NatWest The Action Bank

PRESS FOR ACTION

THE 1988 FIRST-CLASS SEASON
STATISTICAL HIGHLIGHTS

HIGHEST INNINGS TOTALS

628-7d	Worcestershire v Somerset	Taunton
616	Essex v Kent	Chelmsford
614	Nottinghamshire v Derbyshire	Nottingham
592-8d	Essex v Leicestershire	Chelmsford
561-9d	West Indians v Sussex	Hove
553	Surrey v Sussex	Hove
543-8d	Glamorgan v Somerset	Cardiff
539-3d	Kent v Oxford University	Oxford
505-5d	Middlesex v Nottinghamshire	Lord's

LOWEST INNINGS TOTALS

44†	Nottinghamshire v Warwickshire	Birmingham
47	Glamorgan v Lancashire	Swansea
65	Nottinghamshire v Kent	Dartford
68	Oxford University v Leicestershire	Oxford
71	Sussex v Kent	Hastings
74	Warwickshire v Surrey	The Oval

† One man absent

HIGHEST MATCH AGGREGATE

1570 (29 wkts)   Essex v Kent   Chelmsford
(The record aggregate for a County Championship match)

FOUR HUNDREDS IN AN INNINGS

Kent (539-3d)   v Oxford University   Oxford
S.G.Hinks 138, R.F.Pienaar 127, C.J.Tavaré 138*, C.S.Cowdrey 124*

VICTORY AFTER FOLLOWING-ON

Northamptonshire (170 & 363)   v Warwickshire (415 & 112)   Northampton

FIRST TO INDIVIDUAL TARGETS

1000 RUNS   G.A.Hick   Worcestershire   May 28

Hick became the eighth batsman to score 1000 runs before June and set a record aggregate for the month of April with 410 runs, avge 82.00.

2000 RUNS   G.A.Hick   Worcestershire   August 16

100 WICKETS   F.D.Stephenson   Nottinghamshire   August 22

DOUBLE HUNDREDS

K.J.Barnett	239*	Derbyshire v Leicestershire	Leicester
G.Cook	203	Northamptonshire v Yorkshire	Scarborough
M.W.Gatting	210	Middlesex v Nottinghamshire	Lord's
G.A.Gooch	275	Essex v Kent	Chelmsford
R.A.Harper	217*	West Indians v Sussex	Hove
G.A.Hick (2)	212	Worcestershire v Lancashire	Manchester
	405*	Worcestershire v Somerset	Taunton
A.A.Metcalfe	216*	Yorkshire v Middlesex	Leeds
D.W.Randall	237	Nottinghamshire v Derbyshire	Nottingham

HUNDRED IN EACH INNINGS OF A MATCH

G.C.Holmes	100* 107	Glamorgan v Somerset	Taunton
W.N.Slack	163* 105*	Middlesex v Glamorgan	Lord's
F.D.Stephenson	111 117	Nottinghamshire v Yorkshire	Nottingham

FASTEST HUNDRED (WALTER LAWRENCE TROPHY)

G.A.Hick   79 balls   Worcestershire v Surrey   The Oval
In 91 minutes and including 4 sixes and 9 fours.

HUNDRED BEFORE LUNCH

		Day		
K.J.Barnett	114*	1	Derbyshire v Gloucestershire	Derby
G.A.Gooch		1	Essex v Surrey	Chelmsford
N.Hussain		2	Essex v Leicestershire	Chelmsford
M.P.Maynard	108*	3	Glamorgan v Worcestershire	Abergavenny

ELEVEN SIXES IN AN INNINGS

G.A.Hick   Worcestershire v Somerset   Taunton

HUNDRED ON FIRST-CLASS DEBUT

| P.D.Atkins | 114* | Surrey v Cambridge University | The Oval |
| B.M.W.Patterson | 100 | Scotland v Ireland | Dumfries |

P.D.Bowler scored 155* on debut for Derbyshire (v Cambridge U at Cambridge). Having scored 100* for Leicestershire on his first-class debut, he became the first to score hundreds on debut for two counties.

CARRYING BAT THROUGH COMPLETED INNINGS

P.D.Bowler	159*	Derbyshire (340) v Essex	Chesterfield
G.D.Mendis	65*	Lancashire (163) v Glamorgan	Swansea
A.J.Moles	67*	Warwickshire (107†) v Kent	Birmingham
M.Newell	10*	Nottinghamshire (44†) v Warwickshire	Birmingham
N.R.Taylor	67*	Kent (121) v Leicestershire	Leicester
		† One or more batsmen absent	

NOTABLE PARTNERSHIPS   †County record

Second Wicket
276   T.S.Curtis/G.A.Hick, Worcestershire v Hampshire   Worcester

Third Wicket
284   W.N.Slack/M.W.Gatting, Middlesex v Glamorgan   Lord's

Fourth Wicket
345   M.Newell/D.W.Randall, Nottinghamshire v Derbyshire   Nottingham
264   M.W.Gatting/K.R.Brown, Middlesex v Nottinghamshire   Lord's
259   G.A.Gooch/D.R.Pringle, Essex v Kent   Chelmsford
251   G.Fowler/A.N.Hayhurst, Lancashire v Derbyshire   Derby

Sixth Wicket
265†   G.A.Hick/S.J.Rhodes, Worcestershire v Somerset   Taunton
227   I.V.A.Richards/R.A.Harper, West Indians v Sussex   Hove

Seventh Wicket
222   G.R.Cowdrey/S.A.Marsh, Kent v Essex   Chelmsford
205†   G.A.Hick/P.J.Newport, Worcestershire v Yorkshire   Worcester

Eighth Wicket
177* G.A.Hick/R.K.Illingworth, Worcestershire v Somerset   Taunton

Ninth Wicket
123   R.A.Harper/C.E.L.Ambrose, West Indians v Sussex   Hove
113   R.K.Illingworth/N.V.Radford, Worcestershire v Notts   Nottingham

EIGHT OR MORE WICKETS IN AN INNINGS

T.M.Alderman	8-59	Gloucestershire v Somerset	Taunton
M.P.Bicknell	9-45	Surrey v Cambridge University	The Oval
S.D.Fletcher	8-58	Yorkshire v Essex	Sheffield
D.A.Graveney	8-127	Gloucestershire v Worcestershire	Bristol
S.T.Jefferies	8-97	Hampshire v Gloucestershire	Gloucester
K.T.Medlycott	8-52	Surrey v Sussex	Hove
P.G.Newman	8-29	Derbyshire v Yorkshire	Leeds
P.J.Newport	8-52	Worcestershire v Middlesex	Lord's
S.L.Watkin	8-59	Glamorgan v Warwickshire	Birmingham

TEN OR MORE WICKETS IN A MATCH

J.P.Agnew	11-122	Leicestershire v Northamptonshire	Leicester
J.H.Childs	11-180	Essex v Leicestershire	Chelmsford
S.T.Clarke (2)	11-107	Surrey v Gloucestershire	Cheltenham
	10-89	Surrey v Lancashire	The Oval
N.G.Cowans	10-97	Middlesex v Warwickshire	Uxbridge
K.M.Curran (3)	12-162	Gloucestershire v Derbyshire	Derby
	11-109	Gloucestershire v Leicestershire	Gloucester
	10-82	Gloucestershire v Hampshire	Southampton
W.W.Davis (2)	10-185	Northamptonshire v Warwickshire	Northampton
	10-136	Northamptonshire v Sussex	Northampton
N.A.Foster (2)	10-86	Essex v Yorkshire	Sheffield
	10-128	Essex v Worcestershire	Worcester
A.R.C.Fraser (2)	10-117	Middlesex v Nottinghamshire	Lord's
	11-102	Middlesex v Hampshire	Basingstoke
D.A.Graveney	14-165	Gloucestershire v Worcestershire	Bristol
A.P.Igglesden	10-91	Kent v Hampshire	Bournemouth
R.K.Illingworth (2)	10-153	Worcestershire v Lancashire	Manchester
	10-132	Worcestershire v Gloucestershire	Bristol
P.W.Jarvis	10-115	Yorkshire v Kent	Canterbury
C.C.Lewis	10-70	Leicestershire v Oxford University	Oxford
V.J.Marks	10-116	Somerset v Nottinghamshire	Taunton
M.D.Marshall	10-92	West Indies v England (2nd Test)	Lord's
K.T.Medlycott (3)	10-192	Surrey v Kent	Guildford
	10-88	Surrey v Somerset	Weston-s-Mare
	12-105	Surrey v Sussex	Hove
T.A.Merrick	10-69	Warwickshire v Hampshire	Birmingham
P.J.Newport	10-89	Worcestershire v Somerset	Taunton
N.H.Peters	10-67	Surrey v Warwickshire	The Oval
R.J.Shastri	11-90	Glamorgan v Lancashire	Swansea
G.C.Small	10-84	Warwickshire v Somerset	Birmingham
	12-121	Warwickshire v Glamorgan	Birmingham
F.D.Stephenson (3)	12-103	Nottinghamshire v Derbyshire	Derby
	10-95	Nottinghamshire v Northamptonshire	Nottingham
	11-222	Nottinghamshire v Yorkshire	Nottingham
T.D.Topley	12-179	Essex v Derbyshire	Chesterfield

SIX WICKETS IN TEN BALLS

T.A.Merrick   Warwickshire v Derbyshire   Derby

HAT-TRICKS

T.A.Merrick	Warwickshire v Derbyshire	Derby
Wasim Akram	Lancashire v Surrey	Southport

WICKET WITH FIRST BALL IN FIRST-CLASS CRICKET

J.R.Ayling   Hampshire v Oxford University   Oxford

THE SEASON'S 'DOUBLE'

F.D.Stephenson (Nottinghamshire) 1018 runs and 125 wickets

1000 RUNS AND 50 WICKETS

K.M.Curran (Gloucestershire)   1005 runs and 65 wickets

MATCH DOUBLE (100 RUNS AND 10 WICKETS)

G.C.Small	31	69 6-79 6-42	Warwickshire v Glamorgan	Birmingham
F.D.Stephenson	111 117	4-105 7-117	Nottinghamshire v Yorkshire	Nottingham

SIX WICKET-KEEPING DISMISSALS IN AN INNINGS

C.P.Metson (6 ct)	Glamorgan v Leicestershire	Neath
S.J.Rhodes (6 ct)	Worcestershire v Sussex	Kidderminster
C.J.Richards (6 ct)	Surrey v Warwickshire	The Oval
D.Ripley (6 ct)	Northamptonshire v Sussex	Northampton
A.J.Stewart (6 ct)	Surrey v Lancashire	Southport

NINE OR MORE WICKET-KEEPING DISMISSALS IN A MATCH

C.W.Scott (10 ct)	Nottinghamshire v Derbyshire	Derby
S.J.Rhodes (9 ct)	Worcestershire v Sussex	Kidderminster

STUMPED BY A SUBSTITUTE

C.L.Hooper (West Indians) by W.Noon (Northamptonshire)   Northampton

FIVE CATCHES IN AN INNINGS IN THE FIELD

A.C.Storie   Warwickshire v Leicestershire   Birmingham

SEVEN CATCHES IN A MATCH IN THE FIELD

C.S.Cowdrey	Kent v Sussex	Maidstone
R.J.Maru	Hampshire v Northamptonshire	Bournemouth

WORCESTERSHIRE MAKE THEIR POINT

The Britannic Assurance Championship consistently provided the best cricket-watching of another poor English summer and an inspired performance by unfancied Kent produced a dramatic title chase which was resolved by a single point on the competition's penultimate afternoon.

History was made on 21 April 1988 when four-day matches were introduced. As a trial measure for three years, each county will play six four-day matches in two instalments (at the start and end of the season), with 16 of the traditional three-day contests sandwiched in between. Despite much unpleasant weather and some of the most atrocious pitches in memory the experiment was eminently successful. It enabled batsmen to play some long innings, particularly those in the middle-order and, in a drier season, would provide more opportunities for the spinners. Only the parochial interests of counties with several home grounds to accommodate will prevent the Championship being decided by the logical format of 16 four-day matches in 1991.

That season will have special significance for Graeme Ashley Hick as he will then be qualified by residence for England. He was still 17 days short of his 22nd birthday when he amassed 405 not out at Taunton; the highest score in Britain this century, it was just 19 runs short of the record when ended by a declaration. He went on to complete his 1000 runs before June and equal the County record with 10 hundreds. His aggregate of 2443 runs in the Championship was the largest since its fixtures were substantially pruned in 1972. Hick's calm and basically simple method countered many pitches of uneven bounce, especially those on his home ground; in a commendable effort to produce hard and fast surfaces the most important quality of predictable bounce was sacrificed.

Worcestershire were far from being a one-man band. Adroitly and tirelessly led by Phil Neale who played a series of crucial innings when the going was toughest, they were a most cohesive and confident unit. Curtis, Newport and Rhodes deservedly won national selection.

After losing their first three matches, Kent won the next six and, one hiccup apart, led the table until the last round. Tavaré's departure will be severely felt; with Pienaar, the happily repaired Ellison and a much-improved Penn, he enjoyed an exceptional season.

Ken Turner, that ace assessor of overseas talent, deserved a special award for recruiting Franklyn Stephenson to Trent Bridge. The gangling Bajan grinned his way to a 'double' which he completed with a brace of hundreds on the last day. Capable of awesome pace, he pulverised many of his 121 Championship victims with a lethal slower ball.

BRITANNIC ASSURANCE
COUNTY CHAMPIONSHIP 1988
FINAL TABLE

Win = 16 points*

Position		P	W	L	D	Bonus Points Bat	Bowl	Total Points
1	WORCESTERSHIRE (9)	22	10	3	9	55	75	290
2	Kent (14)	22	10	5	7	57	72	289
3	Essex (12)	22	9	5	8	61	69	282
4	Surrey (4)	22	7	5	10	57	72	241
5	Nottinghamshire (1)	22	8	8	6	34	71	229
6	Warwickshire (15)	22	6	8	8	48	74	218
7	Middlesex (16)	22	7	3	12	49	54	215
8	Leicestershire (3)	22	6	3	13	56	63	215
9	Lancashire (2)	22	6	7	9	41	67	212
10	Gloucestershire (10)	21	6	7	8	52	59	207
11	Somerset (11)	22	5	6	11	48	65	201
12	Northamptonshire (7)	22	5	7	10	48	71	199
13	Yorkshire (8)	22	4	6	12	48	65	177
14	Derbyshire (6)	22	4	3	15	53	54	171
15	Hampshire (5)	22	4	6	12	33	69	166
16	Sussex (17)	22	3	11	8	37	65	150
17	Glamorgan (13)	21	1	8	12	42	53	111

1987 final positions are shown in brackets.

*The Essex, Lancashire and Somerset totals include eight points for levelling the scores in a drawn match. Nottinghamshire gained 12 points for winning a match reduced to one innings.

The following match was abandoned and is not included in the above table: May 28, 30, 31 – Glamorgan v Gloucestershire at Swansea.

BRITANNIC ASSURANCE CHAMPIONSHIP

1. Scoring of Points
(a) For a win, 16 points, plus any points scored in the first innings.
(b) In a tie, each side to score eight points, plus any points scored in the first innings.
(c) If the scores are equal in a drawn match, the side batting in the fourth innings to score eight points, plus any points scored in the first innings.
(d) **First Innings Points** (awarded only for performances in the first 100 overs of each first innings and retained whatever the result of the match).
    (i) A maximum of four batting points to be available as under:
        150 to 199 runs – 1 point
        200 to 249 runs – 2 points
        250 to 299 runs – 3 points
        300 runs or over – 4 points
    (ii) A maximum of four bowling points to be available as under:
        3 to 4 wickets taken – 1 point
        5 to 6 wickets taken – 2 points
        7 to 8 wickets taken – 3 points
        9 to 10 wickets taken – 4 points
(e) If play starts when less than eight hours playing time remains and a one innings match is played, no first innings points shall be scored. The side winning on the one innings to score 12 points.
(f) The side which has the highest aggregate of points gained at the end of the season shall be the Champion County. Should any sides in the Championship table be equal on points, the side with most wins will have priority.

COUNTY CHAMPIONS

The English County Championship was not officially constituted until December 1889. Prior to that date there was no generally accepted method of awarding the title; although the 'least matches lost' method existed, it was not consistently applied. Rules governing playing qualifications were not agreed until 1873, and the first unofficial points system was not introduced until 1888.

Recent research has produced a list of champions dating back to 1826, but at least seven different versions exist for the period from 1864 to 1889 (see 'The Wisden Book of Cricket Records'). Only from 1890 can any authorised list of county champions commence.

From 1977 to 1983 the Championship was sponsored by Schweppes. BRITANNIC ASSURANCE have been its benefactors since 1984.

1890	Surrey	1930	Lancashire	1970	Kent
1891	Surrey	1931	Yorkshire	1971	Surrey
1892	Surrey	1932	Yorkshire	1972	Warwickshire
1893	Yorkshire	1933	Yorkshire	1973	Hampshire
1894	Surrey	1934	Lancashire	1974	Worcestershire
1895	Surrey	1935	Yorkshire	1975	Leicestershire
1896	Yorkshire	1936	Derbyshire	1976	Middlesex
1897	Lancashire	1937	Yorkshire	1977	Kent / Middlesex
1898	Yorkshire	1938	Yorkshire		
1899	Surrey	1939	Yorkshire	1978	Kent
1900	Yorkshire	1946	Yorkshire	1979	Essex
1901	Yorkshire	1947	Middlesex	1980	Middlesex
1902	Yorkshire	1948	Glamorgan	1981	Nottinghamshire
1903	Middlesex	1949	Middlesex / Yorkshire	1982	Middlesex
1904	Lancashire			1983	Essex
1905	Yorkshire	1950	Lancashire / Surrey	1984	Essex
1906	Kent			1985	Middlesex
1907	Nottinghamshire	1951	Warwickshire	1986	Essex
1908	Yorkshire	1952	Surrey	1987	Nottinghamshire
1909	Kent	1953	Surrey	1988	Worcestershire
1910	Kent	1954	Surrey		
1911	Warwickshire	1955	Surrey		
1912	Yorkshire	1956	Surrey		
1913	Kent	1957	Surrey		
1914	Surrey	1958	Surrey		
1919	Yorkshire	1959	Yorkshire		
1920	Middlesex	1960	Yorkshire		
1921	Middlesex	1961	Hampshire		
1922	Yorkshire	1962	Yorkshire		
1923	Yorkshire	1963	Yorkshire		
1924	Yorkshire	1964	Worcestershire		
1925	Yorkshire	1965	Worcestershire		
1926	Lancashire	1966	Yorkshire		
1927	Lancashire	1967	Yorkshire		
1928	Lancashire	1968	Yorkshire		
1929	Nottinghamshire	1969	Glamorgan		

cricketcall

0898 12 14

Then add the number you want.

66	Derby	30	Glamorgan
16	Essex	14	Middlesex
34	Gloucs.	50	Northants.
22	Hants.	24	Somerset
21	Kent	56	Warwicks.
69	Lancs.	33	Surrey
42	Leics.	55	Worcs.
12	Sussex	44	Yorks.
60	Notts.		

Live ball-by-ball commentary on all first-class games. Prospects of play. 24 hours every day. For Test matches and one day Internationals call 0898 121 134.

Calls cost 38p min./peak. 25p min./off peak. ℡ SUPERCALL *Sport*

RAMPRAKASH PREVENTS TREBLE

A precocious innings of considerable calm and maturity by Mark Ramprakash steered Middlesex to a thrilling three-wicket victory in the eighth final of the NatWest Trophy. It was a rousing display from a player making his debut in the competition on the eve of his 19th birthday and confronted by a capacity Lord's crowd for the first time.

With excessive dampness in the pitch the toss virtually decided the match. To be victims of this unnecessary lottery, make such a disastrous start and yet bat out their full 60 overs to take the game to 27 balls short of its allotted span was a considerable achievement by Worcestershire. When even the redoubtable Hick could make only one scoring stroke off 26 balls, a tedious day was in prospect. Only a skilled captain's innings from Neale prevented a complete rout as Fraser and Cowans extracted maximum benefit from the conditions. Valiant support from Leatherdale and Weston gave hopes of 200 but a decisive 4-wicket burst from Hughes left Middlesex with a more modest target.

It was quickly expanded to vast proportions by an extremely rapid spell from Dilley. Ignoring the discomfort of ailing knees he steamed in from the Nursery to restore Worcestershire's hopes of the unique treble by removing the first three batsmen. When Gatting contrived to run himself out without facing a ball the Midlanders' hopes of a first win in five Lord's finals grew large. They had merely set the stage for Ramprakash to confirm his prodigious talent with a combination of sound defence and audacious strokeplay which, assisted by the idiosyncratic technique of Emburey, won Middlesex their fourth September final.

GILLETTE CUP WINNERS

1963	Sussex	1969	Yorkshire	1975	Lancashire
1964	Sussex	1970	Lancashire	1976	Northamptonshire
1965	Yorkshire	1971	Lancashire	1977	Middlesex
1966	Warwickshire	1972	Lancashire	1978	Sussex
1967	Kent	1973	Gloucestershire	1979	Somerset
1968	Warwickshire	1974	Kent	1980	Middlesex

NATWEST BANK TROPHY WINNERS

1981	Derbyshire	1984	Middlesex	1987	Nottinghamshire
1982	Surrey	1985	Essex	1988	Middlesex
1983	Somerset	1986	Sussex		

1988 NATWEST TROPHY FINAL

MIDDLESEX v WORCESTERSHIRE

Played at Lord's, London, on 3 September
Toss: Middlesex. Result: Middlesex won by 3 wickets
Match Award: M.R. Ramprakash (adjudicator: G. Boycott)

WORCESTERSHIRE	Runs	Mins	Balls	6s	4s
T.S. Curtis b Fraser	4	7	7	—	—
S.J. O'Shaughnessy c Downton b Cowans	1	32	23	—	—
G.A. Hick b Fraser	4	36	26	—	1
D.A. Leatherdale b Needham	29	96	89	—	—
*P.A. Neale b Hughes	64	144	143	—	5
M.J. Weston c Downton b Fraser	31	46	41	—	3
†S.J. Rhodes c Emburey b Hughes	1	4	5	—	—
P.J. Newport b Hughes	4	9	8	—	—
N.V. Radford b Hughes	5	8	8	—	—
R.K. Illingworth not out	6	11	7	—	—
G.R. Dilley not out	2	5	5	—	—
Extras (LB7, W1, NB2)	10				
Total (60 overs; 207 minutes)	161-9 closed				

MIDDLESEX	Runs	Mins	Balls	6s	4s
W.N. Slack b Dilley	14	58	47	—	2
J.D. Carr c Rhodes b Dilley	1	8	5	—	—
A. Needham b Dilley	6	38	22	—	—
*M.W. Gatting run out (O'Shaughnessy)	0	1	0	—	—
R.O. Butcher run out (Hick/Illingworth)	24	65	47	—	2
M.R. Ramprakash c Radford b Dilley	56	154	123	—	4
J.E. Emburey b Dilley	35	87	78	—	2
†P.R. Downton not out	8	14	11	—	1
S.P. Hughes not out	0	6	3	—	—
A.R.C. Fraser } did not bat					
N.G. Cowans }					
Extras (B4, LB5, W7, NB2)	18				
Total (55.3 overs; 221 minutes)	162-7				

MIDDLESEX	O	M	R	W		FALL OF WICKETS		
Cowans	12	6	23	1	*Wkt*	*W*		*M*
Fraser	12	5	36	3	1st	5		3
Carr	4	1	9	0	2nd	9		21
Hughes	8	0	30	4	3rd	9		21
Needham	12	1	25	1	4th	71		25
Emburey	12	3	31	0	5th	137		64
WORCESTERSHIRE					6th	140		149
Dilley	12	3	29	5	7th	145		159
Radford	11.3	3	37	0	8th	148		—
Illingworth	12	4	24	0	9th	153		—
Newport	10	1	20	0	10th	—		—
Weston	2	0	9	0				
Hick	5	0	19	0				
O'Shaughnessy	3	0	15	0				

Umpires: H.D. Bird and D.R. Shepherd   *Captain †Wicket-keeper

49

THE NATWEST BANK TROPHY 1988

FIRST ROUND 22 June	SECOND ROUND 6, 7, 8 July	QUARTER-FINALS 27 July	SEMI-FINALS 10 August	FINAL 3 September
MIDDLESEX†	MIDDLESEX†	MIDDLESEX†	MIDDLESEX	MIDDLESEX (£21,000)
Hertfordshire	Yorkshire	Kent (£2,500)		
YORKSHIRE				
Berkshire†				
KENT†	KENT†			
Buckinghamshire	Warwickshire			
WARWICKSHIRE†				
Cambridgeshire				
SURREY	SURREY	SURREY†	Surrey† (£5,000)	
Staffordshire†	Essex†	Glamorgan (£2,500)		
ESSEX†				
Wiltshire				
GLAMORGAN	GLAMORGAN†			
Scotland†	Lancashire			
LANCASHIRE†				
Lincolnshire				
Shropshire†	HAMPSHIRE†	HAMPSHIRE	Hampshire (£5,000)	Worcestershire (£10,000)
HAMPSHIRE	Somerset	Derbyshire† (£2,500)		
SOMERSET				
Durham†				
Sussex†	DERBYSHIRE			
DERBYSHIRE	Cheshire†			
CHESHIRE†				
Northamptonshire				
WORCESTERSHIRE†	WORCESTERSHIRE	WORCESTERSHIRE†	WORCESTERSHIRE†	
Cumberland	Nottinghamshire†	Gloucestershire (£2,500)		
NOTTINGHAMSHIRE				
Devon†				
Suffolk	Leicestershire†			
LEICESTERSHIRE†	GLOUCESTERSHIRE			
Ireland				
GLOUCESTERSHIRE†				

† Home team. Winning teams are in capitals. Amounts in brackets show prize-money won by that county.

50

Congratulations Middlesex on winning the 1988 NatWest Trophy.

NatWest
The Action Bank

NATWEST BANK TROPHY
PRINCIPAL RECORDS 1963-1988

(Including The Gillette Cup)

Highest Total		404-3	Worcs v Devon	Worcester	1987
Highest Total in a Final		317-4	Yorkshire v Surrey	Lord's	1965
Highest Total by a Minor County		256	Oxon v Warwicks	Birmingham	1983
Highest Total Batting Second		326-9	Hampshire v Leics	Leicester	1987
Highest Losing Total		326-9	Hampshire v Leics	Leicester	1987
Lowest Total		39	Ireland v Sussex	Hove	1985
Lowest Total in a Final		118	Lancashire v Kent	Lord's	1974
Lowest Total to Win Batting First		98	Worcs v Durham	Chester-le-S	1968
Highest Score		206	A.I.Kallicharran	Warwicks v Oxon	Birmingham	1984
HS (Minor County)		132	G.Robinson	Lincs v Northumb	Jesmond	1971
Hundreds		162 have been scored in GC (93) and NWT (69) matches			
Fastest Hundred		77 min – R.E.Marshall	Hants v Beds	Bedford	1968

Highest Partnerships for each Wicket

1st	227	R.E.Marshall/B.L.Reed	Hampshire v Beds	Bedford	1968
2nd	286	I.S.Anderson/A.Hill	Derbys v Cornwall	Derby	1986
3rd	209	P.Willey/D.I.Gower	Leics v Ireland	Leicester	1986
4th	234*	D.Lloyd/C.H.Lloyd	Lancs v Glos	Manchester	1978
5th	166	M.A.Lynch/G.R.J.Roope	Surrey v Durham	The Oval	1982
6th	105	G.St A.Sobers/R.A.White	Notts v Worcs	Worcester	1974
7th	160*	C.J.Richards/I.R.Payne	Surrey v Lincs	Sleaford	1983
8th	71*	R.C.Ontong/T.Davies	Glamorgan v Staffs	Stone	1986
9th	87	M.A.Nash/A.E.Cordle	Glamorgan v Lincs	Swansea	1974
10th	81	S.Turner/R.E.East	Essex v Yorkshire	Leeds	1982

Best Bowling

	8-21	M.A.Holding	Derbys v Sussex	Hove	1988
	8-31	D.L.Underwood	Kent v Scotland	Edinburgh	1987
	7-15	A.L.Dixon	Kent v Surrey	Oval	1967
	7-30	P.J.Sainsbury	Hants v Norfolk	Southampton	1965
	7-32	S.P.Davis	Durham v Lancs	Chester-le-S	1983
	7-33	R.D.Jackman	Surrey v Yorkshire	Harrogate	1970
	7-37	N.A.Mallender	Northants v Worcs	Northampton	1984

Hat Tricks

J.D.F.Larter	Northants v Sussex	Northampton	1963
D.A.D.Sydenham	Surrey v Cheshire	Hoylake	1964
R.N.S.Hobbs	Essex v Middlesex	Lord's	1968
N.M.McVicker	Warwicks v Lincs	Birmingham	1971
G.S.Le Roux	Sussex v Ireland	Hove	1985
M.Jean-Jacques	Derbyshire v Notts	Derby	1987
J.F.M.O'Brien	Cheshire v Derbys	Chester	1988

Most Wicket-Keeping Dismissals

6 (5ct, 1st)	R.W.Taylor	Derbys v Essex	Derby	1981
6 (4ct, 2st)	T.Davies	Glamorgan v Staffs	Stone	1986

Most Catches in the Field

4	A.S.Brown	Glos v Middlesex	Bristol	1963
4	G.Cook	Northants v Glam	Northampton	1972
4	C.G.Greenidge	Hants v Cheshire	Southampton	1981
4	D.C.Jackson	Durham v Northants	Darlington	1984
4	T.S.Smith	Herts v Somerset	St Albans	1984
4	H.Morris	Glam v Scotland	Edinburgh	1988

Most Match Awards: 8 – C.H.Lloyd (Lancs); 7 – Imran Khan (Worcs/Sussex),
B.Wood (Lancs/Cheshire); 6 – B.L.D'Oliveira (Worcs), G.A.Gooch (Essex),
T.E.Jesty (Hants/Surrey), P.Willey (Northants/Leics).

1988 BENSON & HEDGES CUP FINAL

DERBYSHIRE v HAMPSHIRE

Played at Lord's, London, on 9 July
Toss: Hampshire. Result: Hampshire won by 7 wickets
Match Award: S.T. Jefferies (adjudicator: C.H. Lloyd)

DERBYSHIRE	Runs	Mins	Balls	6s	4s
*K.J. Barnett b Jefferies	13	23	19	—	1
P.D. Bowler c Nicholas b Jefferies	4	29	22	—	1
B. Roberts c Nicholas b Jefferies	0	9	5	—	—
J.E. Morris run out (Cowley/Parks)	42	108	78	—	4
S.C. Goldsmith lbw b Jefferies	0	6	2	—	—
†B.J.M. Maher b Ayling	8	66	52	—	—
M.A. Holding c Turner b Cowley	7	8	16	—	1
P.G. Newman b Connor	10	62	57	—	—
A.E. Warner b Jefferies	4	31	25	—	—
O.H. Mortensen not out	0	9	5	—	—
D.E. Malcolm b Connor	0	1	1	—	—
Extras (LB14, W12, NB3)	29				
Total (46.3 overs; 184 minutes)	117				

HAMPSHIRE	Runs	Mins	Balls	6s	4s
V.P. Terry c Roberts b Malcolm	2	16	13	—	—
C.L. Smith c Maher b Mortensen	20	71	51	—	3
*M.C.J. Nicholas not out	35	108	89	—	4
R.A. Smith c Goldsmith b Warner	38	30	27	—	7
D.R. Turner not out	7	21	16	—	—
J.R. Ayling					
S.T. Jefferies					
†R.J. Parks } did not bat					
N.G. Cowley					
C.A. Connor					
S.J.W. Andrew					
Extras (LB8, W3, NB5)	16				
Total (31.5 overs; 126 minutes)	118-3				

HAMPSHIRE	O	M	R	W	FALL OF WICKETS		
					Wkt	D	H
Connor	7.3	1	27	2	1st	27	10
Jefferies	10	3	13	5	2nd	28	44
Andrew	9	0	25	0	3rd	29	90
Ayling	9	2	21	1	4th	32	—
Cowley	11	2	17	1	5th	71	—
DERBYSHIRE					6th	80	—
Holding	11	2	36	0	7th	101	—
Malcolm	7	2	25	1	8th	114	—
Newman	3	1	11	0	9th	117	—
Mortensen	5	1	19	1	10th	117	—
Warner	5.5	0	19	1			

Umpires: D.J. Constant and N.T. Plews   *Captain   †Wicket-keeper

1988 BENSON AND HEDGES CUP

ZONAL POINTS TABLE

	P	W	L	NR	Pts	Run Rate
GROUP A						
DERBYSHIRE	4	3	—	1	7	64.89
WARWICKSHIRE	4	2	1	1	5	75.15
Leicestershire	4	2	1	1	5	60.10
Lancashire	4	1	3	—	2	68.25
Scotland	4		3	1	1	50.10
GROUP B						
WORCESTERSHIRE	4	2	1	1	5	68.78
NOTTINGHAMSHIRE	4	2	1	1	5	65.36
Northamptonshire	4	2	1	1	5	56.46
Yorkshire	4	1	1	2	4	59.19
Minor Counties	4	—	3	1	1	50.20
GROUP C						
ESSEX	4	3	1	—	6	72.15
MIDDLESEX	4	3	1	—	6	70.01
Kent	4	2	2	—	4	73.53
Sussex	4	1	3	—	2	60.90
Surrey	4	1	3	—	2	58.89
GROUP D						
GLAMORGAN	4	3	1	—	6	63.36
HAMPSHIRE	4	3	1	—	6	62.61
Gloucestershire	4	3	1	—	6	60.94
Somerset	4	1	3	—	2	67.47
Combined Universities	4	—	4	—	0	48.63

FINAL ROUNDS

QUARTER-FINALS 25, 26, 27 May	SEMI-FINALS 8, 9, 10 June	FINAL 9 July
Middlesex / DERBYSHIRE† (£2,500)	DERBYSHIRE	
GLAMORGAN† (£2,500) / Nottinghamshire	Glamorgan† (£5,000)	Derbyshire (£10,500)
ESSEX† / Warwickshire (£2,500)	Essex† (£5,000)	
HAMPSHIRE / Worcestershire† (£2,500)	HAMPSHIRE	HAMPSHIRE (£21,000)

† Home team.   Winning teams are in capitals.   Prize-money in brackets.

BENSON AND HEDGES CUP

PRINCIPAL RECORDS 1972-1988

Highest Total	350-3	Essex v Comb Univs	Chelmsford	1979
Highest Total Batting Second	294-7	Glos v Somerset	Taunton	1982
Highest Losing Total	300	Northants v Derbys	Derby	1987
Lowest Total	56	Leics v Minor C	Wellington	1982
Highest Score	198* G.A.Gooch	Essex v Sussex	Hove	1982
Hundreds	147 have been scored in Benson and Hedges Cup matches			
Fastest Hundred	62 min – M.A.Nash	Glamorgan v Hants	Swansea	1976

Highest Partnerships for each Wicket

1st	241	S.M.Gavaskar/B.C.Rose	Somerset v Kent	Canterbury	1980
2nd	285*	C.G.Greenidge/D.R.Turner	Hants v Minor C (S)	Amersham	1973
3rd	269*	P.M.Roebuck/M.D.Crowe	Somerset v Hants	Southampton	1987
4th	184*	D.Lloyd/B.W.Reidy	Lancashire v Derbys	Chesterfield	1980
5th	160	A.J.Lamb/D.J.Capel	Northants v Leics	Northampton	1986
6th	121	P.A.Neale/S.J.Rhodes	Worcs v Yorkshire	Worcester	1988
7th	149*	J.D.Love/C.M.Old	Yorks v Scotland	Bradford	1981
8th	109	R.E.East/N.Smith	Essex v Northants	Chelmsford	1977
9th	85	P.G.Newman/M.A.Holding	Derbyshire v Notts	Nottingham	1985
10th	80*	D.L.Bairstow/M.Johnson	Yorkshire v Derbys	Derby	1981

Most Wickets	7-12	W.W.Daniel	Middx v Minor C (E)	Ipswich	1978
	7-22	J.R.Thomson	Middx v Hampshire	Lord's	1981
	7-32	R.G.D.Willis	Warwicks v Yorks	Birmingham	1981

Hat Tricks	G.D.McKenzie	Leics v Worcs	Worcester	1972
	K.Higgs	Leics v Surrey	Lord's	1974
	A.A.Jones	Middlesex v Essex	Lord's	1977
	M.J.Procter	Glos v Hampshire	Southampton	1977
	W.Larkins	Northants v Comb Us	Northampton	1980
	E.A.Moseley	Glamorgan v Kent	Cardiff	1981
	G.C.Small	Warwicks v Leics	Leicester	1984
	N.A.Mallender	Somerset v Comb Us	Taunton	1987
	W.K.M.Benjamin	Leics v Notts	Leicester	1987
	A.R.C.Fraser	Middx v Sussex	Lord's	1988

Most Wicket-Keeping Dismissals				
8 (8ct)	D.J.S.Taylor	Somerset v Comb Us	Taunton	1982

Most Catches in the Field				
5	V.J.Marks	Comb Us v Kent	Oxford	1976

Most Match Awards: 14 – G.A.Gooch (Essex); 11 – T.E.Jesty (7 Hants/3 Surrey/1 Lancs), B.Wood (10 Lancs/1 Derbys); 10 – J.C.Balderstone (Leics); 9 – G.Boycott (Yorks), J.H.Edrich (Surrey), C.G.Greenidge (Hants).

BENSON AND HEDGES CUP WINNERS

1972	Leicestershire	1978	Kent	1984	Lancashire
1973	Kent	1979	Essex	1985	Leicestershire
1974	Surrey	1980	Northamptonshire	1986	Middlesex
1975	Leicestershire	1981	Somerset	1987	Yorkshire
1976	Kent	1982	Somerset	1988	Hampshire
1977	Gloucestershire	1983	Middlesex		

REFUGE ASSURANCE FINAL LEAGUE TABLE

			P	W	L	Tie	NR	Pts	Away Wins	Run-Rate
1	**Worcestershire**	(1)	16	12	3	0	1	50	6	5.096
2	Gloucestershire	(3)	16	10	4	0	2	44	4	5.245
3	Lancashire	(9)	16	10	4	0	2	44	3	5.103
4	Middlesex	(10)	16	9	3	0	1	44	3	4.926
5	Surrey	(7)	16	8	5	1	2	38	4	5.087
	Glamorgan	(14)	16	8	5	1	2	38	4	4.791
7	Kent	(6)	16	7	6	0	3	34	3	4.807
8	Yorkshire	(12)	16	7	7	0	2	32	3	4.916
9	Hampshire	(7)	16	7	8	0	1	30	3	4.670
10	Essex	(14)	16	6	8	1	1	28	2	4.715
	Warwickshire	(17)	16	6	8	0	2	28	2	4.377
12	Somerset	(4)	16	6	9	0	1	26	3	4.936
	Derbyshire	(5)	16	5	8	1	2	26	3	4.815
14	Northamptonshire	(10)	16	4	9	0	3	22	2	4.564
	Sussex	(14)	16	4	9	2	1	22	1	4.572
	Leicestershire	(12)	16	4	9	0	3	22	1	4.248
17	Nottinghamshire	(2)	16	3	11	0	2	16	1	4.751

(1987 positions in brackets)

Positions calculated on (a) most points, (b) most wins, (c) most away wins, (d) run-rate.

The top four counties qualified for the Refuge Assurance Cup semi-finals.

REFUGE ASSURANCE CUP

SEMI-FINALS (7 September).
LANCASHIRE beat Gloucestershire by 3 wickets at Bristol.
WORCESTERSHIRE beat Middlesex by 7 wickets at Worcester.

FINAL (18 September)
LANCASHIRE beat Worcestershire by 52 runs at Birmingham.

JOHN PLAYER LEAGUE CHAMPIONS

1969	Lancashire	1975	Hampshire	1981	Essex
1970	Lancashire	1976	Kent	1982	Sussex
1971	Worcestershire	1977	Leicestershire	1983	Yorkshire
1972	Kent	1978	Hampshire	1984	Essex
1973	Kent	1979	Somerset	1985	Essex
1974	Leicestershire	1980	Warwickshire	1986	Hampshire

REFUGE ASSURANCE LEAGUE CHAMPIONS

1987	Worcestershire	1988	Worcestershire

REFUGE ASSURANCE LEAGUE

PRINCIPAL RECORDS 1969-1988
(Including the John Player League)

Highest Total   310-5   Essex v Glamorgan   Southend   1983
Highest Total Batting Second   301-6   Warwicks v Essex   Colchester   1982
Lowest Total   23   Middlesex v Yorks   Leeds   1974
Highest Score   176   G.A.Gooch   Essex v Glamorgan   Southend   1983
Hundreds   305 have been scored in Sunday League matches

Highest Partnerships for each Wicket

1st	239	G.A.Gooch/B.R.Hardie	Essex v Notts	Nottingham	1985
2nd	273	G.A.Gooch/K.S.McEwan	Essex v Notts	Nottingham	1983
3rd	215	W.Larkins/R.G.Williams	Northants v Worcs	Luton	1982
4th	219	C.G.Greenidge/C.L.Smith	Hampshire v Surrey	Southampton	1987
5th	185*	Asif Din/B.M.McMillan	Warwicks v Essex	Chelmsford	1986
6th	121	C.P.Wilkins/A.J.Borrington	Derbys v Warwicks	Chesterfield	1972
7th	132	K.R.Brown/N.F.Williams	Middx v Somerset	Lord's	1988
8th	95*	D.Breakwell/K.F.Jennings	Somerset v Notts	Nottingham	1976
9th	105	D.G.Moir/R.W.Taylor	Derbyshire v Kent	Derby	1984
10th	57	D.A.Graveney/J.B.Mortimore	Glos v Lancashire	Tewkesbury	1973

Most Wickets	8-26	K.D.Boyce	Essex v Lancashire	Manchester	1971
	7-15	R.A.Hutton	Yorkshire v Worcs	Leeds	1969
	7-39	A.Hodgson	Northants v Somerset	Northampton	1976
	7-41	A.N.Jones	Sussex v Notts	Nottingham	1986

Four Wkts in Four Balls   A.Ward   Derbyshire v Sussex   Derby   1970

Hat Tricks: 18 bowlers have achieved this feat in League matches: Derbyshire – A.Ward (1970), C.J.Tunnicliffe (1979); Essex – K.D.Boyce (1971); Glamorgan – M.A.Nash (1975), A.E.Cordle (1979), G.C.Holmes (1987); Hampshire – J.M.Rice (1975), M.D.Marshall (1981). Kent – R.M.Ellison (1983). Leicestershire – G.D.McKenzie (1972). Northamptonshire – A.Hodgson (1976). Nottinghamshire – K.Saxelby (1987). Somerset – R.Palmer (1970), I.V.A.Richards (1982). Sussex – A.Buss (1974). Warwickshire – R.G.D.Willis (1973), W.Blenkiron (1974). Yorkshire – P.W.Jarvis (1982).

Most Economical Analysis

O	M	R	W			
8	8	0	0	B.A.Langford	Somerset v Essex	Yeovil	1969

Most Expensive Analyses

O	M	R	W			
7.5	0	89	3	G.Miller	Derbys v Glos	Gloucester	1984
8	0	88	1	E.E.Hemmings	Notts v Somerset	Nottingham	1983

Most Wicket-Keeping Dismissals
   7 (6ct, 1st)   R.W.Taylor   Derbyshire v Lancs   Manchester   1975

Most Catches in the Field
   5   J.M.Rice   Hants v Warwicks   Southampton 1978

MINOR COUNTIES CHAMPIONSHIP
1988 FINAL

Played at Worcester on 11 September
Toss: Cambridgeshire. Result: Cheshire won by 13 runs

CHESHIRE

B. Wood	c Turner b Benson	24
J.J. Hitchmough	run out	9
I. Cockbain	b Collard	26
D.W. Varey	b Turner	67
*N.T. O'Brien	lbw b Benson	2
S.T. Crawley	c Collard b Lethbridge	16
†S. Bramhall	lbw b Lethbridge	9
J.S. Hitchmough	c Lethbridge b Collard	19
S. Dyson	c Garnham b Lethbridge	0
A.J. Murphy	c Dicks b Lethbridge	5
J.F.M. O'Brien	not out	2
Extras		12
Total (53.3 overs)		**191**

CAMBRIDGESHIRE

*N.T. Gadsby	b Dyson	28
I.S. Lawrence	c and b Dyson	18
†M.A. Garnham	c and b J.S. Hitchmough	4
J.D.R. Benson	b J.M.F. O'Brien	30
P.A. Redfarn	c Dyson b Murphy	37
N.J. Adams	not out	1
S. Turner	run out	1
P.J. Dicks	c Dyson b Murphy	37
C. Lethbridge	b Dyson	0
D.C. Collard	b Murphy	3
M.G. Stephenson	not out	1
Extras		18
Total (54.2 overs)		**178**

CAMBRIDGESHIRE	O	M	R	W		FALL OF WICKETS		
Turner	10	2	34	1		Wkt	Cheshire	Cambs
Lethbridge	10.3	2	47	4		1st	13	40
Benson	11	1	34	2		2nd	54	51
Collard	11	2	54	2		3rd	78	63
Stephenson	11	3	18	0		4th	81	107
CHESHIRE						5th	123	115
Murphy	10.2	1	41	3		6th	135	116
J.S. Hitchmough	11	2	29	1		7th	176	166
Dyson	11	1	30	3		8th	183	168
J.F.M. O'Brien	11	0	27	1		9th	187	171
N.T. O'Brien	6	1	20	0		10th	191	178
Wood	5	1	19	0				

Umpires: C. Smith and R.T. Wilson

MINOR COUNTIES CHAMPIONSHIP

FINAL TABLE 1988

EASTERN DIVISION (Points:)		*Played*	*Won* (10)	*Tied* (5)	*Lost*	*Won 1st Inns* (3)	*Tied 1st Inns* (2)	*Lost 1st Inns* (1)	*No Result* (2)	*Points*
Cambridgeshire	NW	9	5	–	–	1	–	2	1	57
Durham	NW	9	3	–	1	4	–	1	–	43
Staffordshire	NW	9	3	–	2(a)	2	–	1	1	42
Suffolk	NW	9	2	–	2(a)	5	–	–	–	38
Hertfordshire	NW	9	2	–	2(b)	–	–	3	2	33
Cumberland	NW	9	2	–	1(a)	1	1	4	–	32
Northumberland	NW	9	1	–	3(a)	3	1	1	–	25
Norfolk		9	1	–	2	2	–	4	–	20
Bedfordshire		9	–	–	2(b)	2	–	5	–	17
Lincolnshire	NW	9	–	–	4(a)	2	–	1	2	14

WESTERN DIVISION (Points:)		*Played*	*Won* (10)	*Tied* (5)	*Lost*	*Won 1st Inns* (3)	*Tied 1st Inns* (2)	*Lost 1st Inns* (1)	*No Result* (2)	*Points*
Cheshire	NW	9	5	1	1(a)	1	–	1	–	62
Berkshire	NW	9	3	–	2	4	–	–	–	42
Dorset	NW	9	3	–	1	2	1	2	–	40
Oxfordshire	NW	9	1	1	1(a)	4	1	1	–	33
Wiltshire	NW	9	2	–	2	1	–	3	1	28
Shropshire	NW	9	1	–	1(a)	3	–	4	–	26
Devon		9	1	–	1	2	1	3	1	23
Buckinghamshire		9	1	–	3(a)	2	–	3	–	22
Wales		9	–	–	3(b)	3	1	1	1	20
Cornwall		9	1	–	3	–	–	4	1	16

(a) denotes 1st Innings points in 1 match lost.
(b) denotes 1st Innings points in 2 matches lost.
NW denotes qualification for the 1989 NatWest Trophy.

MINOR COUNTIES CHAMPIONSHIP

LEADING AVERAGES 1988

BATTING
(Qualifications: 8 innings, average 35.00)

		I	NO	HS	Runs	Avge
P.R. Oliver	Staffs	11	5	136*	459	76.50
T.A. Lester	Oxon	16	6	97*	679	67.90
I. Cockbain	Cheshire	15	4	119	681	61.91
I.S. Lawrence	Cambs	17	4	144	787	60.54
S.G. Plumb	Norfolk	16	1	204*	830	55.33
A.R. Harwood	Bucks	10	2	142*	434	54.25
N.A. Riddell	Durham	12	5	63	367	52.43
M.J. Roberts	Bucks	8	1	155*	338	48.29
N.G. Roberts	Wales	15	2	103*	617	47.46
P.J. Garner	Oxon	16	3	94*	601	46.23
J.S. Johnson	Shropshire	15	2	99	598	46.00
T. Parton	Shropshire	13	2	95	499	45.36
K.N. Foyle	Wiltshire	8	2	111	272	45.33
P.J. Heseltine	Berkshire	8	1	98*	317	45.29
G.K. Brown	Durham	16	1	114	632	42.13
D. Cartledge	Staffs	15	0	102	627	41.80
J.A. Waterhouse	Staffs	16	4	71	491	40.92
R.D. Huggins	Norfolk	17	5	86	488	40.67
J. Foster	Shropshire	15	3	133*	486	40.50
D.J. Mercer	Wiltshire	17	6	114*	443	40.27
G.C. Ford	Oxon	14	2	113	466	38.83
T. Butler	Bucks	16	5	87	421	38.27
H.V. Patel	Staffs	15	3	120*	449	37.42
S. Williams	Cornwall	17	2	111*	560	37.33
S. Greensword	Durham	13	6	75*	260	37.14
G. Randall-Johnson	Devon	9	2	75	259	37.00
K. Hayes	Cumb'land	8	0	110	293	36.63
D. Gorman	Berkshire	13	5	62	291	36.38
B.W. Reidy	Cumb'land	13	1	81	430	35.83
J.B.R. Jones	Shropshire	12	2	90	358	35.80
S. Hooper	Cornwall	15	3	77	429	35.75
K.G. Rice	Devon	16	1	100	534	35.60
A.S. Patel	Durham	8	2	67	213	35.50
C. Gladwin	Suffolk	14	1	104	461	35.46
K. Gentle	Beds	15	0	80	531	35.40

BOWLING

(Qualifications: 20 wickets, average 25.00)

		O	M	R	W	Avge
S. Dyson	Cheshire	107.2	38	206	23	8.96
P.J. Lewington	Berkshire	302.5	94	658	54	12.19
S. Turner	Cambs	346.4	90	763	58	13.16
G. Edwards	Wales	126.4	52	283	20	14.15
R.C. Green	Suffolk	206.2	51	614	39	15.74
R. Ellwood	Cumb'land	189	52	491	31	15.84
D. Surridge	Herts	156	42	387	23	16.83
D. Marshall	Lincs	206.5	53	509	30	16.97

J. Thompson	Wiltshire	125	28	360	21	17.14
M.G. Boocock	Cheshire	139.5	43	363	21	17.29
T.S. Smith	Herts	123	26	355	20	17.75
T.J.A. Scriven	Bucks	139	25	475	26	18.27
I.E. Conn	Durham	272.5	57	845	45	18.78
B.J. Griffiths	Lincs	157.3	40	455	23	19.78
J.F.M. O'Brien	Cheshire	292.1	98	730	36	20.28
J. Johnston	Durham	169	44	428	21	20.38
C.D. Booden	Bucks	204.1	57	514	25	20.56
N.R. Taylor	Dorset	192.4	53	529	25	21.16
G.J. Blackburn	Cheshire	258	79	637	30	21.23
D. Halliwell	Cumb'land	144.3	39	426	20	21.30
M. Stear	Berkshire	205.2	48	534	25	21.36
A. Wingfield Digby	Dorset	208.2	64	560	26	21.54
J.H. Jones	Berkshire	205.2	38	564	26	21.69
J.S. Roberts	Shropshire	152	33	438	20	21.90
M. Woods	Cumb'land	270.5	62	701	32	21.91
A. Dalby	N'land	169.5	35	548	23	23.83
I.J. Curtis	Oxon	293.2	72	811	34	23.85
D.C. Blank	Staffs	231	49	678	28	24.21

MINOR COUNTIES CHAMPIONS

1895	Norfolk	1925	Buckinghamshire	1960	Lancashire II
1895	Durham	1926	Durham	1961	Somerset II
	Worcestershire	1927	Staffordshire	1962	Warwickshire II
1896	Worcestershire	1928	Berkshire	1963	Cambridgeshire
1897	Worcestershire	1929	Oxfordshire	1964	Lancashire II
1898	Worcestershire	1930	Durham	1965	Somerset II
1899	Northamptonshire	1931	Leicestershire II	1966	Lincolnshire
1899	Buckinghamshire	1932	Buckinghamshire	1967	Cheshire
	Glamorgan	1933	Undecided	1968	Yorkshire II
1900	Durham	1934	Lancashire II	1969	Buckinghamshire
	Northamptonshire	1935	Middlesex II	1970	Bedfordshire
1901	Durham	1936	Hertfordshire	1971	Yorkshire II
1902	Wiltshire	1937	Lancashire II	1972	Bedfordshire
1903	Northamptonshire	1938	Buckinghamshire	1973	Shropshire
1904	Northamptonshire	1939	Surrey II	1974	Oxfordshire
1905	Norfolk	1946	Suffolk	1975	Hertfordshire
1906	Staffordshire	1947	Yorkshire II	1976	Durham
1907	Lancashire II	1948	Lancashire II	1977	Suffolk
1908	Staffordshire	1949	Lancashire II	1978	Devon
1909	Wiltshire	1950	Surrey II	1979	Suffolk
1910	Norfolk	1951	Kent II	1980	Durham
1911	Staffordshire	1952	Buckinghamshire	1981	Durham
1912	In abeyance	1953	Berkshire	1982	Oxfordshire
1913	Norfolk	1954	Surrey II	1983	Hertfordshire
1920	Staffordshire	1955	Surrey II	1984	Durham
1921	Staffordshire	1956	Kent II	1985	Cheshire
1922	Buckinghamshire	1957	Yorkshire II	1986	Cumberland
1923	Buckinghamshire	1958	Yorkshire II	1987	Buckinghamshire
1924	Berkshire	1959	Warwickshire II	1988	Cheshire

SECOND XI CHAMPIONSHIP 1988
FINAL TABLE

Win = 16 points*

Position	P	W	L	D	Bonus Points Bat	Points Bowl	Total Points	Avge Points
1 SURREY (1)	17	8	–	9	45	48	221	13.00
2 Worcestershire (11)	15	7	2	6	38	34	184	12.27
3 Nottinghamshire (15)	15	6	3	6	29	41	166	11.07
4 Essex (1)	15	4	5	6	40	50	154	10.27
5 Lancashire (3)	20	6	2	12	42	57	195	9.75
6 Warwickshire (7)	17	5	3	9	31	47	158	9.29
7 Hampshire (16)	14	4	2	8	24	39	127	9.07
8 Middlesex (14)	15	4	–	11	38	32	134	8.93
9 Yorkshire (2)	16	4	1	11	43	28	135	8.44
10 Sussex (4)	14	2	5	7	28	52	112	8.00
11 Northamptonshire (13)	17	3	4	10	37	41	126	7.41
12 Glamorgan (12)	12	2	5	5	20	27	79	6.58
13 Kent (1)	16	1	6	9	37	52	105	6.56
14 Derbyshire (17)	14	1	5	8	16	39	71	5.07
15 Leicestershire (5)	18	1	6	11	27	48	91	5.06
16 Somerset (9)	15	–	5	10	36	35	71	4.73
17 Gloucestershire (16)	14	–	4	10	19	35	54	3.86

1987 final positions are shown in brackets.
Two matches (both involving Glamorgan) were abandoned without a ball being bowled.

SECOND XI CHAMPIONS

1959	Gloucestershire	1969	Kent	1979	Warwickshire
1960	Northamptonshire	1970	Kent	1980	Glamorgan
1961	Kent	1971	Hampshire	1981	Hampshire
1962	Worcestershire	1972	Nottinghamshire	1982	Worcestershire
1962	Worcestershire	1973	Essex	1983	Leicestershire
1964	Lancashire	1974	Middlesex	1984	Yorkshire
1965	Glamorgan	1975	Surrey	1985	Nottinghamshire
1966	Surrey	1976	Kent	1986	Lancashire
1967	Hampshire	1977	Yorkshire	1987	Kent/Yorkshire
1968	Surrey	1978	Sussex	1988	Surrey

THE FIRST-CLASS COUNTIES HONOURS, REGISTER, RECORDS AND 1988 AVERAGES

Records are complete to the end of the 1988 English season (15 September).

ABBREVIATIONS

General

*	not out/unbroken partnership	f-c	first-class
b	born	HS	Highest Score
BB	Best innings bowling analysis	LOI	Limited-Overs Internationals
Cap	Awarded lst XI County Cap	Tests	Official Test Matches
Tours	Overseas tours involving first-class appearances		

Awards

BHC	Benson and Hedges Cup 'Gold' Award
NWT	NatWest Trophy/Gillette Cup 'Man of the Match' Award
Wisden 1986	One of Wisden Cricketers' Almanack's Five Cricketers of 1986
YC 1987	Cricket Writers' Club Young Cricketer of 1987

Competitions

BHC	Benson and Hedges Cup
GC	Gillette Cup
NWT	NatWest Trophy
RAL	Refuge Assurance League

Playing Categories

LB	Bowls right-arm leg-breaks
LF	Bowls left-arm fast
LFM	Bowls left-arm fast-medium
LHB	Bats left-handed
LM	Bowls left-arm medium pace
LMF	Bowls left-arm medium fast
OB	Bowls right-arm off-breaks
RHB	Bats right-handed
RM	Bowls right-arm medium pace
RMF	Bowls right-arm medium-fast
RF	Bowls right-arm fast
RFM	Bowls right-arm fast-medium
SLA	Bowls left-arm leg-breaks
WK	Wicket-keeper

Education

BHS	Boys' High School
BS	Boy's School
C	College
CE	College of Education
CFE	College of Further Education
CHE	College of Higher Education
CPE	College of Physical Education
CS	Comprehensive School
GS	Grammar School
HS	High School
LSE	London School of Economics
RGS	Royal Grammar School
S	School
SFC	Sixth Form College
SS	Secondary School
TC	Technical College
TGS	Technical Grammar School
THS	Technical High School
U	University

Teams (see also p 161)

Cav	Cavaliers	ND	Northern Districts
DHR	D.H. Robins' XI	NSW	New South Wales
DN	Duke of Norfolk's XI	OFS	Orange Free State
Eng Co	English Counties XI	PIA	Pakistan International Airlines
GW	Griqualand West	RW	Rest of the World XI
Int XI	International XI	SAB	South African Breweries XI
IW	International Wanderers	Zim	Zimbabwe (Rhodesia)

DERBYSHIRE

Formation of Present Club: 4 November 1870
Colours: Chocolate, Amber and Pale Blue
Badge: Rose and Crown
Championships: (1) 1936
NatWest Trophy/Gillette Cup Winners: (1) 1981
Benson and Hedges Cup Winners: (0) Finalists 1978, 1988
Sunday League Champions: (0) Third 1970
Match Awards: NWT 27; BHC 44

Secretary: I.Edwards, County Ground, Nottingham Road, Derby DE2 6DA
Captain: K.J.Barnett
Scorer: S.W.Tacey
Cricketcall: ☎ 0898 1214 66
Benefit 1989: Derbyshire CCC Funds

ADAMS, Christopher John (Repton S), b Whitwell, 6 May 1970. 6′0″. RHB, OB. Debut 1988. HS 21 v Surrey (Oval) 1988.

BARNETT, Kim John (Leek HS), b Stoke-on-Trent, Staffs 17 Jul 1960. 6′1″. RHB, LB. Debut 1979. Cap 1982. Captain 1983-. Boland 1982-88. Staffordshire 1976. Wisden 1988. **Tests:** 1 (1988) HS 66 v SL (Lord's). LOI: 1. Tours: NZ 1979-80 (DHR); SL 1985-86 (Eng B). 1000 runs (6); most – 1734 (1984). HS 239* v Leics (Leicester) 1988. BB 6-115 v Yorks (Bradford) 1985. Awards: NWT 2; BHC 6. **NWT:** HS 88 v Middx (Derby) 1983. BB 6-24 v Cumberland (Kensal) 1984. **BHC:** HS 115 v Glos (Derby) 1987. BB 1-10. **RAL:** HS 131* v Essex (Derby) 1984. BB 3-39 v Yorks (Chesterfield) 1979.

BASE, Simon John (Fish Hoek HS, Cape Town), b Maidstone, Kent 2 Jan 1960. 6′2″. RHB, RMF. W Province 1981-84. Glamorgan 1986-87. Boland 1987-88. Derbyshire debut 1988. HS 38 Glam v Glos (Swansea) 1987. Derbys HS 15 v Notts (Nottingham) 1988. BB 6-28 Boland v Border (Stellenbosch) 1987-88. Derbys BB 4-74 v Lancs (Derby) 1988. **NWT:** HS 4. BB 2-49 Glam v Sussex (Hove) 1986. **BHC:** HS 12 Glam v Kent (Cardiff) 1987. BB 2-34 Glam v Sussex (Swansea) 1986. **RAL:** HS 19 Glam v Kent (Swansea) 1987. BB 3-31 Glam v Surrey (Oval) 1986.

BEARDSHALL, Mark (Holgate GS), b Barnsley, Yorks 10 Jan 1962. 6′0″. RHB, RM. Debut 1987. HS 25 v Glos (Bristol) 1987. BB 4-68 v Kent (Canterbury) 1987. **RAL:** HS 7.

BOWLER, Peter Duncan (Educated at Canberra, Australia), b Plymouth, Devon 30 Jul 1963. 6′1″. RHB, OB. Leicestershire 1986 – first to score hundred on f-c debut for Leics (100* and 62 v Hants at Leicester). Tasmania 1986-87. Derbyshire debut 1988 scoring 155* CU at Cambridge – first to score hundreds on debut for two counties. 1000 runs (1): 1725 (1988). HS 159* v Essex (Chesterfield) 1988. BB 2-63 v Worcs (Derby) 1988. **NWT:** HS 46 v Chester (Cheshire) 1988. **BHC:** HS 64 v Lancs (Liverpool) 1988. BB 1-15. **RAL:** HS 55 Leics v Sussex (Leicester) 1986. BB 2-29 v Leics (Derby) 1988.

GOLDSMITH, Steven Clive (Simon Langton GS, Canterbury), b Ashford, Kent 19 Dec 1964. 5′10″. RHB, RM. Kent 1987. Derbyshire debut 1988. 1000 runs (1): 1071 (1988). HS 89 v Kent (Chesterfield) 1988. BB 1-37. **NWT:** HS 10 v Hants (Derby) 1988. **BHC:** HS 27* v Scotland (Glasgow) 1988. **RAL:** HS 61 v Middx (Repton) 1988.

GRIFFITH, Frank Alexander (Beaconsfield HS; Wm Morris HS; Haringey Cricket C), b Whipps Cross, Essex 15 Aug 1968. 6'0". RHB, RM. Debut 1988. HS 37 v Northants (Northampton) 1988. BB 4-47 v Lancs (Manchester) 1988. **RAL:** HS 9. BB 2-27 v Northants (Northampton) 1988.

HOLDING, Michael Anthony (Kingston College HS), b Kingston, Jamaica 16 Feb 1954. 6'3". RHB, RF. Jamaica 1972-88 (capt 1985-87). Lancashire 1981. Tasmania 1982-83. Derbyshire debut/cap 1983. Canterbury 1987-88. Wisden 1976. **Tests** (WI): 60 (1975-76 to 1986-87); HS 73 v Eng (St John's) 1985-86; BB 8-92 v Eng (Oval) 1976. LOI (WI): 102. Tours (WI): Eng 1976, 1980, 1984; Aus 1975-76, 1979-80, 1981-82, 1984-85, 1986-87; NZ 1979-80, 1986-87; Ind 1983-84; Pak 1980-81, 1981-82 (Int XI). HS 80 v Yorks (Chesterfield) 1985. BB 8-92 (Tests). Derbys BB 7-97 v Worcs (Derby) 1986. Awards: NWT 2; BHC 2. **NWT:** HS 27 v Durham (Derby) 1985. BB 8-21 (world record) v Sussex (Hove) 1988. **BHC:** HS 69 v Lancs (Chesterfield) 1986. BB 5-31 v Glam (Swansea) 1988. **RAL:** HS 58 v Sussex (Hove) 1985. BB 4-22 v Notts (Derby) 1988.

JEAN-JACQUES, Martin (Aylestone SS, London), b Soufriere, Dominica 2 Jul 1960. 6'0". RHB, RMF. Debut 1986. Buckinghamshire 1983-85. HS 73 v Yorks (Sheffield) 1986 (on debut, sharing Derbys record 10th-wkt stand of 132 with A.Hill). BB 8-77 v Kent (Derby) 1986. **NWT:** HS 16 v Surrey (Derby) 1986. BB 3-23 v Cambs (Wisbech) 1987. **BHC:** HS 2*. BB 3-22 v Notts (Nottingham) 1987. **RAL:** HS 15 v Somerset (Derby) 1987. BB 3-36 v Worcs (Worcester) 1986.

KRIKKEN, Karl Matthew (Rivington & Blackrod HS & SFC), b Bolton, Lancs 9 Apr 1969. Son of B.E.Krikken (Lancs and Worcs 1966-69). 5'9". RHB, WK. Awaiting f-c debut. RAL debut 1987 – did not bat.

MAHER, Bernard Joseph Michael (Abbotsfield CS; Bishopshalt GS; Loughborough U), b Hillingdon, Middx 11 Feb 1958. 5'10". RHB, WK. Debut 1981. Cap 1987. HS 126 v NZ (Derby) 1986. BB 2-69 v Glam (Abergavenny) 1986. **NWT:** HS 44 v Hants (Derby) 1988. **BHC:** HS 50 v Northants (Derby) 1987. **RAL:** HS 78 v Lancs (Manchester) 1987.

MALCOLM, Devon Eugene (Richmond C, Sheffield), b Kingston, Jamaica 22 Feb 1963. 6'2". RHB, RF. Debut 1984. HS 29* v Glos (Gloucester) 1986. BB 6-68 v Warwicks (Derby) 1988. Award: BHC 1. **NWT:** HS 1. BB 1-48. **BHC:** HS 0*. BB 5-27 v Middx (Derby) 1988. **RAL:** HS 16 and BB 2-40 v Northants (Finedon) 1986.

MORRIS, John Edward (Shavington CS; Dane Bank CFE), b Crewe, Cheshire 1 Apr 1964. 5'10". RHB, RM. Debut 1982. Cap 1986. 1000 runs (3); most – 1739 (1986). HS 191 v Kent (Derby) 1986. BB 1-13. **NWT:** HS 43* v Sussex (Hove) 1988. **BHC:** HS 65 v Kent (Derby) 1986. **RAL:** HS 104 v Glos (Gloucester) 1984.

MORTENSEN, Ole Henrek (Brondbyoster S; Abedore C, Copenhagen), b Vejle, Denmark 29 Jan 1958. 6'3". RHB, RFM. Debut 1983. Cap 1986. Denmark 1975-82. Hat-trick 1987. HS 74* v Yorks (Chesterfield) 1987. BB 6-27 v Yorks (Sheffield) 1983. Award: NWT 1. **NWT:** HS 11 v Surrey (Derby) 1986. BB 5-15 v Cheshire (Chester) 1988. **BHC:** HS 3*. BB 3-17 v Leics (Chesterfield) 1986. **RAL:** HS 5*. BB 4-10 v Leics (Chesterfield) 1985.

NEWMAN, Paul Geoffrey (Alderman Newton's GS, Leicester), b Evington, Leicester 10 Jan 1959. 6'2½". RHB, RFM. Debut 1980. Cap 1986. Tour: Zim 1984-85 (Eng Co). HS 115 v Leics (Chesterfield) 1985. BB 8-29 v Yorks (Leeds) 1988. **NWT:** HS 35 v Leics (Leicester) 1984. BB 3-23 v Notts (Derby) 1981. **BHC:** HS 56* v Notts (Nottingham) 1985. BB 4-48 v Worcs (Worcester) 1982. **RAL:** HS 52* v Warwicks (Birmingham) 1987. BB 4-21 v Hants (Derby) 1983.

O'GORMAN, Timothy Joseph Gerard (St George's C, Weybridge; Durham U), b Woking, Surrey 15 May 1967. Grandson of J.G.O'Gorman (Surrey 1927). 6'2". RHB, OB. Debut 1987. HS 78 v Kent (Chesterfield) 1988. **BHC:** HS 43 Comb Us v Glam (Cardiff) 1988. **RAL:** HS 14 v Northants (Northampton) 1988.

ROBERTS, Bruce (Peterhouse; Prince Edward S, Salisbury), b Lusaka, N Rhodesia 30 May 1962. 6'2". RHB, RM, WK. Transvaal 1982-88. Derbyshire debut 1984. Cap 1986. 1000 runs (2); most – 1643 (1987). HS 184 v Sussex (Chesterfield) 1987. BB 5-68 Transvaal B v N Transvaal B (Johannesburg) 1986-87. Derbys BB 4-77 v Essex (Ilford) 1984. Awards: BHC 2. **NWT:** HS 60 v Kent (Canterbury) 1987. BB 2-73 v Leics (Leicester) 1984. **BHC:** HS 100 v Northants (Derby) 1987. BB 2-47 v Minor C (Shrewsbury) 1984. **RAL:** HS 101* v Sussex (Hove) 1987. BB 4-29 v Lancs (Derby) 1984.

SHARMA, Rajeshwar ('Reg') (Parklands S, Sidcup; Bexley and Erith TS), b Nairobi, Kenya 27 Jun 1962. 6'3". RHB, RM/OB. Debut 1985. HS 111 v Yorks (Chesterfield) 1987. BB 6-80 v Glos (Bristol) 1987. **NWT:** HS 21 v Kent (Canterbury) 1987. BB 4-29 v Cornwall (Derby) 1986. **BHC:** HS 2. **RAL:** HS 37 v Hants (Heanor) 1986. BB 3-35 v Somerset (Weston) 1988.

WAKEFIELD, Mark (Bishop Henshaw RC Upper School), b Rochdale, Lancs 17 Nov 1968. 5'9". RHB, SLA. Debut 1987. HS 4 and BB 1-30 v CU (Cambridge) 1987.

WARNER, Allan Esmond (Tabernacle S, St Kitts), b Birmingham 12 May 1957. 5'7". RHB, RFM. Worcestershire 1982-84. Derbyshire debut 1985. Cap 1987. HS 91 v Leics (Chesterfield) 1986. BB 5-27 Worcs v Glam (Worcester) 1984. Derbys BB 5-51 v Essex (Colchester) 1985. Awards: NWT 1. **NWT:** HS 32 v Kent (Canterbury) 1987. BB 3-20 v Cambs (Wisbech) 1987. **BHC:** HS 24* Worcs v Derbys (Worcester) 1982. BB 4-36 v Notts (Nottingham) 1987. **RAL:** HS 68 v Hants (Heanor) 1986. BB 5-39 v Worcs (Knypersley) 1985.

NEWCOMERS

BISHOP, Ian Raphael (Belmont SS), b Port-of-Spain, Trinidad 24 Oct 1967. Nephew of R.J.Bishop (Trinidad 1986-87). 6'5". RHB, RF. Trinidad 1986-88. LOI (WI): 2. Tour (WI): Eng 1988. HS 23 and BB 6-39.WI v Kent (Canterbury) 1988.

HALLACK, David, b Rhodesia 22 Jan 1966. RHB, RM. Derbyshire 2nd XI 1985-88.

DEPARTURES

FINNEY, Roger John (Lady Manners S, Bakewell), b Darley Dale 2 Aug 1960. 6'1". RHB, LM. Derbyshire 1982-88 (cap 1985). HS 82 v Glos (Derby) 1985. BB 7-54 v Leics (Chesterfield) 1986. Award: BHC 1. **NWT:** HS 40 v Notts (Derby) 1987. BB 2-8 v Cumberland (Kensal) 1984. **BHC:** HS 46 v Lancs (Derby) 1984. BB 5-40 v Scotland (Aberdeen) 1985. **RAL:** HS 50* v Worcs (Worcester) 1984. BB 4-38 v Northants (Northampton) 1984.

WRIGHT, John Geoffrey (Christ's C, Christchurch; Otago U), b Darfield, NZ 5 July 1954. 6'1". LHB, RM. N Districts 1975-84. Canterbury 1985-88 (capt 1986-87). Derbyshire 1977-88 (cap 1977; benefit 1987). Tests (NZ): 58 (1977-78 to 1987-88, 1 as capt). HS 141 v Aus (Christchurch) 1981-82. LOI (NZ): 110. Tours (NZ): Eng 1978, 1983, 1986; Aus 1980-81, 1985-86, 1987-88; WI 1982-83 (Int XI), 1984-85; Pak 1984-85; SL 1977-78 (DHR), 1983-84. 1000 runs (6+2); most – 1830 (1982). HS 192 Canterbury v Central Districts (New Plymouth) 1987. Derbys HS 190 v Yorks (Derby) 1982. BB 1-4. Awards: NWT 1; BHC 3. **NWT:** HS 87* v Sussex (Hove) 1977. **BHC:** 102 v Worcs (Chesterfield) 1977. **RAL:** 108 v Warwicks (Coventry) 1983.

DERBYSHIRE 1988

RESULTS SUMMARY

	Place	Won	Lost	Tied	Drew	Aban
Britannic Assurance Championship	14th	4	3		15	
All First-class Matches		5	3		16	
Refuge Assurance League	12th	5	4	8	1	2
NatWest Bank Trophy	Quarter-Finalist					
Benson and Hedges Cup	Finalist					

BRITANNIC ASSURANCE CHAMPIONSHIP AVERAGES

BATTING AND FIELDING

Cap		M	I	NO	HS	Runs	Avge	100	50	Ct/St
1982	K.J.Barnett	17	27	2	239*	1406	56.24	4	7	14
1985	R.J.Finney	3	5	2	52*	142	47.33	—	1	—
—	P.D.Bowler	22	40	4	159*	1563	43.41	3	9	12
1977	J.G.Wright	11	20	1	154*	815	42.89	1	5	1
1986	J.E.Morris	21	35	5	175	1163	38.76	2	6	5
—	S.C.Goldsmith	22	37	4	89	956	28.96	—	5	16
1987	B.J.M.Maher	22	38	6	121*	920	28.75	1	4	51/1
1986	B.Roberts	22	37	4	71	903	27.36	—	7	13
—	R.Sharma	9	13	2	80	275	25.00	—	1	5
—	T.J.G.O'Gorman	4	8	—	78	152	19.00	—	1	5
—	F.A.Griffith	4	6	1	37	87	17.40	—	—	2
1987	A.E.Warner	18	25	6	45	300	15.78	—	—	3
1986	P.G.Newman	14	18	5	39	174	13.38	—	—	1
1983	M.A.Holding	11	12	2	30*	129	12.90	—	—	7
1986	O.H.Mortensen	22	12	8	15	46	11.50	—	—	6
—	S.J.Base	7	9	3	15	51	8.50	—	—	2
—	D.E.Malcolm	19	21	5	22	119	7.43	—	—	1
—	M.Jean-Jacques	3	4	—	5	5	1.25	—	—	1

Also batted: C.J.Adams (1 match) 21 (1 ct).

BOWLING

	O	M	R	W	Avge	Best	5 wI	10 wM
O.H.Mortensen	233.3	73	464	34	13.64	6-35	4	—
P.G.Newman	306.5	70	877	32	27.40	8-29	1	—
A.E.Warner	416	92	1091	37	29.48	4-36	—	—
K.J.Barnett	158.1	35	411	13	31.61	3-63	—	—
D.E.Malcolm	468	85	1642	50	32.84	6-68	2	—
M.A.Holding	279.1	49	827	24	34.45	4-74	—	—
S.J.Base	165	12	654	17	38.47	4-74	—	—

Also bowled: P.D.Bowler 169.5-28-577-7; R.J.Finney 45-8-131-0; S.C.Goldsmith 43-8-125-0; F.A.Griffith 80.3-17-268-9; M.Jean-Jacques 84.1-14-262-8; J.E.Morris 5.1-0-19-0; B.Roberts 99-21-300-8; R.Sharma 208.2-47-559-7.

The First-Class Averages (pp 161-175) give the records of Derbyshire players in all first-class county matches, (their other opponents being the Sri Lankans and Cambridge U.), with the exception of:
K.J.Barnett 18-28-2-239*-1557-59.88-5-7-16ct. 161.1-37-414-14-29.57-3/63.

DERBYSHIRE RECORDS

FIRST-CLASS CRICKET

Highest Total	For	645		v Hampshire	Derby	1898
	V	662		by Yorkshire	Chesterfield	1898
Lowest Total	For	16		v Notts	Nottingham	1879
	V	23		by Hampshire	Burton upon T	1958
Highest Innings	For	274	G.Davidson	v Lancashire	Manchester	1896
	V	343*	P.A.Perrin	for Essex	Chesterfield	1904

Highest Partnerships
Wkt

1st	322	H.Storer/J.Bowden	v Essex	Derby	1929
2nd	349	C.S.Elliott/J.D.Eggar	v Notts	Nottingham	1947
3rd	291	P.N.Kirsten/D.S.Steele	v Somerset	Taunton	1981
4th	328	P.Vaulkhard/D.Smith	v Notts	Nottingham	1946
5th	203	C.P.Wilkins/I.R.Buxton	v Lancashire	Manchester	1971
6th	212	G.M.Lee/T.S.Worthington	v Essex	Chesterfield	1932
7th	241*	G.H.Pope/A.E.G.Rhodes	v Hampshire	Portsmouth	1948
8th	182	A.H.M.Jackson/W.Carter	v Leics	Leicester	1922
9th	283	A.Warren/J.Chapman	v Warwicks	Blackwell	1910
10th	132	A.Hill/M.Jean-Jacques	v Yorkshire	Sheffield	1986

Best Bowling	For	10-40	W.Bestwick	v Glamorgan	Cardiff	1921
(Innings)	V	10-47	T.F.Smailes	for Yorkshire	Sheffield	1939
Best Bowling	For	17-103	W.Mycroft	v Hampshire	Southampton	1876
(Match)	V	16-101	G.Giffen	for Australians	Derby	1886

Most Runs – Season	2,165	D.B.Carr	(av 48.11)		1959
Most Runs – Career	20,516	D.Smith	(av 31.41)		1927-1952
Most 100s – Season	8	P.N.Kirsten			1982
Most 100s – Career	30	D.Smith			1927-1952
Most Wkts – Season	168	T.B.Mitchell	(av 19.55)		1935
Most Wkts – Career	1,670	H.L.Jackson	(av 17.11)		1947-1963

LIMITED-OVERS CRICKET

Highest Total	NWT	365-3		v Cornwall	Derby	1986
	BHC	300-6		v Northants	Derby	1987
	RAL	292-9		v Worcs	Knypersley	1985
Lowest Total	NWT	79		v Surrey	The Oval	1967
	BHC	102		v Yorkshire	Bradford	1975
	RAL	70		v Surrey	Derby	1972
Highest Innings	NWT	153	A.Hill	v Cornwall	Derby	1986
	BHC	115	K.J.Barnett	v Glos	Derby	1987
	RAL	131*	K.J.Barnett	v Essex	Derby	1984
Best Bowling	NWT	8-21	M.A.Holding	v Sussex	Hove	1988
	BHC	6-33	E.J.Barlow	v Glos	Bristol	1978
	RAL	6-7	M.Hendrick	v Notts	Nottingham	1972

ESSEX

Formation of Present Club: 14 January 1876
Colours: Blue, Gold and Red
Badge: Three Seaxes above Scroll bearing 'Essex'
Championships: (4) 1979, 1983, 1984, 1986
NatWest Trophy/Gillette Cup Winners: (1) 1985
Benson and Hedges Cup Winners: (1) 1979
Sunday League Champions: (3) 1981, 1984, 1985
Match Awards: NWT 30; BHC 55

Secretary/General Manager: P.J.Edwards, County Cricket Ground, New Writtle
Street, Chelmsford CM2 0PG
Captain: G.A.Gooch
Scorer: C.F.Driver
Cricketcall: ☎ 0898 1214 16
Testimonial 1989: J.K.Lever

CHILDS, John Henry (Audley Park SMS, Torquay), b Plymouth, Devon 15 Aug
1951. 6'0". LHB, SLA. Gloucestershire 1975-84 (cap 1977). Essex debut 1985. Cap
1986. Devon 1973-74. Wisden 1986. **Tests:** 2 (1988); HS 2*; BB 1-13. HS 34* Glos v
Notts (Cheltenham) 1982. Essex HS 34 v NZ (Chelmsford) 1986. BB 9-56 Glos v
Somerset (Bristol) 1981. Essex BB 8-58 v Glos (Colchester) 1986. Awards: BHC 1.
NWT: HS 14* Glos v Hants (Bristol) 1983. BB 2-15 Glos v Ireland (Dublin) 1981.
BHC: HS 10 Glos v Somerset (Bristol) 1979. BB 3-36 Glos v Glam (Bristol) 1982.
RAL: HS 16* Glos v Warwicks (Bristol) 1981. BB 4-15 Glos v Northants
(Northampton) 1976.

EAST, David Edward (Hackney Downs S; E Anglia U), b Clapton 27 Jul 1959.
5'9". RHB, WK. Debut 1981. Cap 1982. HS 134 v Glos (Ilford) 1988. Set world f-c
record by catching the FIRST eight wickets to fall in an innings (v Somerset at
Taunton 1985 on his 26th birthday). Awards: NWT 1. **NWT:** HS 28 v Northumberland (Jesmond) 1984. **BHC:** HS 33 v Glos (Chelmsford) 1984. **RAL:** HS 43 v
Derbys (Derby) 1982.

FOSTER, Neil Alan (Philip Morant CS), b Colchester 6 May 1962. 6'3". RHB,
RFM. Debut 1980. Cap 1983. YC 1983. Wisden 1987. **Tests:** 25 (1983 to 1988); HS
39 v Pak (Lahore) 1987-88; BB 8-107 v Pak (Leeds) 1987. **LOI:** 45. Tours: Aus
1986-87, 1987-88; WI 1985-86; NZ 1983-84, 1987-88; Ind/SL 1984-85; Pak 1983-84,
1987-88. 100 wickets (1) – 105 (1986). HS 74* Eng XI v Queensland (Brisbane)
1986-87. Essex HS 63 v Lancs (Ilford) 1985. BB 8-107 England v Pakistan (Leeds)
1987. Essex BB 7-33 v Warwicks (Chelmsford) 1987. Awards: NWT 1; BHC 2.
NWT: HS 26 v Worcs (Chelmsford) 1987. BB 4-9 v Northumb (Jesmond) 1987.
BHC: HS 37* v Somerset (Taunton) 1987. BB 5-32 v Surrey (Oval) 1985. **RAL:** HS
40 v Warwicks (Birmingham) 1988. BB 5-17 v Derbys (Derby) 1986.

GOOCH, Graham Alan (Norlington Jr HS), b Leytonstone 23 Jul 1953. 6'0". RHB,
RM. Debut 1973. Cap 1975. Captain 1986-87, 1989. Benefit 1985. W Province
1982-84. Wisden 1979. **Tests:** 68 (1975 to 1988, 2 as captain); HS 196 v Aus (Oval)
1985; BB 2-12 v Ind (Delhi) 1981-82. **LOI:** 67. Tours: Aus 1978-79, 1979-80; SA
1981-82 (SAB); WI 1980-81, 1985-86; Ind 1979-80, 1981-82; Pak 1987-88; SL
1981-82. 1000 runs (12+1); most – 2559 (1984). HS 275 v Kent (Chelmsford) 1988.
BB 7-14 v Worcs (Ilford) 1982. Shared Essex record 2nd-wkt stand of 321 with
K.S.McEwan v Northants (Ilford) 1978. Awards: NWT 6; BHC 14 (record). **NWT:**
HS 133 v Scotland (Chelmsford) 1984. BB 3-31 v Warwicks (Birmingham) 1986.
BHC: HS 198* v Sussex (Hove) 1982. BB 3-24 v Sussex (Hove) 1982. **RAL:** HS 176
v Glam (Southend) 1983. BB 4-33 v Worcs (Chelmsford) 1984.

HARDIE, Brian Ross (Larbert HS), b Stenhousemuir, Scotland 14 Jan 1950. Brother of K.M. (Scotland 1966-76). 5'11". RHB, RM. Scotland 1970-72. Essex debut 1973. Cap 1974. Benefit 1983. 1000 runs (11); most – 1522 (1975). HS 162 v Warwicks (Birmingham) 1975, and 162 v Somerset (Southend) 1985. BB 2-39 v Glamorgan (Ilford) 1979. Awards: NWT 1; BHC 2. **NWT:** HS 110 v Notts (Lord's) 1985. BB 1-16. **BHC:** HS 119* v Sussex (Hove) 1986. **RAL:** HS 109 v Northants (Colchester) 1986. BB 1-4.

HUSSAIN, Nasser (Forest S, Snaresbrook; Durham U), b Madras, India 28 Mar 1968. Brother of M. (Worcs 1985). 5'11". RHB, LB. Debut 1987. HS 165* v Leics (Chelmsford) 1988. **BHC:** HS 76* Comb Us v Glam (Cardiff) 1988. **RAL:** HS 38 v Glam (Chelmsford) 1988.

ILOTT, Mark Christopher (Francis Combe S, Garston), b Watford, Herts 27 Aug 1970. 6'0½". LHB, LMF. Debut 1988. Hertfordshire 1987-88. HS 6. BB 2-23 v CU (Cambridge) 1988.

LEVER, John Kenneth (Dane SM), b Stepney 24 Feb 1949. 6'0½". RHB, LFM. Debut 1967. Cap 1970. Benefit 1980. Testimonial 1989. Natal 1982-85. Wisden 1978. **Tests:** 21 (1976-77 to 1986); HS 53 and BB 7-46 (10-70 match) v India (Delhi) 1976-77 on debut. LOI: 22. Tours: Aus 1976-77, 1978-79, 1979-80; SA 1972-73 (DHR), 1973-74 (DHR), 1981-82 (SAB); NZ 1977-78; Ind/SL 1976-77, 1981-82; Ind 1979-80, 1980-81 (Overseas XI); Pak 1977-78; SL 1977-78 (DHR). 100 wickets (4); most – 116 (1984). HS 91 v Glamorgan (Cardiff) 1970. BB 8-37 v Glos (Bristol) 1984. Awards: NWT 4; BHC 2. **NWT:** HS 15* v Surrey (Chelmsford) 1984. BB 5-8 v Middx (Westcliff) 1972. **BHC:** HS 13 v Lancs (Chelmsford) 1984. BB 5-13 v Middx (Lord's) 1985. **RAL:** HS 23 v Worcs (Worcester) 1974. BB 5-13 v Glam (Ebbw Vale) 1975.

LILLEY, Alan William (Caterham HS, Ilford), b Ilford 8 May 1959. 5'11". RHB, RM. Debut 1978 scoring 22 and 100* v Notts (Nottingham). Cap 1986. HS 102 v Middx (Chelmsford) 1987. BB 3-116 v Glamorgan (Swansea) 1985. Awards: NWT 1; BHC 1. **NWT:** HS 113 v Northumb (Jesmond) 1986. BB 2-19 v Scotland (Chelmsford) 1984. **BHC:** HS 119 v Cambridge U (Chelmsford) 1979. BB 1-4. **RAL:** HS 60 v Northants (Chelmsford) 1980. BB 2-0 v Glos (Bristol) 1984.

MILLER, Geoffrey (Chesterfield GS), b Chesterfield, Derbys 8 Sep 1952. 6'1". RHB, OB. Derbyshire 1973-86 (cap 1976; captain 1979-81; benefit 1985). Natal 1983-84. Essex debut 1987. Cap 1988. YC 1976. **Tests:** 34 (1976 to 1984); HS 98* v Pak (Lahore) 1977-78; BB 5-44 v Aus (Sydney) 1978-79. LOI: 25. Tours: Aus 1976-77, 1978-79, 1979-80, 1982-83; WI 1980-81; NZ 1977-78; Ind and SL 1976-77; Pak 1977-78. HS 130 Derbys v Lancs (Manchester) 1984. Essex HS 77 v Lancs (Southend) 1988. BB 8-70 Derbys v Leics (Coalville) 1982. Essex BB 7-59 v Lancs (Manchester) 1987. Awards: BHC 4. **NWT:** HS 59* Derbys v Worcs (Worcester) 1978. BB 3-23 v Wilts (Chelmsford) 1988. **BHC:** HS 88* Derbys v Minor C (Derby) 1982. BB 3-23 Derbys v Surrey (Derby) 1979. **RAL:** HS 84 Derbys v Somerset (Chesterfield) 1980. BB 4-22 Derbys v Yorks (Huddersfield) 1978.

POOK, Robert Neil (Chafford CS), b Rainham 9 Feb 1967. 5'10". RHB, RM. Debut 1988. MCC Staff 1985. HS 6.

PRICHARD, Paul John (Brentwood HS), b Billericay 7 Jan 1965. 5'10". RHB. Debut 1984. Cap 1986. 1000 runs (2); most – 1342 (1986). HS 147* v Notts (Chelmsford) 1986. **NWT:** HS 94 v Oxon (Chelmsford) 1985. **BHC:** HS 68* v Surrey (Chelmsford) 1988. **RAL:** HS 103* v Lancs (Manchester) 1986.

PRINGLE, Derek Raymond (Felsted S; Fitzwilliam C, Cambridge), b Nairobi, Kenya 18 Sep 1958. Son of D.J. (East Africa). 6'4½". RHB, RMF. Debut 1978. Cap 1982. Cambridge U 1979-82 (blue 1979-80-81; capt 1982). **Tests**: 19 (1982 to 1988); HS 63 v Ind (Lord's) 1986; BB 5-95 v WI (Leeds) 1988. LOI: 20. Tours: Aus 1982-83; SL 1985-86 (Eng B). HS 128 v Kent (Chelmsford) 1988. BB 7-32 v Middx (Chelmsford) 1983. Awards: NWT 2; BHC 4. **NWT**: HS 80* v Wilts (Chelmsford) 1988. BB 5-12 v Oxon (Chelmsford) 1985. **BHC**: HS 68 Comb Us v Somerset (Taunton) 1982. BB 5-35 v Lancs (Chelmsford) 1984. **RAL**: HS 81* v Warwicks (Birmingham) 1985. BB 5-41 v Glos (Southend) 1985.

SEYMOUR, Adam Charles (Millfield S), b Royston, Cambs 7 Dec 1967. 6'2". LHB. Debut 1988. HS 33* v CU (Cambridge) 1988.

STEPHENSON, John Patrick (Felsted S; Durham U), b Stebbing 14 Mar 1965. 6'1". RHB, RM. Debut 1985. HS 99 v Leics (Chelmsford) 1988. BB 2-66 v Surrey (Oval) 1988. **NWT**: HS 55 v Warwicks (Birmingham) 1986. **BHC**: HS 75 Comb Us v Somerset (Taunton) 1987. BB 1-27. **RAL**: HS 45 v Lancs (Manchester) 1986. BB 1-11.

TOPLEY, Thomas Donald (Royal Hospital S, Holbrook, Suffolk), b Canterbury, Kent 25 Feb 1964. Brother of P.A. (Kent 1972-75). 6'3". RHB, RMF. Surrey (v CU) and Essex debuts 1985. Cap 1988. Griqualand West 1987-88. Norfolk 1984-85. HS 66 v Yorks (Leeds) 1987. BB 7-75 (12-179 match) v Derbys (Chesterfield) 1988. Awards: NWT 1; BHC 1. **NWT**: HS 15* v Worcs (Chelmsford) 1987. BB 4-21 v Northumb (Jesmond) 1987. **BHC**: HS 6*. BB 4-22 v Surrey (Chelmsford) 1988. **RAL**: HS 23 v Middx (Lord's) 1988. BB 6-33 v Notts (Colchester) 1988.

WAUGH, Mark Edward (E Hills, HS), b Canterbury, Sydney, Aus 2 Jun 1965. Twin of S.R. (NSW, Somerset and Aus). 6'1". RHB, RM. NSW 1985-88. Essex debut 1988. Tour: Zim 1987-88 (NSW). HS 116 NSW v Tasmania (Sydney) 1987-88. Essex HS 86 v Leics (Chelmsford) 1988. BB 4-130 NSW v Queensland (Brisbane) 1985-86. **RAL**: HS 103 and BB 2-16 v Notts (Colchester) 1988 (on debut).

NEWCOMERS

GARNHAM, Michael Anthony (Camberwell GS, Melbourne; Scotch C, Perth; Barnstaple GS; N Devon SFC; East Anglia U), b Johannesburg, SA 20 Aug 1960. 5'10". RHB, WK. Gloucestershire 1979. Leicestershire 1980-85 and 1988. Cambridgeshire 1986-88. HS 100 Leics v OU (Oxford) 1985. Awards: NWT 1; BHC 1. **NWT**: HS 110 Cambs v Warwks (Birmingham) 1988. **BHC**: HS 55 Leics v Derbys (Leicester) 1982. **RAL**: HS 79* Leics v Lancs (Leicester) 1982.

KNIGHT, Nicholas Verity (Felsted S; Loughborough U), Watford, Herts 28 Nov 1969. 6'0". LHB. Represented Young England at hockey.

VAN-LINT, Alan Terence (Caterham S, Ilford), b Newbury Park, Essex 3 Jul 1969. 6'0". RHB, RM.

THOMAS, Kevin Oliver (Wanstead HS), b Mile End, London 20 Jun 1963. 6'3". RHB, RFM.

DEPARTURES – see page 150

ESSEX 1988

RESULTS SUMMARY

	Place	Won	Lost	Tied	Drew	Aban
Britannic Assurance Championship	3rd	9	5		8	
All First-class Matches		10	5		9	
Refuge Assurance League	10th	6	8	1		1
NatWest Bank Trophy	2nd Round					
Benson and Hedges Cup	Semi-Finalist					

BRITANNIC ASSURANCE CHAMPIONSHIP AVERAGES

BATTING AND FIELDING

Cap		M	I	NO	HS	Runs	Avge	100	50	Ct/St
1975	G.A.Gooch	14	23	0	275	1631	70.91	5	9	19
1986	A.R.Border	19	30	7	169*	1361	59.17	4	4	26
—	N.Hussain	8	11	3	165*	469	58.62	1	2	5
—	M.E.Waugh	3	4	0	86	178	44.50	—	1	2
1986	P.J.Prichard	22	36	7	80	1051	36.24	—	7	12
1963	K.W.R.Fletcher	12	14	3	58	303	27.54	—	2	9
	J.P.Stephenson	17	29	3	99	707	27.19	—	5	10
1982	D.R.Pringle	13	17	0	128	446	26.23	1	3	5
1986	A.W.Lilley	19	30	2	80*	730	26.07	—	4	16
1982	D.E.East	18	26	2	134	580	24.16	1	1	53/4
1974	B.R.Hardie	12	19	3	58	353	22.06	—	2	9
1988	G.Miller	17	19	4	77	329	21.93	—	1	18
	I.L.Pont	6	6	2	29	76	19.00	—	—	1
1988	T.D.Topley	15	20	6	56*	233	16.64	—	1	8
1986	J.H.Childs	16	15	8	25*	71	10.14	—	—	4
1983	N.A.Foster	13	16	2	22	108	7.71	—	—	7
—	A.D.Brown	4	5	3	6*	13	6.50	—	—	9/2
1970	J.K.Lever	13	13	1	20	53	4.41	—	—	2

Also batted: M.C.Ilott (1 match) 6.

BOWLING

	O	M	R	W	Avge	Best	5 wI	10 wM
N.A.Foster	471.1	95	1423	66	21.56	6-53	4	2
T.D.Topley	500	81	1520	62	24.51	7-75	4	1
D.R.Pringle	352.3	71	1031	41	25.14	6-39	3	—
J.H.Childs	505.2	160	1239	49	25.28	6-92	3	1
J.K.Lever	422.4	90	1120	43	26.04	4-61	—	—
G.Miller	376.1	95	1025	35	29.28	5-76	1	—
I.L.Pont	158	16	591	16	36.93	5-103	1	—

Also bowled: G.A.Gooch 135-37-342-9; J.P.Stephenson 59.2-12-187-4; A.R.Border 28-8-74-1; A.W.Lilley 11-0-119-0; P.J.Prichard 1-0-7-0; N.Hussain 9-0-47-0; M.C.Ilott 15-1-48-0; M.E.Waugh 12-0-75-0.

The First-Class Averages (pp 161-175) give the records of Essex players in all first-class county matches (their other opponents being the West Indians and Cambridge U.), with the exception of N.A.Foster, whose full county figures are as above, and:

J.H.Childs 18-15-8-25*-71-10.14-0-0-5ct. 568.5-179-1399-59-23.71-6/92-4-1.
G.A.Gooch 15-25-1-275-1754-73.08-5-11-19ct. 152-39-401-10-40.10-2/29.
D.R.Pringle 14-19-0-128-450-23.68-1-3-5ct. 378.3-75-1119-43-26.02-6/39-3-0.

72

ESSEX RECORDS

FIRST-CLASS CRICKET

Highest Total	For	692	v Somerset	Taunton	1895
	V	803-4d	by Kent	Brentwood	1934
Lowest Total	For	30	v Yorkshire	Leyton	1901
	V	14	by Surrey	Chelmsford	1983
Highest Innings	For	343* P.A.Perrin	v Derbyshire	Chesterfield	1904
	V	332 W.H.Ashdown	for Kent	Brentwood	1934

Highest Partnerships
Wkt

1st	270	A.V.Avery/T.C.Dodds	v Surrey	The Oval	1946
2nd	321	G.A.Gooch/K.S.McEwan	v Northants	Ilford	1978
3rd	343	P.A.Gibb/R.Horsfall	v Kent	Blackheath	1951
4th	298	A.V.Avery/R.Horsfall	v Worcs	Clacton	1948
5th	287	C.T.Ashton/J.O'Connor	v Surrey	Brentwood	1934
6th {	206	J.W.H.T.Douglas/J.O'Connor	v Glos	Cheltenham	1923
	206	B.R.Knight/R.A.G.Luckin	v Middlesex	Brentwood	1962
7th	261	J.W.H.T.Douglas/J.Freeman	v Lancashire	Leyton	1914
8th	263	D.R.Wilcox/R.M.Taylor	v Warwicks	Southend	1946
9th	251	J.W.H.T.Douglas/S.N.Hare	v Derbyshire	Leyton	1921
10th	218	F.H.Vigar/T.P.B.Smith	v Derbyshire	Chesterfield	1947

Best Bowling	For	10-32 H.Pickett	v Leics	Leyton	1895
(Innings)	V	10-40 E.G.Dennett	for Glos	Bristol	1906
Best Bowling	For	17-119 W.Mead	v Hampshire	Southampton	1895
(Match)	V	17-56 C.W.L.Parker	for Glos	Gloucester	1925

Most Runs – Season	2,559	G.A.Gooch	(av 67.34)	1984
Most Runs – Career	29,434	K.W.R.Fletcher	(av 36.88)	1962-1988
Most 100s – Season	9	J.O'Connor		1934
	9	D.J.Insole		1955
Most 100s – Career	71	J.O'Connor		1921-1939
Most Wkts – Season	172	T.P.B Smith	(av 27.13)	1947
Most Wkts – Career	1,610	T.P.B.Smith	(av 26.68)	1929-1951

LIMITED-OVERS CRICKET

Highest Total	NWT	386-5	v Wiltshire	Chelmsford	1988
	BHC	350-3	v Comb Univs	Chelmsford	1979
	RAL	310-5	v Glamorgan	Southend	1983
Lowest Total	NWT	100	v Derbyshire	Brentwood	1965
	BHC	100	v Hampshire	Chelmsford	1987
	RAL	69	v Derbyshire	Chesterfield	1974
Highest Innings	NWT	133 G.A.Gooch	v Scotland	Chelmsford	1984
	BHC	198* G.A.Gooch	v Sussex	Hove	1982
	RAL	176 G.A.Gooch	v Glamorgan	Southend	1983
Best Bowling	NWT	5-8 J.K.Lever	v Middlesex	Westcliff	1972
	BHC	5-13 J.K.Lever	v Middlesex	Lord's	1985
	RAL	8-26 K.D.Boyce	v Lancashire	Manchester	1971

GLAMORGAN

Formation of Present Club: 6 July 1888
Colours: Blue and Gold
Badge: Gold Daffodil
Championships: (2) 1948, 1969
NatWest Trophy/Gillette Cup Winners: (0) Finalists 1977
Benson and Hedges Cup Winners: (0) Semi-Finalists 1988
Sunday League Champions: (0) Fifth 1988
Match Awards: NWT 20; BHC 34

Chief Executive: P.G.Carling
Secretary: A.P.Dilloway, Sophia Gardens, Cardiff, CF1 9XR
Captain: H.Morris
Scorer: B.T.Denning
Cricketcall: ☎ 0898 1214 30
Benefit 1989: R.C.Ontong

BARWICK, Stephen Royston (Cwrt Sart CS; Dwr-y-Felin CS), b Neath 6 Sep 1960. 6'2". RHB, RMF. Debut 1981. Cap 1987. HS 30 v Hants (Bournemouth) 1988. BB 8-42 v Worcs (Worcester) 1983. Awards: BHC 1. NWT: HS 6. BB 4-14 v Hants (Bournemouth) 1981. BHC: HS 18 v Kent (Canterbury) 1984. BB 4-11 v Minor C (Swansea) 1985. RAL: HS 29* v Worcs (Worcester) 1986. BB 4-23 v Yorks (Cardiff) 1987.

BASTIEN, Steven (St Bonaventure S, Forest Gate; Haringey Cricket C), b Stepney, London 13 Mar 1963 (of Dominican parents). 6'1". RHB, RMF. Debut 1988. HS 36* v Warwicks (Birmingham) 1988 (his first innings). BB 5-90 v Leics (Neath) 1988 (on debut).

BUTCHER, Alan Raymond (Heath Clark GS), b Croydon, Surrey 7 Jan 1954. Brother of I.P. (Leics 1980-87 and Glos) and M.S. (Surrey 1982). 5'8½". LHB, SLA/LM. Surrey 1972-86 (cap 1975; benefit 1985). Glamorgan debut/cap 1987. Tests: 1 (1979); HS 20 v India (Oval). LOI: 1. Tours: WI 1982-83 (Int XI); Ind 1980-81 (Overseas XI). 1000 runs (9); most – 1713 (1980). HS 216* Surrey v CU (Cambridge) 1980. Glam HS 166 v CU (Cambridge) 1988. BB 6-48 Surrey v Hants (Guildford) 1972. Glam BB 3-35 v Middx (Cardiff) 1987. Awards: NWT 2; BHC 5. NWT: HS 86* Surrey v Warwicks (Lord's) 1982. BB 1-27. BHC: HS 80 Surrey v Sussex (Oval) 1982. BB 4-36 Surrey v Middx (Lord's) 1985. RAL: HS 113* Surrey v Warwicks (Birmingham) 1978. BB 5-19 Surrey v Glos (Bristol) 1975

CANN, Michael James (St Illtyds C, Cardiff; Swansea U), b Cardiff 4 July 1965. 5'9". LHB, OB. Debut 1986. HS 28 and BB 2-20 v Worcs (Worcester) 1988. BHC: HS 46 Comb Us v Somerset (Taunton) 1987. BB 1-1.

COTTEY, Phillip Anthony (Bishopston CS, Swansea), b Swansea 2 Jun 1966. 5'4". RHB. Debut 1986. HS 92 v CU (Cambridge) 1988. BHC: HS 15 v Hants (Southampton) 1988. RAL: HS 10 v Notts (Ebbw Vale) 1987.

DERRICK, John (Blaengwawr CS), b Cwmaman 15 Jan 1963. 6'1". RHB, RM. Debut 1983. Cap 1988. HS 78* v Derbys (Abergavenny) 1986. BB 6-54 v Leics (Leicester) 1988. NWT: HS 4. BB 4-14 v Scotland (Edinburgh) 1985. BHC: HS 42 v Kent (Cardiff) 1985. BB 4-53 v Comb Us (Cardiff) 1988. RAL: HS 26 v Northants (Northampton) 1983 and v Kent (Maidstone) 1986. BB 5-32 v Middx (Lord's) 1987.

HOLMES, Geoffrey Clark (West Denton HS), b Newcastle-upon-Tyne 16 Sep 1958. 5'10". RHB, RM. Debut 1978. Cap 1985. 1000 runs (3); most – 1129 (1985). HS 117 v Glos (Bristol) 1988. BB 5-38 v Essex (Colchester) 1988. Awards: NWT 2. **NWT:** HS 57 v Cheshire (Cardiff) 1987. BB 5-24 v Scotland (Edinburgh) 1985. **BHC:** HS 70 v Somerset (Taunton) 1985. BB 3-26 v Minor C (Swansea) 1985. **RAL:** HS 73 v Warwicks (Birmingham) 1984. BB 5-2 v Derbys (Ebbw Vale) 1984.

JAMES, Stephen Peter (Monmouth S; Swansea U; now at Cambridge U), b Lydney, Glos 7 Sep 1967. 5'11". RHB. Debut 1985. HS 106 v OU (Oxford) 1987 – sharing Glam record 2nd-wkt stand of 249 with H.Morris. **NWT:** HS 26 v Cheshire (Cardiff) 1987.

MAYNARD, Matthew Peter (David Hughes S, Anglesey), b Oldham, Lancs 21 Mar 1966. 5'10½". RHB. Debut 1985 scoring 102 out of 117 in 87 min v Yorks (Swansea), reaching 100 with 3 sixes off successive balls. Cap 1987. YC 1988. Tests: 1 (1988); HS 10 v WI (Oval). 1000 runs (3); most – 1606 (1985). HS 160 v Sussex (Weston) 1987. BB 3-21 v OU (Oxford) 1987. Awards: BHC 3. **NWT:** HS 64 v Surrey (Oval) 1988. **BHC:** HS 115 v Comb Us (Cardiff) 1988. **RAL:** HS 92* v Sussex (Eastbourne) 1988.

METSON, Colin Peter (Enfield GS; Stanborough S, Welwyn Garden City), b Goffs Oak, Herts 2 Jul 1963. 5'5½". RHB, WK. Middlesex 1981-86. Glamorgan debut/ cap 1987. HS 96 Middx v Glos (Uxbridge) 1984. Glamorgan HS 81 v Yorks (Cardiff) 1987. **NWT:** HS 4*. **BHC:** HS 11 v Hants (Southampton) 1988. **RAL:** HS 23* v Middx (Lord's) 1987.

MORRIS, Hugh (Blundell's S), b Cardiff 5 Oct 1963. 5'8". LHB, RM. Debut 1981. Cap 1986. 1000 runs (2); most – 1522 (1986). HS 143 v OU (Oxford) 1987. BB 1-6. Shared Glam record 2nd-wkt stand of 249 with S.P.James v OU (Oxford) 1987. Award: BHC 1. **NWT:** HS 75 v Worcs (Swansea) 1985. **BHC:** HS 115 v Kent (Cardiff) 1987. BB 1-14. **RAL:** HS 100 v Derbys (Ebbw Vale) 1986.

NORTH, Philip David (St Julian's CS; Nash CFE), b Newport 16 May 1965. 5'5". RHB, SLA. Debut 1985. HS 41* v Northants (Wellingborough) 1988. BB 4-43 v Worcs (Neath) 1987. **RAL:** HS 0. BB 3-20 v Northants (Wellingborough) 1988.

ONTONG, Rodney Craig (Selbourne C, East London, SA), b Johannesburg, SA 9 Sep 1955. 5'11". RHB, OB. Border 1972-76 (debut aged 17yr 7m) and 1982-85 (captain 1983-85). Transvaal 1976-78. N Transvaal 1978-82 and 1985-88. Glamorgan debut 1975. Cap 1979. Captain 1984-86. Benefit 1989. 1000 runs (5); most – 1320 (1984). HS 204* v Middx (Swansea) 1984. BB 8-67 (13-106 and 130 in match) v Notts (Nottingham) 1983. Awards: NWT 2; BHC 5. **NWT:** HS 64 v Somerset (Cardiff) 1978. BB 4-49 v Norfolk (Norwich) 1983. **BHC:** HS 81 v Somerset (Swansea) 1984. BB 5-30 v Somerset (Taunton) 1985. **RAL:** HS 100 v Northants (Abergavenny) 1984. BB 4-28 v Glos (Cardiff) 1986.

ROBERTS, Martin Leonard (Helston CS), b Mullion, Cornwall 12 Apr 1966. 6'1". RHB, WK. Debut 1985. Cornwall 1983-84. HS 8. **RAL:** HS 6*.

SHASTRI, Ravishankar Jayadritha (Don Bosco HS, Bombay), b Bombay, India 27 May 1962. 6'3". RHB, SLA. Bombay 1979-88 (capt 1987-88). Glamorgan debut 1987. Cap 1988. Tests (Ind): 58 (1980-81 to 1987-88); HS 142 v Eng (Bombay) 1984-85; BB 5-75 v Pak (Nagpur) 1983-84. LOI (Ind): 102. Tours (Ind): Eng 1982, 1986; Aus 1985-86; WI 1982-83; NZ 1980-81; Pak 1982-83, 1984-85; SL 1985-86. 1000 runs (0+1): 1027 (1983-84). HS 200* Bombay v Baroda (Bombay) 1984-85 (including 6 sixes off one over and 200 in 113 min – world records). Glam HS 157 v

SHASTRI (contd.)
Somerset (Cardiff) 1988. BB 9-101 Bombay v Rest (Indore) 1981-82. Glam BB 7-49 v Lancs (Swansea) 1988. Award: NWT 1. **NWT:** HS 59* v Surrey (Oval) 1988. BB 5-13 v Scotland (Edinburgh) 1988. **BHC:** HS 55 v Hants (Southampton) 1988. BB 1-17. **RAL:** HS 84* v Glos (Bristol) 1988. BB 2-19 v Somerset (Cardiff) 1988.

SMITH, Ian (Ryton CS), b Chopwell, Co Durham 11 Mar 1967. 6'2". RHB, RM. Debut 1985. HS 45 v Derbys (Cardiff) 1987. BB 3-65 v Glos (Swansea) 1987. **NWT:** HS 5. BB 1-18. **BHC:** HS 6. BB 1-21. **RAL:** HS 34 v Derbys (Cheadle) 1987. BB 2-19 v Yorks (Cardiff) 1987.

WATKIN, Steven Llewellyn (Cymer Afan CS; S Glamorgan CHE), b Maesteg 15 Sep 1964. 6'3". RHB, RMF. Debut 1986. HS 23 v Worcs (Abergavenny) 1988. BB 8-59 v Warwicks (Birmingham) 1988. **BHC:** HS 4*. **RAL:** HS 7. BB 2-19 v Yorks (Cardiff) 1988.

NEWCOMERS

DALE, Adrian (Chepstow CS; Swansea U), b Germiston, SA 24 Oct 1968 (to UK at 6 mths). 5'11½"in. RHB, RM. Represented Glamorgan at soccer, basketball and swimming.

DENNIS, Simon John (Scarborough C), b Scarborough 18 Oct 1960. Nephew of F.Dennis (Yorkshire 1928-33) and Sir Leonard Hutton (Yorkshire and England 1934-55). 6'1". RHB, LFM. Yorkshire 1980-88 (cap 1983). OFS 1982-83. Tour: WI 1986-87 (Yorks). HS 53* Yorks v Notts (Nottingham) 1984. BB 5-35 Yorks v Somerset (Sheffield) 1981. **NWT:** HS 14 Yorks v Salop (Telford) 1984. BB 2-45 Yorks v Northants (Leeds) 1983. **BHC:** HS 10 Yorks v Warwicks (Birmingham) 1984. BB 3-41 Yorks v Northants (Bradford) 1984. **RAL:** HS 16* (twice for Yorks). BB 3-19 Yorks v Hants (Middlesbrough) 1981.

RICHARDS, Isaac Vivian Alexander (Antigua GS), b St John's, Antigua 7 Mar 1952. 5'11". RHB, OB. Leeward Is 1971-88. Somerset 1974-86 (cap 1974; benefit 1982). Queensland 1976-77. Wisden 1976. **Tests** (WI): 99 (1974-75 to 1988, 28 as captain); HS 291 v Eng (Oval) 1976; BB 2-17 v Pak (P-of-S) 1987-88. LOI (WI): 149. Tours (WI)(C=Capt): Eng 1976, 1980, 1984, 1988C; Aus 1975-76, 1979-80, 1981-82, 1984-85, 1986-87C; NZ 1986-87C; Ind 1974-75, 1983-84, 1987-88C; Pak 1974-75, 1980-81, 1986-87C; SL 1974-75. 1000 runs (12+3); most – 2161 (1977). Shared record Somerset 8th-wkt stand of 172 with I.T.Botham v Leics (Leicester) 1983. HS 322 (Somerset record) v Warwicks (Taunton) 1985. BB 5-88 WI v Queensland (Brisbane) 1981-82. Awards: NWT 4; BHC 6. **NWT:** HS 139* Somerset v Warwicks (Taunton) 1978. BB 3-15 Somerset v Beds (Bedford) 1982. **BHC:** HS 132* Somerset v Surrey (Lord's) 1981. BB 1-9. **RAL:** HS 126* Somerset v Glos (Bristol Imp) 1975. BB 6-24 Somerset v Lancs (Manchester) 1983

DEPARTURES

HOPKINS, John Anthony (Ynysawdre CS; Trinity CE), b Maesteg 16 Jun 1953. Brother of J.D. (Middlesex 1969-72). 5'10". RHB, WK. Glamorgan 1970-88 (cap 1977; benefit 1986). E Province 1981-82. 1000 runs (7); most – 1500 (1984). HS 230 v Worcs (Worcester) 1977. Awards: NWT 1; BHC 4. **NWT:** HS 63 v Leics (Swansea) 1977. **BHC:** HS 103* v Minor C (Swansea) 1980. **RAL:** HS 130* v Somerset (Bath) 1983.

MONKHOUSE, Steven (Derby TGS; Peel C, Bury), b Bury, Lancs 24 Nov 1962. 6'3". RHB, LFM. Warwickshire 1985-86. Glamorgan 1987-88. HS 15 v Northants (Swansea) 1987. BB 3-37 v CU (Cambridge) 1988. **NWT:** BB 5-32 v Cheshire (Cardiff) 1987. **RAL:** HS 0. BB 3-14 v Northants (Luton) 1987.

continued on p 150
76

GLAMORGAN 1988

RESULTS SUMMARY

	Place	Won	Lost	Drew	Abandoned
Britannic Assurance Championship	**17th**	1	8	12	1
All First-class Matches		1	8	14	1
Refuge Assurance League	**5th**	8	5	1	2
NatWest Bank Trophy	Quarter-Finalist				
Benson and Hedges Cup	Semi-Finalist				

BRITANNIC ASSURANCE CHAMPIONSHIP AVERAGES

BATTING AND FIELDING

Cap		M	I	NO	HS	Runs	Avge	100	50	Ct/St
1987	M.P.Maynard	19	35	6	126	1361	46.93	3	11	21
1979	R.C.Ontong	16	24	8	120*	734	45.87	1	4	7
1988	R.J.Shastri	12	19	2	157	575	33.82	1	2	5
1985	G.C.Holmes	18	30	3	117	912	33.77	4	3	6
1987	A.R.Butcher	21	38	2	93	1098	30.50	—	9	12
1986	H.Morris	18	32	3	87	820	28.27	—	6	13
—	P.D.North	5	7	3	41*	107	26.75	—	—	2
—	P.A.Cottey	12	21	3	73	443	24.61	—	3	4
1986	J.G.Thomas	15	25	4	110	515	24.52	2	—	5
1977	J.A.Hopkins	11	20	1	71	368	19.36	—	2	8
1987	C.P.Metson	21	29	7	48	347	15.77	—	—	51/6
—	P.G.P.Roebuck	2	4	0	46	60	15.00	—	—	1
—	S.Bastien	8	6	2	36*	57	14.25	—	—	1
—	M.J.Cann	6	7	0	28	78	11.14	—	—	5
1988	J.Derrick	19	26	5	50*	212	10.09	—	1	8
—	S.L.Watkin	15	19	7	23	115	9.58	—	—	2
1987	S.R.Barwick	12	7	2	30	40	8.00	—	—	2
—	C.J.P.G. van Zyl	3	5	1	11	30	7.50	—	—	1

Also batted: S.Monkhouse (2 matches) 0*

BOWLING

	O	M	R	W	Avge	Best	5 wI	10 wM
S.L.Watkin	505.3	125	1347	44	30.61	8-59	2	—
J.G.Thomas	400.2	60	1444	47	30.72	6-68	2	—
J.Derrick	504.1	123	1418	45	31.51	6-54	1	—
S.R.Barwick	383.5	102	1014	32	31.68	5-37	1	—
R.J.Shastri	304.2	91	709	20	35.45	7-49	1	1
G.C.Holmes	116.2	12	440	11	40.00	5-38	1	—
R.C.Ontong	376.1	88	1078	24	44.91	4-38	—	—

Also bowled: S.Bastien 119.1-35-289-8; A.R.Butcher 47-8-172-5; M.J.Cann 14-2-63-4; J.A.Hopkins 5-1-46-0; M.P.Maynard 5-2-13-0; S.Monkhouse 44-8-118-2; H.Morris 4.3-0-58-0; P.D.North 64.5-12-195-5; C.J.P.G.van Zyl 99.1-27-291-2.

The First-Class Averages (pp 161-175) give the records of Glamorgan players in all first-class county matches, (their other opponents being the West Indians and Cambridge U), with the exception of:
    M.P.Maynard 21-38-6-126-1439-44.96-3-11-21ct. 5-2-13-0.

GLAMORGAN RECORDS

FIRST-CLASS CRICKET

Highest Total	For	587-8d		v Derbyshire	Cardiff	1951
	V	653-6d		by Glos	Bristol	1928
Lowest Total	For	22		v Lancashire	Liverpool	1924
	V	33		by Leics	Ebbw Vale	1965
Highest Innings	For	287*	D.E.Davies	v Glos	Newport	1939
	V	⎰302*	W.R.Hammond	for Glos	Bristol	1934
		⎱302	W.R.Hammond	for Glos	Newport	1939

Highest Partnerships
Wkt

1st	330	A.Jones/R.C.Fredericks	v Northants	Swansea	1972
2nd	249	S.P.James/H.Morris	v Oxford U	Oxfordgs	1987
3rd	313	D.E.Davies/W.E.Jones	v Essex	Brentwood	1948
4th	306*	Javed Miandad/Younius Ahmed	v Australians	Neath	1985
5th	264	M.Robinson/S.W.Montgomery	v Hampshire	Bournemouth	1949
6th	230	W.E.Jones/B.L.Muncer	v Worcs	Worcester	1953
7th	195*	W.Wooller/W.E.Jones	v Lancashire	Liverpool	1947
8th	202	D.Davies/J.J.Hills	v Sussex	Eastbourne	1928
9th	203*	J.J.Hills/J.C.Clay	v Worcs	Swansea	1929
10th	143	T.Davies/S.A.B.Daniels	v Glos	Swansea	1982

Best Bowling	For	10-51	J.Mercer	v Worcs	Worcester	1936
(Innings)	V	10-18	G.Geary	for Leics	Pontypridd	1929
Best Bowling	For	17-212	J.C.Clay	v Worcs	Swansea	1937
(Match)	V	16-96	G.Geary	for Leics	Pontypridd	1929
Most Runs – Season		2,083	Javed Miandad	(av 69.43)		1981
Most Runs – Career		34,056	A.Jones	(av 33.03)		1957-1983
Most 100s – Season		8	Javed Miandad			1981
Most 100s – Career		52	A.Jones			1957-1983
Most Wkts – Season		176	J.C.Clay	(av 17.34)		1937
Most Wkts – Career		2,174	D.J.Shepherd	(av 20.95)		1950-1972

LIMITED-OVERS CRICKET

Highest Total	NWT	283-3		v Warwicks	Birmingham	1976
	BHC	302-6		v Comb Univs	Cardiff	1988
	RAL	277-6		v Derbyshire	Ebbw Vale	1984
Lowest Total	NWT	76		v Northants	Northampton	1968
	BHC	68		v Lancashire	Manchester	1973
	RAL	42		v Derbyshire	Swansea	1979
Highest Innings	NWT	124*	A.Jones	v Warwicks	Birmingham	1976
	BHC	⎰115	H.Morris	v Kent	Cardiff	1987
		⎱115	M.P.Maynard	v Comb Univs	Cardiff	1988
	RAL	130*	J.A.Hopkins	v Somerset	Bath	1983
Best Bowling	NWT	5-13	R.J.Shastri	v Scotland	Edinburgh	1988
	BHC	5-17	A.H.Wilkins	v Worcs	Worcester	1978
	RAL	6-29	M.A.Nash	v Worcs	Worcester	1975

GLOUCESTERSHIRE

Formation of Present Club: 1871
Colours: Blue, Gold, Brown, Silver, Green and Red
Badge: Coat of Arms of the City and County of Bristol
Championships (since 1890): (0) Second 1930, 1931, 1947, 1959, 1969, 1986
NatWest Trophy/Gillette Cup Winners: (1) 1973
Benson and Hedges Cup Winners: (1) 1977
Sunday League Champions: (0) Second 1988
Match Awards: NWT 31; BHC 35

Secretary: P.G.M.August, Phoenix County Ground, Nevil Road, Bristol BS7 9EJ
Captain: C.W.J.Athey
Scorer: B.H.Jenkins
Cricketcall: ☎ 0898 1214 34
Benefit 1989: P.Bainbridge

ALDERMAN, Terence Michael (Aquinas C and Churchlands C, Perth), b Subiaco, Perth, Aus 12 Jun 1956. 6'2½". RHB, RFM. W Australia 1974-85. Perth 1984-88 (cap 1984). Gloucestershire debut 1988. Wisden 1981. **Tests** (Aus): 22 (1981 to 1984-85); HS 23 and BB 6-128 v WI (Perth) 1984-85. **LOI:** 23. Tours (Aus): Eng 1981; SA (Aus XI) 1985-86, 1986-87; WI 1983-84; NZ 1981-82; Pak 1982-83. HS 52* Kent v Sussex (Hastings) 1984. Glos HS 43* v Surrey (Cheltenham) 1988. BB 8-46 Kent v Derbys (Derby) 1986. Glos BB 8-59 v Somerset (Taunton) 1988. **NWT:** BB 5-34 v Ireland (Bristol) 1988. **BHC:** HS 8. BB 2-9 Kent v Middx (Lord's) 1984. **RAL:** HS 11 and BB 5-36 Kent v Lancs (Maidstone) 1984.

ALLEYNE, Mark Wayne (Harrison C, Barbados; Cardinal Pole S, London E9; Haringey Cricket C), b Tottenham, London 23 May 1968. 5'10". RHB, RM. Debut 1986. Tour: SL 1986-87 (Glos). HS 116* v Sussex (Bristol) 1986. BB 4-48 v Glam (Bristol) 1988. **NWT:** HS 9. BB 1-12. **BHC:** HS 36 v Derbys (Derby) 1987. BB 5-27 v Comb Us (Bristol) 1988. **RAL:** HS 49* and BB 3-36 v Derbys (Heanor) 1988.

ATHEY, Charles William Jeffrey (Stainsby SS; Acklam Hall HS), b Middlesbrough, Yorks 27 Sep 1957. 5'9½". RHB, RM. Yorkshire 1976-83 (cap 1980). Gloucestershire debut 1984. Cap 1985. Captain 1989. **Tests:** 23 (1980 to 1988); HS 123 v Pak (Lord's) 1987. **LOI:** 31. Tours: Aus 1986-87, 1987-88; WI 1980-81; NZ 1979-80 (DHR), 1987-88; Pak 1987-88; SL 1985-86 (Eng B). 1000 runs (7); most - 1812 (1984). HS 184 England B v Sri Lanka (Galle) 1985-86. Glos HS 171* v Northants (Northampton) 1986. BB 3-3 v Hants (Bristol) 1985. Awards: NWT 3; BHC 4. **NWT:** HS 115 Yorks v Kent (Leeds) 1980. BB 1-18. **BHC:** HS 95 v Northants (Northampton) 1987. BB 4-48 v Comb Us (Bristol) 1984. **RAL:** HS 121* v Worcs (Moreton) 1985. BB 5-35 Yorks v Derbys (Chesterfield) 1981.

BAINBRIDGE, Philip (Hanley HS; Stoke-on-Trent SFC, Borough Road CE), b Sneyd Green, Stoke-on-Trent, Staffs 16 Apr 1958. 5'10". RHB, RM. Debut 1977. Cap 1981. Benefit 1989. Wisden 1985. Tours: SL 1986-87 (Glos); Zim 1984-85 (Eng Co). 1000 runs (7); most – 1644 (1985). HS 169 v Yorks (Cheltenham) 1988. BB 8-53 v Somerset (Bristol) 1986. Awards: NWT 1; BHC 1. **NWT:** HS 89 v Leics (Leicester) 1988. BB 3-49 v Scotland (Bristol) 1983. **BHC:** HS 96 v Hants (Southampton) 1988. BB 3-21 v Notts (Gloucester) 1981. **RAL:** HS 106* v Somerset (Bristol) 1986. BB 5-22 v Middx (Lord's) 1987.

BALL, Martyn Charles John (King Edmund SS; Bath CFE), b Bristol 26 Apr 1970. 5'8". RHB, OB. Debut 1988. HS 2. BB 1-8.

79

BUTCHER, Ian Paul (John Ruskin HS), b Farnborough, Kent 1 Jul 1962. Brother of A.R. (Surrey, Glam and England) and M.S. (Surrey 1982). 6'0". RHB, RM. Leicestershire 1980-87 (cap 1984). Gloucestershire debut 1988. 1000 runs (2); most - 1349 (1984). HS 139 Leics v Notts (Leicester) 1983. Glos HS 75 v OU (Oxford) 1988. BB 1-2. **NWT:** HS 81 Leics v Northants (Northampton) 1984. BB 1-6. **BHC:** HS 103* Leics v Minor C (Leicester) 1986. **RAL:** HS 71 Leics v Northants (Leics) 1982.

CURRAN, Kevin Malcolm (Marandellas HS), b Rusape, S Rhodesia 7 Sep 1959. Son of K.P. (Rhodesia 1947-54). 6'1". RHB, RMF. Zimbabwe 1980-88. Gloucestershire debut/cap 1985. LOI (Zim): 11. Tours (Zim): E 1982; SL 1983-84. 1000 runs (3); most – 1353 (1986). HS 142 v Middx (Lord's) 1988. BB 7-54 v Leics (Gloucester) 1988. Awards: NWT 2; BHC 1. **NWT:** HS 58* v Leics (Leicester) 1988. BB 4-34 v Northants (Bristol) 1985. **BHC:** HS 57 v Derbys (Derby) 1987. BB 4-43 v Leics (Bristol) 1987. **RAL:** HS 71* v Notts (Nottingham) 1986. BB 5-15 v Leics (Gloucester) 1988.

GRAVENEY, David Anthony (Millfield S), b Bristol 2 Jan 1953. Son of J.K. (Glos 1947-64); nephew of T.W. (Glos, Worcs, Queensland and England). 6'4". RHB, SLA. Debut 1972. Cap 1976. Captain 1981-88. Tour: SL 1986-87 (Glos – capt). Hat-trick 1983. HS 119 v OU (Oxford) 1980. BB 8-85 v Notts (Cheltenham) 1974. Match analysis of 14-165 v Worcs (Bristol) 1988. Awards: NWT 2. **NWT:** HS 44 v Surrey (Bristol) 1973. BB 5-11 v Ireland (Dublin) 1981. **BHC:** HS 49* v Somerset (Taunton) 1982. BB 3-13 v Scotland (Glasgow) 1983. **RAL:** HS 56* v Notts (Bristol) 1985. BB 4-22 v Hants (Lydney) 1974.

GREENE, Victor Sylvester ('Vibert') (Garrison SC), b Christ Church, Barbados 24 Sep 1960. 5'10". RHB, RMF. Barbados 1985-88. Gloucestershire debut 1987. Tour (WI B): Zim 1986-87. HS 62* v Leics (Cheltenham) 1987. BB 7-96 v Notts (Nottingham) 1987. **RAL:** 21* v Notts (Nottingham) 1988. BB 4-25 v Lancs (Manchester) 1988.

IBADULLA, Kassem Ben Khalid, b Birmingham 13 Oct 1964. Son of Khalid Ibadulla (Pakistan, Warwicks, Otago & Tasmania). RHB, OB. Otago 1982-88. Gloucestershire debut 1987. Cheshire 1985. HS 107 Otago v C Districts (New Plymouth) 1987-88. Glos HS 77 v Kent (Bristol) 1988. BB 5-22 Otago v Canterbury (Invercargill) 1982-83. Glos BB 3-37 v Lancs (Manchester) 1987. **RAL:** HS 12 v Notts (Moreton) 1987.

JARVIS, Kevin Bertram Sidney (Springhead S, Northfleet; Thames Polytechnic) b Dartford, Kent 23 Apr 1953. 6'3". RHB, RFM. Kent 1975-87 (cap 1977; benefit 1987). Gloucestershire debut 1988. Tours: WI 1982-83 (Int XI); SL 1977-78 (DHR). Hat-trick 1987 (Kent). HS 19 Kent v Derbys (Maidstone) 1984. Glos HS 1*. BB 8-97 Kent v Worcs (Worcester) 1978. Glos BB 1-32. Awards: NWT 1; BHC 1. **NWT:** HS 5*. BB 4-19 Kent v Warwicks (Canterbury) 1983. **BHC:** HS 4*. BB 4-34 Kent v Worcs (Lord's) 1976. **RAL:** HS 8*. BB 5-24 Kent v Notts (Nottingham) 1985.

LAWRENCE, David Valentine (Linden S), b Gloucester 28 Jan 1964. 6'2". RHB, RF. Debut 1981. Cap 1985. **Tests:** 1 (1988) HS 4 and BB 2-74 v SL (Lord's). Tours: SL 1985-86 (Eng B); 1986-87 (Glos). HS 65* v Glam (Swansea) 1987. BB 7-47 v Surrey (Cheltenham) 1988. Awards: NWT 1; BHC 1. **NWT:** HS 2*. BB 4-36 v Berks (Reading) 1986. **BHC:** HS 22* v Scotland (Bristol) 1985. BB 5-48 v Hants (Bristol) 1984. **RAL:** HS 21* v Leics (Leicester) 1986. BB 4-32 v Lancs (Moreton) 1984.

LLOYDS, Jeremy William (Blundell's S), b Penang, Malaya 17 Nov 1954. 6'0".
LHB, OB. Somerset 1979-84 (cap 1982). OFS 1983-88. Gloucestershire debut/cap
1985. Tour: SL 1986-87 (Glos). 1000 runs (2); most – 1295 (1986). HS 132*
Somerset v Northants (Northampton) 1982. Glos HS 130 v Glam (Swansea) 1987.
BB 7-88 Somerset v Essex (Chelmsford) 1982. Glos BB 6-57 v Middx (Bristol)
1987. **NWT:** HS 40 v Northants (Bristol) 1985. BB 2-35 v Berks (Reading) 1986.
BHC: HS 51 Somerset v Sussex (Taunton) 1983. BB 3-21 v Glam (Swansea) 1986.
RAL: HS 57 v Essex (Chelmsford) 1987. BB 2-1 Somerset v Hants (Taunton) 1981.

POOLEY, Malcolm William (Pool S), b Truro, Cornwall 27 Jul 1969. 5'10". RHB,
RM. Debut 1988. Cornwall 1986-87. HS 38 v Middx (Lord's) 1988. BB 4-80 v Kent
(Bristol) 1988. **RAL:** HS 1*. BB 2-40 v Middx (Lord's) 1988.

ROMAINES, Paul William (Leeholm S), b Bishop Auckland, Co Durham 25 Dec
1955. 6'0". RHB. Northants 1975-76. Gloucestershire debut 1982. Cap 1983. GW
1984-85. Durham 1977-81. Tour: SL 1986-87 (Glos). 1000 runs (3); most – 1844
(1984). HS 186 v Warwicks (Nuneaton) 1982. BB 3-42 v Surrey (Oval) 1985.
Awards: BHC 2. **NWT:** HS 82 v Hants (Bristol) 1983. **BHC:** HS 125 v Notts
(Bristol) 1985. **RAL:** HS 105 v Northants (Northampton) 1985.

RUSSELL, Robert Charles (**Jack**) (Archway CS), b Stroud 15 Aug 1963. 5'8½".
LHB, WK. Debut 1981. Cap 1985. **Tests:** 1 (1988); HS 94 v SL (Lord's). LOI: 2.
Tours: Pak 1987-88; SL 1986-87 (Glos). HS 94 (Tests). Glos HS 72 v Hants
(Gloucester) 1988. Award: BHC 1. **NWT:** HS 39 v Leics (Bristol) 1986. **BHC:** HS
36* v Scotland (Glasgow) 1983. **RAL:** HS 108 v Worcs (Hereford) 1986.

SMITH, Oliver Charles Kennedy (Cotham GS; York U), b Meriden, Warwicks 29
Oct 1967. 5'11". LHB, OB. Debut 1987. HS 14 v Rest of World XI (Bristol) 1987.

STOVOLD, Andrew WILLIS- (Filton HS; Loughborough C), b Bristol 19 Mar
1953. Brother of Martin (Glos 1979-82). 5'8". RHB, WK. Debut 1973. Cap 1976.
Benefit 1987. OFS 1974-76. Tour: SL 1986-87 (Glos). 1000 runs (8); most – 1671
(1983). HS 212* v Northants (Northampton) 1982. BB 1-0. Awards: NWT 4; BHC
8. **NWT:** HS 104* v Ireland (Bristol) 1988. **BHC:** HS 123 v Comb Us (Oxford)
1982. **RAL:** HS 98* v Kent (Cheltenham) 1977.

WALSH, Courtney Andrew (Excelsior HS), b Kingston, Jamaica 30 Oct 1962.
6'5½". RHB, RF. Jamaica 1981-88. Gloucestershire debut 1984. Cap 1985. Wisden
1986. **Tests** (WI): 25 (1984-85 to 1988); HS 18* v Aus (Melbourne) 1984-85; BB
5-54 v Ind (Delhi) 1987-88. LOI (WI): 54. Tours (WI): Eng 1984, 1988; Aus
1984-85, 1987-88; NZ 1986-87; Ind 1987-88; Pak 1986-87; Zim 1983-84 (Young
WI). 100 wickets (1): 118 (1986). HS 52 v Yorks (Bristol) 1986. BB 9-72 v Somerset
(Bristol) 1986. **NWT:** HS 25* v Berks (Reading) 1986. BB 3-25 v Lancs (Manchester) 1987. **BHC:** HS 8. BB 2-19 v Scotland (Glasgow) 1985. **RAL:** HS 35 v Glam (Cardiff)
1986. BB 4-19 v Kent (Cheltenham) 1987.

WRIGHT, Anthony John (Alleyn's GS) b Stevenage, Herts 27 Jun 1962. 6'0".
RHB, RM. Gloucestershire debut 1982. Cap 1987. Tour: SL 1986-87 (Glos). 1000
runs (2); most – 1268 (1988). HS 161 v Glam (Bristol) 1987. **NWT:** HS 88 v Lancs
(Manchester) 1987. **BHC:** HS 66 v Somerset (Bristol) 1988. **RAL:** HS 81 v Kent
(Moreton) 1988.

DEPARTURES

BRASSINGTON, Andrew James (Endon SS), b Bagnall, Staffs 9 Aug 1954. 5'11".
RHB, WK. Gloucestershire 1974-88 (cap 1978; benefit 1988). HS 35 v Sussex
(Hastings) 1982. **NWT:** HS 20 v Hants (Bristol) 1982. **BHC:** HS 9*. **RAL:** HS 14* v
Northants (Bristol) 1982. Gloucestershire CCC Marketing Manager 1988-.

81   continued on p 150

GLOUCESTERSHIRE 1988

RESULTS SUMMARY

	Place	Won	Lost	Drew	Abandoned
Britannic Assurance Championship	10th	6	7	8	1
All First-class Matches		6	7	11	1
Refuge Assurance League	2nd	10	4	2	
NatWest Bank Trophy	Quarter-Finalist				
Benson and Hedges Cup	3rd in Group D				

BRITANNIC ASSURANCE CHAMPIONSHIP AVERAGES

BATTING AND FIELDING

Cap		M	I	NO	HS	Runs	Avge	100	50	Ct/St
1985	C.W.J.Athey	12	20	6	168*	1037	74.07	2	6	18
1985	K.M.Curran	19	34	5	142	1005	37.22	2	4	15
1976	A.W.Stovold	21	39	2	136	1296	35.02	2	6	14
1981	P.Bainbridge	21	36	1	169	1213	34.65	3	6	7
—	K.B.K.Ibadulla	3	6	2	77	122	30.50	—	1	1
1985	R.C.Russell	19	30	6	72	658	27.41	—	4	46/9
1987	A.J.Wright	21	38	0	136	1023	26.92	1	4	13
1983	P.W.Romaines	18	34	2	101*	859	26.84	1	5	12
—	M.W.Pooley	6	12	4	38	146	18.25	—	—	4
1985	J.W.Lloyds	14	22	2	68	331	16.55	—	1	20
1976	D.A.Graveney	20	23	8	47	227	15.13	—	—	6
—	M.W.Alleyne	11	18	0	56	224	12.44	—	1	11
—	T.M.Alderman	20	22	11	43*	135	12.27	—	—	12
1985	D.V.Lawrence	20	24	3	29	217	10.33	—	—	7

Also batted (1 match each): M.C.J.Ball 2; A.J.Brassington (cap 1978) 1 (1 ct, 1 st); I.P.Butcher 11, 8 (2 ct); V.S.Greene 2; K.B.S.Jarvis 1*; D.J.Thomas 7, 3.

BOWLING

	O	M	R	W	Avge	Best	5 wI	10 wM
K.M.Curran	414.2	86	1385	65	21.30	7-54	4	3
T.M.Alderman	601	135	1711	75	22.81	8-59	3	—
D.A.Graveney	561.5	163	1268	49	25.87	8-127	2	1
D.V.Lawrence	580.2	94	2037	77	26.45	7-47	4	—
M.W.Pooley	104.4	25	311	11	28.27	4-80	—	—
P.Bainbridge	284.4	58	913	12	76.08	3-85	—	—

Also bowled: M.W.Alleyne 61-11-206-6; C.W.J.Athey 5-0-20-0; M.C.J.Ball 5-3-2-1; V.S.Greene 18-3-49-0; K.B.K.Ibadulla 26.2-6-94-3; K.B.S.Jarvis 22-1-104-1; J.W.Lloyds 214.3-37-696-9; P.W.Romaines 0.1-0-6-0; D.J.Thomas 24.4-5-66-3.

The First-Class Averages (pp 161-175) give the records of Gloucestershire players in all first-class county matches (their other opponents being the West Indians, the Sri Lankans and Oxford U.), with the exception of C.W.J.Athey, whose full county figures are as above, and:

D.V.Lawrence 21-25-3-29-221-10.04-0-0-3ct. 611.2-94-2185-81-26.97-7/47-4-0.

R.C.Russell 22-33-7-72-757-29.11-0-5-52ct/12st. 1-0-12-0.

GLOUCESTERSHIRE RECORDS

FIRST-CLASS CRICKET

Highest Total	For	653-6d		v	Glamorgan	Bristol	1928
	V	774-7d		by	Australians	Bristol	1948
Lowest Total	For	17		v	Australians	Cheltenham	1896
	V	12		by	Northants	Gloucester	1907
Highest Innings	For	318*	W.G.Grace	v	Yorkshire	Cheltenham	1876
	V	296	A.O.Jones	for	Notts	Nottingham	1903

Highest Partnerships
Wkt

1st	395	D.M.Young/R.B.Nicholls	v	Oxford U	Oxford	1962
2nd	256	C.T.M.Pugh/T.W.Graveney	v	Derbyshire	Chesterfield	1960
3rd	336	W.R.Hammond/B.H.Lyon	v	Leics	Leicester	1933
4th	321	W.R.Hammond/W.L.Neale	v	Leics	Gloucester	1937
5th	261	W.G.Grace/W.O.Moberley	v	Yorkshire	Cheltenham	1876
6th	320	G.L.Jessop/J.H.Board	v	Sussex	Hove	1903
7th	248	W.G.Grace/E.L.Thomas	v	Sussex	Hove	1896
8th	239	W.R.Hammond/A.E.Wilson	v	Lancashire	Bristol	1938
9th	193	W.G.Grace/S.A.P.Kitcat	v	Sussex	Bristol	1896
10th	131	W.R.Gouldsworthy/J.G.Bessant	v	Somerset	Bristol	1923

Best Bowling	For	10-40	E.G.Dennett	v	Essex	Bristol	1906
(Innings)	V	10-66	A.A.Mailey	for	Australians	Cheltenham	1921
		10-66	K.Smales	for	Notts	Stroud	1956
Best Bowling	For	17-56	C.W.L.Parker	v	Essex	Gloucester	1925
(Match)	V	15-87	A.J.Conway	for	Worcs	Moreton-in-M	1914

Most Runs – Season		2,860	W.R.Hammond	(av 69.75)		1933
Most Runs – Career		33,664	W.R.Hammond	(av 57.05)		1920-1951
Most 100s – Season		13	W.R.Hammond			1938
Most 100s – Career		113	W.R.Hammond			1920-1951
Most Wkts – Season		222	T.W.J.Goddard	(av 16.80)		1937
		222	T.W.J.Goddard	(av 16.37)		1947
Most Wkts – Career		3,170	C.W.L.Parker	(av 19.43)		1903-1935

LIMITED-OVERS CRICKET

Highest Total	NWT	327-7		v	Berkshire	Reading	1966
	BHC	300-4		v	Comb Univs	Oxford	1982
	RAL	272-4		v	Middlesex	Lord's	1983
Lowest Total	NWT	82		v	Notts	Bristol	1987
	BHC	62		v	Hampshire	Bristol	1975
	RAL	49		v	Middlesex	Bristol	1978
Highest Innings	NWT	158	Zaheer Abbas	v	Leics	Leicester	1983
	BHC	154*	M.J.Procter	v	Somerset	Taunton	1972
	RAL	131	Sadiq Mohd	v	Somerset	Bristol (Imp)	1975
Best Bowling	NWT	5-11	D.A.Graveney	v	Ireland	Dublin	1981
	BHC	6-13	M.J.Procter	v	Hampshire	Southampton	1977
	RAL	6-52	D.J.Shepherd	v	Kent	Bristol	1983

HAMPSHIRE

Formation of Present Club: 12 August 1863
Colours: Blue, Gold and White
Badge: Tudor Rose and Crown
Championships: (2) 1961, 1973
NatWest Trophy/Gillette Cup Semi-Finalists: (5) 1966, 1976, 1983, 1985, 1988
Benson and Hedges Cup Winners: (1) 1988
Sunday League Champions: (3) 1975, 1978, 1986
Match Awards: NWT 37; BHC 44

Chief Executive: A.F.Baker, County Cricket Ground, Northlands Road, Southampton SO9 2TY
Captain: M.C.J.Nicholas
Scorer: V.H Isaacs
Cricketcall: ☎ 0898 1214 22
Testimonial 1989: M.N.S.Taylor

ANDREW, Stephen Jon Walter (Milton Abbey S; Portchester SS), b London 27 Jan 1966. 6'3". RHB, RMF. Debut 1984. HS 12* v Middx (Basingstoke) 1988. BB 7-92 v Glos (Southampton) 1987. Awards: BHC 2. **NWT:** HS 0*. BB 2-37 v Somerset (Southampton) 1988. **BHC:** HS 4*. BB 5-24 v Essex (Chelmsford) 1987. **RAL:** HS 1*. BB 4-50 v Middx (Southampton) 1988.

AYLING, Jonathan Richard (Portsmouth GS), b Portsmouth 13 Jun 1967. 6'4". RHB, RM. Debut 1988. Took wicket of D.A.Polkinghorne (OU) with first ball in f-c cricket. HS 88* v Lancs (Liverpool) 1988. BB 4-57 v Glos (Gloucester) 1988. **NWT:** HS 25 v Worcs (Worcester) 1988. BB 2-35 v Somerset (Southampton) 1988. **BHC:** HS 1. BB 1-21. **RAL:** HS 41* v Derbys (Portsmouth) 1988. BB 3-30 v Kent (Maidstone) 1987.

AYMES, Adrian Nigel (Bellemoor SM, Southampton), b Southampton 4 Jun 1964. 6'0". RHB, WK. Debut 1987. HS 58 v Surrey (Oval) 1987 (on debut).

BAKKER, Paul-Jan (Hugo De Groot C, The Hague), b Vlaardingen, Holland 19 Aug 1957. 5'11". RHB, RMF. Debut 1986. HS 16 v Kent (Bournemouth) 1988. BB 7-31 v Kent (Bournemouth) 1987. **NWT:** HS 2. BB 3-34 v Worcs (Worcester) 1988. **BHC:** BB 2-19 v Comb Us (Oxford) 1986. **RAL:** HS 6*. BB 5-26 v Derbys (Portsmouth) 1988.

CONNOR, Cardigan Adolphus (The Valley SS, Anguilla; Langley C, Berkshire), b The Valley, Anguilla 24 Mar 1961. 5'9". RHB, RFM. Debut 1984. Cap 1988. Buckinghamshire 1979-83. HS 36 v Northants (Northampton) 1985. BB 7-37 v Kent (Bournemouth) 1988. **NWT:** HS 5. BB 3-52 v Essex (Southampton) 1985. **BHC:** HS 5*. BB 4-27 v Kent (Canterbury) 1985. **RAL:** HS 5*. BB 4-16 v Yorks (Bournemouth) 1984.

COWLEY, Nigel Geoffrey (Dutchy Manor SS, Mere), b Shaftesbury, Dorset 1 Mar 1953. 5'7". RHB, OB. Debut 1974. Cap 1978. Benefit 1988. Dorset 1972. 1000 runs (1): 1042 (1984). HS 109* v Somerset (Taunton) 1977. BB 6-48 v Leics (Southampton) 1982. Award: NWT 1. **NWT:** HS 63* v Glos (Bristol) 1979. BB 5-24 v Norfolk (Norwich) 1984. **BHC:** HS 59 v Glos (Southampton) 1977. BB 3-39 v Sussex (Bournemouth) 1982. **RAL:** HS 74 v Warwicks (Birmingham) 1981. BB 4-42 v Surrey (Portsmouth) 1983.

JAMES, Kevan David (Edmonton County HS), b Lambeth, London 18 Mar 1961. 6'0". LHB, LMF. Middlesex 1980-84. Wellington 1982-83. Hampshire debut 1985. Shared record Hants 8th-wkt stand of 227 with T.M.Tremlett v Somerset (Taunton) 1985. HS 142* v Notts (Bournemouth) 1987. BB 6-22 v Australians (Southampton) 1985. **NWT:** HS 19 v Worcs (Southampton) 1986. BB 3-22 v Dorset (Southampton) 1987. **BHC:** HS 29 v Comb Us (Oxford) 1987. BB 3-31 v Middx 1987 and v Glam 1988. **RAL:** HS 54* v Surrey (Oval) 1986. BB 4-23 v Lancs (Southampton) 1986.

JEFFERIES, Stephen Thomas (Plumstead HS), b Cape Town, SA 8 Dec 1959. 6'0". LHB, LFM. W Province 1978-88. Derbyshire 1982. Lancashire 1983-85. Hampshire debut 1988. HS 93 Lancs v Sussex (Manchester) 1985. Hants HS 60 v Surrey (Southampton) 1988. BB 10-59 W Province v OFS (Cape Town) 1987-88. Hants BB 8-97 v Glos (Gloucester) 1988. Awards: BHC 3. **NWT:** HS 39 v Salop (Telford) 1988. BB 3-43 Lancs v Glos (Bristol) 1984. **BHC:** HS 39 Lancs v Worcs (Manchester) 1984. BB 5-13 v Derbys (Lord's) 1988. **RAL:** HS 39 v Surrey (Southampton) 1988. BB 4-20 Lancs v Worcs (Manchester) 1984.

MARSHALL, Malcolm Denzil (Parkinson CS, Barbados), b St Michael, Barbados 18 Apr 1958. 5'11". RHB, RF. Barbados 1977-88 (capt 1987-88). Hampshire debut 1979. Cap 1981. Benefit 1987. Wisden 1982. **Tests** (WI): 58 (1978-79 to 1988); HS 92 v Ind (Kanpur) 1983-84; BB 7-22 v Eng (Manchester) 1988. LOI (WI): 90. Tours (WI): Eng 1980, 1984, 1988; Aus 1979-80, 1981-82, 1984-85; NZ 1979-80, 1986-87; Ind 1978-79, 1983-84; Pak 1980-81, 1986-87; SL 1978-79; Zim 1981-82 (Young WI). 100 wickets (2); most – 134 (1982). 2 hat-tricks: 1978-79 (Barbados), 1983 (4 wkts in 5 balls). HS 116* v Lancs (Southampton) 1982. BB 8-71 v Worcs (Southampton) 1982. **NWT:** HS 51 v Leics (Leicester) 1987. BB 4-15 v Kent (Canterbury) 1983. **BHC:** HS 34 v Essex (Chelmsford) 1987. BB 4-26 v Kent (Canterbury) 1983. **RAL:** HS 46 v Leics (Leicester) 1982. BB 5-13 v Glam (Portsmouth) 1979.

MARU, Rajesh Jamandass (Rook's Heath HS, Harrow; Pinner SFC), b Nairobi, Kenya 28 Oct 1962. 5'6". RHB, SLA. Middlesex 1980-82. Hampshire debut 1984. Cap 1986. Tour: Zim 1980-81 (Middx). HS 74 v Glos (Gloucester) 1988. BB 7-79 v Middx (Bournemouth) 1984. **NWT:** BB 2-5 v Dorset (Southampton) 1987. **RAL:** HS 6*. BB 3-30 v Leics (Leicester) 1988.

MIDDLETON, Tony Charles (Montgomery of Alamein S, and Peter Symonds SFC, Winchester), b Winchester 1 Feb 1964. 5'10½". RHB, SLA. Debut 1984. HS 68* v Somerset (Taunton) 1986. BB 1-13.

NICHOLAS, Mark Charles Jefford (Bradfield C), b London 29 Sep 1957. Grandson of F.W.H. (Essex 1912-29). 5'11". RHB, RM. Debut 1978. Cap 1982. Captain 1985-. Tours (C=Capt): SL 1984-85C (Eng B); Zim 1984-85C (Eng Co). 1000 runs (6); most – 1559 (1984). HS 206* v OU (Oxford) 1982. BB 5-45 v Worcs (Southampton) 1983. Award: BHC 1. **NWT:** HS 63 v Norfolk (Norwich) 1984. BB 2-39 v Berks (Southampton) 1985. **BHC:** HS 74 v Glam (Southampton) 1985. BB 4-34 v Minor C (Reading) 1985. **RAL:** HS 108 v Glos (Bristol) 1984. BB 4-41 v Northants (Southampton) 1986.

PARKS, Robert James (Eastbourne GS; Southampton Inst of Technology), b Cuckfield, Sussex 15 Jun 1959. Son of J.M. (Sussex, Somerset and England 1949-76) and grandson of J.H. (Sussex and England 1924-52). 5'8". RHB, WK. Debut 1980. Cap 1982. Tour: Zim 1984-85 (Eng Co). Held 10 catches in match v Derbys (Portsmouth) 1981. HS 89 v CU (Cambridge) 1984. Award: BHC 1. **NWT:** HS 25 v Kent (Southampton) 1984. **BHC:** HS 23* v Somerset (Taunton) 1988. **RAL:** HS 38* v Essex (Portsmouth) 1987.

SCOTT, Richard John (Queen Elizabeth S, Bournemouth), b Bournemouth 2 Nov 1963. 5'11". LHB, RM. Debut 1988. Dorset 1981-85. HS 107* v SL (Southampton) 1988. **NWT:** HS 0. **BHC:** HS 41 v Glos (Southampton) 1988. **RAL:** HS 48 v Lancs (Manchester) 1987.

SMITH, Christopher Lyall ('Kippy') (Northlands HS, Durban), b Durban, SA 15 Oct 1958. Brother of R.A. and grandson of Dr V.L.Shearer (Natal). RHB, OB. Natal 1977-83. Glamorgan 1979. Hampshire debut 1980. Cap 1981. Wisden 1983. **Tests:** 8 (1983 to 1986); HS 91 v NZ (Auckland) 1983-84; BB 2-31 v NZ (Nottingham) 1983. LOI: 4. Tours: NZ 1983-84; Pak 1983-84; SL 1985-86 (Eng B). 1000 runs (7); most – 2000 (1985). HS 217 v Warwicks (Birmingham) 1987 – sharing record Hants 1st-wkt stand of 347 with V.P.Terry. BB 5-69 v Sussex (Southampton) 1988. Awards: NWT 4; BHC 2. **NWT:** HS 140* v Dorset (Southampton) 1987. BB 3-32 v Berks (Southampton) 1985. **BHC:** HS 82* v Comb Us (Southampton) 1984. **RAL:** HS 95 v Leics (Basingstoke) 1984. BB 2-3 v Glos (Bristol) 1984.

SMITH, Robin Arnold (Northlands HS), b Durban, SA 13 Sep 1963. Brother of C.L. and grandson of Dr V.L.Shearer (Natal). 5'11". RHB, LB. Natal 1980-85. Hampshire debut 1982. Cap 1985. **Tests:** 3 (1988); HS 57 v WI (Oval). LOI: 1. 1000 (3); most – 1533 (1985). HS 209* v Essex (Southend) 1987. BB 2-11 v Surrey (Southampton) 1985. Awards: NWT 1; BHC 1. **NWT:** HS 110 v Somerset (Taunton) 1985. BB 2-13 v Berks (Southampton) 1985. **BHC:** HS 87* v Worcs (Worcester) 1988. **RAL:** HS 104 v Glam (Cardiff) 1984 and v Surrey (Southampton) 1985.

TERRY, Vivian Paul (Millfield S), b Osnabruck, W Germany 14 Jan 1959. 6'0". RHB, RM. Debut 1978. Cap 1983. **Tests:** 2 (1984); HS 8. Tour: Zim 1984-85 (Eng Co). 1000 runs (5); most – 1382 (1987). Shared record Hants 1st-wkt stand of 347 with C.L.Smith v Warwicks (Birmingham) 1987. HS 190 v SL (Southampton) 1988. Awards: NWT 3; BHC 3. **NWT:** HS 165* v Berks (Southampton) 1985. **BHC:** HS 109 v Essex (Chelmsford) 1988. **RAL:** HS 142 v Leics (Southampton) 1986.

TREMLETT, Timothy Maurice (Bellemoor SM; Richard Taunton SFC, Southampton), b Wellington, Somerset 26 Jul 1956. Son of M.F. (Somerset and England 1947-60). 6'2". RHB, RMF. Debut 1976. Cap 1983. Tours: SL 1985-86 (Eng B); Zim 1984-85 (Eng Co). HS 102* v Somerset (Taunton) 1985 – sharing record Hants 8th-wkt stand of 227 with K.D.James. BB 6-53 v Somerset (Weston) 1983. Awards: BHC 2. **NWT:** HS 43* v Leics (Leicester) 1987. BB 4-38 v Kent (Canterbury) 1983. **BHC:** HS 36* v Kent (Southampton) 1986. BB 4-30 v Surrey (Oval) 1986. **RAL:** HS 35 v Worcs (Worcester) 1984. BB 5-28 v Kent (Canterbury) 1985.

TURNER, David Roy (Chippenham BHS), b Chippenham, Wilts 5 Feb 1949. 5'6". LHB, RM. Debut 1966. Cap 1970. W Province 1977-78. Benefit 1981. Tour: SA 1972-73 (DHR). 1000 runs (9); most – 1365 (1984). HS 184* v Glos (Gloucester) 1987. BB 2-7 v Glam (Bournemouth) 1981. Awards: NWT 1; BHC 4. **NWT:** HS 100* v Dorset (Southampton) 1987. **BHC:** HS 123* v Minor C (S) (Amersham) 1973. **RAL:** HS 114 v Essex (Colchester) 1984.

NEWCOMER

WOOD, Julian Ross (Leighton Park S, Reading), b Winchester 21 Nov 1968. 5'8". LHB. MCC staff.

DEPARTURE

MULLALLY, Alan David (Educated in Perth, Aus), b Southend-on-Sea, Essex 12 Jul 1969. 6'3½". RHB, LFM. Debut for W Australia v Queensland (Perth) in 1987-88 Sheffield Shield Final. Hampshire debut 1988. HS 2*. BB 1-17.

HAMPSHIRE 1988

RESULTS SUMMARY

	Place	Won	Lost	Drew	Abandoned
Britannic Assurance Championship	15th	4	6	12	
All First-class Matches		4	6	14	
Refuge Assurance League	9th	7	8		1
NatWest Bank Trophy	Semi-Finalist				
Benson and Hedges Cup	Winners				

BRITANNIC ASSURANCE CHAMPIONSHIP AVERAGES

BATTING AND FIELDING

Cap		M	I	NO	HS	Runs	Avge	100	50	Ct/St
1978	N.G.Cowley	4	5	2	55	139	46.33	—	1	1
1981	C.L.Smith	22	43	3	124*	1436	35.90	3	8	14
1970	D.R.Turner	21	38	5	150*	1121	33.96	2	5	5
—	S.T.Jefferies	14	19	5	60	462	33.00	—	2	4
1985	R.A.Smith	16	32	4	141*	912	32.57	2	2	10
1982	M.C.J.Nicholas	22	42	3	132*	1146	29.38	2	4	18
1983	V.P.Terry	22	42	3	126*	992	25.43	2	5	30
—	J.R.Ayling	18	31	4	88*	667	24.70	—	4	5
—	S.J.W.Andrew	10	9	7	12*	41	20.50	—	—	1
—	R.J.Scott	7	13	0	58	255	19.61	—	2	9
—	P.J.Bakker	10	11	8	16	50	16.66	—	—	1
1982	R.J.Parks	22	33	8	38*	392	15.68	—	—	59/10
—	K.D.James	10	19	2	77	238	14.00	—	1	2
1983	T.M.Tremlett	6	10	2	38	111	13.87	—	—	3
1986	R.J.Maru	21	28	5	74	302	13.13	—	1	30
1988	C.A.Connor	17	22	4	24	135	7.50	—	—	3

BOWLING

	O	M	R	W	Avge	Best	5 wI	10 wM
O.H.Mortensen	233.3	73	464	34	13.64	6-35	4	—
P.J.Bakker	293.4	86	670	30	22.33	5-54	1	—
J.R.Ayling	409.1	84	1065	45	23.66	4-57	—	—
K.D.James	250.5	56	639	26	24.57	5-25	1	—
S.J.W.Andrew	233.3	60	681	26	26.19	4-52	—	—
C.A.Connor	470.5	86	1451	53	27.37	5-70	1	—
S.T.Jefferies	355.1	53	1216	34	35.76	8-97	2	—
R.J.Maru	622.0	171	1618	45	35.95	5-69	1	—

Also bowled: N.G.Cowley 96.1-22-246-8; M.C.J.Nicholas 33-3-114-1; R.J.Scott 13.3-2-52-0; C.L.Smith 49-1-171-5; R.A.Smith 5.1-1-34-0; D.R.Turner 0.2-0-8-0.

The First-Class Averages (pp 161-175) give the records of Hampshire players in all first-class county matches (their other opponents being the Sri Lankans and Oxford U.), with the exception of:
  M.C.J.Nicholas 24-45-3-132*-1262-30.04-2-5-18ct. 34-3-115-1-115.00-1/58.
  R.A.Smith 18-36-7-141*-1211-41.75-4-3-13ct. 6.1-1-35-0.

HAMPSHIRE RECORDS

FIRST-CLASS CRICKET

Highest Total	For	672-7d		v Somerset	Taunton	1899
	V	742		by Surrey	The Oval	1909
Lowest Total	For	15		v Warwicks	Birmingham	1922
	V	23		by Yorkshire	Middlesbrough	1965
Highest Innings	For	316	R.H.Moore	v Warwicks	Bournemouth	1937
	V	302*	P.Holmes	for Yorkshire	Portsmouth	1920

Highest Partnerships
Wkt

1st	347	V.P.Terry/C.L.Smith	v Warwicks	Birmingham	1987
2nd	321	G.Brown/E.I.M.Barrett	v Glos	Southampton	1920
3rd	344	C.P.Mead/G.Brown	v Yorks	Portsmouth	1927
4th	263	R.E.Marshall/D.A.Livingstone	v Middlesex	Lord's	1970
5th	235	G.Hill/D.F.Walker	v Sussex	Portsmouth	1937
6th	411	R.M.Poore/E.G.Wynyard	v Somerset	Taunton	1899
7th	325	G.Brown/C.H.Abercrombie	v Essex	Leyton	1913
8th	227	K.D.James/T.M.Tremlett	v Somerset	Taunton	1985
9th	230	D.A.Livingstone/A.T.Castell	v Surrey	Southampton	1962
10th	192	H.A.W.Bowell/W.H.Livsey	v Worcs	Bournemouth	1921

Best Bowling	For	9-25	R.M.H.Cottam	v Lancashire	Manchester	1965
(Innings)	V	10-46	W.Hickton	for Lancashire	Manchester	1870
Best Bowling	For	16-88	J.A.Newman	v Somerset	Weston-s-M	1921
(Match)	V	17-119	W.Mead	for Essex	Southampton	1895

Most Runs – Season	2,854	C.P.Mead	(av 79.27)		1928
Most Runs – Career	48,892	C.P.Mead	(av 48.84)		1905-1936
Most 100s – Season	12	C.P.Mead			1928
Most 100s – Career	138	C.P.Mead			1905-1936
Most Wkts – Season	190	A.S.Kennedy	(av 15.61)		1922
Most Wkts – Career	2,669	D.Shackleton	(av 18.23)		1948-1969

LIMITED-OVERS CRICKET

highest total	nwt	371-4		v Glamorgan	Southampton	1975
	BHC	321-1		v Minor C(S)	Amersham	1973
	RAL	292-1		v Surrey	Portsmouth	1983
Lowest Total	NWT	98		v Lancashire	Manchester	1975
	BHC	94		v Glamorgan	Swansea	1973
	RAL	43		v Essex	Basingstoke	1972
Highest Innings	NWT	177	C.G.Greenidge	v Glamorgan	Southampton	1975
	BHC	173*	C.G.Greenidge	v Minor C(S)	Amersham	1973
	RAL	172	C.G.Greenidge	v Surrey	Southampton	1987
Best Bowling	NWT	7-30	P.J.Sainsbury	v Norfolk	Southampton	1965
	BHC	5-13	S.T.Jefferies	v Derbyshire	Lord's	1988
	RAL	6-20	T.E.Jesty	v Glamorgan	Cardiff	1975

KENT

Formation of Present Club: 1 March 1859
Substantial Reorganisation: 6 December 1870
Colours: Maroon and White
Badge: White Horse on a Red Ground
Championships: (6) 1906, 1909, 1910, 1913, 1970, 1978.
Joint Championship: (1) 1977
NatWest Trophy/Gillette Cup Winners: (2) 1967, 1974
Benson and Hedges Cup Winners: (3) 1973, 1976, 1978
Sunday League Champions: (3) 1972, 1973, 1976
Match Awards: NWT 39; BHC 55

Chief Executive: A.J.P.Woodhouse
Secretary: D.B.Dalby, St Lawrence Ground, Canterbury, CT1 3NZ
Captain: C.S.Cowdrey
Scorer: J.Foley
Cricketcall: ☎ 0898 1214 21
Benefit 1989: C.S.Cowdrey

ALLEYNE, Hartley Leroy (St John's Baptist SS, Bridgetown), b Bridgetown, Barbados 27 Feb 1957. 6'0". RHB, RFM. Barbados 1978-83. Worcestershire 1980-82 (cap 1981). Natal 1986-88. Kent debut 1988. Lincolnshire 1979. Buckinghamshire 1984-86. Tour: SA 1983-84 (WI XI); Zim 1981-82 (Young WI). HS 72 Worcs v Lancs (Stourport) 1980. Kent HS 9. BB 8-43 (inc hat-trick) Worcs v Middx (Lord's) 1981. Kent BB 5-54 v Leics (Leicester) 1988. **NWT:** HS 19 and BB 3-27 Worcs v Somerset (Taunton) 1980. **BHC:** HS 10 Worcs v Essex (Worcester) 1980. BB 3-39 Worcs v Lancs (Manchester) 1980. **RAL:** HS 32 Worcs v Kent (Worcester) 1980. BB 4-24 Worcs v Lancs (Worcester) 1980.

BENSON, Mark Richard (Sutton Valence S), b Shoreham, Sussex 6 Jul 1958. 5'10". LHB, OB. Debut 1980. Cap 1981. Tests: 1 (1986); HS 30 v Ind (Birmingham) 1986. LOI: 1. 1000 runs (7); most – 1725 (1987). HS 162 v Hants (Southampton) 1985. BB 2-55 v Surrey (Dartford) 1986. Awards: NWT 2; BHC 1. **NWT:** HS 113* v Warwicks (Birmingham) 1984. **BHC:** HS 113 v Essex (Canterbury) 1988. **RAL:** HS 97 v Surrey (Oval) 1982.

COWDREY, Christopher Stuart (Tonbridge S), b Farnborough 20 Oct 1957. Brother of G.R., son of M.C. (Kent and England 1950-76), grandson of E.A. (Europeans). 6'1". RHB, RM. Kent 2nd XI debut when aged 15. Debut 1977. Cap 1979. Captain 1985-. Benefit 1989. Tests: 6 (1984-85 to 1988, 1 as captain); HS 38 v Ind (Delhi) 1984-85; BB 2-65 v Ind (Madras) 1984-85. LOI: 3. Tours: NZ 1979-80 (DHR); Ind/SL 1984-85; SL 1977-78 (DHR). 1000 runs (3); most – 1364 (1983). HS 159 v Surrey (Canterbury) 1985. BB 5-46 v Hants (Canterbury) 1988. Awards: NWT 3; BHC 5. **NWT:** HS 122* v Essex (Chelmsford) 1983. BB 4-36 v Hants (Canterbury) 1983. **BHC:** HS 114 v Sussex (Canterbury) 1977. BB 4-14 v Sussex (Canterbury) 1987. **RAL:** HS 95 v Worcs (Canterbury) 1983. BB 5-28 v Leics (Canterbury) 1984.

COWDREY, Graham Robert (Tonbridge S; Durham U), b Farnborough 27 Jun 1964. Brother of C.S., son of M.C. (Kent and England 1950-76), grandson of E.A. (Europeans). 5'11". RHB, RM. Debut 1984. Cap 1988. HS 145 v Essex (Chelmsford) 1988. BB 1-5. Award: BHC 1. **NWT:** HS 25 v Middx (Lord's) 1988. BB 2-19 v Warwicks (Canterbury) 1988. **BHC:** HS 69 v Sussex (Canterbury) 1987. BB 1-6. **RAL:** HS 53 v Warwicks (Birmingham) 1987. BB 4-15 v Essex (Ilford) 1987.

89

DAVIS, Richard Peter (King Ethelbert's S, Birchington; Thanet TC), b Westbrook, Margate 18 Mar 1966. 6'3". RHB, SLA. Debut 1986. HS 23 v Hants (Canterbury) 1988. BB 5-132 v Essex (Chelmsford) 1988. **NWT:** HS 0. BB 3-19 v Bucks (Canterbury) 1988. **BHC:** HS 0*. BB 2-33 v Sussex (Hove) 1988. **RAL:** HS 7*. BB 3-19 v Glam 1987 and v Sussex 1988.

ELLISON, Richard Mark (Tonbridge S; Exeter U), b Ashford 21 Sep 1959. Brother of C.C. (Cambridge U). 6'2". LHB, RMF. Debut 1981. Cap 1983. Tasmania 1986-87. Wisden 1985. **Tests:** 11 (1984 to 1986); HS 41 v SL (Lord's) 1984; BB 6-77 v Aus (Birmingham) 1985. LOI: 14. Tours: WI 1985-86; Ind/SL 1984-85. HS 108 v OU (Oxford) 1984. BB 7-75 v Notts (Dartford) 1988. Awards: NWT 1; BHC 4. **NWT:** HS 49* v Warwicks (Birmingham) 1984. BB 4-19 v Cheshire (Canterbury) 1983. **BHC:** HS 72 v Middx (Lord's) 1984. BB 4-28 v Glam (Canterbury) 1984. **RAL:** HS 84 v Glos (Canterbury) 1984. BB 4-25 v Hants (Canterbury) 1983.

FARBRACE, Paul (Geoffrey Chaucer S, Canterbury), b Ash 7 Jul 1967. 5'10". RHB, WK. Debut 1987. HS 75* v Yorks (Canterbury) 1987. **NWT:** HS 4.

FLEMING, Matthew Valentine (St Aubyns S, Rottingdean; Eton C), b Macclesfield, Cheshire 12 Dec 1964. 5'11½". RHB, RM. Army and Combined Services. Awaiting f-c debut. **RAL:** HS 3*. BB 1-34.

HARMAN, Mark David (Frome C; Loughborough U), b Aylesbury, Bucks 30 June 1964. 5'11". RHB, OB. Somerset 1986-87. Kent debut 1988. HS 41 Somerset v Kent (Bath) 1987. Kent HS 17* v Hants (Canterbury) 1988. BB 5-55 v OU (Oxford) 1988. **NWT:** HS 0. BB 1-38. **RAL:** HS 8*. BB 2-58 v Glos (Moreton) 1988.

HINKS, Simon Graham (St George's S, Gravesend), b Northfleet 12 Oct 1960. 6'2". LHB, RM. Debut 1982. Cap 1985. 1000 runs (1): 1536 (1985). HS 138 v OU (Oxford) 1988. BB 1-10. Awards: NWT 1; BHC 1. **NWT:** HS 95 v Surrey (Canterbury) 1985. **BHC:** HS 85 v Sussex (Canterbury) 1987. BB 1-15. **RAL:** HS 99 v Glam (Maidstone) 1986. BB 1-3.

IGGLESDEN, Alan Paul (Churchill S, Westerham), b Farnborough 8 Oct 1964. 6'5". RHB, RFM. Debut 1986. W Province 1987-88. HS 41 and BB 6-34 v Surrey (Canterbury) 1988. **NWT:** BB 3-54 v Derbys (Canterbury) 1988. **BHC:** HS 5*. BB 1-25. **RAL:** HS 13* v Glos (Cheltenham) 1987. BB 3-40 v Lancs (Manchester) 1987.

KELLEHER, Daniel John Michael (St Mary's GS, Sidcup; Erith TC), b Southwark, London 5 May 1966. Nephew of H.R.A.Kelleher (Surrey 1955, Northants 1956-58). 6'1". RHB, RMF. Debut 1987. HS 51 v West Indians (Canterbury) 1988. BB 6-109 v Somerset (Bath) 1987. **NWT:** HS 0*. BB 2-73 v Derbys (Canterbury) 1987. **BHC:** HS 0*. BB 1-30. **RAL:** HS 19 v Notts (Nottingham) 1987. BB 2-25 (twice in 1987).

MARSH, Steven Andrew (Walderslade SS; Mid-Kent CFE), b Westminster, London 27 Jan 1961. 5'10". RHB, WK. Debut 1982. Cap 1986. HS 120 v Essex (Chelmsford) 1988. **NWT:** HS 24* v Middx (Lord's) 1988. **BHC:** HS 17 v Surrey (Oval) 1988. **RAL:** HS 36 v Notts (Nottingham) 1987.

PENN, Christopher (Dover GS), b Dover 19 Jun 1963. 6'1". LHB, RFM. Debut 1982. Cap 1987. HS 115 v Lancs (Manchester) 1984. BB 7-70 v Middx (Lord's) 1988. **NWT:** HS 5. BB 3-30 v Warwicks (Canterbury) 1988. **BHC:** HS 17 v Somerset (Canterbury) 1984. BB 4-34 v Surrey (Canterbury) 1982. **RAL:** HS 40 v Sussex (Maidstone) 1982. BB 4-22 v Lancs (Canterbury) 1988.

PIENAAR, Roy Francois (Stithians C; Cape Town U), b Johannesburg, SA 17 Jul 1961. 6'2". RHB, RMF. Transvaal B 1977-78 (aged 16yr 4m). W Province 1984-85. N Transvaal 1985-88. Kent debut 1987. Cap 1988. 1000 runs (1): 1228 (1988). HS 153 v Derbys (Derby) 1987. BB 5-24 W Province v Natal (Durban) 1984-85. Kent BB 5-27 v Middx (Tunbridge Wells) 1988. Award: NWT 2. **NWT:** HS 58* v Warwicks (Canterbury) 1988. BB 3-19 v Bucks (Canterbury) 1988. **RAL:** HS 84 v Surrey (Oval) 1988. BB 4-34 v Middx (Canterbury) 1988.

SABINE, David John (St Anselms CS; Canterbury TC), b Papakura, Auckland, NZ 2 Jun 1966. 5'11½". RHB, RM. Debut 1988. HS 7.

TAYLOR, Neil Royston (Cray Valley THS), b Orpington 21 Jul 1959. 6'1". RHB, OB. Debut 1979 scoring 110 and 11 v SL at Canterbury. Cap 1982. 1000 runs (5); most – 1340 (1982). HS 155* v Glam (Cardiff) 1983. BB 2-20 v Somerset (Canterbury) 1985. Awards: BHC 6. **NWT:** HS 85 v Derbys (Canterbury) 1987. **BHC:** HS 137 v Surrey (Oval) 1988. **RAL:** HS 85 v Lancs (Canterbury) 1988.

WARD, Trevor Robert (Hextable CS, nr Swanley), b Farningham 18 Jan 1968. 5'11". RHB, RM. Debut 1986. HS 72 v Surrey (Guildford) 1988. **NWT:** HS 34 v Warwicks (Canterbury) 1988. **RAL:** HS 25 v Middx (Canterbury) 1988.

WELLS, Vincent John (Sir William Nottidge S, Whitstable), b Dartford 6 Aug 1965. 6'0". RHB, WK. Debut 1988. HS 6. BB 1-51. **BHC:** HS 15* v Middx (Canterbury) 1988. **RAL:** HS 10* v Yorks (Canterbury) 1988. BB 3-17 v Somerset (Canterbury) 1988.

NEWCOMERS

DOBSON, Mark Christopher (Simon Langton GS), b Canterbury 24 Oct 1967. 5'10". RHB, SLC.

EALHAM, Mark Alan (Stour Valley SS, Chartham), b Willesborough, Ashford 27 Aug 1969. 5'9". Son of A.G.E. Ealham (Kent), RHB, RM.

DEPARTURE

TAVARÉ, C.J. – see SOMERSET

KENT 1988

RESULTS SUMMARY

	Place	Won	Lost	Drew	Abandoned
Britannic Assurance Championship	2nd	10	5	7	
All First-class Matches		10	6	8	
Refuge Assurance League	7th	7	6		3
NatWest Bank Trophy	Quarter-Finalist				
Benson and Hedges Cup	3rd in Group C				

BRITANNIC ASSURANCE CHAMPIONSHIP AVERAGES

BATTING AND FIELDING

Cap		M	I	NO	HS	Runs	Avge	100	50	Ct/St
1978	C.J.Tavaré	21	35	1	129*	1292	38.00	3	5	29
1988	R.F.Pienaar	19	32	2	144	1070	35.66	2	7	5
1981	M.R.Benson	21	37	1	110	1227	34.08	2	8	13
1988	G.R.Cowdrey	18	29	4	145	790	31.60	1	4	10
1982	N.R.Taylor	20	36	2	114	915	26.91	2	4	15
1985	S.G.Hinks	14	24	1	92	611	26.56	—	3	11
1979	C.S.Cowdrey	19	33	6	108	714	26.44	1	2	31
—	T.R.Ward	9	15	0	72	345	23.00	—	3	9
1987	C.Penn	19	30	12	40	407	22.61	—	—	7
—	D.J.M.Kelleher	4	5	1	43*	86	21.50	—	—	2
1986	S.A.Marsh	22	34	5	120	613	21.13	1	1	51/5
—	A.P.Igglesden	7	8	2	41	103	17.16	—	—	1
1983	R.M.Ellison	19	27	6	50*	345	16.42	—	1	7
—	M.D.Harman	10	11	6	17*	71	14.20	—	—	6
—	R.P.Davis	17	19	6	23	103	7.92	—	—	12
—	H.L.Alleyne	3	5	1	9	16	4.00	—	—	—

BOWLING

	O	M	R	W	Avge	Best	5 wI	10 wM
A.P.Igglesden	234.3	46	805	37	21.75	6-34	3	1
R.M.Ellison	571.4	156	1652	69	23.94	7-75	3	—
C.Penn	629.1	142	1918	80	23.97	7-70	6	—
H.L.Alleyne	74.3	13	260	10	26.00	5-54	1	—
M.D.Harman	238.4	76	537	20	26.85	5-68	1	—
C.S.Cowdrey	384.5	96	1114	39	28.56	5-46	1	—
R.F.Pienaar	368.2	90	1055	32	32.96	5-27	1	—
R.P.Davis	529.2	163	1333	34	39.20	5-132	1	—

Also bowled: M.R.Benson 3.3-0-39-0; G.R.Cowdrey 88.4-17-351-5; S.G.Hinks 2-0-28-0; D.J.M.Kelleher 72-18-188-7; N.R.Taylor 8-4-7-1; T.R.Ward 4-1-4-0.

The First-Class Averages (pp 161-175) give the records of Kent players in all first-class county matches (their other opponents being the West Indians and Oxford U.), with the exception of:
  C.S.Cowdrey 20-34-7-124*-838-31.03-2-2-33ct. 385.5-96-1120-39-28.71-5/46-1-0.

KENT RECORDS

FIRST-CLASS CRICKET

Highest Total	For	803-4d		v Essex	Brentwood	1934
	V	676		by Australians	Canterbury	1921
Lowest Total	For	18		v Sussex	Gravesend	1867
	V	16		by Warwicks	Tonbridge	1913
Highest Innings	For	332	W.H.Ashdown	v Essex	Brentwood	1934
	V	344	W.G.Grace	for MCC	Canterbury	1876

Highest Partnerships
Wkt

1st	283	A.E.Fagg/P.R.Sunnucks	v Essex	Colchester	1938
2nd	352	W.H.Ashdown/F.E.Woolley	v Essex	Brentwood	1934
3rd	321*	A.Hearne/J.R.Mason	v Notts	Nottingham	1899
4th	297	H.T.W.Harding/A.P.F.Chapman	v Hampshire	Southampton	1926
5th	277	F.E.Woolley/L.E.G.Ames	v New Zealand	Canterbury	1931
6th	284	A.P.F.Chapman/G.B.Legge	v Lancashire	Maidstone	1927
7th	248	A.P.Day/E.Humphreys	v Somerset	Taunton	1908
8th	157	A.L.Hilder/A.C.Wright	v Essex	Gravesend	1924
9th	161	B.R.Edrich/F.Ridgway	v Sussex	Tunbridge W	1949
10th	235	F.E.Woolley/A.Fielder	v Worcs	Stourbridge	1909

Best Bowling	For	10-30	C.Blythe	v Northants	Northampton	1907
(Innings)	V	10-48	C.H.G.Bland	for Sussex	Tonbridge	1899
Best Bowling	For	17-48	C.Blythe	v Northants	Northampton	1907
(Match)	V	17-106	T.W.J.Goddard	for Glos	Bristol	1939

Most Runs – Season	2,894	F.E.Woolley	(av 59.06)		1928
Most Runs – Career	47,868	F.E.Woolley	(av 41.77)		1906-1938
Most 100s – Season	10	F.E.Woolley			1928
	10	F.E.Woolley			1934
Most 100s – Career	122	F.E.Woolley			1906-1938
Most Wkts – Season	262	A.P.Freeman	(av 14.74)		1933
Most Wkts – Career	3,340	A.P.Freeman	(av 17.64)		1914-1936

LIMITED-OVERS CRICKET

Highest Total	NWT	297-3		v Worcs	Canterbury	1970
	BHC	293-6		v Somerset	Taunton	1985
	RAL	290-4		v Lancashire	Manchester	1987
Lowest Total	NWT	60		v Somerset	Taunton	1979
	BHC	73		v Middlesex	Canterbury	1979
	RAL	83		v Middlesex	Lord's	1984
Highest Innings	NWT	129*	B.W.Luckhurst	v Durham	Canterbury	1974
	BHC	143	C.J.Tavaré	v Somerset	Taunton	1985
	RAL	142	B.W.Luckhurst	v Somerset	Weston-s-M	1970
Best Bowling	NWT	8-31	D.L.Underwood	v Scotland	Edinburgh	1987
	BHC	5-21	B.D.Julien	v Surrey	The Oval	1973
	RAL	6-9	R.A.Woolmer	v Derbyshire	Chesterfield	1979

LANCASHIRE

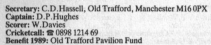

Formation of Present Club: 12 January 1864
Colours: Red, Green and Blue.
Badge: Red Rose.
Championships (since 1890): (7) 1897, 1904, 1926, 1927,
1928, 1930, 1934
Joint Championship: (1) 1950
NatWest Trophy/Gillette Cup Winners: (4) 1970, 1971,
1972, 1975
Benson and Hedges Cup Winners: (1) 1984
Sunday League Champions: (2) 1969, 1970
Match Awards: NWT 46; BHC 41

Secretary: C.D.Hassell, Old Trafford, Manchester M16 0PX
Captain: D.P.Hughes
Scorer: W.Davies
Cricketcall: ☎ 0898 1214 69
Benefit 1989: Old Trafford Pavilion Fund

ABRAHAMS, John (Heywood GS), b Cape Town, SA 21 Jul 1952. 5'8". LHB, OB. Debut 1973. Cap 1982. Captain 1984-85. Benefit 1988. 1000 runs (4); most – 1261 (1983). HS 201* v Warwicks (Nuneaton) 1984. BB 3-27 v Worcs (Manchester) 1981. Awards: NWT 1; BHC 2. **NWT:** HS 67* and BB 2-26 v Cumberland (Manchester) 1986. **BHC:** HS 66* v Minor C (Bowdon) 1984. BB 2-32 v Scotland (Southport) 1987. **RAL:** HS 103* v Somerset (Taunton) 1986. BB 2-11 v Kent (Canterbury) 1986.

ALLOTT, Paul John Walter (Altrincham GS; Durham U), b Altrincham, Cheshire 14 Sep 1956. 6'4". RHB, RFM. Debut 1978. Cap 1981. Wellington 1986-87. Cheshire 1976. **Tests:** 13 (1981 to 1985); HS 52* v Aus (Manchester) 1981 – on debut. BB 6-61 v WI (Leeds) 1984. LOI: 13. Tours: WI 1982-83 (Int XI), 1986-87 (Lancs); Ind/SL 1981-82, 1984-85. HS 88 v Hants (Southampton) 1987. BB 8-48 v Northants (Northampton) 1981. Award: BHC 1. **NWT:** HS 19* v Worcs (Worcester) 1980. BB 4-28 v Leics (Leicester) 1986. **BHC:** HS 23* v Notts (Liverpool) 1986. BB 3-15 v Warwicks (Lord's) 1984. **RAL:** HS 43 v Warwicks (Manchester) 1988. BB 4-28 v Kent (Manchester) 1985.

ATHERTON, Michael Andrew (Manchester GS, Downing C, Cambridge), b Manchester 23 Mar 1968. 5'11". RHB, LB. CU debut 1987 (blue 1987-88; captain 1988-89). Lancs debut 1987. 1000 runs (2); most – 1193 (1987 – first to score 1,000 runs in season of f-c debut since P.W.G.Parker in 1976). HS 152* v Sussex (Hove) 1988. BB 3-32 v Middx (Manchester) 1988. **BHC:** HS 57 Comb Us v Somerset (Taunton) 1987. **RAL:** HS 22 v Essex (Chelmsford) 1987.

AUSTIN, Ian David (Haslingden HS), b Haslingden 30 May 1966. 5'10". LHB, RM. Debut 1987. HS 64 v Derbys (Manchester) 1988. BB 5-79 v Surrey (Oval) 1988. **NWT:** HS 10 v Glos (Manchester) 1987. **BHC:** HS 80 v Worcs (Worcester) 1987 (on county debut). BB 1-17. **RAL:** HS 41 and BB 3-34 v Derbys (Manchester) 1988.

FAIRBROTHER, Neil Harvey (Lymm GS), b Warrington 9 Sep 1963. 5'8". LHB, LM. Debut 1982. Cap 1985. **Tests:** 4 (1987 and 1987-88); HS 3. LOI: 11. Tours: WI 1987-88 (Lancs); NZ 1987-88; Pak 1987-88. 1000 runs (5); most – 1395 (1985). HS 164* v Hants (Liverpool) 1985. BB 2-91 v Notts (Manchester) 1987. Awards: NWT 3; BHC 1. **NWT:** HS 93* v Leics (Leicester) 1986. **BHC:** HS 116* v Scotland (Manchester) 1988. **RAL:** HS 116* v Notts (Nottingham) 1988.

FITTON, John Dexter(Redbrook HS; Oulder Hill S), b Littleborough 24 Aug 1965. 5'10". LHB, OB. Debut 1987. HS 36 and BB 6-59 v Yorks (Manchester) 1988. **RAL:** HS 0. BB 1-25.

FOLLEY, Ian (Mansfield HS; Colne C), b Burnley 9 Jan 1963. 5'9½". RHB, SLA. Debut 1982. Cap 1987. Tours: WI 1986-87 (Lancs), 1987-88 (Lancs). HS 69 v Yorks (Manchester) 1985. BB 7-15 (12-57 match) v Warwicks (Southport) 1987. **NWT:** HS 3*. BB 2-10 v Lancs (Chester-le-St) 1983. **BHC:** HS 11* v Notts (Nottingham) 1982. BB 4-18 v Middx (Lord's) 1982. **RAL:** HS 19 v Northants (Tring) 1987. BB 3-23 v Glos (Manchester) 1987.

FOWLER, Graeme (Accrington GS; Durham U), b Accrington 20 Apr 1957. 5'9½". LHB, RM. Debut 1979. Cap 1981. **Tests:** 21 (1982 to 1984-85); HS 201 v Ind (Madras) 1984-85. LOI: 26. Tours: Aus 1982-83 (Int XI), 1987-88 (Lancs); NZ 1983-84; Ind/SL 1984-85; Pak 1983-84. 1000 runs (7); most – 1800 (1987). HS 226 v Kent (Maidstone) 1984. BB 2-34 v Warwicks (Manchester) 1986. Awards: NWT 2; BHC 2. **NWT:** HS 122 v Glos (Bristol) 1984. **BHC:** HS 97 v Northants (Manchester) 1983. **RAL:** HS 112 v Kent (Canterbury) 1986.

HAYHURST, Andrew Neil (Worsley Wardley HS; Eccles SFC; Leeds Polytechnic), b Davyhulme, Manchester 23 Nov 1962. 5'11". RHB, RM. Debut 1985. Tours: WI 1986-87 (Lancs), 1987-88 (Lancs). HS 107 v Derbys (Derby) 1988. BB 4-27 v Middx (Manchester) 1987. **NWT:** HS 49 v Sussex (Lord's) 1986. BB 4-40 v Leics (Leicester) 1986. **BHC:** HS 12 v Derbys (Liverpool) 1988. BB 4-50 v Worcs (Worcester) 1987. **RAL:** HS 84 v Leics (Manchester) 1988. BB 4-37 v Glam (Pontypridd) 1988.

HEGG, Warren Kevin (Unsworth HS, Bury; Stand C, Whitefield), b Whitefield 23 Feb 1968. 5'8". RHB, WK. Debut 1986. Tours: WI 1986-87 (Lancs), 1987-88 (Lancs). HS 130 v Northants (Northampton) 1987. **NWT:** HS 20 v Glam (Cardiff) 1988. **BHC:** HS 11 v Leics (Leicester) 1988. **RAL:** HS 9*.

HUGHES, David Paul (Newton-le-Willows GS), b Newton-le-Willows 13 May 1947. 5'11". RHB, SLA. Debut 1967. Cap 1970. Captain 1987-. Benefit 1981. Tasmania 1975-77. Wisden 1987. Tours: SA 1972-73 (DHR); WI 1986-87 (Lancs), 1987-88 (Lancs). 1000 runs (2); most – 1303 (1982). HS 153 v Glam (Manchester) 1983. BB 7-24 v OU (Oxford) 1970. Awards: NWT 1; BHC 1. **NWT:** HS 71 v Durham (Chester-le-St) 1983. BB 4-61 v Somerset (Manchester) 1972. **BHC:** HS 52 v Derbys (Manchester) 1981. BB 5-23 v Minor C (W)(Watford) 1978. **RAL:** HS 92 v Kent (Maidstone) 1984. BB 6-29 v Somerset (Manchester) 1977.

JESTY, Trevor Edward (Privet County SS, Gosport), b Gosport, Hants 2 Jun 1948. 5'8½". RHB. RM. Hampshire 1966-84 (cap 1971; benefit 1982). Surrey 1985-87 (cap 1985; captain 1985). Lancashire debut 1988. Border 1973-74. GW 1974-76, 1980-81. Canterbury 1979-80. Wisden 1982. LOI: 10. Tours: WI 1982-83 (Int XI), 1987-88 (Lancs). 1000 runs (9); most – 1645 (1982). HS 248 Hants v CU (Cambridge) 1984. Lancs HS 73 v Essex (Southend) 1988. BB 7-75 Hants v Worcs (Southampton) 1976. Awards: NWT 6: BHC 11. **NWT:** HS 118 Hants v Derbys (Derby) 1980. BB 6-46 Hants v Glos (Derby) 1979. **BHC:** HS 105 Hants v Glam (Swansea) 1977. BB 5-39 v Leics (Leicester) 1988. **RAL:** HS 166* Hants v Surrey (Portsmouth) 1983. BB 6-20 v Glam (Cardiff) 1976.

LLOYD, Graham David (Hollins County HS), b Accrington 1 Jul 1969. Son of D. Lloyd (Lancs and England 1965-83). 5'9". RHB. Debut 1988. HS 22 v Derbys (Derby) 1988.

MENDIS, Gehan Dixon (St Thomas C, Colombo; Brighton, Hove & Sussex GS; Durham U), b Colombo, Ceylon 24 Apr 1955. 5'9". RHB. RM. Sussex 1974-85 (cap 1980). Lancashire debut/cap 1986. Tours: WI 1982-83 (Int XI), 1986-87 (Lancs), 1987-88 (Lancs); Pak 1981-82 (Int XI). 1000 runs (9); most – 1756 (1985). HS 209* Sussex v Somerset (Hove) 1984. Lancs HS 203* v Middx (Manchester) 1987. BB 1-65. Awards: NWT 3; BHC 3. **NWT:** HS 141* Sussex v Warwicks (Hove) 1980. **BHC:** HS 109 Sussex v Glos (Hove) 1980. **RAL:** HS 125* Sussex v Glos (Hove) 1981.

MURPHY, Anthony John (Xaverian C, Swansea U), b Manchester 6 Aug 1962. 6'0". RHB, RMF. Debut 1985. Cheshire 1984-85. Tours: WI 1986-87 (Lancs), 1987-88 (Lancs). HS 6. BB 4-115 v Somerset (Taunton) 1987. **RAL:** HS 2*. BB 1-33.

PATTERSON, Balfour Patrick(Happy Grove HS; Wolmer's HS), b Portland, Jamaica 15 Sep 1961. 6'2½". RHB, RF. Jamaica 1982-88. Lancashire debut 1984. Cap 1987. **Tests**(WI): 13 (1985-86 to 1988); HS 21* v Ind (Bombay) 1987-88; BB 5-24 v Ind (Delhi) 1987-88. LOI (WI): 26. Tours (WI): Eng 1988; NZ 1986-87; Ind 1987-88; Pak 1986-87. HS 29 v Northants (Northampton) 1987. BB 7-24 Jamaica v Guyana (Kingston) 1985-86. Lancs BB 7-49 v OU (Oxford) 1985. **NWT:** HS 4. BB 1-69. **BHC:** HS 15* v Leics (Manchester) 1985. BB 3-31 v Scotland (Perth) 1986. **RAL:** HS 3*. BB 3-25 v Essex (Chelmsford) 1987.

SIMMONS, Jack (Accrington TS; Blackburn TC), b Clayton-le-Moors 28 Mar 1941. 6'1½". RHB, OB. Debut 1968. Cap 1971. Benefit 1980. Tasmania 1972-79. Wisden 1984. Tours: WI 1987-88 (Lancs); Ind 1980-81 (Overseas XI). Hat-trick 1977. HS 112 v Sussex (Hove) 1970. BB 7-59 Tasmania v Queensland (Brisbane) 1978-79. Lancs BB 7-64 v Hants (Southport) 1973. Awards: NWT 1; BHC 2. **NWT:** HS 54* v Essex (Manchester) 1979. BB 5-37 v Glos (Bristol) 1984. **BHC:** HS 64 v Derbys (Manchester) 1978. BB 4-31 v Yorks (Manchester) 1975. **RAL:** HS 65 v Essex (Manchester) 1980. BB 5-17 v Worcs (Worcester) 1982.

SPEAK, Nicholas Jason (Parrs Wood HS, Manchester), b Manchester 21 Nov 1966. 6'0". RHB, RM/OB. Debut v Jamaica (Kingston) 1986-87. Tour: WI 1986-87 (Lancs). HS 35 v Glos (Manchester) 1988. **RAL:** HS 13 v Glos (Manchester) 1987.

STANWORTH, John (Chadderton GS), b Oldham 30 Sep 1960. 5'10". RHB, WK. Debut 1983. HS 50* v Glos (Bristol) 1985. **NWT:** HS 8*. **BHC:** HS 4*. **RAL:** HS 4*.

WASIM AKRAM (Islamia C), b Lahore, Pakistan 3 Jun 1966. 6'3". LHB, LFM. PACO 1984-86. Lahore Whites 1985-86. Lancashire debut 1988. **Tests**(Pak): 25 (1984-85 to 1987-88); HS 66 and BB 6-91 v Pak (Faisalabad) 1986-87. LOI (Pak): 57. Tours (Pak): Eng 1987; WI 1987-88; NZ 1984-85; Ind 1986-87; SL 1984-85 (Pak U-23), 1985-86. Hat-trick 1988. HS 116* v Somerset (Manchester) 1988. BB 7-50 Patron's XI v New Zealanders (Rawalpindi) 1984-85 (on debut). Lancs BB 7-53 v Northants (Northampton) 1988. **NWT**: HS 14 and BB 4-37 v Lincs (Manchester) 1988. **BHC**: HS 23 v Derbys (Liverpool) 1988. BB 3-37 v Warwicks (Birmingham) 1988. **RAL**: HS 29 v Yorks (Scarborough) 1988. BB 3-24 v Somerset (Manchester) 1988.

WATKINSON, Michael (Rivington and Blackrod HS, Horwich), b Westhoughton 1 Aug 1961. 6'1". RHB, RMF. Debut 1982. Cap 1987. Cheshire 1982. Tour: WI 1987-88 (Lancs). HS 106 v Surrey (Southport) 1985. BB 7-25 v Sussex (Lytham) 1987. **NWT**: HS 56 v Worcs (Manchester) 1985. BB 3-44 v Somerset (Taunton) 1986. **BHC**: HS 70* v Derbys (Liverpool) 1988. BB 4-39 v Notts (Manchester) 1983. **RAL**: HS 58 v Sussex (Hove) 1988. BB 4-17 v Middx (Blackpool) 1988.

NEWCOMERS

DEFREITAS, Phillip Anthony Jason (Willesden HS, London), b Scotts Head, Dominica 18 Feb 1966. 6'0". RHB, RFM. UK resident since 1976. Leicestershire 1985-88 (cap 1986). **Tests**: 12 (1986-87 to 1988): HS 40 v Aus (Brisbane) 1986-87; BB 5-86 v Pak (Karachi) 1987-88. LOI: 38. Tours: Aus 1986-87; NZ 1987-88; Pak 1987-88. HS 113 Leics v Notts (Worksop) 1988. BB 7-44 (13-86 match) Leics v Essex (Southend) 1986. Award: NWT 1. **NWT**: HS 69 Leics v Lancs (Leicester) 1986. BB 5-34 Leics v Yorks (Leeds) 1987. **BHC**: HS 57 Leics v Derbys (Derby) 1988. BB 4-27 Leics v Lancs (Leicester) 1988. **RAL**: HS 37 Leics v Derby (Derby) 1988. BB 4-20 Leics v Middx and v Worcs 1986.

IRANI, Ronald (Smithills S, Bolton), b Leigh 26 Oct 1971. 6'4". RHB, RM. Represented North of England at basketball.

MARTIN, Peter James (Danum S, Doncaster), b Accrington 15 Nov 1968. 6'4". RHB, RFM. Awaiting f-c debut.

DEPARTURES

MAKINSON, David John (St Mary's HS, Leyland), b Eccleston 12 Jan 1961. 6'3". RHB, LFM. Lancashire 1984-88. HS 58* v Northants (Lytham) 1985. BB 5-60 v Derbys (Manchester) 1985. **NWT**: HS 17 v Worcs (Manchester) 1985. BB 2-49 v Somerset (Taunton) 1986. **BHC**: HS 5. BB 3-36 v Worcs (Worcester) 1986. **RAL**: HS 13 v Hants (Manchester) 1985.

MATTHEWS, Christopher Darrell, b Cunderdin, Aus 22 Sep 1962. LHB, LFM. W Australia 1984-88. Lancashire 1988. **Tests**(Aus): 2 (1986-87); HS 11 and BB 3-95 v Eng (Brisbane) 1986-87. HS 65 W Australia v Victoria (Perth) 1986-87. BB 8-101 W Australia v Queensland (Perth) 1987-88. Lancs HS 31 and BB 4-47 v Warwicks (Manchester) 1988. **BHC**: HS 43 v Leics (Leicester) 1988. **RAL**: HS 1*. BB 2-44 v Worcs (Manchester) 1988.

LANCASHIRE 1988

	Place	Won	Lost	Tied	Drew	Aban
Britannic Assurance Championship	9th	6	7		9	
All First-class Matches		6	7		11	
Refuge Assurance League	3rd	10	4		2	
NatWest Bank Trophy	2nd Round					
Benson and Hedges Cup	4th in Group A					

BRITANNIC ASSURANCE CHAMPIONSHIP AVERAGES

BATTING AND FIELDING

Cap		M	I	NO	HS	Runs	Avge	100	50	Ct/St
—	M.A.Atherton	8	14	2	152*	456	38.00	2	—	5
1986	G.D.Mendis	22	40	4	151	1166	32.38	1	7	9
—	Wasim Akram	10	18	2	116*	496	31.00	1	3	2
—	I.D.Austin	6	9	2	64	216	30.85	—	2	—
1981	G.Fowler	20	36	1	172	1061	30.31	2	4	19
1985	N.H.Fairbrother	22	40	3	111	1090	29.45	2	6	9
—	T.E.Jesty	13	25	3	73	587	26.68	—	2	3
—	A.N.Hayhurst	12	21	2	107	477	25.10	1	2	1
1987	M.Watkinson	22	37	4	85*	725	21.96	—	6	13
1971	J.Simmons	20	26	9	57*	335	19.70	—	1	9
1970	D.P.Hughes	21	33	3	62	465	15.50	—	2	25
—	W.K.Hegg	22	32	5	76	406	15.03	—	1	50/8
1987	I.Folley	17	19	13	30	90	15.00	—	—	6
1981	P.J.W.Allott	19	28	4	31*	308	12.83	—	—	13

Also batted: J.Abrahams (1 match – cap 1982) 9, 1 (1 ct); J.D.Fitton (1 match) 36; C.D.Matthews (2 matches) 7, 0, 31; G.D.Lloyd (1 match) 22, 0 (1 ct); A.J.Murphy (2 matches) 0, 0, 3 (1 ct); N.J.Speak (1 match) 35, 10 (2 ct).

BOWLING

	O	M	R	W	Avge	Best	5 wI	10 wM
P.J.W.Allott	590.2	162	1378	67	20.56	6-59	5	—
Wasim Akram	291.4	76	666	31	21.48	7-53	2	—
J.Simmons	585	150	1457	60	24.28	5-53	2	—
I.D.Austin	137.1	43	367	15	24.46	5-79	1	—
I.Folley	547.3	142	1564	52	30.07	6-20	2	—
M.Watkinson	600.3	149	1632	50	32.64	6-43	2	—
A.N.Hayhurst	159.3	31	518	15	34.53	4-45	—	—

Also bowled: M.A.Atherton 89.5-23-242-4; N.H.Fairbrother 10.1-0-59-0; J.D.Fitton 42-13-77-7; T.E.Jesty 25-10-56-0; C.D.Matthews 60-16-177-5; G.D.Mendis 8-0-35-0; A.J.Murphy 47.1-7-184-3.

The First-Class Averages (pp 161-175) give the records of Lancashire players in all first-class county matches (their other opponents being the West Indians and Oxford U.), with the exception of M.A.Atherton and G.Fowler whose full county figures are as above.

LANCASHIRE RECORDS

FIRST-CLASS CRICKET

Highest Total	For	801		v Somerset	Taunton	1895
	V	634		by Surrey	The Oval	1898
Lowest Total	For	25		v Derbyshire	Manchester	1871
	V	22		by Glamorgan	Liverpool	1924
Highest Innings	For	424	A.C.MacLaren	v Somerset	Taunton	1895
	V	315*	T.W.Hayward	for Surrey	The Oval	1898

Highest Partnerships
Wkt

1st	368	A.C.MacLaren/R.H.Spooner	v Glos	Liverpool	1903
2nd	371	F.B.Watson/G.E.Tyldesley	v Surrey	Manchester	1928
3rd	306	E.Paynter/N.Oldfield	v Hampshire	Southampton	1938
4th	324	A.C.MacLaren/J.T.Tyldesley	v Notts	Nottingham	1904
5th	249	B.Wood/A.Kennedy	v Warwicks	Birmingham	1975
6th	278	J.Iddon/H.R.W.Butterworth	v Sussex	Manchester	1932
7th	245	A.H.Hornby/J.Sharp	v Leics	Manchester	1912
8th	158	J.Lyon/R.M.Ratcliffe	v Warwicks	Manchester	1979
9th	142	L.O.S.Poidevin/A.Kermode	v Sussex	Eastbourne	1907
10th	173	J.Briggs/R.Pilling	v Surrey	Liverpool	1885

Best Bowling	For	10-46	W.Hickton	v Hampshire	Manchester	1870
(Innings)	V	10-40	G.O.B.Allen	for Middlesex	Lord's	1929
Best Bowling	For	17-91	H.Dean	v Yorkshire	Liverpool	1913
(Match)	V	16-65	G.Giffen	for Australians	Manchester	1886
Most Runs – Season		2,633	J.T.Tyldesley	(av 56.02)		1901
Most Runs – Career		34,222	G.E.Tyldesley	(av 45.20)		1909-1936
Most 100s – Season		11	C.Hallows			1928
Most 100s – Career		90	G.E.Tyldesley			1909-1936
Most Wkts – Season		198	E.A.McDonald	(av 18.55)		1925
Most Wkts – Career		1,816	J.B.Statham	(av 15.12)		1950-1968

LIMITED-OVERS CRICKET

Highest Total	NWT	349-6		v Glos	Bristol	1984
	BHC	317-5		v Scotland	Manchester	1988
	RAL	255-5		v Somerset	Manchester	1970
Lowest Total	NWT	59		v Worcs	Worcester	1963
	BHC	82		v Yorkshire	Bradford	1972
	RAL	71		v Essex	Chelmsford	1987
Highest Innings	NWT	131	A.Kennedy	v Middlesex	Manchester	1978
	BHC	124	C.H.Lloyd	v Warwicks	Manchester	1981
	RAL	134*	C.H.Lloyd	v Somerset	Manchester	1970
Best Bowling	NWT	5-28	J.B.Statham	v Leics	Manchester	1963
	BHC	6-10	C.E.H.Croft	v Scotland	Manchester	1982
	RAL	6-29	D.P.Hughes	v Somerset	Manchester	1977

LEICESTERSHIRE

Formation of Present Club: 25 March 1879
Colours: Dark Green and Scarlet
Badge: Gold Running Fox on Green Ground
Championships: (1) 1975
NatWest Trophy/Gillette Cup Semi-Finalists: (2) 1977, 1987
Benson and Hedges Cup Winners: (3) 1972, 1975, 1985
Sunday League Champions: (2) 1974, 1977
Match Awards: NWT 27; BHC 49

Chief Executive: F.M.Turner
Secretary: K.P.Hill, County Ground, Grace Road, Leicester LE2 8AD
Captain: D.I.Gower
Scorer: G.R.Blackburn
Cricketcall: ☎ 0898 1214 42
Benefit 1989: L.B.Taylor

AGNEW, Jonathan Philip (Uppingham S), b Macclesfield, Cheshire 4 Apr 1960. 6'3½". RHB, RFM. Debut 1978. Cap 1984. Wisden 1987. **Tests:** 3 (1984 to 1985); HS 5; BB 2-51 v WI (Oval) 1984. **LOI:** 3. **Tours:** Ind 1984-85; SL 1985-86 (Eng B); Zim 1980-81 (Leics). 100 wickets (1): 101 (1987). HS 90 v Yorks (Scarborough) 1987. BB 9-70 v Kent (Leicester) 1985. **Award:** NWT 1. **NWT:** HS 8*. BB 3-31 v Oxon (Leicester) 1987. **BHC:** HS 23* v Warwicks (Leicester) 1984. BB 5-30 v Glos (Bristol) 1987. **RAL:** HS 23* v Notts (Nottingham) 1987. BB 3-16 v Northants (Leicester) 1987.

BENJAMIN, Winston Keithroy Matthew (All Saints S, Antigua), b St John's, Antigua 31 Dec 1964. 6'3". RHB, RFM. Debut for Rest of World XI 1985. Leicestershire debut 1986. Leeward Is 1985-88. Cheshire 1985. **Tests:** (WI): 7 (1987-88 and 1988); HS 40* v Pak (Bridgetown) 1987-88; BB 4-52 v Eng (Oval) 1988. **LOI** (WI): 30. **Tours** (WI): Eng 1988; Aus 1986-87; Ind 1987-88; Pak 1986-87. HS 95* v Indians (Leicester) 1986. BB 6-33 v Notts (Leicester) 1986. **Award:** BHC 1. **NWT:** HS 5. BB 3-28 v Glos (Bristol) 1986. **BHC:** HS 21 v Northants (Northampton) 1987. BB 5-17 v Minor C (Leicester) 1986. **RAL:** HS 19* v Glam (Swansea) 1986. BB 4-19 v Lancs (Leicester) 1986.

BENSON, Justin David Ramsay (The Leys S, Cambridge), b Dublin, Ireland 1 Mar 1967. 6'2". RHB, RM. Debut 1988. Cambridgeshire 1984-87. HS 3. **Award:** NWT 1. **NWT:** HS 85 Cambs v Yorks (Leeds) 1986. **BHC:** HS 37* v Lancs (Leicester) 1988. **RAL:** HS 42* v Hants (Leicester) 1988.

BOON, Timothy James (Edlington CS, Doncaster), b Doncaster, Yorks 1 Nov 1961. 6'0". RHB, RM. Debut 1980. Cap 1986. **Tour:** Zim 1980-81 (Leics). 1000 runs (3); most – 1233 (1984). Shared record Leics 4th-wkt stand of 290* with P.Willey v Warwicks (Leicester) 1984. HS 144 v Glos (Bristol) 1984. BB 3-40 v Yorks (Leicester) 1986. **NWT:** HS 22* v Derbys (Leicester) 1984. **BHC:** HS 58* v Northants (Northampton) 1987. **RAL:** HS 61 v Essex (Chelmsford) 1987.

BRIERS, Nigel Edwin (Lutterworth GS; Borough Road CE), b Leicester 15 Jan 1955. 6'0". RHB, RM. Debut 1971 (aged 16yr 103d – youngest Leicestershire player). Cap 1981. **Tour:** Zim 1980-81 (Leics). 1000 runs (5); most –1335 (1988). Shared record Leics 5th-wkt stand of 233 with R.W.Tolchard v Somerset (Leicester) 1979. HS 201* v Warwicks (Birmingham) 1983. BB 4-29 v Derbys (Leicester) 1985. **Award:** BHC 1. **NWT:** HS 59 v Wilts (Swindon) 1984. BB 2-6 v Worcs (Leicester) 1979. **BHC:** HS 71* v Hants (Southampton) 1979. BB 1-26. **RAL:** HS 119* v Hants (Bournemouth) 1981. BB 3-29 v Middx (Leicester) 1984.

COBB, Russell Alan (Trent C), b Leicester 18 May 1961. 5'11". RHB, SLA. Debut 1980. Cap 1986. Tours: NZ 1979-80 (DHR); Zim 1980-81 (Leics). 1000 runs (1): 1092 (1986). HS 91 v Northants (Leicester) 1986. Award: NWT 1. **NWT:** HS 66* v Oxon (Leicester) 1987. **BHC:** HS 22 v Warwicks (Leicester) 1986. **RAL:** HS 24 v Worcs (Leicester) 1981.

FERRIS, George John Fitzgerald (Jennings SS, Antigua), b Urlings Village, Antigua 18 Oct 1964. 6'3". RHB, RF. Leeward Is 1982-88. Leicestershire debut 1983. Cap 1988. Tours (WI B): Zim 1983-84; 1986-87. Hat-trick 1983. HS 36* v Hants (Leicester) 1988. BB 7-42 v Glam (Hinckley) 1983. Award: BHC 1. **NWT:** HS 2*. BB 2-47 v Yorks (Leeds) 1987. **BHC:** HS 1*. BB 5-28 v Warwicks (Leicester) 1988. **RAL:** HS 13* v Worcs (Leicester) 1988. BB 4-24 v Lancs (Manchester) 1988.

GOWER, David Ivon (Kings S, Canterbury; London U), b Tunbridge Wells, Kent 1 Apr 1957. 6'0". LHB, OB. Debut 1975. Cap 1977. Captain 1984-86, 1988-. Benefit 1987. Wisden 1978. YC 1978. Tests: 100 (1978 to 1988, 26 as captain); HS 215 v Aus (Birmingham) 1985; BB 1-1. LOI: 102. Tours (C=Capt): Aus 1978-79, 1979-80, 1982-83, 1986-87; WI 1980-81, 1985-86C; NZ 1983-84; Ind 1979-80, 1981-82, 1984-85C; Pak 1983-84; SL 1977-78 (DHR), 1981-82, 1984-85C. 1000 runs (8); most – 1530 (1982). Shared record Leics 2nd-wkt stand of 289* with J.C.Balderstone v Essex (Leicester) 1981. HS 215 (Tests). Leics HS 176* v Pakistanis (Leicester) 1982. BB 3-47 v Essex (Leicester) 1977. Awards: NWT 5; BHC 1. **NWT:** HS 156 v Derbys (Leicester) 1984. **BHC:** HS 114* v Derbys (Derby) 1980. **RAL:** HS 135* v Warwicks (Leicester) 1977.

HEPWORTH, Peter Nash, b Ackworth, Yorks 4 May 1967. 6'1". RHB, OB. Debut 1988. HS 51 v Sussex (Leicester) 1988. **RAL:** HS 38 v Sussex (Leicester) 1988.

LEWIS, Clairmonte Christopher (Willesden HS, London), b Georgetown, Guyana 14 Feb 1968. 6'2½". RHB, RMF. Debut 1987. HS 42 v Notts (Leicester) 1987. BB 6-22 v OU (Oxford) 1988. **NWT:** HS 53 v Glos (Leicester) 1988. BB 2-32 v Suffolk (Leicester) 1988. **BHC:** HS 13* v Warwicks (Leicester) 1988. BB 3-41 v Lancs (Leicester) 1988. **RAL:** HS 40 v Northants (Leicester) 1988. BB 4-13 v Essex (Leicester) 1988.

PARSONS, Gordon James (Woodside County SS, Slough), b Slough, Bucks 17 Oct 1959. 6'1". LHB, RMF. Leicestershire 1978-85 (cap 1984). Warwickshire 1986-88 (cap 1987). Boland 1983-85. GW 1985-87. Buckinghamshire 1977. Tours: NZ 1979-80 (DHR); Zim 1980-81 (Leics). HS 76 Boland v W Province B (Cape Town) 1984-85. Leics HS 63 v Yorks (Leicester) 1984. BB 9-72 Boland v Transvaal B (Johannesburg) 1984-85. Leics BB 6-11 v OU (Oxford) 1985. Award: BHC 1. **NWT:** HS 23 v Northants (Northampton) 1984. BB 2-11 v Wilts (Swindon) 1984. **BHC:** HS 29* v Northants (Leicester) 1983. BB 4-33 v Worcs (Leicester) 1981. **RAL:** HS 26* Warwicks v Derbys (Birmingham) 1987. BB 4-19 v Essex (Harlow) 1982.

POTTER, Laurie (Kelmscott HS, Perth, Aus), b Bexleyheath, Kent 7 Nov 1962. 6'1". RHB, SLA. Kent 1981-85. Leicestershire debut 1986. Cap 1988. GW 1984-86 (captain 1985-86). OFS 1987-88. HS 165* GW v Border (East London) 1988. Leics HS 107 v Derbys (Derby) 1988. BB 4-52 GW v Boland (Stellenbosch) 1985-86. Leics BB 3-37 v Glam (Leicester) 1986. Award: BHC 1. **NWT:** HS 45 Kent v Essex (Chelmsford) 1982. BB 1-28. **BHC:** HS 112 and BB 2-70 v Minor C (Leicester) 1986. **RAL:** HS 105 v Derbys (Leicester) 1986. BB 4-9 Kent v Derbys (Folkestone) 1985.

SUCH, Peter Mark (Harry Carlton CS, E Leake, Notts), b Helensburgh, Dunbartonshire 12 Jun 1964. 5'11". RHB, OB. Nottinghamshire 1982-86. Leicestershire debut 1987. HS 16 Notts v Middx (Lord's) 1984. Leics HS 12 v Essex (Leicester) 1987. BB 6-123 Notts v Kent (Nottingham) 1983. Leics BB 4-14 v CU (Cambridge) 1987. **BHC:** BB 3-50 Notts v Scotland (Glasgow) 1985. **RAL:** HS 0*. BB 2-50 Notts v Glos (Bristol) 1985.

TAYLOR, Leslie Brian (Heathfield HS), b Earl Shilton 25 Oct 1953. 6'3½". RHB, RFM. Debut 1977. Cap 1981. Benefit 1989. Natal 1981-84. **Tests:** 2 (1985); HS 1* and BB 2-34 v Aus (Oval). LOI: 2. Tours: SA 1981-82 (SAB); WI 1985-86; Zim 1980-81 (Leics). Hat-trick 1979. HS 60 v Essex (Chelmsford) 1988. BB 7-28 v Derbys (Leicester) 1981. Award: NWT 1. **NWT:** HS 6*. BB 4-14 v Norfolk (Norwich) 1985. **BHC:** HS 5. BB 6-35 v Worcs (Worcester) 1982. **RAL:** HS 15* v Somerset (Taunton) 1980. BB 5-23 v Notts (Nottingham) 1978.

TENNANT, Lloyd (Shellfield CS), b Walsall, Staffs 9 Apr 1968. 5'11". RHB, RMF. Debut 1986. HS 12* v Sussex (Leicester) 1986. BB 1-0. **RAL:** HS 17* v Somerset (Leicester) 1988. BB 3-25 v Somerset (Leicester) 1988.

WHITAKER, John James (Uppingham S), b Skipton, Yorks 5 May 1962. 5'10". RHB, OB. Debut 1983. Cap 1986. Wisden 1986. YC 1986. **Test:** 1 (1986-87); HS 11 v Aus (Adelaide) 1986-87. LOI: 2. Tour: Aus 1986-87. 1000 runs (5); most – 1526 (1986). HS 200* v Notts (Leicester) 1986. BB 1-41. Awards: NWT 1; BHC 1. **NWT:** HS 155 v Wilts (Swindon) 1984. **BHC:** HS 73* v Warwicks (Birmingham) 1985. **RAL:** HS 132 v Glam (Swansea) 1984.

WHITTICASE, Philip (Crestwood CS, Kingswinford), b Marston Green, Solihull 15 Mar 1965. 5'11". RHB, WK. Debut 1984. Cap 1987. HS 71 v Somerset (Hinckley) 1988. **NWT:** HS 32 v Lancs (Leicester) 1986. **BHC:** HS 36 v Derbys (Leicester) 1987. **RAL:** HS 29* v Worcs (Worcester) 1986.

WILLEY, Peter (Seaham SS) b Sedgefield, Co Durham 6 Dec 1949. 6'1". RHB, OB. Northamptonshire 1966-83 (cap 1971; benefit 1981). Leicestershire debut/cap 1984. Captain 1987. E Province 1982-85. **Tests:** 26 (1976-86); HS 102* v WI (St John's) 1980-81; BB 2-73 v WI (Lord's) 1980. LOI: 26. Tours: Aus 1979-80; SA 1972-73 (DHR), 1981-82 (SAB); WI 1980-81, 1985-86; Ind 1979-80; SL 1977-78 (DHR). 1000 runs (8); most – 1783 (1982). Shared record Northants 4th-wkt stand of 370 with R.T.Virgin v Somerset (Northampton) 1976. Shared record Leics 4th-wkt stand of 290* with T.J.Boon v Warwicks (Leicester) 1984. HS 227 Northants v Somerset (Northampton) 1976. Leics HS 172* v Hants (Leicester) 1986. BB 7-37 Northants v OU (Oxford) 1975. Leics BB 6-43 v Hants (Leicester) 1985. Awards: NWT 6; BHC 7. **NWT:** HS 154 v Hants (Leicester) 1987. BB 3-33 v Derby (Leicester) 1984. **BHC:** HS 88* v Northants (Leicester) 1984. BB 3-12 Northants v Minor C (E) (Horton) 1977. **RAL:** HS 107 Northants v Warwicks 1975 and v Hants 1976. BB 4-37 v Somerset (Leicester) 1986.

NEWCOMERS

NIXON, Paul Andrew, b Carlisle 21 Oct 1970. LHB, WK.

ROSEBERRY, Andrew (Durham S), b Sunderland, Co Durham 2 Apr 1971. 6'0". Younger brother of M.A.Roseberry (Middlesex). RHB, RM.

DEPARTURES

DEFREITAS, P.A.J. – see LANCASHIRE.

GARNHAM, M.A. – see ESSEX.

LEICESTERSHIRE 1988

RESULTS SUMMARY

	Place	Won	Lost	Drew	Abandoned
Britannic Assurance Championship	8th	6	3	13	
All First-class Matches		7	3	14	
Refuge Assurance League	14th	4	9		3
NatWest Bank Trophy	2nd Round				
Benson and Hedges Cup	3rd in Group A				

BRITANNIC ASSURANCE CHAMPIONSHIP AVERAGES

BATTING AND FIELDING

Cap		M	I	NO	HS	Runs	Avge	100	50	Ct/St
1977	D.I.Gower	17	29	3	172	1080	41.53	2	4	14
1986	J.J.Whitaker	21	36	5	145	1160	37.41	3	4	13
1981	N.E.Briers	22	38	2	125*	1231	34.19	2	8	14
1988	L.Potter	21	31	4	107	796	29.48	1	4	13
1986	P.A.J.DeFreitas	12	17	1	113	458	28.62	1	3	5
1984	P.Willey	22	37	1	130	946	26.27	2	3	11
1986	T.J.Boon	13	20	1	131	459	24.15	1	2	7
1986	R.A.Cobb	11	20	2	65	432	24.00	—	2	10
—	P.N.Hepworth	4	6	0	51	132	22.00	—	1	—
1987	P.Whitticase	21	30	9	71	453	21.57	—	2	60/4
—	C.C.Lewis	14	20	3	40	337	19.82	—	—	9
1984	J.P.Agnew	22	28	8	38	263	13.15	—	—	1
1981	L.B.Taylor	15	15	6	60	111	12.33	—	1	3
1988	G.J.F.Ferris	18	20	8	36*	139	11.58	—	—	1
	P.M.Such	6	5	2	6	2	2.33	—	—	—

Also batted (1 match each): L.Tennant 3, 0*; J.D.R.Benson 3. M.A.Garnham (2 ct) did not bat.

BOWLING

	O	M	R	W	Avge	Best	5 wI	10 wM
O.H. Mortensen	233.3	73	464	34	13.64	6-35	4	—
P.A.J.DeFreitas	412.3	91	1188	54	22.00	5-38	5	—
G.J.F.Ferris	452.1	82	1380	62	22.25	5-47	2	—
J.P.Agnew	718.5	156	2139	88	24.30	7-61	8	1
L.B.Taylor	283.3	58	850	31	27.41	6-49	1	—
C.C.Lewis	342.2	68	1102	31	35.54	5-73	1	—
P.Willey	333	104	775	18	43.05	4-153	—	—

Also bowled: L.Potter 93.1-25-269-6; P.M.Such 115-20-331-8; L.Tennant 7-2-19-1.

The First-Class Averages (pp 161-175) give the records of Leicestershire players in all first-class county matches (their other opponents being the West Indians and Oxford U.), with the exception of:

P.J.Agnew 23-29-8-38-271-12.90-0-0-2ct. 747.5-159-2253-90-25.03-7/61-8-1.
P.A.J.DeFreitas 14-20-1-113-481-25.31-1-3-6ct. 465.3-111-1302-61-21.34-5/38-5-0.
D.I.Gower 18-30-3-172-1106-40.96-2-4-14ct. Did not bowl.

LEICESTERSHIRE RECORDS

FIRST-CLASS CRICKET

Highest Total	For	701-4d		v Worcs	Worcester	1906
	V	739-7d		by Notts	Nottingham	1903
Lowest Total	For	25		v Kent	Leicester	1912
	V	{ 24		by Glamorgan	Leicester	1971
		{ 24		by Oxford U	Oxford	1985
Highest Innings	For	252*	S.Coe	v Northants	Leicester	1914
	V	341	G.H.Hirst	for Yorks	Leicester	1905

Highest Partnerships
Wkt

1st	390	B.Dudleston/J.F.Steele	v Derbyshire	Leicester	1979
2nd	289*	J.C.Balderstone/D.I.Gower	v Essex	Leicester	1981
3rd	316*	W.Watson/A.Wharton	v Somerset	Taunton	1961
4th	290*	P.Willey/T.J.Boon	v Warwicks	Leicester	1984
5th	233	N.E.Briers/R.W.Tolchard	v Somerset	Leicester	1979
6th	262	A.T.Sharpe/G.H.S.Fowke	v Derbyshire	Chesterfield	1911
7th	206	B.Dudleston/J.Birkenshaw	v Kent	Canterbury	1969
8th	164	M.R.Hallam/C.T.Spencer	v Essex	Leicester	1964
9th	160	W.W.Odell/R.T.Crawford	v Worcs	Leicester	1902
10th	228	R.Illingworth/K.Higgs	v Northants	Leicester	1977

Best Bowling	For	10-18	G.Geary	v Glamorgan	Pontypridd	1929
(Innings)	V	10-32	H.Pickett	for Essex	Leyton	1895
Best Bowling	For	16-96	G.Geary	v Glamorgan	Pontypridd	1929
(Match)	V	16-102	C.Blythe	for Kent	Leicester	1909

Most Runs – Season	2,446	L.G.Berry	(av 52.04)		1937
Most Runs – Career	30,143	L.G.Berry	(av 30.32)		1924-1951
Most 100s – Season	{ 7	L.G.Berry			1937
	{ 7	W.Watson			1959
	{ 7	B.F.Davison			1982
Most 100s – Career	45	L.G.Berry			1924-1951
Most Wkts – Season	170	J.E.Walsh	(av 18.96)		1948
Most Wkts – Career	2,130	W.E.Astill	(av 23.19)		1906-1939

LIMITED-OVERS CRICKET

Highest Total	NWT	354-7		v Wiltshire	Swindon	1984
	BHC	327-4		v Warwicks	Coventry	1972
	RAL	291-5		v Glamorgan	Swansea	1984
Lowest Total	NWT	56		v Northants	Leicester	1964
	BHC	56		v Minor C	Wellington	1982
	RAL	36		v Sussex	Leicester	1973
Highest Innings	NWT	156	D.I.Gower	v Derbyshire	Leicester	1984
	BHC	158*	B.F.Davison	v Warwicks	Coventry	1972
	RAL	152	B.Dudleston	v Lancashire	Manchester	1975
Best Bowling	NWT	6-20	K.Higgs	v Staffs	Longton	1975
	BHC	6-35	L.B.Taylor	v Worcs	Worcester	1982
	RAL	6-17	K.Higgs	v Glamorgan	Leicester	1973

MIDDLESEX

Formation of Present Club: 2 February 1864
Colours: Blue
Badge: Three Seaxes
Championships (since 1890): (8) 1903, 1920, 1921, 1947, 1976, 1980, 1982, 1985.
Joint Championships: (2) 1949, 1977
NatWest Trophy/Gillette Cup Winners: (4) 1977, 1980, 1984, 1988
Benson and Hedges Cup Winners: (2) 1983, 1986
Sunday League Champions: (0) Second 1982
Match Awards: NWT 41; BHC 42

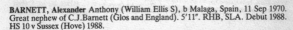

Secretary/Gen Manager: Lt Col P.F.Packham MBE, Lord's Cricket Ground, London NW8 8QN
Captain: M.W.Gatting
Scorer: H.P.H.Sharp
Cricketcall: ☎ 0898 1214 14
Benefit 1989: R.O.Butcher

BARNETT, Alexander Anthony (William Ellis S), b Malaga, Spain, 11 Sep 1970. Great nephew of C.J.Barnett (Glos and England). 5'11". RHB, SLA. Debut 1988. HS 10 v Sussex (Hove) 1988.

BROWN, Keith Robert (Chace S, Enfield), b Edmonton 18 Mar 1963. Brother of G.K. (Middlesex 1986). 5'11". RHB, WK. Debut 1984. HS 131* v Notts (Lord's) 1988. BB 2-7 v Glos (Bristol) 1987. **NWT:** HS 37* v Kent (Lord's) 1988. **BHC:** HS 32* v Surrey (Oval) 1988. **RAL:** HS 102 v Somerset (Lord's) 1988.

BUTCHER, Roland Orlando (Shephalbury SS, Stevenage), b East Point, Barbados 14 Oct 1953. 5'8". UK resident since 1967. RHB, RM. Debut 1974. Cap 1979. Benefit 1989. Barbados 1974-75. Tasmania 1982-83. **Tests:** 3 (1980-81); HS 32 v WI (Kingston) 1980-81. **LOI:** 3. Tours: WI 1980-81, 1982-83 (Int XI); Pak 1981-82 (Int XI); Zim 1980-81 (Middx) 1000 runs (4); most – 1326 (1984). HS 197 v Yorks (Lord's) 1982. BB 2-37 v Glos (Cheltenham) 1986. Awards: NWT 2; BHC 2. **NWT:** HS 65 v Surrey (Oval) 1988. BB 1-18. **BHC:** HS 85 v Surrey (Oval) 1983. **RAL:** HS 100 v Glos (Lord's) 1983.

CARR, John Donald (Repton S; Worcester C, OU), b St John's Wood 15 Jun 1963. Son of D.B. (Derbyshire, OU and England 1945-63). 5'11". RHB, RM/OB. OU 1983-85 (blue 1983-84-85). Middlesex debut 1983. Cap 1987. Hertfordshire 1982-84. 1000 runs (2); most – 1541 (1987). HS 156 v Essex (Lord's) 1987. BB 6-61 v Glos (Lord's) 1985. **NWT:** HS 42 v Herts (Lord's) 1988. 2-19 v Surrey (Oval) 1988. **BHC:** HS 67 Comb Us v Essex (Chelmsford) 1985. BB 3-22 Comb Us v Glos (Bristol) 1984. **RAL:** HS 84 v Worcs (Worcester) 1987. BB 2-10 v Glam (Cardiff) 1986.

COWANS, Norman George (Park High SS, Stanmore), b Enfield St Mary, Jamaica 17 Apr 1961. 6'3". RHB, RF. Debut 1980. Cap 1984. YC 1982. **Tests:** 19 (1982-83 to 1985); HS 36 v Aus (Perth) 1982-83; BB 6-77 v Aus (Melbourne) 1982-83. **LOI:** 23. Tours: Aus 1982-83; NZ 1983-84; Ind 1984-85; Pak 1983-84; SL 1984-85, 1985-86 (Eng B); Zim 1980-81 (Middx). HS 66 v Surrey (Lord's) 1984. BB 6-31 v Leics (Leicester) 1985. Awards: NWT 1; BHC 1. **NWT:** HS 12* v Lancs (Lord's) 1984. BB 4-24 v Yorks (Leeds) 1986. **BHC:** HS 6. BB 4-33 v Lancs (Lord's) 1983. **RAL:** HS 20 v Notts (Nottingham) 1985. BB 4-44 v Sussex (Hove) 1982.

DOWNTON, Paul Rupert (Sevenoaks S; Exeter U), b Farnborough, Kent 4 Apr 1957. Son of G.C. (Kent 1948). 5'10". RHB, WK, OB. Kent 1977-79 (cap 1979). Middlesex debut 1980. Cap 1981. **Tests**: 30 (1980-81 to 1988); HS 74 v Ind (Delhi) 1984-85. LOI: 28. Tours: WI 1980-81, 1985-86; NZ 1977-78; Ind/SL 1984-85; Pak 1977-78; Zim 1980-81 (Middx). 1000 runs (1): 1120 (1987). HS 126* v OU (Oxford) 1986. **NWT**: HS 62 v Notts (Nottingham) 1984. **BHC**: HS 80* v Hants (Southampton) 1987. **RAL**: HS 70 v Notts (Nottingham) 1985.

EMBUREY, John Ernest (Peckham Manor SS), b Peckham, London 20 Aug 1952. 6'2". RHB, OB. Debut 1973. Cap 1977. Wisden 1983. W Province 1982-84. Benefit 1986. **Tests**: 57 (1978 to 1988, 2 as captain); HS 75 v NZ (Nottingham) 1986; BB 7-78 v Aus (Sydney) 1986-87. LOI: 55. Tours: Aus 1978-79, 1979-80, 1986-87, 1987-88; SA 1981-82 (SAB); WI 1980-81, 1985-86; NZ 1987-88; Ind 1979-80, 1981-82; Pak 1987-88; SL 1977-78 (DHR), 1981-82; Zim 1980-81 (Middx). 100 wickets (1): 103 (1983). HS 133 v Essex (Chelmsford) 1983. BB 7-36 v CU (Cambridge) 1981. Awards: NWT 1; BHC 6. **NWT**: HS 36* v Lancs (Manchester) 1978. BB 3-20 v Northumb (Jesmond) 1984. **BHC**: HS 50 v Kent (Lord's) 1984. BB 4-22 v Notts (Lord's) 1986. **RAL**: HS 50 v Lancs (Blackpool) 1988. BB 5-36 v Warwicks (Lord's) 1983.

FRASER, Alastair Gregory James (Gayton HS, John Lyon S, Harrow; Harrow Weald SFC), b Edgware 17 Oct 1967. Brother of A.R.C. 6'1". RHB, RFM. Debut 1986. HS 19* v Warwicks (Uxbridge) 1986. BB 3-46 v NZ (Lord's) 1986. **RAL**: HS 2*. BB 1-19.

FRASER, Angus Robert Charles (Gayton HS, Harrow), b Billinge, Lancs 8 Aug 1965. Brother of A.G.J. 6'5". RHB, RFM. Debut 1984. Cap 1988. HS 41 v Sri Lankans (Lord's) 1988. BB 6-68 v Hants (Basingstoke) 1988. **NWT**: BB 4-34 v Yorks (Leeds) 1988. **BHC**: HS 13* v Essex (Lord's) 1988. BB 3-39 v Sussex (Lord's) 1988. **RAL**: HS 30* v Kent (Canterbury) 1988. BB 3-8 v Derbys (Repton) 1988.

GATTING, Michael William (John Kelly HS), b Kingsbury 6 Jun 1957. 5'10". RHB, RM. Debut 1975. Cap 1977. Captain 1983-. Benefit 1988. YC 1981. Wisden 1983. OBE 1987. **Tests**: 67 (1977-78 to 1988, 23 as captain); HS 207 v Ind (Madras) 1984-85; BB 1-14. LOI: 82. Tours (C=Capt): Aus 1986-87C, 1987-88C; WI 1980-81, 1985-86; NZ 1977-78, 1983-84, 1987-88C; Ind/SL 1981-82, 1984-85; Pak 1977-78, 1983-84, 1987-88C; Zim 1980-81 (Middx). 1000 runs (10+1); most – 2257 (1984). HS 258 v Somerset (Bath) 1984. BB 5-34 v Glam (Swansea) 1982. Awards: NWT 3; BHC 8. **NWT**: HS 118* v Northants (Northampton) 1986. BB 2-14 (twice). **BHC**: HS 143* v Sussex (Hove) 1985. BB 4-49 v Sussex (Lord's) 1984. **RAL**: HS 109 v Leics (Leicester) 1984. BB 4-32 v Kent (Lord's) 1978.

HUGHES, Simon Peter (Latymer Upper S, Hammersmith; Durham U), b Kingston upon Thames 20 Dec 1959. 5'10". RHB, RFM. Debut 1980. Cap 1981. N Transvaal 1982-83. Tours: Ind 1980-81 (Overseas XI); Zim 1980-81 (Middx). HS 53 v CU (Cambridge) 1988. BB 7-35 v Surrey (Oval) 1986. Award: NWT 1. **NWT**: HS 6. BB 4-30 v Worcs (Lord's) 1988. **BHC**: HS 8*. BB 4-34 v Somerset (Lord's) 1987. **RAL**: HS 25* v Surrey (Lord's) 1985. BB 3-26 v Worcs (Lord's) 1988.

HUTCHINSON, Ian James Frederick (Shrewsbury S), b Welshpool, Montgomeryshire, 31 Oct 1964. 6'1". RHB, RMF. Debut 1988. Shropshire 1984-86. MCC staff 1984-86. Scored 204 off 124 balls (14 sixes) before lunch for Cross Arrows 1985. HS 25 v Northants (Luton) 1988. **RAL**: HS 22* v Lancs (Lord's) 1987.

RAMPRAKASH, Mark Ravin (Gayton HS; Harrow Weald SFC), b Bushey, Herts 5 Sep 1969. 5'9". RHB, RM. Debut 1987. HS 71 v Essex (Chelmsford) 1987. Award: NWT 1. **NWT:** HS 56 v Worcs (Lord's) 1988. **RAL:** HS 82* v Sussex (Lord's) 1987.

ROSEBERRY, Michael Anthony (Durham S), b Houghton-le-Spring, Co Durham 28 Nov 1966. 6'1". RHB, RM. Debut 1986. HS 70* v Northants (Northampton) 1986. BB 1-1. **BHC:** HS 6. **RAL:** HS 27 v Glos (Lord's) 1987.

SYKES, James Frederick (**'Jamie'**) (Bow CS), b Shoreditch, London 30 Dec 1965. 6'1". RHB, OB. Debut 1983. HS 126 v CU (Cambridge) 1985. BB 4-49 v Glam (Cardiff) 1987. **BHC:** HS 24 v Derbys (Derby) 1988. **RAL:** HS 57 v Hants (Southampton) 1988. BB 3-26 v Sussex (Lord's) 1987.

TUFNELL, Philip Clive Roderick (Highgate S), b Barnet, Herts 29 Apr 1966. 6'0". RHB, SLA. Debut 1986. HS 20 v Kent (Lord's) 1988. BB 6-60 v Kent (Canterbury) 1987. Award: NWT 1. **NWT:** BB 3-29 v Herts (Lord's) 1988. **RAL:** BB 1-32.

WILLIAMS, Neil FitzGerald (Acland Burghley CS), b Hope Well, St Vincent 2 Jul 1962. 5'11". RHB, RFM. Debut 1982. Cap 1984. Windward Is 1982-83. Tasmania 1983-84. Tour: Zim 1984-85 (Eng Co). HS 67 v CU (Cambridge) 1985. BB 7-55 Eng Co XI v Zimbabwe (Harare) 1984-85. Middx BB 6-42 v Essex (Lord's) 1988. Award: BHC 1. **NWT:** HS 10 v Northumb (Jesmond) 1984. BB 4-36 v Derbys (Derby) 1983. **BHC:** HS 29* v Surrey (Lord's) 1985. BB 3-16 v Comb Us (Cambridge) 1982. **RAL:** HS 43 v Somerset (Lord's) 1988. BB 4-39 v Surrey (Oval) 1988.

NEWCOMERS

HABIB, Aftab (Millfield S), b Reading, Berks 7 Feb 1972. 5'11". RHB, RMF.

POOLEY, Jason Calvin (Acton HS), b Hammersmith, London 8 Aug 1969. 6'0". LHB, OB.

DEPARTURES

DANIEL, Wayne Wendell (Princess Margaret S), b St Philip, Barbados 16 Jan 1956. 6'1". RHB, RF. Barbados 1975-85. Middlesex 1977-88 (cap 1977; benefit 1985). W Australia 1981-82. **Tests** (WI): 10 (1975-76 to 1983-84); HS 11 v Ind (Kingston) 1975-76; BB 5-39 v Ind (Ahmedabad) 1983-84. LOI (WI): 18. **Tours:** Eng 1976; Ind 1983-84; Zim 1981-82 (Young WI). Hat-trick 1981. HS 53* Barbados v Jamaica (Bridgetown) 1979-80 and 53* v Yorks (Lord's) 1981. BB 9-61 v Glam (Swansea) 1982. Awards: NWT 2; BHC 2. **NWT:** HS 14 v Lancs (Manchester) 1978. BB 6-15 v Sussex (Hove) 1980. **BHC:** HS 20* v Derbys (Derby) 1978. BB 7-12 v Minor C (E) (Ipswich) 1978. **RAL:** HS 14 v Kent (Lord's) 1980. BB 5-27 v Lancs (Lord's) 1982.

MACLAURIN, Neil Ralph Charter (Malvern C), b Welwyn Garden City, Herts 22 Mar 1966. 5'11". RHB, RM. Middlesex 1988. HS 35 v CU (Cambridge) 1988. **RAL:** HS 15* v Worcs (Lord's) 1988.

NEEDHAM, Andrew (Ecclesbourne GS; Paisley GS; Watford GS), b Calow, Derbys 23 Mar 1957. 5'9". RHB, OB. Surrey 1977-86 (cap 1985). Middlesex 1987-88. 1000 (1): 1223 (1985). HS 138 Surrey v Warwicks (Oval) 1985. Middx HS 66* v Derbys (Derby) 1988. BB 6-30 Surrey v OU (Oval) 1983. Middx BB 5-125 v Glam (Lord's) 1988. **NWT:** HS 30 v Yorks (Leeds) 1988. BB 4-32 Surrey v Derbys (Derby) 1986. **BHC:** HS 30 Surrey v Glos (Oval) 1984. **RAL:** HS 55 Surrey v Essex (Southend) 1982. BB 3-24 Surrey v Glos (Bristol) 1986.

continued on p 151

MIDDLESEX 1988

RESULTS SUMMARY

	Place	Won	Lost	Drew	Abandoned
Britannic Assurance Championship	7th	7	3	12	
All First-class Matches		7	3	14	
Refuge Assurance League	4th	9	3		4
NatWest Bank Trophy	Winners				
Benson and Hedges Cup	Quarter-Finalist				

BRITANNIC ASSURANCE CHAMPIONSHIP AVERAGES

BATTING AND FIELDING

Cap		M	I	NO	HS	Runs	Avge	100	50	Ct/St
—	M.R.Ramprakash	8	11	4	68*	401	57.28	—	3	1
1977	M.W.Gatting	18	29	2	210	1431	53.00	3	9	14
1981	W.N.Slack	19	32	5	163*	1228	45.48	3	6	11
1977	J.E.Emburey	15	20	4	102	584	36.50	1	4	19
1987	J.D.Carr	22	39	6	144	1194	36.18	2	7	20
1981	P.R.Downton	14	18	4	120	506	36.14	1	2	30/5
—	A.Needham	7	10	3	66*	231	33.00	—	2	5
1979	R.O.Butcher	17	25	2	134	673	29.26	1	3	13
—	K.R.Brown	19	30	4	131*	668	25.69	1	2	28
—	M.A.Roseberry	12	18	3	67	357	23.80	—	1	5
1984	N.F.Williams	8	11	2	63*	186	20.66	—	1	1
1981	S.P.Hughes	16	18	5	34	248	19.07	—	—	3
—	J.F.Sykes	7	10	1	86	164	18.22	—	1	3
—	I.J.F.Hutchinson	3	4	0	25	48	12.00	—	—	—
1988	A.R.C.Fraser	22	27	10	17	182	10.70	—	—	1
1984	N.G.Cowans	20	21	7	27*	119	8.50	—	—	4
—	P.C.R.Tufnell	9	10	2	20	41	5.12	—	—	4

Also batted: A.A.Barnett (1 match) 10; W.W.Daniel (2 matches – cap 1977) 0; 0; M.W.C.Olley (3 matches) 16, 16, 4 (8 ct).

BOWLING

	O	M	R	W	Avge	Best	5 wI	10 wM
N.F.Williams	178.3	33	511	30	17.03	6-42	2	—
N.G.Cowans	491.5	123	1290	71	18.16	6-49	3	1
A.R.C.Fraser	674.1	190	1484	77	19.27	6-68	6	2
J.E.Emburey	543.1	167	1201	49	24.51	6-24	2	—
P.C.R.Tufnell	349.2	90	876	19	46.10	4-88	—	—
S.P.Hughes	385.3	70	1136	22	51.63	3-45	—	—

Also bowled: A.A.Barnett 27-9-65-0; K.R.Brown 1-1-0-0; J.D.Carr 65.1-15-154-5; W.W.Daniel 16-2-37-2; M.W.Gatting 96-21-287-4; A.Needham 113.4-19-399-8; M.R.Ramprakash 8-0-53-0; M.A.Roseberry 11.4-1-61-2; W.N.Slack 2-1-14-0; J.F.Sykes 30-0-142-0.

The First-Class Averages (pp 161-175) give the records of Middlesex players in all first-class county matches (their other opponents being the Sri Lankans and Cambridge U.), with exception of M.W.Gatting, whose full county figures are as above, and:

P.R.Downton 15-19-4-120-530-35.33-1-2-31ct/5st. Did not bowl.

J.E.Emburey 16-21-4-102-627-36.88-1-4-21ct. 589.5-191-1277-54-23.64-6/24-2-0.

MIDDLESEX RECORDS

FIRST-CLASS CRICKET

Highest Total	For	642-3d		v Hampshire	Southampton	1923
	V	665		by W Indians	Lord's	1939
Lowest Total	For	20		v MCC	Lord's	1864
	V	31		by Glos	Bristol	1924
Highest Innings	For	331*	J.D.B.Robertson	v Worcester	Worcester	1949
	V	316*	J.B.Hobbs	for Surrey	Lord's	1926

Highest Partnerships
Wkt

1st	367*	G.D.Barlow/W.N.Slack	v Kent	Lord's	1981
2nd	380	F.A.Tarrant/J.W.Hearne	v Lancashire	Lord's	1914
3rd	424*	W.J.Edrich/D.C.S.Compton	v Somerset	Lord's	1948
4th	325	J.W.Hearne/E.H.Hendren	v Hampshire	Lord's	1919
5th	338	R.S.Lucas/T.C.O'Brien	v Sussex	Hove	1895
6th	227	C.T.Radley/F.J.Titmus	v S Africans	Lord's	1965
7th	271*	E.H.Hendren/F.T.Mann	v Notts	Nottingham	1925
8th	182*	M.H.C.Doll/H.R.Murrell	v Notts	Lord's	1913
9th	160*	E.H.Hendren/F.J.Durston	v Essex	Leyton	1927
10th	230	R.W.Nicholls/W.Roche	v Kent	Lord's	1899

Best Bowling	For	10-40	G.O.B.Allen	v Lancashire	Lord's	1929
(Innings)	V	9-38	R.C.Glasgow†	for Somerset	Lord's	1924
Best Bowling	For	16-114	G.Burton	v Yorkshire	Sheffield	1888
(Match)		16-114	J.T.Hearne	v Lancashire	Manchester	1898
	V	16-109	C.W.L.Parker	for Glos	Cheltenham	1930

Most Runs – Season	2,669	E.H.Hendren	(av 83.41)		1923
Most Runs – Career	40,302	E.H.Hendren	(av 48.81)		1907-1937
Most 100s – Season	13	D.C.S.Compton			1947
Most 100s – Career	119	E.H.Hendren			1907-1937
Most Wkts – Season	158	F.J.Titmus	(av 14.63)		1955
Most Wkts – Career	2,361	F.J.Titmus	(av 21.27)		1949-1982

LIMITED-OVERS CRICKET

Highest Total	NWT	283-9		v Cumberland	Uxbridge	1985
	BHC	303-7		v Northants	Northampton	1977
	RAL	270-5		v Glos	Lord's	1983
Lowest Total	NWT	41		v Essex	Westcliff	1972
	BHC	73		v Essex	Lord's	1985
	RAL	23		v Yorkshire	Leeds	1974
Highest Innings	NWT	158	G.D.Barlow	v Lancashire	Lord's	1984
	BHC	143*	M.W.Gatting	v Sussex	Hove	1985
	RAL	133*	C.T.Radley	v Glamorgan	Lord's	1969
Best Bowling	NWT	6-15	W.W.Daniel	v Sussex	Hove	1980
	BHC	7-12	W.W.Daniel	v Minor C(E)	Ipswich	1978
	RAL	6-6	R.W.Hooker	v Surrey	Lord's	1969

† R.C.Robertson-Glasgow

NORTHAMPTONSHIRE

Formation of Present Club: 31 July 1878
Colours: Maroon
Badge: Tudor Rose
Championships: (0) Second 1912, 1957, 1965, 1976
NatWest Trophy/Gillette Cup Winners: (1) 1976
Benson and Hedges Cup Winners: (1) 1980
Sunday League Champions: (0) Fourth 1974
Match Awards: NWT 31; BHC 32

Secretary/Manager: S.P.Coverdale, County Ground, Wantage Road, Northampton, NN1 4TJ
Captain: A.J.Lamb
Scorer: B.H.Clarke
Cricketcall: ☎ 0898 1214 50
Benefit 1989: R.G.Williams

BAILEY, Robert John (Biddulph HS), b Biddulph, Staffs 28 Oct 1963. 6'3". RHB, OB. Debut 1982. Cap 1985. Staffordshire 1980. YC 1984. **Tests:** 1 (1988); HS 43 v WI (Oval). LOI: 3. 1000 runs (5); most – 1915 (1986). HS 224* v Glam (Swansea) 1986. BB 3-27 v Glam (Wellingborough) 1988. Awards: BHC 3. **NWT:** HS 56* v Middx (Lord's) 1984. BB 1-2. **BHC:** HS 134 v Glos (Northampton) 1987. BB 1-22. **RAL:** HS 125* v Derbys (Derby) 1987. BB 3-23 v Leics (Leicester) 1987.

BROWN, Simon John (Boldon CS), b Cleadon, Co Durham 29 Jun 1969. 6'3". RHB, LFM. Debut 1987. HS 25* v Glos (Northampton) 1988. BB 3-20 v OU (Oxford) 1988. **RAL:** HS 1. BB 2-25 v Worcs (Worcester) 1988.

CAPEL, David John (Roade CS), b Northampton 6 Feb 1963. 5'11". RHB, RMF. Debut 1981. Cap 1986. E Province 1985-87. **Tests:** 10 (1987 to 1988); HS 98 v Pak (Karachi) 1987-88; BB 2-13 v Aus (Sydney) 1987-88. LOI: 11. Tours: Aus 1987-88; NZ 1987-88; Pak 1987-88. 1000 runs (1): 1040 (1988). HS 134 E Province v W Province (Port Elizabeth) 1986-87. Northants HS 111 v Leics (Northampton) 1986. BB 7-46 v Yorks (Northampton) 1987. Award: NWT 1. **NWT:** HS 48 v Ireland (Northampton) 1987. BB 3-43 v Leics (Leicester) 1987. **BHC:** HS 97 v Yorks (Lord's) 1987. BB 4-29 v Warwicks (Birmingham) 1987. **RAL:** HS 83 v Sussex (Northampton) 1988. BB 4-30 v Yorks (Middlesbrough) 1982.

COOK, Geoffrey (Middlesbrough HS), b Middlesbrough, Yorks 9 Oct 1951. 6'0". RHB, SLA. Debut 1971. Cap 1975. E Province 1978-81. Captain 1981-88. Benefit 1985. **Tests:** 7 (1981-82 to 1982-83); HS 66 v Ind (Manchester) 1982. LOI: 6. Tours: Aus 1982-83; Ind/SL 1981-82. 1000 runs (11); most – 1759 (1981). Shared record Northants 2nd-wkt stand of 344 with R.J.Boyd-Moss v Lancs (Northampton) 1986. HS 203 v Yorks (Scarborough) 1988. BB 3-47 England XI v S Australia (Adelaide) 1982-83. Awards: NWT 5; BHC 3. **NWT:** HS 130 v Shropshire (Telford) 1985. **BHC:** HS 108 v Glos (Northampton) 1987. **RAL:** HS 98 v Lancs (Northampton) 1985.

COOK, Nicholas Grant Billson (Lutterworth GS), b Leicester 17 June 1956. 6'0". RHB, SLA. Leicestershire 1978-85 (cap 1982). Northamptonshire debut 1986. Cap 1987. **Tests:** 12 (1983 to 1987-88). LOI: 2. Tours: NZ 1979-80 (DHR), 1983-84; Pak 1983-84, 1987-88; SL 1985-86 (Eng B); Zim 1980-81, 1984-85 (Eng Co). HS 75 Leics v Somerset (Taunton) 1980. Northants HS 64 v Lancs (Manchester) 1987.

BB 7-63 Leics v Somerset (Taunton) 1982. Northants BB 6-56 v Essex (Chelmsford) 1988. **NWT:** HS 13 v Middx (Northampton) 1986. BB 4-24 v Ireland (Northampton) 1987. **BHC:** HS 23 Leics v Warwicks (Leicester) 1984. BB 2-21 v Minor C (Darlington) 1988. **RAL:** HS 13* (4 times). BB 3-23 v Sussex (Hastings) 1986.

DAVIS, Winston Walter (Emmanuel HS, St Vincent), b Sion Hill, St Vincent 18 Sep 1958. RHB, RF. Combined Is/Windward Is 1979-87 (capt 1987-88). Glamorgan 1982-84. Northamptonshire debut/cap 1987. Tasmania 1985-86. **Tests** (WI): 15 (1982-83 to 1987-88); HS 77 v Eng (Manchester) 1984; BB 4-19 v NZ (Kingston) 1984-85. LOI (WI): 35; BB 7-51 v Aus (Leeds) 1983 – LOI world record. Tours (WI): Eng 1984; Aus 1984-85; Ind 1983-84, 1987-88; Zim 1981-82 (Young WI). HS 77 (Tests). Northants HS 43 v Warwicks (Northampton) 1988. BB 7-52 v Sussex (Northampton) 1988. Award: BHC 1. **NWT:** HS 14* v Ireland (Northampton) 1987. BB 3-26 Glam v Norfolk (Norwich) 1983. **BHC:** HS 15* v Derbys (Derby) 1987. BB 5-29 Glam v Middx (Cardiff) 1984. **RAL:** HS 34 v Middx (Luton) 1988. BB 4-24 Glam v Derbys (Derby) 1982.

FORDHAM, Alan (Bedford Modern S; Durham U), b Bedford 9 Nov 1964. 6'1". RHB, RM. Debut 1986. Bedfordshire 1982-85. HS 125* v Surrey (Oval) 1988. **BHC:** HS 19 Comb Us v Hants (Oxford) 1987. **RAL:** HS 30 v Warwicks (Birmingham) 1988.

LAMB, Allan Joseph (Wynberg HS; Abbotts C) b Langebaanweg, Cape Province, SA 20 Jun 1954. 5'8". RHB, RM. W Province 1972-82. OFS 1987-88. Northants debut/cap 1978. Benefit 1988. Captain 1989. Wisden 1980. **Tests:** 56 (1982 to 1988); HS 137* v NZ (Nottingham) 1983; BB 1-6. LOI: 80. Tours: Aus 1982-83, 1986-87; WI 1985-86; NZ 1983-84; Ind/SL 1984-85; Pak 1983-84. 1000 runs (8); most – 2049 (1981). HS 294 OFS v E Province (Bloemfontein) 1987-88 – sharing record SA 5th-wkt stand of 355 with J.J.Strydom. Northants HS 178 v Leics (Leicester) 1979. BB 1-1. Awards: NWT 2; BHC 7. **NWT:** HS 101 v Sussex (Hove) 1979. BB 1-4. **BHC:** HS 126* v Kent (Canterbury) 1987. BB 1-11. **RAL:** HS 132* v Surrey (Guildford) 1985.

LARKINS, Wayne (Bushmead SS, Eaton Socon), b Roxton, Beds 22 Nov 1953. 5'11". RHB, RM. Debut 1972. Cap 1976. Benefit 1986. E Province 1982-84. **Tests:** 6 (1979-80 to 1981); HS 34 v Aus (Oval) 1981. LOI: 6. Tours: Aus 1979-80; SA 1981-82 (SAB); Ind 1979-80, 1980-81 (Overseas XI). 1000 runs (10); most – 1863 (1982). HS 252 v Glam (Cardiff) 1983. BB 5-59 v Worcs (Worcester) 1984. Awards: NWT 2; BHC 5. **NWT:** HS 121* v Essex (Chelmsford) 1987. BB 2-38 v Glos (Bristol) 1985. **BHC:** HS 132 v Warwicks (Birmingham) 1982. BB 4-37 v Comb Us (Northampton) 1980. **RAL:** HS 172* v Warwicks (Luton) 1983. BB 5-32 v Essex (Ilford) 1978.

NOON, Wayne Michael (Caistor S), b Grimsby, Lincs 5 Feb 1971. 5'9". RHB, WK. Awaiting f-c debut. Worcestershire 2nd XI debut aged 15yr 199d. **RAL:** HS 9*.

RIPLEY, David (Royds SS, Leeds), b Leeds, Yorks 13 Sep 1966. 5'9". RHB, WK. Debut 1984. Cap 1987. HS 134* v Yorks (Scarborough) 1986. BB 2-89 v Essex (Ilford) 1987. Award: BHC 1. **NWT:** HS 27* v Durham (Darlington) 1984. **BHC:** HS 33 v Derbys (Derby) 1987. **RAL:** HS 36* v Hants (Southampton) 1986.

ROBINSON, Mark Andrew (Hull GS), b Hull, Yorks, 23 Nov 1966. 6'3". RHB, RFM. Debut 1987. HS 19* v Essex (Chelmsford) 1988. BB 4-19 v Glam (Wellingborough) 1988. **RAL:** HS 1. BB 1-13.

SMITH, Gareth (Boldon CS; South Tyneside C), b Jarrow, Co Durham 20 Jul 1966. 6'1". RHB, LFM. Debut 1986 (dismissing S.M.Gavaskar with his second ball). HS 29* v Lancs (Manchester) 1987. BB 6-72 v Sussex (Hove) 1987.

STANLEY, Neil Alan (Bedford Modern S), b Bedford 16 May 1968. 6'2". RHB, RM. Debut 1988. Bedfordshire 1987. HS 66 v OU (Oxford) 1988 (on debut). **BHC:** HS 8. BB 1-3. **RAL:** HS 18 v Warwicks (Birmingham) 1988.

WALKER, Alan (Shelley HS), b Emley, Yorks 7 Jul 1962. 5'11". LHB, RFM. Debut 1983. Cap 1987. HS 41* v Warwicks (Birmingham) 1987. BB 4-7 v Ireland (Northampton) 1986. Award: NWT 1. **NWT:** HS 7. BB 4-7 v Ireland (Northampton) 1987. **BHC:** HS 15* v Notts (Nottingham) 1987. BB 4-46 v Glos (Northampton) 1985. **RAL:** HS 13 v Yorks (Tring) 1983. BB 4-21 v Worcs (Worcester) 1985.

WILD, Duncan James (Northampton GS), b Northampton 28 Nov 1962. Son of John Wild (Northamptonshire 1953-61). 5'11½". LHB, RM. Debut 1980. Cap 1986. HS 144 v Lancs (Southport) 1984. BB 4-4 v CU (Cambridge) 1986. Award: BHC 1. **NWT:** HS 11 (twice). BB 3-43 v Surrey (Northampton) 1987. **BHC:** HS 48 v Warwicks (Northampton) 1984. BB 4-32 v Notts (Northampton) 1988. **RAL:** HS 91 v Derbys (Northampton) 1988. BB 5-7 v Derbys (Finedon) 1986.

WILLIAMS, Richard Grenville (Ellesmere Port GS), Bangor, Caernarvonshire 10 Aug 1957. 5'6½". RHB, OB. Debut 1974. Cap 1979. Benefit 1989. Tours: NZ 1979-80 (DHR); Zim 1984-85 (Eng Co). Hat-trick 1980. 1000 runs (6); most – 1262 (1980). HS 175* v Leics (Leicester) 1980. BB 7-73 v CU (Cambridge) 1980. Awards: NWT 1; BHC 4. **NWT:** HS 94 v Worcs (Northampton) 1984. BB 4-10 v Leics (Leicester) 1987. **BHC:** HS 83 v Yorks (Bradford) 1980. BB 4-41 v Glos (Northampton) 1987. **RAL:** HS 82 v Glos (Bristol) 1982. BB 5-30 v Warwicks (Luton) 1983.

NEWCOMERS

AMBROSE, Curtly Elconn Lynwall (All Saints Village SS), b Swetes Village, Antigua 21 Sep 1963. Cousin of R.M.Otto (Leeward Is). 6'7". LHB, RF. Leeward Is 1985-88. **Tests** (WI): 8 (1987-88 and 1988). HS 43 and BB 4-53 v Eng (Nottingham) 1988. LOI (WI): 5. Tour (WI): Eng 1988. HS 59 WI v Sussex (Hove) 1988. BB 7-61 Leeward Is v Guyana (St John's) 1988.

FELTON, Nigel Alfred (Millfield S; Loughborough U), b Guildford, Surrey 24 Oct 1960. 5'8". LHB. Somerset 1982-88 (cap 1986). 1000 runs (2); most – 1094 (1987). HS 173* v Kent (Taunton) 1983. Award: NWT 1. **NWT:** HS 87 v Kent (Taunton) 1984. **BHC:** HS 50 v Hants (Taunton) 1988. **RAL:** HS 96 v Essex (Chelmsford) 1986.

THOMAS, John Gregory (Cwmtawe HS; Cardiff CE), b Trebanos 12 Aug 1960. 6'3". RHB, RF. Glamorgan 1979-88 (cap 1986). Border 1983-87. E Province 1987-88. **Tests:** 5 (1985-86 and 1986); HS 31* v WI (P-of-S) 1985-86; BB 4-70 v WI (Bridgetown) 1985-86. LOI: 3. Tour: WI 1985-86. HS 110 Glam v Warwicks (Birmingham) 1988. BB 6-68 Glam v Notts (Nottingham) 1988. Awards: NWT 1. **NWT:** HS 34 Glam v Cheshire (Cardiff) 1987. BB 5-17 Glam v Sussex (Cardiff) 1985. **BHC:** HS 32 Glam v Kent (Cardiff) 1987. BB 4-38 Glam v Hants (Southampton) 1985. **RAL:** HS 37 Glam v Notts (Nottingham) 1983. BB 5-38 Glam v Yorks (Cardiff) 1983.

continued on p 151

112

NORTHAMPTONSHIRE 1988

RESULTS SUMMARY

	Place	Won	Lost	Tied	Drew	Aban
Britannic Assurance Championship	12th	5	7		10	
All First-class Matches		6	7		11	
Refuge Assurance League	14th	4	9			3
NatWest Bank Trophy	1st Round					
Benson and Hedges Cup	3rd in Group B					

BRITANNIC ASSURANCE CHAMPIONSHIP AVERAGES

BATTING AND FIELDING

Cap		M	I	NO	HS	Runs	Avge	100	50	Ct/St
1978	A.J.Lamb	9	15	2	155	731	56.23	3	3	4
1986	D.J.Capel	17	29	4	92	981	39.24	—	7	4
1985	R.J.Bailey	20	36	1	127*	1203	34.37	2	8	19
1979	R.G.Williams	18	31	7	119	770	32.08	1	4	8
1975	G.Cook	17	29	1	203	836	29.85	2	3	9
—	A.Fordham	15	28	6	125*	627	28.50	1	3	13
1976	W.Larkins	20	37	2	134	905	25.85	2	2	23
1987	A.Walker	16	19	10	40*	208	23.11	—	—	7
—	M.R.Gouldstone	7	12	1	71	239	21.72	—	2	4
1987	W.W.Davis	15	18	3	43	306	20.40	—	—	5
—	N.A.Stanley	6	10	2	62	142	17.75	—	1	3
1986	D.J.Wild	17	26	1	75	408	16.32	—	2	3
1987	D.Ripley	22	30	5	49	390	15.60	—	—	66/6
—	D.K.Lillee	7	10	2	22	98	12.25	—	—	3
—	S.J.Brown	3	6	1	25*	34	6.80	—	—	2
1987	N.G.B.Cook	20	24	1	24	133	5.78	—	—	12
—	M.A.Robinson	13	16	7	19*	32	3.55	—	—	3

BOWLING

	O	M	R	W	Avge	Best	5 wI	10 wM
W.W.Davis	538.2	91	1614	73	22.10	7-52	7	2
M.A.Robinson	347.4	72	932	42	22.19	4-19	—	—
N.G.B.Cook	632.2	228	1285	56	22.94	6-56	2	—
A.Walker	406.1	81	1240	46	26.95	5-64	1	—
R.G.Williams	295	61	888	31	28.64	5-86	1	—
D.J.Wild	164.5	33	486	16	30.37	4-18	—	—
D.J.Capel	371.4	68	1235	34	36.32	4-40	—	—
D.K.Lillee	232	42	731	20	36.55	6-68	1	—

Also bowled: R.J.Bailey 59.1-8-201-5; S.J.Brown 65-13-176-4; G.Cook 5-1-7-0; W.Larkins 5-1-18-0.

The First-Class Averages (pp 161-175) give the records of Northamptonshire players in all first-class county matches (their other opponents being the West Indians and Oxford U.), with the exception of D.K.Lillee, whose full county figures are as above, and:

R.J.Bailey 22-38-1-127*-1349-36.45-3-8-23ct. 76.1-10-278-7-39.71-3/27.
D.J.Capel 18-30-4-92-983-37.80-0-7-4ct. 398.4-72-1321-37-35.70-4/40.
N.G.B.Cook 22-26-2-24-171-7.12-0-0-13ct. 725.4-256-1491-66-22.59-6/56-2-0.
A.J.Lamb 11-17-3-155-838-59.85-4-3-6ct. 4-0-19-0.
W.Larkins 22-39-2-134-921-24.89-2-2-23ct. 24-13-39-2-19.50-1/0.
D.Ripley 24-32-6-49-439-16.88-0-0-75ct/6st. Did not bowl.
R.G.Williams 19-32-7-119-798-31.92-1-4-8ct. 304-66-901-32-28.15-5/86-1-0.
A.Walker 17-19-10-40*-208-23.11-0-0-7ct. 440.5-95-1300-51-25.49-5/64-1-0.

113

NORTHAMPTONSHIRE RECORDS

FIRST-CLASS CRICKET

Highest Total	For	557-6d	v Sussex	Hove	1914
	V	670-9d	by Sussex	Hove	1921
Lowest Total	For	12	v Glos	Gloucester	1907
	V	33	by Lancashire	Northampton	1977
Highest Innings	For	300 R.Subba Row	v Surrey	The Oval	1958
	V	333 K.S.Duleepsinhji	for Sussex	Hove	1930

Highest Partnerships

Wkt

1st	361	N.Oldfield/V.Broderick	v Scotland	Peterborough	1953
2nd	344	G.Cook/R.J.Boyd-Moss	v Lancashire	Northampton	1986
3rd	320	L.Livingston/F.Jakeman	v S Africans	Northampton	1951
4th	370	R.T.Virgin/P.Willey	v Somerset	Northampton	1976
5th	347	D.Brookes/D.W.Barrick	v Essex	Northampton	1952
6th	376	R.Subba Row/A.Lightfoot	v Surrey	The Oval	1958
7th	229	W.W.Timms/F.A.Walden	v Warwicks	Northampton	1926
8th	155	F.R.Brown/A.E.Nutter	v Glamorgan	Northampton	1952
9th	156	R.Subba Row/S.Starkie	v Lancashire	Northampton	1955
10th	148	B.W.Bellamy/J.V.Murdin	v Glamorgan	Northampton	1925

Best Bowling	For	10-127 V.W.C.Jupp	v Kent	Tunbridge W	1932
(Innings)	V	10-30 C.Blythe	for Kent	Northampton	1907
Best Bowling	For	15-31 G.E.Tribe	v Yorkshire	Northampton	1958
(Match)	V	17-48 C.Blythe	for Kent	Northampton	1907
Most Runs – Season		2,198 D.Brookes	(av 51.11)		1952
Most Runs – Career		28,980 D.Brookes	(av 36.13)		1934-1959
Most 100s – Season		8 R.A.Haywood			1921
Most 100s – Career		67 D.Brookes			1934-1959
Most Wkts – Season		175 G.E.Tribe	(av 18.70)		1955
Most Wkts – Career		1,097 E.W.Clark	(av 21.31)		1922-1947

LIMITED-OVERS CRICKET

Highest Total	NWT	285-6	v Wiltshire	Swindon	1983
	BHC	300-9	v Derbyshire	Derby	1987
	RAL	306-2	v Surrey	Guildford	1985
Lowest Total	NWT	62	v Leics	Leicester	1974
	BHC	85	v Sussex	Northampton	1978
	RAL	41	v Middlesex	Northampton	1972
Highest Innings	NWT	130 G.Cook	v Shropshire	Telford	1985
	BHC	134 R.J.Bailey	v Glos	Northampton	1987
	RAL	172* W.Larkins	v Warwicks	Luton	1983
Best Bowling	NWT	7-37 N.A.Mallender	v Worcs	Northampton	1984
	BHC	5-21 Sarfraz Nawaz	v Middlesex	Lord's	1980
	RAL	7-39 A.Hodgson	v Somerset	Northampton	1976

NOTTINGHAMSHIRE

Formation of Present Club: March/April 1841
Substantial Reorganisation: 11 December 1866
Colours: Green and Gold
Badge: County Badge of Nottinghamshire
Championships (since 1890): (4) 1907, 1929, 1981, 1987
NatWest Trophy/Gillette Cup Winners: (1) 1987
Benson and Hedges Cup Finalists: (1) 1982
Sunday League Champions: (0) Second 1984, 1987
Match Awards: NWT 29; BHC 43

Secretary: B.Robson, Trent Bridge, Nottingham NG2 6AG
Captain: R.T.Robinson
Scorers: L.Beaumont
Cricketcall: ☎ 0898 1214 60
Benefit 1989: J.D.Birch

AFFORD, John Andrew (Spalding GS; Stamford CFE), b Crowland, Lincs 12 May 1964. 6'1½". RHB, SLA. Debut 1984. HS 16 v Surrey (Nottingham) 1987. BB 6-81 v Kent (Nottingham) 1986. **RAL:** BB 1-27.

BIRCH, John Dennis (William Crane Bilateral S), b Nottingham 18 Jun 1955. 5'11". RHB, RM. Debut 1973. Cap 1981. Benefit 1989. 1000 runs (2); most – 1086 (1983). HS 125 v Leics (Nottingham) 1982. BB 6-64 v Hants (Bournemouth) 1975. Award: BHC 1. **NWT:** HS 55* v Devon (Torquay) 1988. BB 1-58. **BHC:** HS 85 v Minor C (N) (Nottingham) 1979. BB 2-14 v Minor C (N) (Newark) 1975. **RAL:** HS 92 v Sussex (Nottingham) 1983. BB 3-26 v Warwicks (Birmingham) 1988.

BROAD, Brian Christopher (Colston's S, Bristol; St. Paul's C, Cheltenham), b Bristol 29 Sep 1957. 6'4". LHB, RM. Gloucestershire 1979-83 (cap 1981). Nottinghamshire debut/cap 1984. OFS 1985-86 (captain). **Tests:** 23 (1984 to 1988); HS 162 v Aus (Perth) 1986-87. LOI: 34. Tours: Aus 1986-87, 1987-88; NZ 1987-88; Pak 1987-88;Zim 1984-85 (Eng Co). 1000 runs (6); most –1786 (1985). HS 171 v Derbys (Derby) 1985. BB 2-14 Glos v WI (Bristol) 1980. Awards: NWT 2; BHC 1. **NWT:** HS 98 Glos v Middx (Bristol) 1982. **BHC:** HS 122 v Derbys (Derby) 1984. BB 2-73 v Lancs (Nottingham) 1984. **RAL:** HS 104* v Derbys (Nottingham) 1986. BB 3-46 Glos v Worcs (Bristol) 1982.

CAIRNS, Christopher Lance (Christchurch BHS), b Picton, NZ 13 Jun 1970. Son of B.L.Cairns (C Districts, Otago, N Districts and NZ). 6'2". RHB, RFM. Debut 1988. HS 15 and BB 4-70 v Kent (Dartford) 1988 (on debut). **RAL:** HS 4.

COOPER, Kevin Edwin (Hucknall National SS), b Hucknall 27 Dec 1957. 6'1". LHB, RFM. Debut 1976. Cap 1980. 100 wickets (1): 101 (1988). HS 46 v Middlesex (Nottingham) 1985. BB 8-44 v Middlesex (Lord's) 1984. Award: NWT 1. **NWT:** HS 11 v Glos (Nottingham) 1982. BB 4-49 v Warwicks (Nottingham) 1985. **BHC:** HS 25* v Lancs (Manchester) 1983. BB 4-23 v Kent (Canterbury) 1979. **RAL:** HS 31 v Glos (Nottingham) 1984. BB 4-25 v Hants (Nottingham) 1976.

EVANS, Kevin Paul (Colonel Frank Seely S) b Calverton 10 Sep 1963. Brother of R.J. 6'2". RHB, RMF. Debut 1984. HS 54 v Derbys (Nottingham) 1988. BB 3-22 v Derbys (Nottingham) 1988. **NWT:** HS 10 v Devon (Exmouth) 1986. BB 4-30 v Kent (Nottingham) 1986. **BHC:** HS 31* v Northants (Northampton) 1988. BB 3-36 v Worcs (Worcester) 1988. **RAL:** HS 28 v Glos and v Kent 1985. BB 3-26 v Essex (Colchester) 1988.

EVANS, Russell John (Colonel Frank Seely S), b Calverton 1 Oct 1965. Brother of K.P. 6'0". RHB, RM. Debut 1987. HS 50* v SL (Nottingham) 1988. BB 3-40 v OU (Oxford) 1988. **RAL:** HS 20 v Hants (Nottingham) 1985.

FRENCH, Bruce Nicholas (The Meden CS), b Warsop 13 Aug 1959. 5'6". RHB, WK. Debut 1976 (aged 16yr 287d). Cap 1980. **Tests:** 16 (1986 to 1987-88); HS 59 v Pak (Manchester) 1987. LOI: 13. Tours: Aus 1986-87, 1987-88; WI 1985-86; NZ 1987-88; Ind/SL 1984-85; Pak 1987-88. HS 98 v Lancs (Nottingham) 1984. Award: BHC 1. **NWT:** HS 49 v Staffs (Nottingham) 1985. **BHC:** HS 48* v Worcs (Nottingham) 1984. **RAL:** HS 37 v Glos (Bristol) 1985.

HEMMINGS, Edward Ernest (Campion S), b Leamington Spa, Warwicks 20 Feb 1949. 5'10". RHB, OB. Warwickshire 1966-1978 (cap 1974). Nottinghamshire debut 1979. Cap 1980. Benefit 1987. **Tests:** 8 (1982 to 1987-88); HS 95 v Aus (Sydney) 1982-83; BB 3-53 v Aus (Sydney) 1987-88. LOI: 13. Tours: Aus 1982-83, 1987-88; SA 1974-75 (DHR); WI 1982-83 (Int XI); NZ 1987-88; Pak 1981-82 (Int XI), 1987-88. 2 hat-tricks: 1977 (Warwicks), 1984. HS 127* v Yorks (Worksop) 1982. BB 10-175 Int XI v WI XI (Kingston) 1982-83. Notts BB 7-23 v Lancs (Nottingham) 1983. Awards: NWT 1; BHC 1. **NWT:** HS 31* v Staffs (Nottingham) 1985. BB 3-27 v Warwicks (Nottingham) 1985. **BHC:** HS 61* Warwicks v Leics (Birmingham) 1974. BB 3-12 v Surrey (Nottingham) 1984. **RAL:** HS 44* Warwicks v Kent (Birmingham) 1971. BB 5-22 Warwicks v Notts (Birmingham) 1974.

JOHNSON, Paul (Grove CS, Balderton), b Newark 24 Apr 1965. 5'7". RHB, RM. Debut 1982. Cap 1986. 1000 runs (3); most – 1389 (1988). HS 140 v Hants (Southampton) 1988. BB 1-9. Award: NWT 1. **NWT:** HS 101* v Staffs (Nottingham) 1985. **BHC:** HS 49 v Northants (Nottingham) 1987. **RAL:** HS 90 v Leics (Leicester) 1986.

MARTINDALE, Duncan John Richardson (Lymm GS; Trent Polytechnic), b Harrogate, Yorks 13 Dec 1963. 5'11". RHB, OB. Debut 1985. HS 104* v Lancs (Manchester) 1985. **NWT:** HS 20* v Essex (Lord's) 1985. **RAL:** HS 39 v Somerset (Taunton) 1988.

MIKE, Gregory Wentworth, b Nottingham 14 Jul 1966. 6'0". RHB, RMF. Awaiting f-c debut. **RAL:** HS 0. BB 1-57.

MILLNS, David James (Garibaldi CS), b Clipstone 27 Feb 1965. 6'3". LHB, RMF. Debut 1988. HS 7*. BB 3-37 v Glam (Nottingham) 1988 (on debut). **RAL:** HS 0*. BB 1-31.

NEWELL, Michael (West Bridgford CS), b Blackburn, Lancs 25 Feb 1965. 5'8". RHB, LB. Debut 1984. Cap 1987. 1000 runs (1): 1054 (1987). HS 203* v Derbys (Derby) 1987. BB 2-38 v SL (Nottingham) 1987. **NWT:** HS 60 v Derbys (Derby) 1987. **BHC:** HS 31* v Minor C (Nottingham) 1988. **RAL:** HS 58 v Northants (Nottingham) 1988.

PICK, Robert Andrew (Alderman Derbyshire CS; High Pavement SFC), b Nottingham 19 Nov 1963. 5'10". LHB, RMF. Debut 1983. Cap 1987. HS 63 v Warwicks (Nuneaton) 1985. BB 6-68 v Yorks (Worksop) 1986. Awards: NWT 1; BHC 1. **NWT:** HS 34* v Sussex (Hove) 1983. BB 5-22 v Glos (Bristol) 1987. **BHC:** HS 4. BB 4-42 v Northants (Nottingham) 1987. **RAL:** HS 24 v Yorks (Hull) 1986. BB 4-32 v Glos (Moreton) 1987.

POLLARD, Paul (Gedling CS), b Carlton, Nottingham, 24 Sep 1968. 5'11". LHB, RM. Debut 1987. HS 142 v Kent (Dartford) 1988. **RAL:** HS 25 v Sussex and v Derbys 1988.

RANDALL, Derek William (Sir Frederick Milner SS), b Retford 24 Feb 1951. 5'9". RHB, RM. Debut 1972. Cap 1973. Benefit 1983. Wisden 1979. **Tests:** 47 (1976-77 to 1984); HS 174 v Aus (Melbourne) 1976-77. LOI: 49. Tours: Aus 1976-77, 1978-79, 1979-80, 1982-83; SA 1975-76 (DHR); NZ 1977-78, 1983-84; Ind/SL 1976-77; Pak 1977-78, 1983-84; Zim 1985-86 (Eng B). 1000 runs (11); most – 2151 (1985). HS 237 v Derbys (Nottingham) 1988. BB 3-15 v MCC (Lord's) 1982. Awards: NWT 3; BHC 5. **NWT:** HS 149* v Devon (Torquay) 1988. **BHC:** HS 103* v Minor C (N) (Nottingham) 1979. **RAL:** HS 123 v Yorks (Nottingham) 1987.

ROBINSON, Robert Timothy (Dunstable GS; High Pavement SFC; Sheffield U), b Sutton-in-Ashfield 21 Nov 1958. 6'0". RHB, RM. Debut 1978. Cap 1983. Captain 1988-. Wisden 1985. **Tests:** 28 (1984-85 to 1988); HS 175 v Aus (Leeds) 1985. LOI: 26. Tours: Aus 1987-88; NZ 1987-88; WI 1985-86; Ind/SL 1984-85; Pak 1987-88. 1000 runs (6); most – 2032 (1984). HS 207 v Warwicks (Nottingham) 1983. BB 1-22. Awards: NWT 4; BHC 2. **NWT:** HS 139 v Worcs (Worcester) 1985. **BHC:** HS 120 v Scotland (Glasgow) 1985. **RAL:** HS 100 v Surrey (Nottingham) 1988.

SAXELBY, Kevin (Magnus GS), b Worksop 23 Feb 1959. 6'2". RHB, RMF. Debut 1978. Cap 1984. HS 59* v Derbys (Chesterfield) 1982. BB 6-49 v Sussex (Nottingham) 1987. Award: BHC 1. **NWT:** HS 12 v Worcs (Worcester) 1983. BB 4-28 v Middx (Nottingham) 1984. **BHC:** HS 13* v Lancs (Nottingham) 1982. BB 5-21 v Minor C (Nottingham) 1988. **RAL:** HS 23* v Middx (Cleethorpes) 1983. BB 5-21 v Kent (Nottingham) 1987.

SCOTT, Christopher Wilmot (Robert Pattinson CS), b Thorpe-on-the-Hill, Lincs 23 Jan 1964. 5'8". RHB, WK. Debut 1981. Cap 1988. HS 78 v CU (Cambridge) 1983. Held 10 catches in match v Derbys (Derby) 1988. **BHC:** HS 18 v Northants (Northampton) 1988. **RAL:** HS 26 v Yorks (Nottingham) 1987.

STEPHENSON, Franklyn Dacosta (Samuel Jackson Prescod Polytechnic), b St James, Barbados 8 Apr 1959. 6'3½". RHB, RFM. Barbados 1981-82. Tasmania 1981-82. Gloucestershire 1982-83. Nottinghamshire debut/cap 1988. Staffordshire 1980. Wisden 1988. Tour (WI XI): SA 1982-83, 1983-84. 1000 runs (1): 1018 (1988). 100 wickets (1): 125 (1988). Double 1988. HS 165 Barbados v Leeward Is (Basseterre) 1981-82. Notts HS 117 v Yorks (Nottingham) 1988 (111 and 117, plus 11-222 in match). BB 7-56 v Northants (Nottingham) 1988. **NWT:** HS 7. BB 2-17 Glos v Notts (Nottingham) 1982. **BHC:** HS 10 v Glam (Cardiff) 1988. BB 4-14 v Minor C (Nottingham) 1988. **RAL:** HS 43 v Lancs (Nottingham) 1988. BB 4-23 v Surrey (Nottingham) 1988.

NEWCOMERS

FIELD-BUSS, Michael Gwyn (Wanstead HS), b Mtarfa, Malta 23 Sep 1964. 5'10". RHB, OB. Essex 1987. HS 34* Essex v Middx (Lord's) 1987.

SAXELBY, Mark (Nottingham HS), b Worksop 4 Jan 1969. 6'3". LHB, RM. Younger brother of K.

DEPARTURES

BORE, Michael Kenneth (Mayberry SM, Hull), b Hull, Yorks 2 Jun 1947. 5'11". RHB, LM/SLA. Yorkshire 1969-78. Nottinghamshire 1979-88 (cap 1980). HS 37* Yorks v Notts (Bradford) 1973. BB 8-89 v Kent (Folkestone) 1979. Awards BHC 1. **NWT:** HS 4*. BB 3-35 Yorks v Kent (Canterbury) 1971. **BHC:** HS 7*. BB 6-22 v Leics (Leicester) 1980. **RAL:** HS 28* v Northants (Northampton) 1979. BB 4-21 Yorks v Sussex (Middlesbrough) 1971 and v Worcs (Worcester) 1970.

continued on p 151

117

NOTTINGHAMSHIRE 1988

RESULTS SUMMARY

	Place	Won	Lost	Drew	Abandoned
Britannic Assurance Championship	5th	8	8	6	
All First-class Matches		8	8	10	
Refuge Assurance League	17th	3	11		2
NatWest Bank Trophy	2nd Round				
Benson and Hedges Cup	Quarter-Finalist				

BRITANNIC ASSURANCE CHAMPIONSHIP AVERAGES

BATTING AND FIELDING

Cap		M	I	NO	HS	Runs	Avge	100	50	Ct/St
1973	D.W.Randall	21	37	4	237	1286	38.96	2	9	9
1983	R.T.Robinson	18	30	3	134*	988	36.59	3	4	17
1986	P.Johnson	21	37	0	140	1104	29.83	2	4	10
1988	F.D.Stephenson	20	34	0	117	962	28.29	2	6	9
—	P.Pollard	7	13	0	142	323	24.84	1	—	6
1984	B.C.Broad	16	27	0	68	647	23.96	—	3	13
1987	M.Newell	16	30	1	105	619	21.34	1	2	28
—	K.P.Evans	13	22	3	54	359	18.89	—	1	18
1981	J.D.Birch	20	35	2	75	596	18.06	—	2	12
1980	E.E.Hemmings	16	25	10	31*	245	16.33	—	—	8
1980	B.N.French	6	11	1	28	135	13.50	—	—	12
1988	C.W.Scott	16	25	4	47*	273	13.00	—	—	39/2
—	D.J.R.Martindale	6	10	0	46	125	12.50	—	—	3
1980	K.E.Cooper	22	33	9	39	263	10.95	—	—	7
1987	R.A.Pick	2	4	1	19	31	10.33	—	—	—
—	C.L.Cairns	2	4	1	15	29	9.66	—	—	—
1984	K.Saxelby	7	12	1	17	41	3.72	—	—	4
—	D.J.Millns	8	11	5	7*	19	3.16	—	—	4
—	J.A.Afford	4	8	3	4	4	0.80	—	—	2

Also batted: M.K.Bore (1 match – cap 1980) 5, 0.

BOWLING

	O	M	R	W	Avge	Best	5 wI	10 wM
F.D.Stephenson	776.1	191	2161	121	17.85	7-56	10	3
K.E.Cooper	776	213	2035	99	20.55	5-41	5	—
E.E.Hemmings	495.5	137	1265	41	30.85	4-50	—	—
D.J.Millns	101	13	374	12	31.16	3-37	—	—
K.P.Evans	201.5	34	665	18	36.94	3-22	—	—
K.Saxelby	193	29	690	12	57.50	3-30	—	—

Also bowled: J.A.Afford 83-19-270-9; J.D.Birch 68.4-16-226-5; M.K.Bore 9-2-41-0; C.L.Cairns 49-6-179-8; M.Newell 1-0-11-0; R.A.Pick 51-7-236-5; R.T.Robinson 4-0-38-0.

The First-Class Averages (pp 161-175) give the records of Nottinghamshire players in all first-class county matches (their other opponents being MCC, the West Indians, the Sri Lankans and Oxford U.), with the exception of:
B.C.Broad 18-30-0-73-801-26.70-0-4-13ct. 4-0-30-0.
R.T.Robinson 20-33-3-134*-1141-38.03-4-4-17ct. 4-0-38-0.

NOTTINGHAMSHIRE RECORDS

FIRST-CLASS CRICKET

Highest Total	For	653-6d		v Glamorgan	Bristol	1928
Highest Total	For	739-7d		v Leics	Nottingham	1903
	V	706-4d		by Surrey	Nottingham	1947
Lowest Total	For	13		v Yorkshire	Nottingham	1901
	V	16		by Derbyshire	Nottingham	1879
		16		by Surrey	The Oval	1880
Highest Innings	For	312*	W.W.Keeton	v Middlesex	The Oval	1939
	V	345	C.G.Macartney	for Australians	Nottingham	1921

Highest Partnerships
Wkt

1st	391	A.O.Jones/A.Shrewsbury	v Glos	Bristol	1899
2nd	398	A.Shrewsbury/W.Gunn	v Sussex	Nottingham	1890
3rd	369	W.Gunn/J.R.Gunn	v Leics	Nottingham	1903
4th	361	A.O.Jones/J.R.Gunn	v Essex	Leyton	1905
5th	266	A.Shrewsbury/W.Gunn	v Sussex	Hove	1884
6th	303*	F.H.Winrow/P.F.Harvey	v Derbyshire	Nottingham	1947
7th	204	M.J.Smedley/R.A.White	v Surrey	The Oval	1967
8th	220	G.F.H.Heane/R.Winrow	v Somerset	Nottingham	1935
9th	165	W.McIntyre/G.Wootton	v Kent	Nottingham	1869
10th	152	E.B.Alletson/W.Riley	v Sussex	Hove	1911

Best Bowling	For	10-66	K.Smales	v Glos	Stroud	1956
(Innings)	V	10-10	H.Verity	for Yorkshire	Leeds	1932
Best Bowling	For	17-89	F.C.Matthews	v Northants	Nottingham	1923
(Match)	V	17-89	W.G.Grace	for Glos	Cheltenham	1877

Most Runs – Season	2,620	W.W.Whysall	(av 53.46)		1929
Most Runs – Career	31,592	G.Gunn	(av 35.69)		1902-1932
Most 100s – Season	9	W.W.Whysall			1928
	9	M.J.Harris			1971
Most 100s – Career	65	J.Hardstaff, jr			1930-1955
Most Wkts – Season	181	B.Dooland	(av 14.96)		1954
Most Wkts – Career	1,653	T.G.Wass	(av 20.34)		1896-1920

LIMITED-OVERS CRICKET

Highest Total	NWT	302-3		v Devon	Torquay	1988
	BHC	282-4		v Derbyshire	Derby	1984
	RAL	283-6		v Yorkshire	Nottingham	1987
Lowest Total	NWT	123		v Yorkshire	Scarborough	1969
	BHC	74		v Leics	Leicester	1987
	RAL	66		v Yorkshire	Bradford	1969
Highest Innings	NWT	149*	D.W.Randall	v Devon	Torquay	1988
	BHC	130*	C.E.B.Rice	v Scotland	Glasgow	1982
	RAL	123	D.W.Randall	v Yorkshire	Nottingham	1987
Best Bowling	NWT	6-18	C.E.B.Rice	v Sussex	Hove	1982
	BHC	6-22	M.K.Bore	v Leics	Leicester	1980
		6-22	C.E.B.Rice	v Northants	Northampton	1981
	RAL	6-12	R.J.Hadlee	v Lancashire	Nottingham	1980

SOMERSET

Formation of Present Club: 18 August 1875
Colours: Black, White and Maroon
Badge: Somerset Dragon
Championships: (0) Third in 1892, 1958, 1963, 1966, 1981
NatWest Trophy/Gillette Cup Winners: (2) 1979, 1983
Benson and Hedges Cup Winners: (2) 1981, 1982
Sunday League Champions: (1) 1979
Match Awards: NWT 36; BHC 42

Secretary: P.W.Anderson, County Ground, St James Street, Taunton TA1 1JT
Captain: V.J.Marks
Scorer: D.A.Oldam
Cricketcall: ☎ 0898 1214 24
Benefit 1989: D.Breakwell and T.Gard

ATKINSON, Jonathon Colin Mark (Millfield S), b Butleigh 10 July 1968. Son of C.R.M. (Somerset 1960-67). 6'3". RHB, RMF. Debut 1985. Cambridge U debut/blue 1988. HS 79 v Northants (Weston) 1985 – on debut. BB 2-80 v Indians (Taunton) 1986. **NWT:** BB 1-16. **BHC:** HS 24 Comb Us v Glos (Bristol) 1988. **RAL:** HS 2.

BARTLETT, Richard James (Taunton S), b Ash Priors 8 Oct 1966. 5'9". RHB, OB. Debut 1986 scoring 117* v OU (Oxford). HS 117* (above). BB : 1-9. **NWT:** HS 85 v Hants (Southampton) 1988. **BHC:** HS 4. **RAL:** HS 55 v Lancs (Manchester) 1988.

BURNS, Neil David (Moulsham HS, Chelmsford), b Chelmsford 19 Sep 1965. 5'10". LHB, WK. W Province B 1985-86. Essex 1986. Somerset debut/cap 1987. HS 133* v Sussex (Chelmsford) 1987. **NWT:** HS 18 v Hants (Southampton) 1988. **BHC:** HS 51 v Middx (Lord's) 1987. **RAL:** HS 34 v Glos (Bristol) 1988.

CLEAL, Matthew William (Preston CS, Yeovil), b Yeovil 23 Jul 1969. 6'2". RHB, RMF. Debut 1988. HS 19 and BB 4-41 v WI (Taunton) 1988 (on debut). **RAL:** HS 1.

FOSTER, Daren Joseph (Somerset S; Southgate TS, Haringey Cricket C), b Tottenham, London 14 Mar 1966. 5'9". RHB, RFM. Debut 1986. HS 20 v Hants (Southampton) 1988. BB 4-46 v Worcs (Worcester) 1988. **BHC:** BB 1-57. **RAL:** HS 3*. BB 3-28 v Notts (Taunton) 1988.

GARD, Trevor (Huish Episcopi CS), b West Lambrook 2 Jun 1957. 5'7". RHB, WK. Debut 1976. Cap 1983. Joint benefit with D.Breakwell 1989. HS 51* v Indians (Taunton) 1979. Award: NWT 1. **NWT:** HS 17 v Shropshire (Wellington) 1983. **BHC:** HS 34 v Sussex (Hove) 1986. **RAL:** HS 19 v Hants (Taunton) 1986.

HARDEN, Richard John (King's C, Taunton), b Bridgwater 16 Aug 1965. 5'11". RHB, LM. Debut 1985. C Districts 1987-88. 1000 runs (1): 1093 (1986). HS 108 v Sussex (Taunton) 1986. BB 2-7 C Districts v Canterbury (Blenheim) 1987-88. Somerset BB 2-24 v Hants (Taunton) 1986. **NWT:** HS 17 v Lancs (Taunton) 1986. **BHC:** HS 35 v Middx (Lord's) 1987. **RAL:** HS 73 v Derbys (Derby) 1987.

HARDY, Jonathan James Ean (Canford S), b Nakaru, Kenya 2 Oct 1960. 6'3½". LHB. Hampshire 1984-85. Somerset debut 1986. Cap 1987. W. Province 1987-88. 1000 runs (1): 1089 (1987). HS 119 v Glos (Taunton) 1987. Award: NWT 1. **NWT:** HS 100 v Durham (Darlington) 1988. **BHC:** HS 70* v Glos (Bristol) 1988. **RAL:** HS 94* v Essex (Taunton) 1987.

120

JONES, Adrian Nicholas (Seaford C), b Woking, Surrey 22 Jul 1961. 6'2". LHB, RFM. Sussex 1981-86 (cap 1986). Somerset debut/cap 1987. Border 1981-82. HS 38 v Glos (Bristol) 1988. **BB** 7-30 v Hants (Southampton) 1988. Award: BHC 1. **NWT:** HS 3*. **BB** 4-26 Sussex v Yorks (Leeds) 1986. **BHC:** HS 20 Sussex v Middx (Lord's) 1986. **BB** 4-19 v Comb Us (Oxford) 1988. **RAL:** HS 17* and BB 7-41 Sussex v Notts (Nottingham) 1986.

MALLENDER, Neil Alan (Beverley GS), b Kirk Sandall, Yorks 13 Aug 1961. 6'0". RHB, RFM. Northamptonshire 1980-86 (cap 1984). Somerset debut/cap 1987. Otago 1983-88. HS 88 Otago v Central Districts (Oamaru) 1984-85. Somerset HS 44 v Sussex (Hove) 1988. **BB** 7-27 Otago v Auckland (Auckland) 1984-85. Somerset BB 7-61 v Derbys (Taunton) 1987. Awards: NWT 1; BHC 1. **NWT:** HS 11* Northants v Yorks (Leeds) 1983. BB 7-37 Northants v Worcs (Northampton) 1984. **BHC:** HS 16* v Hants (Taunton) 1988. BB 5-53 Northants v Leics (Northampton) 1986. **RAL:** HS 23* v Worcs (Taunton) 1988. BB 5-34 Northants v Middlesex (Tring) 1981.

MARKS, Victor James (Blundell's S; St John's C, Oxford), b Middle Chinnock 25 Jun 1955. 5'9". RHB, OB. Oxford U 1975-78 (blue 1975-76-77-78; capt 1976-77). Somerset debut 1975. Cap 1979. Benefit 1988. Captain 1988-. W Australia 1986-87. **Tests:** 6 (1982 to 1983-84); HS 83 v Pak (Faisalabad) 1983-84; BB 3-78 v NZ (Oval) 1983. LOI: 34. Tours: Aus 1982-83; NZ 1983-84; Ind/SL 1984-85; Pak 1983-84. 1000 runs (2); most – 1262 (1984). HS 134 v Worcs (Weston) 1984. BB 8-17 v Lancs (Bath) 1985. Awards: NWT 2; BHC 4. **NWT:** HS 55 v Warwicks (Taunton) 1982. BB 3-15 v Herts (St Albans) 1984. **BHC:** HS 81* v Hants (Bournemouth) 1980. BB 3-25 v Sussex (Taunton) 1982. **RAL:** HS 80 v Derbys (Weston) 1988. BB 4-11 v Surrey (Taunton) 1984.

PALMER, Gary Vincent (Queen's C), b Taunton 1 Nov 1965. Son of K.E. (Somerset and England 1955-69) – see 1989 UMPIRES. 6'1". RHB, RMF. Debut 1982. HS 78 v Glos (Bristol) 1983. BB 5-38 v Warwicks (Taunton) 1983. **NWT:** 17 and BB 3-24 v Durham (Darlington) 1988. **BHC:** HS 53 v Sussex (Hove) 1986. BB 2-9 v Comb Us (Oxford) 1988. **RAL:** HS 33 v Worcs (Weston) 1986. BB 5-24 v Kent (Canterbury) 1987.

PRINGLE, Nicholas John (Taunton S), b Weymouth, Dorset 20 Sep 1966. 5'10½". RHB, RMF. MCC Staff. Debut 1986. HS 79 v Warwicks (Birmingham) 1987. BB 2-35 v Glam (Weston) 1987. **NWT:** HS 17 v Hants (Southampton) 1988. **RAL:** HS 22 v Glam (Weston) 1987.

ROEBUCK, Peter Michael (Millfield S; Emmanuel C, Cambridge), b Oxford 6 Mar 1956. Brother of P.G.P. (CU, Glos and Glam 1983-88). 6'0". RHB, LB. Debut 1974. CU 1975-77; blue 1975-76-77. Cap 1978. Captain 1986-88. 2nd XI debut 1969 (aged 13). Wisden 1987. 1000 runs (7); most – 1702 (1984). Shared record Somerset 3rd-wkt stand of 319 with M.D.Crowe v Leics (Taunton) 1984. HS 221* v Notts (Nottingham) 1986. BB 6-50 CU v Kent (Canterbury) 1977. Award: BHC 1. **NWT:** HS 98 v Sussex (Hove) 1984. **BHC:** HS 120 v Comb Us (Taunton) 1987. BB 2-13 v Comb Us (Taunton) 1982. **RAL:** HS 105 v Glos (Bath) 1983. BB 2-4 v Warwicks (Birmingham) 1982.

ROSE, Graham David (Northumberland Park S, Tottenham), b Tottenham, London 12 Apr 1964. 6'4". RHB, RM. Middlesex 1985-86. Somerset debut 1987. Cap 1988. HS 95 v Lancs (Taunton) 1988. BB 6-41 Middx v Worcs (Worcester) 1985 – on debut. Somerset BB 6-47 v Warwicks (Bath) 1988. **NWT:** HS 26 and BB 2-30 v Bucks (High Wycombe) 1987. **BHC:** HS 42 v Middx (Lord's) 1987. 3-32 v Glam (Taunton) 1988. **RAL:** HS 93* v Notts (Taunton) 1988. BB 4-28 v Derbys (Derby) 1987.

121

TRUMP, Harvey Russell John (Millfield S), b Taunton 11 Oct 1968. 6'0". RHB, OB. Debut 1988. HS 48 v Notts (Taunton) 1988 (on debut). BB 4-17 v Kent (Canterbury) 1988. **RAL:** HS 4.

WAUGH, Stephen Rodger (East Hills BHS), b Canterbury, Sydney, Australia 2 Jun 1965. Twin of M.E. (NSW and Essex). 5'11". RHB, RMF. NSW 1984-88. Somerset debut 1987. Cap 1988. Wisden 1988. **Tests** (Aus): 18 (1985-86 to 1987-88); HS 79* v Eng (Adelaide) 1986-87; BB 5-69 v Eng (Perth) 1986-87. LOI (Aus): 58. Tours (Aus): NZ 1985-86; Ind 1986-87; Zim 1985-86 (Young Aus). 1000 runs (1): 1314 (1988). HS 170 NSW v Victoria (Sydney) 1987-88. Somerset HS 161 v Kent (Canterbury) 1988. BB 5-50 NSW v Tasmania (Sydney) 1987-88. Somerset BB 3-48 v Surrey (Oval) 1987. Award: BHC 1. **NWT:** HS 21 and BB 2-45 v Durham (Darlington) 1988. **BHC:** HS 79 and BB 2-16 v Comb Us (Oxford) 1988. **RAL:** HS 140* v Middx (Lord's) 1988. BB 1-27

WYATT, Julian George (Wells Cathedral S), b Paulton 19 Jun 1963. 5'10". RHB, RM. Debut 1983. HS 145 v OU (Oxford) 1985. BB 1-0. **NWT:** HS 8. **BHC:** HS 55 v Glos (Bristol) 1988. **RAL:** HS 89 v Yorks (Scarborough) 1988.

NEWCOMERS

COOK, Stephen James (Hyde Park HS; Witwatersrand U), b Johannesburg, SA 31 Jul 1953. RHB. Transvaal 1972-88. 1000 runs (0+2); most – 1142 (1982-83). Has played in every international against unofficial touring teams since 1981-82. HS 201* Transvaal v E Province (Pt Elizabeth) 1982-83. BB 1-15.

PHILLIPS, Alan Russell (Millfield S), b Weston-s-Mare 4 Oct 1968. RHB, RMF.

RENDELL, Perry John (Broad Oak CS), Weston-s-Mare 20 Jan 1970. 5'11½". RHB, RM.

ROBINSON, Andrew Nathan (Haringey Cricket C), b Croydon, Surrey 22 Feb 1966. 5'7". LHB.

TAVARÉ, Christopher James (Sevenoaks S; St John's, Oxford), b Orpington, Kent 27 Oct 1954. 6'1½". RHB, RM. Kent 1974-88 (cap 1978; captain 1983-84; benefit 1988). Oxford U 1975-77 (blue 1975-76-77). **Tests:** 30 (1980 to 1984); HS 149 v Ind (Delhi) 1981-82. LOI: 29. Tours: Aus 1982-83; NZ 1983-84; Ind/SL 1981-82; Pak 1983-84. 1000 runs (12); most – 1770 (1981). HS 168* Kent v Essex (Chelmsford) 1982. BB 1-3. Awards: NWT 3; BHC 6. **NWT:** HS 118* Kent v Yorks (Canterbury) 1981. **BHC:** HS 143 Kent v Somerset (Taunton) 1985. **RAL:** HS 136* Kent v Glos (Canterbury) 1978.

DEPARTURES

CROWE, Martin David (Auckland GS), b Henderson, Auckland, NZ, 22 Sep 1962. Son of D.W. (Wellington and Canterbury); brother of J.J. (Auckland, S Australia and NZ). 6'1½". RHB, RMF. Auckland 1979-83. C Districts 1983-87 (capt 1984-87). Somerset 1984-88 (cap 1984). MCC staff 1981. **Tests** (NZ): 42 (1981-82 to 1987-88); HS 188 v WI (Georgetown) 1984-85 and 188 v Aus (Brisbane) 1985-86; BB 2-25 v WI (Bridgetown) 1984-85. LOI (NZ): 65. Tours (NZ): Eng 1983, 1986; Aus 1982-83, 1985-86; WI 1984-85; Pak 1984-85; SL 1983-84, 1986-87. 1000 runs (2+3); most – 1870 (1984). Shared record Somerset 3rd-wkt stand of 319 with P.M.Roebuck v Leics (Taunton) 1984. Scored 4045 f-c runs during 1987. HS 242* NZ v S Australia (Adelaide) 1985-86. Somerset HS 206* v Warwicks (Birmingham) 1987. BB 5-18 Central Districts v Auckland (Auckland) 1983-84. Somerset BB 5-66 v Leics (Leicester) 1984. Awards: NWT 1; BHC 3. **NWT:** HS 114 v Sussex (Hove) 1984. BB 3-33 v Kent (Taunton) 1984. **BHC:** HS 155* v Hants (Southampton) 1987. BB 4-24 v Kent (Canterbury) 1984. **RAL:** HS 82 v Warwicks (Bath) 1987. BB 2-14 v Derbys (Taunton) 1984.

continued on p 152

SOMERSET 1988

RESULTS SUMMARY

	Place	Won	Lost	Drew	Abandoned
Britannic Assurance Championship	11th	5	6	11	
All First-class Matches		5	7	11	
Refuge Assurance League	12th	6	9		1
NatWest Bank Trophy	2nd Round				
Benson and Hedges Cup	4th in Group D				

BRITANNIC ASSURANCE CHAMPIONSHIP AVERAGES

BATTING AND FIELDING

Cap		M	I	NO	HS	Runs	Avge	100	50	Ct/St
1988	S.R.Waugh	14	22	6	161	1286	80.37	6	4	19
1984	M.D.Crowe	4	7	1	136*	473	78.83	2	2	4
1986	N.A.Felton	13	25	2	127	706	30.69	1	4	6
—	R.J.Harden	6	11	1	78	295	29.50	—	3	3
1978	P.M.Roebuck	12	19	3	112*	454	28.37	1	1	6
1987	N.D.Burns	22	32	7	133*	708	28.32	1	2	55/2
1987	J.J.E.Hardy	21	37	3	97	902	26.52	—	6	23
1979	V.J.Marks	22	29	2	68	673	24.92	—	3	8
—	R.J.Bartlett	18	29	3	102*	648	24.92	1	2	12
—	J.G.Wyatt	14	24	1	69	532	23.13	—	3	9
—	N.J.Pringle	8	15	4	54	244	22.18	—	1	8
1988	G.D.Rose	19	23	6	69*	359	21.11	—	1	10
1978	C.H.Dredge	2	4	0	37	73	18.25	—	—	—
—	D.J.Foster	12	12	7	20	64	12.80	—	—	—
1987	N.A.Mallender	16	19	6	44	157	12.07	—	—	8
1987	A.N.Jones	20	21	8	38	130	10.00	—	—	8
—	M.W.Cleal	8	10	1	13	72	8.00	—	—	1
—	H.R.J.Trump	8	10	1	48	62	6.88	—	—	7

Also batted: G.V.Palmer (1 match) 0, 23; T.J.A.Scriven (2 matches) 7, 4.

BOWLING

	O	M	R	W	Avge	Best	5 wI	10 wM
N.A.Mallender	411.1	108	969	47	20.61	5-12	1	—
G.D.Rose	483.5	112	1455	54	26.94	6-47	1	—
H.R.J.Trump	258	70	653	23	28.39	4-17	—	—
V.J.Marks	856.5	220	2201	76	28.96	7-118	5	1
A.N.Jones	512	86	1658	55	30.14	7-30	1	—
M.W.Cleal	153	22	541	16	33.81	3-16	—	—
D.J.Foster	282.3	44	967	25	38.68	4-46	—	—

Also bowled: R.J.Bartlett 30-4-145-4; C.H.Dredge 53.5-15-181-3; R.J.Harden 16-1-61-0; J.J.E.Hardy 0.3-0-12-0; G.V.Palmer 18.2-2-54-1; N.J.Pringle 13-1-40-1; P.M.Roebuck 28.4-2-106-1; T.J.A.Scriven 96-25-237-3; S.R.Waugh 23-5-60-3; J.G.Wyatt 9-4-30-1.

The First-Class Averages (pp 161-175) give the records of Somerset players in all first-class county matches (their other opponents being the West Indians), with the exception of R.J.Bartlett, N.A.Mallender and H.R.J.Trump whose full county figures are as above.

SOMERSET RECORDS

FIRST-CLASS CRICKET

Highest Total	For	675-9d	v Hampshire	Bath	1924
	V	811	by Surrey	The Oval	1899
Lowest Total	For	25	v Glos	Bristol	1947
	V	22	by Glos	Bristol	1920
Highest Innings	For	322 I.V.A.Richards	v Warwicks	Taunton	1985
	V	424 A.C.MacLaren	for Lancashire	Taunton	1895

Highest Partnerships
Wkt

1st	346 H.T.Hewett/L.C.H.Palairet	v Yorkshire	Taunton	1892
2nd	290 J.C.W.MacBryan/M.D.Lyon	v Derbyshire	Buxton	1924
3rd	319 P.M.Roebuck/M.D.Crowe	v Leics	Taunton	1984
4th	310 P.W.Denning/I.T.Botham	v Glos	Taunton	1980
5th	235 J.C.White/C.C.C.Case	v Glos	Taunton	1927
6th	265 W.E.Alley/K.E.Palmer	v Northants	Northampton	1961
7th	240 S.M.J.Woods/V.T.Hill	v Kent	Taunton	1898
8th	172 I.V.A.Richards/I.T.Botham	v Leics	Leicester	1983
9th	183 C.H.M.Greetham/H.W.Stephenson	v Leics	Weston-s-Mare	1963
10th	143 J.J.Bridges/A.H.D.Gibbs	v Essex	Weston-s-Mare	1919

Best Bowling	For	10-49 E.J.Tyler	v Surrey	Taunton	1895
(Innings)	V	10-35 A.Drake	for Yorkshire	Weston-s-Mare	1914
Best Bowling	For	16-83 J.C.White	v Worcs	Bath	1919
(Match)	V	17-137 W.Brearley	for Lancashire	Manchester	1905
Most Runs – Season		2,761 W.E.Alley	(av 58.74)		1961
Most Runs – Career		21,142 H.Gimblett	(av 36.96)		1935-1954
Most 100s – Season		10 W.E.Alley			1961
Most 100s – Career		49 H.Gimblett	1935-1954		
Most Wkts – Season		169 A.W.Wellard	(av 19.24)		1938
Most Wkts – Career		2,166 J.C.White	(av 18.02)		1909-1937

LIMITED-OVERS CRICKET

Highest Total	NWT	330-4	v Glamorgan	Cardiff	1978
	BHC	319-2	v Hampshire	Southampton	1987
	RAL	286-7	v Hampshire	Taunton	1981
Lowest Total	NWT	59	v Middlesex	Lord's	1977
	BHC	98	v Middlesex	Lord's	1982
	RAL	58	v Essex	Chelmsford	1977
Highest Innings	NWT	145 P.W.Denning	v Glamorgan	Cardiff	1978
	BHC	155* M.D.Crowe	v Hampshire	Southampton	1987
	RAL	175* I.T.Botham	v Northants	Wellingborough	1986
Best Bowling	NWT	6-29 J.Garner	v Northants	Lord's	1979
	BHC	5-14 J.Garner	v Surrey	Lord's	1981
	RAL	6-24 I.V.A.Richards	v Lancashire	Manchester	1983

124

SURREY

Formation of Present Club: 22 August 1845
Colours: Chocolate
Badge: Prince of Wales' Feathers
Championships (since 1890): (15) 1890, 1891, 1892, 1894, 1895, 1899, 1914, 1952, 1953, 1954, 1955, 1956, 1957, 1958, 1971. **Joint:** (1) 1950
NatWest Trophy/Gillette Cup Winners: (1) 1982
Benson and Hedges Cup Winners: (1) 1974
Sunday League Champions: (0) Fifth 1969, 1980
Match Awards: NWT 29; BHC 43

Secretary: D.G.Seward, Kennington Oval, London, SE11 5SS
Captain: I.A.Greig
Scorer: T.Billson
Cricketcall: ☎ 0898 1214 33
Benefit 1989: G.S.Clinton

ATKINS, Paul David (Aylesbury G.S.), b Aylesbury, Bucks 11 Jun 1966. 6'1". RHB, OB. Debut 1988 v CU (Oval) scoring 114* and 8. Buckinghamshire 1985-88 (cap 1986). HS 114* (above). Award: NWT 1. **NWT:** HS 82 v Glam (Oval) 1988. **RAL:** HS 2.

BICKNELL, Darren John (Robert Haining SS; Guildford TC), b Guildford 24 Jun 1967. Elder brother of M.P. 6'4". LHB, LM. Debut 1987. HS 105 v Hants (Oval) 1987 (his third match). **BHC:** HS 17 v Worcs (Oval) 1987. **RAL:** HS 31 v Glam (Ebbw Vale) 1988.

BICKNELL, Martin Paul (Robert Haining SS), b Guildford 14 Jan 1969. Younger brother of D.J. 6'3". RHB, RFM. Debut 1986. HS 33 v SL (Oval) 1988. BB 9-45 v CU (Oval) 1988. **NWT:** HS 2 and BB 2-36 v Cheshire (Birkenhead) 1986. **BHC:** HS 1*. HS 3-29 v Yorks (Leeds) 1987. **RAL:** HS 13 v Northants (Tring) 1986. BB 2-14 v Essex (Chelmsford) 1988.

BOILING, James (Rutlish S, Merton; Durham U), b New Delhi, India 8 Apr 1968. 6'4". RHB, OB. Debut 1988. HS 8*. **BHC:** HS 9*. BB 2-44 Comb Us v Glos (Bristol) 1988.

BROWN, Graham Elliott (Spencer Park S, Wandsworth; South London C), b Balham 11 Oct 1966. 5'7". RHB, WK. Debut 1986. HS 13* v Pak (Oval) 1987.

BULLEN, Christopher Keith (Rutlish S, Merton) b Clapham 5 Nov 1962. 6'4½". RHB, OB. Debut 1982. HS 65 v Pakistanis (Oval) 1987. BB 6-119 v Middx (Lord's) 1987. **NWT:** HS 22 v Essex (Chelmsford) 1988. BB 2-55 v Middx (Oval) 1988. **BHC:** HS 33 and BB 2-38 v Yorks (Leeds) 1987. **RAL:** HS 25 v Hants (Southampton) 1987. BB 3-23 v Leics (Oval) 1988.

CLARKE, Sylvester Theophilus (St Bartholomew's BS), b Christ Church, Barbados 11 Dec 1954. 6'1". RHB, RF. Barbados 1977-1982. Surrey debut 1979. Cap 1980. Benefit 1987. Transvaal 1983-86. OFS 1987-88. **Tests** (WI): 11 (1977-78 to 1981-82); HS 35* v Pak (Faisalabad) 1980-81; BB 5-126 v Ind (Bangalore) 1978-79. LOI (WI): 10. Tours (WI): Aus 1981-82; SA (WI XI) 1982-83, 1983-84; Ind/SL 1978-79; Pak 1980-81. 3 hat-tricks: 1977-78 (Barbados), 1980, 1987 (4 wkts in 5 balls). HS 100* v Glam (Swansea) 1981. BB 8-62 v Northants (Oval) 1987. Awards:

NWT 1; BHC 3. **NWT:** HS 45* v Leics (Oval) 1981. BB 4-10 v Middx (Oval) 1982. **BHC:** HS 39 v Hants (Southampton) 1982. BB 5-23 v Kent (Oval) 1980. **RAL:** HS 34* v Hants (Oval) 1980. BB 4-38 v Somerset (Bath) 1988.

CLINTON, Grahame Selvey (Chislehurst and Sidcup GS), b Sidcup, Kent 5 May 1953. 5'10". LHB, RM. Kent 1974-78. Surrey debut 1979. Cap 1980. Benefit 1989. Rhodesia 1979-80. 1000 runs (6); most – 1240 (1980). HS 192 v Yorks (Oval) 1984. BB 2-8 Kent v Pak (Canterbury) 1978. Awards: BHC: 3. **NWT:** HS 146 v Kent (Canterbury) 1985. **BHC:** HS 121* v Kent (Oval) 1988. **RAL:** HS 105* v Yorks (Scarborough) 1981.

FELTHAM, Mark Andrew (Tiffin S), b St John's Wood, London 26 June 1963. 6'2½". RHB, RM. Debut 1983. HS 76 v Glos (Oval) 1986. BB 5-45 v Lancs (Oval) 1988. Award: BHC 1. **NWT:** HS 16* v Staffs (Burton) 1988. BB 2-27 v Cheshire (Birkenhead) 1986. **BHC:** HS 22* v Hants (Oval) 1984. BB 3-25 v Glos (Oval) 1984. **RAL:** HS 37 and BB 4-35 v Sussex (Guildford) 1986.

FROST, Mark (Alexander HS, Tipton; St Peter's S, Wolverhampton; Durham U), b Barking, Essex 21 Oct 1962. 6'2". RHB, RMF. Debut 1988. Staffordshire 1987. HS 7. BB 4-56 v CU (Cambridge) 1988 (on debut).

GREIG, Ian Alexander (Queen's S, Queenstown; Downing C, Cambridge), b Queenstown, SA 8 Dec 1955. Brother of A.W. (Border, Sussex, E Province and England 1965-78). 5'11½". RHB, RMF. Border 1974-75, 1979-80. GW 1975-76. Cambridge U 1977-79 (blue 1977-78-79; captain 1979). Sussex 1980-85 (cap 1981). Surrey debut/cap 1987. Captain 1987-. Tests: 2 (1982); HS 14 and BB 4-53 v Pak (Birmingham) 1982. HS 147* Sussex v OU (Oxford) 1983. Surrey HS 104* v CU (Cambridge) 1987. BB 7-43 Sussex v CU (Cambridge) 1981. Surrey BB 6-34 v CU (Cambridge) 1988. Awards: NWT 1; BHC 1. **NWT:** HS 82 and BB 4-31 Sussex v Warwicks (Birmingham) 1981. **BHC:** HS 51 and BB 5-35 Sussex v Hants (Hove) 1981. **RAL:** HS 56* v Northants (Oval) 1988. BB 5-30 v Kent (Oval) 1988.

KENDRICK, Neil Michael (Wilson's GS), b Bromley, Kent 11 Nov 1967. 5'11". RHB, SLA. Debut 1988. HS 8*. BB 1-92.

LYNCH, Monte Alan (Ryden's S, Walton-on-Thames), b Georgetown, British Guiana 21 May 1958. 5'8". RHB, RM/OB. Debut 1977. Cap 1982. Guyana 1982-83. LOI: 3. Tours: SA 1983-84 (WI XI); Pak 1981-82 (Int XI). 1000 (6); most – 1714 (1985). HS 152 v Notts (Oval) 1986. BB 3-6 v Glam (Swansea) 1981. Awards: NWT 1; BHC 3. **NWT:** HS 129 v Durham (Oval) 1982. BB 1-11. **BHC:** HS 112* v Kent (Oval) 1987. **RAL:** HS 136 v Yorks (Bradford) 1985. BB 2-2 v Northants (Guildford) 1987.

MAYS, Christopher Sean (Lancing C; Middlesex Hospital Medical S), b Brighton 11 May 1966. 5'9". RHB, OB. Sussex 1986. Surrey debut 1987. HS 13* v Essex (Chelmsford) 1988. BB 3-77 Sussex v NZ (Hove) 1986. Surrey BB 1-36.

MEDLYCOTT, Keith Thomas (Parmiters GS, Wandsworth), b Whitechapel 12 May 1965. 5'11". RHB, SLA. Debut 1984 scoring 117* v CU (Banstead). Cap 1988. HS 153 v Kent (Oval) 1987 -sharing Surrey record 7th-wkt stand of 262 with C.J.Richards. BB 8-52 v Sussex (Hove) 1988. **RAL:** HS 34 v Glam (Ebbw Vale) 1988. BB 2-29 v Lancs (Oval) 1988.

126

PETERS, Nicholas Howard (Sherborne S; West London IHE), b Guildford 21 Feb 1968. 6'2". RHB, RFM. Debut 1988. HS 25* v Leics (Oval) 1988. BB 6-31 v Warwicks (Oval) 1988 (taking 10-67 in his fifth match). **NWT:** BB 2-28 v Essex (Chelmsford) 1988. **BHC:** HS 1*. BB 1-24. **RAL:** HS 4*. BB 2-16 v Middx (Oval) 1988.

ROBINSON, Jonathan David (Lancing C; West Sussex IHE), b Epsom 3 Aug 1966. Son of P.M.H. (L.C.Stevens' XI 1961). 5'10". LHB, RM. Debut 1988. HS 20 v Notts (Nottingham) 1988. BB 2-41 v Worcs (Oval) 1988. **RAL:** HS 14 v Notts (Nottingham) 1988.

SADIQ, Zahid Asa (Rutlish S.), b Nairobi, Kenya, 6 May 1965. 5'11". RHB. Debut 1988. HS 64 v CU (Oval) 1988 (on debut). **RAL:** HS 53 v Leics (Oval) 1988.

STEWART, Alec James (Tiffin S) b Merton 8 Apr 1963. Son of M.J. (Surrey and England 1954-72). 5'11". RHB, WK. Debut 1981. Cap 1985. 1000 runs (4); most – 1665 (1986). HS 166 v Kent (Oval) 1986. BB 1-18. Awards: NWT 1; BHC 1. **NWT:** HS 107* v Middx (Oval) 1986. **BHC:** HS 63* v Comb Us (Oval) 1986. **RAL:** HS 86 v Warwicks (Oval) 1985.

THORPE, Graham Paul (Weydon CS; Farnham C), b Farnham 1 Aug 1969. 5'11". LHB, RM. Debut 1988. HS 100* v CU (Oval) 1988 (second match). BB 2-33 v Leics (Oval) 1988 (on debut). **RAL:** HS 15 v Glam (Ebbw Vale) 1988.

WARD, David Mark (Haling Manor HS), b Croydon 10 Feb 1961. 6'1". RHB, OB. Debut 1985. HS 143 v Derbys (Derby) 1985. **NWT:** HS 27 v Glam (Oval) 1988. **BHC:** HS 7. **RAL:** HS 73* v Kent (Oval) 1987.

SMITH, Andrew (Sutton Manor S), b 30 May 1969. Son of W.A. (Surrey 1961-70) RHB, OB.

DEPARTURES

GRAY, Anthony Hollis (Malick SS), b Port-of-Spain, Trinidad 23 May 1963. 6'7". RHB, RF. Debut (N E Trinidad in Beaumont Cup) 1983-84. Trinidad 1984-88. Surrey 1985-88 (cap 1985). **Tests** (WI): 5 (1986-87); HS 12* and BB 4-39 v Pak (Faisalabad) 1986-87. LOI (WI): 21. Tours (WI): NZ 1986-87; Pak 1986-87. HS 54* Trinidad v Leeward Is (Basseterre) 1985-86. Surrey HS 35 v Glam (Oval) 1987. BB 8-40 v Yorks (Sheffield) 1985 (inc hat-trick and 4 wkts in 5 balls). **NWT:** HS 3 and BB 3-23 v Cheshire (Birkenhead) 1986. **RAL:** HS 24* v Essex (Chelmsford) 1986. BB 4-21 v Leics (Oval) 1986.

RICHARDS, Clifton James ('**Jack**') (Humphrey Davy GS, Penzance) b Penzance, Cornwall 10 Aug 1958. 5'11". RHB, WK, OB. Surrey 1976-88 (cap 1978; benefit 1988). OFS 1983-84. **Tests**: 8 (1986-87 to 1988); HS 133 v Aus (Perth) 1986-87. LOI: 22. Tours: Aus 1986-87; WI 1982-83 (Int XI); NZ 1979-80 (DHR), 1987-88; Ind/SL 1981-82. 1000 runs (1): 1006 (1986). HS 172* v Kent (Oval) 1987 – sharing Surrey record 7th-wkt stand of 262 with K.T.Medlycott. BB 2-42 v Somerset (Oval) 1985. Awards: NWT 2. **NWT:** HS 105* v Lincs (Sleaford) 1983. **BHC:** HS 45 v Kent (Canterbury) 1986. **RAL:** HS 113 v Somerset (Oval) 1987.

SMITH, D.M. – see SUSSEX.

SURREY 1988

RESULTS SUMMARY

	Place	Won	Lost	Tied	Drew	Aban
Britannic Assurance Championship	4th	7	5		10	
All First-class Matches		9	5		11	
Refuge Assurance League	5th	8	5	1		2
NatWest Bank Trophy	Semi-Finalist					
Benson and Hedges Cup	5th in Group C					

BRITANNIC ASSURANCE CHAMPIONSHIP AVERAGES

BATTING AND FIELDING

Cap		M	I	NO	HS	Runs	Avge	100	50	Ct/St
1978	C.J.Richards	17	21	4	102*	861	50.64	1	6	58/1
1980	D.M.Smith	10	17	5	157*	585	48.75	2	1	2
1980	G.S.Clinton	17	28	5	158	980	42.60	4	3	7
1985	A.J.Stewart	20	30	3	133	992	36.74	2	6	11/1
1982	M.A.Lynch	20	28	3	103	893	35.72	1	4	16
—	D.M.Ward	22	31	5	126	835	32.11	1	7	16
—	P.D.Atkins	5	9	0	99	235	26.11	—	1	—
—	M.A.Feltham	20	24	9	74	352	23.46	—	1	9
1988	K.T.Medlycott	21	27	4	77*	483	21.00	—	3	26
—	J.D.Robinson	2	4	2	20	37	18.50	—	—	1
1987	I.A.Greig	22	27	1	47	462	17.76	—	—	16
—	G.P.Thorpe	2	4	1	19	50	16.66	—	—	1
—	D.J.Bicknell	9	16	1	50	247	16.46	—	1	3
1980	S.T.Clarke	12	10	1	28	141	15.66	—	—	11
—	N.H.Peters	11	14	7	25*	83	11.85	—	—	4
—	C.K.Bullen	9	11	1	24	101	10.10	—	—	5
—	M.P.Bicknell	15	12	3	25	60	6.66	—	—	3

Also batted: J.Boiling (1 match) 1, 8*; G.E.Brown (1 match) 0 (1 ct, 1 st); M.Frost (2 matches) 0, 0, 4 (1 ct); C.S.Mays (2 matches) 13* (2 ct); Z.A.Sadiq (2 matches) 13, 37, 0.

BOWLING

	O	M	R	W	Avge	Best	5 wI	10 wM
S.T.Clarke	396.4	108	913	63	14.49	6-52	4	2
K.T.Medlycott	522.1	143	1445	62	23.30	8-52	6	3
I.A.Greig	371.3	74	1082	41	26.39	6-56	1	—
N.H.Peters	263.2	48	907	34	26.67	6-31	1	1
M.A.Feltham	521.4	116	1536	51	30.11	5-45	2	—
M.P.Bicknell	439.2	115	1280	36	35.55	4-34	—	—

Also bowled: D.J.Bicknell 1-0-18-0; J.Boiling 15-3-40-0; C.K.Bullen 60.1-7-209-5; G.S.Clinton 0.4-0-16-0; M.Frost 28-4-115-2; M.A.Lynch 29.2-8-88-4; C.S.Mays 25-2-102-1; C.J.Richards 4-1-26-0; J.D.Robinson 13-1-67-3; A.J.Stewart 13.1-2-45-1; G.P.Thorpe 24-2-60-3; D.M.Ward 5-0-31-0.

The First-Class Averages (pp 161-175) give the records of Surrey players in all first-class county matches (their other opponents being the Sri Lankans and Cambridge U. twice), with the exception of:
C.J.Richards 18-21-4-102*-861-50.64-1-6-60ct/1st. 4-1-26-0.

SURREY RECORDS

FIRST-CLASS CRICKET

Highest Total	For	811		v Somerset	The Oval	1899
	V	705-8d		by Sussex	Hastings	1902
Lowest Total	For	14		v Essex	Chelmsford	1983
	V	16		by MCC	Lord's	1872
Highest Innings	For	357*	R.Abel	v Somerset	The Oval	1899
	V	{300*	F.B.Watson	for Lancashire	Manchester	1928
		{300	R.Subba Row	for Northants	The Oval	1958

Highest Partnerships
Wkt

st	428	J.B.Hobbs/A.Sandham	v Oxford U	The Oval	1926
nd	371	J.B.Hobbs/E.G.Hayes	v Hampshire	The Oval	1909
rd	353	A.Ducat/E.G.Hayes	v Hampshire	Southampton	1919
th	448	R.Abel/T.W.Hayward	v Yorkshire	The Oval	1899
5th	308	J.N.Crawford/F.C.Holland	v Somerset	The Oval	1908
6th	298	A.Sandham/H.S.Harrison	v Sussex	The Oval	1913
7th	262	C.J.Richards/K.T.Medlycott	v Kent	The Oval	1987
8th	204	T.W.Hayward/L.C.Braund	v Lancashire	The Oval	1898
9th	168	E.R.T.Holmes/E.W.J.Brooks	v Hampshire	The Oval	1936
10th	173	A.Ducat/A.Sandham	v Essex	Leyton	1921

Best Bowling	For	10-43	T.Rushby	v Somerset	Taunton	1921
(Innings)	V	10-28	W.P.Howell	for Australians	The Oval	1899
Best Bowling	For	16-83	G.A.R.Lock	v Kent	Blackheath	1956
(Match)	V	15-57	W.P.Howell	for Australians	The Oval	1899
Most Runs – Season		3,246	T.W.Hayward	(av 72.13)		1906
Most Runs – Career		43,554	J.B.Hobbs	(av 49.72)		1905-1934
Most 100s – Season		13	T.W.Hayward			1906
		13	J.B.Hobbs			1925
Most 100s – Career		144	J.B.Hobbs			1905-1934
Most Wkts – Season		252	T.Richardson	(av 13.94)		1895
Most Wkts – Career		1,775	T.Richardson	(av 17.87)		1892-1904

LIMITED-OVERS CRICKET

Highest Total	NWT	297-6		v Lincs	Sleaford	1983
	BHC	276-6		v Essex	The Oval	1982
	RAL	304-6		v Warwicks	The Oval	1985
Lowest Total	NWT	74		v Kent	The Oval	1967
	BHC	89		v Notts	Nottingham	1984
	RAL	64		v Worcs	Worcester	1978
Highest Innings	NWT	146	G.S.Clinton	v Kent	Canterbury	1985
	BHC	121*	G.S.Clinton	v Kent	The Oval	1988
	RAL	136	M.A.Lynch	v Yorkshire	Bradford	1985
Best Bowling	NWT	7-33	R.D.Jackman	v Yorkshire	Harrogate	1970
	BHC	5-21	P.H.L.Wilson	v Comb Univs	The Oval	1979
	RAL	6-25	Intikhab Alam	v Derbyshire	The Oval	1974

SUSSEX

Formation of Present Club: 1 March 1839
Substantial Reorganisation: August 1857
Colours: Dark Blue, Light Blue and Gold
Badge: County Arms of Six Martlets
Championships: (0) Second 1902, 1903, 1932, 1933, 1934, 1953, 1981
NatWest Trophy/Gillette Cup Winners: (4) 1963, 1964, 1978, 1986
Benson and Hedges Cup Winners: (0) Semi-Finalists 1982
Sunday League Champions: (1) 1982
Match Awards: NWT 40; BHC 40

Secretary: N.Bett, County Ground, Eaton Road, Hove BN3 3AN
Captain: P.W.G.Parker
Scorer: L.V.Chandler
Cricketcall: ☎ 0898 1214 12
Benefit 1989: Sussex CCC 150th Anniversary Fund

BABINGTON, Andrew Mark (Reigate GS; Borough Road PE College), b Middlesex Hospital, London 22 Jul 1963. 6'2". LHB, RFM. Debut 1986. HS 16 v Middx (Uxbridge) 1987. BB 4-18 (inc hat-trick) v Glos (Bristol) 1986. **NWT:** HS 4*. BB 2-9 v Suffolk (Hove) 1986. **BHC:** HS 4*. BB 4-29 v Surrey (Hove) 1988. **RAL:** HS 1. BB 3-33 v Derbys (Hove) 1987.

BUNTING, Rodney Alan (King Edward VII GS, King's Lynn), b East Winch, Norfolk, 25 Apr 1965. 6'5". RHB, RFM. Debut 1988 taking 5-86 v Glos (Bristol). Norfolk 1985-87 (cap 1986). HS 17* v Hants (Southampton) 1988. BB 5-44 v Warwicks (Hove) 1988. **BHC:** HS 0*. BB 2-43 Minor C v Glam (Oxford) 1987. **RAL:** HS 5*. BB 2-8 v Glos (Bristol) 1988.

CLARKE, Andrew Russell (Longhill HS), b Patcham 23 Dec 1961. 5'9". RHB, LB. Debut 1988. HS 68 and BB 5-60 v Hants (Eastbourne) 1988. **NWT:** HS 24 v Derbys (Hove) 1988. **RAL:** HS 7. BB 4-24 v Glam (Eastbourne) 1988.

FALKNER, Nicholas James (Reigate GS), b Redhill, Surrey 30 Sep 1962. 5'10". RHB, RM. Surrey 1984-87, scoring 101* v CU (Banstead) on debut. HS 102 Surrey v Middx (Uxbridge) 1986. Sussex HS 55 v Yorks (Hove) 1988. BB 1-3. **NWT:** HS 36 Surrey v Derbys (Derby) 1986. **BHC:** HS 58 Surrey v Glam (Oval) 1987. **RAL:** HS 52 Surrey v Hants (Southampton) 1987.

GOULD, Ian James (Westgate SS, Cippenham), b Slough, Bucks 19 Aug 1957. 5'8". LHB, WK. Middlesex 1975-80 (cap 1977). Auckland 1979-80. Sussex debut/cap 1981. LOI: 18. Tours: Aus 1982-83; Pak 1980-81 (Int XI); Zim 1980-81 (Middx). HS 128 Middx v Worcs (Worcester) 1978. Sussex HS 111 v Northants (Hove) 1987. BB 2-48 v Hants (Eastbourne) 1988. Awards: NWT 1; BHC 3. **NWT:** HS 88 v Yorks (Leeds) 1986. **BHC:** HS 72 v Kent (Hove) 1982. BB 1-0. **RAL:** HS 74 v Essex (Chelmsford) 1987.

GREEN, Allan Michael (Knoll S, Hove; Brighton SFC), b Pulborough 28 May 1960. 5'11". RHB, OB. Debut 1980. Cap 1985. OFS 1984-87. 1000 runs (3): most – 1646 (1985). HS 179 v Glam (Cardiff) 1986. BB 6-82 v Hants (Southampton) 1988. Awards: NWT 2. **NWT:** HS 102 v Glam (Hove) 1986. **BHC:** HS 53 v Essex (Chelmsford) 1988. BB 1-4. **RAL:** HS 83 v Derbys (Heanor) 1984. BB 3-16 v Kent (Maidstone) 1988.

130

GREENFIELD, Keith (Falmer HS), b Brighton 6 Dec 1968. 6'0". RHB, RM. Debut 1987. HS 18 v Lancs (Lytham) 1987. **RAL:** HS 8*.

KIMBER, Simon Julian Spencer (Educated in Durban, SA), b Ormskirk, Lancs 6 Oct 1963. 6'2". RHB, RMF. Worcestershire 1985. Sussex debut 1987. Natal B 1986-87. HS 54 v Notts (Eastbourne) 1987. BB 4-76 Natal B v E Province B (Uitenhage) 1986-87. Sussex BB 3-44 v Derbys (Horsham) 1988. **NWT:** HS 0. **BHC:** HS 15 v Middx (Lord's) 1988. BB 3-36 v Essex (Chelmsford) 1988. **RAL:** HS 15* v Somerset (Hove) 1988. BB 3-35 v Leics (Leicester) 1988.

LENHAM, Neil John (Brighton C), b Worthing 17 Dec 1965. Son of L.J. (Sussex 1956-70). 5'11". RHB, RMF. Debut 1984. HS 104* v Pakistanis (Hove) 1987. BB 4-85 v Leics (Leicester) 1986. Award: BHC 1. **NWT:** HS 6. BB 1-48. **BHC:** HS 82 v Somerset (Hove) 1986. BB 1-17. **RAL:** HS 39 v Surrey (Hove) 1988. BB 1-16.

MOORES, Peter (King Edward VI S, Macclesfield), b Macclesfield, Cheshire 18 Dec 1962. 6'0". RHB, WK. Worcestershire 1983-84. Sussex debut 1985. HS 97* v Lancs (Hove) 1988. **NWT:** HS 20 v Derbys (Hove) 1988. **RAL:** HS 34 v Derbys (Horsham) 1988.

PARKER, Paul William Giles (Collyer's GS; St Catharine's C, CU), b Bulawayo, Rhodesia 15 Jan 1956. 5'10". RHB, RM. CU and Sussex debuts 1976. Blue 1976-77-78. Cap 1979. Captain 1988-. Benefit 1988. YC 1979. **Tests:** 1 (1981); HS 13 v Aus (Oval). 1000 runs (8); most – 1692 (1984). HS 215 CU v Essex (Cambridge) 1976. Sussex HS 181 v SL (Hove) 1981. BB 2-21 v Surrey (Guildford) 1984. Awards: NWT 3; BHC 3. **NWT:** HS 109 v Ireland (Hove) 1985. BB 1-10. **BHC:** HS 77 v Hants (Bournemouth) 1982. BB 2-3 v Minor C (Hove) 1987. **RAL:** HS 121* v Northants (Hastings) 1983. BB 1-2.

PIGOTT, Anthony Charles Shackleton (Harrow S), b London 4 Jun 1958. 6'1". RHB, RFM. Debut 1978. Cap 1982. Tour: NZ 1979-80 (DHR). Wellington 1982-84. **Tests:** 1 (1983-84); HS 8* and BB 2-75 v NZ (Christchurch) 1983-84. Hat-trick 1978 (his first f-c wkts). HS 104* v Warwicks (Birmingham) 1986. BB 7-74 v Northants (Eastbourne) 1982. **NWT:** HS 53 v Derbys (Hove) 1988. BB 3-4 v Ireland (Hove) 1985. **BHC:** HS 21 v Somerset (Hove) 1986. BB 3-33 v Hants 1982 and v Somerset 1986. **RAL:** HS 49 v Warwicks (Hove) 1979. BB 5-24 v Lancs (Manchester) 1986.

SPEIGHT, Martin Peter (Hurstpierpoint C; Durham U), b Walsall, Staffs 24 Oct 1967. 5'9". RHB, WK. Debut 1986. HS 58 v Hants (Southampton) 1988. BB 1-2. **BHC:** HS 83 Comb Us v Glos (Bristol) 1988. **RAL:** HS 37 v Lancs (Hove) 1988.

THRELFALL, Philip Walter (Barrow GS; Parkview S), b Barrow-in-Furness, Lancs 11 Feb 1967. 6'3". RHB, RMF. Debut 1988 (did not bat). Cumberland 1987.

WELLS, Alan Peter (Tideway CS, Newhaven), b Newhaven 2 Oct 1961. Younger brother of C.M. 6'0". RHB, RM. Debut 1981. Cap 1986. Border 1981-82. 1000 runs (3); most – 1286 (1988). HS 161* v Kent (Hove) 1987. BB 3-67 v Worcs (Worcester) 1987. **NWT:** HS 55 v Glos (Hove) 1987. **BHC:** HS 72 v Glam (Swansea) 1987. BB 1-17. **RAL:** HS 71* v Hants (Southampton) 1984. BB 1-0.

WELLS, Colin Mark (Tideway CS, Newhaven), b Newhaven 3 Mar 1960. Elder brother of A.P. 5'11". RHB, RMF. Debut 1979. Cap 1982. Border 1980-81. W Province 1984-85. LOI: 2. 1000 runs (5); most – 1456 (1987). HS 203 v Hants (Hove) 1984. BB 6-34 v Lancs (Lytham) 1987. Awards: BHC 2. **NWT:** HS 76 v Ireland (Hove) 1985. BB 2-20 v Suffolk (Hove) 1979. **BHC:** HS 101* v Minor C

WELLS, Colin (contd.)

(Hove) 1987. BB 4-21 v Middx (Lord's) 1980. **RAL:** HS 104* v Warwicks (Hove) 1983. BB 4-15 v Worcs (Worcester) 1983.

NEWCOMERS

BOARER, Paul Vincent, b Haslemere, Surrey 19 Jul 1967. RHB, RFM.

DODEMAIDE, Anthony Ian Christopher, b 5 Oct 1963. RHB, RFM. Victoria 1983-88. **Tests (Aus):** 3 (1987-88); HS 50 and BB 6-58 v NZ (Melbourne) 1987-88 (on debut). LOI (Aus): 11. Tour (Young Aus): Zim 1985-86. Esso scholarship to Sussex 1985. HS 81* Victoria v W Australia (Perth) 1986-87. BB 6-58 (Tests).

SMITH, David Mark (Battersea GS), b Balham 9 Jan 1956. 6'4". LHB, RM. Surrey 1973-83 and 1987-88 (cap 1980). Worcestershire 1984-86 (cap 1984). **Tests:** 2 (1985-86); HS 47 v WI (P-of-S). LOI: 1. Tour: WI 1985-86. 1000 runs (4); most − 1113 (1985). HS 189* Worcs v Kent (Worcester) 1984. BB 3-40 Surrey v Sussex (Oval) 1976. Awards: NWT 2; BHC 3. **NWT:** HS 109 Worcs v Lancs (Manchester) 1985. BB 3-39 Surrey v Derbys (Ilkeston) 1976. **BHC:** HS 126 Worcs v Warwicks (Worcester) 1985. BB 4-29 Surrey v Kent (Oval) 1980. **RAL:** HS 87* Surrey v Hants (Oval) 1980. BB 2-21 Surrey v Worcs (Byfleet) 1973.

DEPARTURES

ALIKHAN, Rehan Iqbal ('Ray') (KCS, Wimbledon), b Westminster Hospital, London 28 Dec 1962. 6'1½". RHB, OB. Sussex 1986-88. HS 98 v Somerset (Bath) 1988. BB 2-19 v WI (Hove) 1988. **NWT:** HS 41 v Worcs (Worcester) 1986. **BHC:** HS 71 v Glam (Swansea) 1987. **RAL:** HS 23 v Essex (Chelmsford) 1987.

HESELTINE, Peter Anthony William (Queen Elizabeth GS, Wakefield; King's C, London U), b Barnsley, Yorks 5 Apr 1965. 5'10". RHB, OB. Brother of P.J. (OU blue 1983). Sussex 1987-88. HS 26 v Kent (Dartford) 1987. BB 3-33 v Notts (Eastbourne) 1987. **BHC:** BB 2-12 v Surrey (Hove) 1987. **RAL:** HS 6*. BB 1-34.

IMRAN KHAN NIAZI (Aitchison C; Cathedral S; Worcester RGS; Keble C, OU), b Lahore, Pakistan 25 Nov 1952. 6'0". RHB, RF. Lahore, PIA, etc 1969-81. Worcestershire 1971-76 (cap 1976). Oxford U 1973-75 (blue 1973-74-75; captain 1974). Sussex 1977-88 (cap 1978; benefit 1987). Wisden 1982. **Tests (Pak):** 73 (1971 to 1987-88, 33 as captain); HS 135* v Ind (Madras) 1986-87; BB 8-58 (14-116 match) v SL (Faisalabad) 1981-82. LOI (Pak): 106. Tours (Pak)(C=Capt): Eng 1971, 1974, 1982C, 1987C; Aus 1976-77, 1978-79, 1981-82, 1983-84C; WI 1976-77, 1987-88C; NZ 1978-79; Ind 1979-80, 1986-87C; SL 1975-76; 1985-86C. 1000 runs (4); most − 1339 (1978). Hat-trick 1983. HS 170 OU v Northants (Oxford) 1974. Sussex HS 167 v Glos (Hove) 1978. BB 8-34 v Middx (Lord's) 1986. Awards: NWT 7; BHC 8. **NWT:** HS 114* v Notts (Hove) 1983. BB 4-27 v Staffs (Stone) 1978. **BHC:** HS 112* v Essex (Hove) 1986. BB 5-8 v Northants (Northampton) 1978. **RAL:** HS 104* v Hants (Hove) 1985. BB 5-29 Worcs v Leics (Leicester) 1973.

PRINGLE, Meyrick Wayne (Dale C; Kingswood C), b Adelaide, SA 22 June 1966. 6'4". RHB, RMF. OFS 1985-86. SA Us 1986-87. E Province 1987-88. Sussex 1987-88. HS 50* E Province B v Border (Pt Elizabeth) 1987-88. Sussex HS 35 v Glos (Bristol) 1988. BB 6-33 E Province B v W Province B (Plumstead) 1987-88. Sussex BB 2-45 v Pak (Hove) 1988. **BHC:** HS 19* v Kent (Hove) 1988. BB 1-33. **RAL:** HS 11 v Worcs (Worcester) 1988. BB 3-37 v Somerset (Hove) 1988.

STANDING, David Kevin (Tideway CS, Newhaven; Brighton and Hove GS), b Brighton 21 Oct 1963. 5'7". RHB, OB. Sussex 1983-88. HS 65 v Warwicks (Birmingham) 1986. BB 2-28 v NZ (Hove) 1986. **NWT:** HS 4. BB 2-27 v Suffolk (Hove) 1986. **BHC:** HS 42* v Kent (Hove) 1988. BB 2-29 v Surrey (Hove) 1988. **RAL:** HS 8*. BB 3-28 v Glos (Swindon) 1987.

SUSSEX 1988

RESULTS SUMMARY

	Place	Won	Lost	Tied	Drew	Aban
Britannic Assurance Championship	16th	3	11		8	
All First-class Matches		3	11		9	
Refuge Assurance League	14th	4	9	2		1
NatWest Bank Trophy	1st Round					
Benson and Hedges Cup	4th in Group C					

BRITANNIC ASSURANCE CHAMPIONSHIP AVERAGES

BATTING AND FIELDING

Cap		M	I	NO	HS	Runs	Avge	100	50	Ct/St
1979	P.W.G.Parker	20	39	5	124	1270	37.35	5	4	14
1986	A.P.Wells	22	41	5	120	1269	35.25	1	9	17
1981	I.J.Gould	18	30	4	82*	842	32.38	—	6	29
1982	C.M.Wells	22	39	4	109*	906	25.88	1	4	8
1982	A.C.S.Pigott	20	34	8	56	668	25.69	—	3	16
—	N.J.Lenham	17	31	2	74	721	24.86	—	3	7
1985	A.M.Green	15	28	2	68	607	23.34	—	4	10
1978	Imran Khan	4	6	1	55	116	23.20	—	1	—
—	R.I.Alikhan	9	18	0	98	400	22.22	—	3	8
—	M.P.Speight	7	13	0	58	258	19.84	—	2	5
—	P.Moores	14	24	2	97*	395	17.95	—	1	30/3
—	N.J.Falkner	7	14	0	55	232	16.57	—	1	4
—	M.W.Pringle	4	6	0	35	90	15.00	—	—	1
—	A.R.Clarke	20	31	8	68	336	14.60	—	1	5
—	S.J.S.Kimber	4	7	3	32*	54	13.50	—	—	2
—	R.A.Bunting	16	20	4	17*	92	5.75	—	—	2
—	A.M.Babington	18	25	8	12	85	5.00	—	—	7

Also batted: P.A.W.Heseltine (2 matches) 6, 8; D.K.Standing (2 matches) 0, 9, 4. P.W.Threlfall (1 match) did not bat.

BOWLING

	O	M	R	W	Avge	Best	5 wI	10 wM
Imran Khan	109.3	26	255	13	19.61	5-50	1	—
A.C.S.Pigott	627	108	2078	74	28.08	6-100	2	—
R.A.Bunting	351	66	1088	36	30.22	5-44	2	—
A.M.Babington	514.5	108	1496	48	31.16	4-66	—	—
C.M.Wells	495.4	109	1359	42	32.35	4-43	—	—
A.R.Clarke	577	153	1481	42	35.26	5-60	2	—
A.M.Green	148.5	39	387	10	38.70	6-82	1	—

Also bowled: R.I.Alikhan 0.3-0-7-0; I.J.Gould 21-2-84-2; P.A.W.Heseltine 28-5-106-1; S.J.S.Kimber 83-19-272-7; N.J.Lenham 19.5-2-60-3; P.Moores 1-0-6-0; P.W.G.Parker 1-0-1-1; M.W.Pringle 98-19-323-6; M.P.Speight 0.3-0-2-1; P.W.Threlfall 12-3-31-0; A.P.Wells 5-1-11-0.

The First-Class Averages (pp 161-175) give the records of Sussex players in all first-class county matches (their other opponents being the West Indians), with the exception of Imran Khan, whose full county figures are as above, and:
   C.M.Wells 23-40-4-109*-907-25.19-1-4-8ct. 524.4-116-1429-43-33.23-4/43.

SUSSEX RECORDS

FIRST-CLASS CRICKET

Highest Total	For	705-8d		v Surrey	Hastings	1902
	V	726		by Notts	Nottingham	1895
Lowest Total	For	⎰ 19		v Surrey	Godalming	1830
		⎱ 19		v Notts	Hove	1873
	V	18		by Kent	Gravesend	1867
Highest Innings	For	333	K.S.Duleepsinhji	v Northants	Hove	1930
	V	322	E.Paynter	for Lancashire	Hove	1937

Highest Partnerships
Wkt

1st	490	E.H.Bowley/J.G.Langridge	v Middlesex	Hove	1933
2nd	385	E.H.Bowley/M.W.Tate	v Northants	Hove	1921
3rd	298	K.S.Ranjitsinhji/E.H.Killick	v Lancashire	Hove	1901
4th	326*	J.Langridge/G.Cox	v Yorkshire	Leeds	1949
5th	297	J.H.Parks/H.W.Parks	v Hampshire	Portsmouth	1937
6th	255	K.S.Duleepsinhji/M.W.Tate	v Northants	Hove	1930
7th	344	K.S.Ranjitsinhji/W.Newham	v Essex	Leyton	1902
8th	229*	C.L.A.Smith/G.Brann	v Kent	Hove	1902
9th	178	H.W.Parks/A.F.Wensley	v Derbyshire	Horsham	1930
10th	156	G.R.Cox/H.R.Butt	v Cambridge U	Cambridge	1908

Best Bowling	For	10-48	C.H.G.Bland	v Kent	Tonbridge	1899
(Innings)	V	9-11	A.P.Freeman	for Kent	Hove	1922
Best Bowling	For	17-106	G.R.Cox	v Warwicks	Horsham	1926
(Match)	V	17-67	A.P.Freeman	for Kent	Hove	1922

Most Runs – Season	2,850	J.G.Langridge	(av 64.77)	1949
Most Runs – Career	34,152	J.G.Langridge	(av 37.69)	1928-1955
Most 100s – Season	12	J.G.Langridge		1949
Most 100s – Career	76	J.G.Langridge		1928-1955
Most Wkts – Season	198	M.W.Tate	(av 13.47)	1925
Most Wkts – Career	2,211	M.W.Tate	(av 17.41)	1912-1937

LIMITED-OVERS CRICKET

Highest Total	NWT	314-7		v Kent	Tunbridge W	1963
	BHC	305-6		v Kent	Hove	1982
	RAL	293-4		v Worcs	Horsham	1980
Lowest Total	NWT	49		v Derbyshire	Chesterfield	1969
	BHC	60		v Middlesex	Hove	1978
	RAL	61		v Derbyshire	Derby	1978
Highest Innings	NWT	141*	G.D.Mendis	v Warwicks	Hove	1980
	BHC	117	R.D.V.Knight	v Surrey	The Oval	1977
	RAL	129	A.W.Greig	v Yorkshire	Scarborough	1976
Best Bowling	NWT	6-30	D.L.Bates	v Glos	Hove	1968
	BHC	5-8	Imran Khan	v Northants	Northampton	1978
	RAL	7-41	A.N.Jones	v Notts	Nottingham	1986

WARWICKSHIRE

Formation of Present Club: 8 April 1882
Substantial Reorganisation: 19 January 1884.
Colours: Dark Blue, Gold and Silver
Badge: Bear and Ragged Staff
Championships: (3) 1911, 1951, 1972
NatWest Trophy/Gillette Cup Winners: (2) 1966, 1968
Benson and Hedges Cup Winners: (0) Finalists 1984
Sunday League Champions: (1) 1980
Match Awards: NWT 33; BHC 39

Secretary: D.M.W.Heath, County Ground, Edgbaston, Birmingham, B5 7QU
Captain: T.A.Lloyd
Scorer: A.Davies (home) and S.P.Austin (away)
Cricketcall: ☎ 0898 1214 56
Benefit 1989: none

ASIF DIN, Mohamed (Ladywood CS, Birmingham), b Kampala, Uganda 21 Sep 1960. 5'9½". RHB, LB. Debut 1981. Cap 1987. 1000 (2); most – 1425 (1988). HS 158* v CU (Cambridge) 1988. BB 5-100 v Glam (Birmingham) 1982. NWT: HS 45 v Surrey (Lord's) 1982. BHC: HS 107 v Scotland (Birmingham) 1988. BB 1-26. RAL: HS 108* v Essex (Chelmsford) 1986. BB 1-11.

BANKS, David Andrew (Pensnett SM; Dudley TC), b Pensnett, Staffs 11 Jan 1961. RHB, RM. Worcestershire 1983-85. Warwickshire debut 1988. Staffordshire 1986-88. HS 100 Worcs v OU (Oxford) 1984. Warwicks HS 61 v SL (Birmingham) 1988. Award: NWT 1. NWT: HS 62* and BB 2-49 Staffs v Surrey (Burton) 1988. RAL: HS 51* v Derbys (Derby) 1988.

BENJAMIN, Joseph Emmanuel (Cayon HS, St Kitts; Mount Pleasant S, Highgate, Birmingham), b Christ Church, St Kitts 2 Feb 1961. 6'2". RHB, RMF. Debut 1988 (did not bat). Staffordshire 1986-88. NWT: HS 19 Staffs v Glam (Stone) 1986.

DONALD, Allan Anthony (Grey College HS), b Bloemfontein, SA 20 Oct 1966. 6'2". RHB, RFM. OFS 1985-88. Warwickshire debut 1987. HS 37* v Sussex (Nuneaton) 1987. BB 8-37 OFS v Transvaal (Johannesburg) 1986-87. Warwicks BB 6-74 v Essex (Chelmsford) 1987. NWT: BB 5-24 v Staffs (Burton) 1987. BHC: HS 0. BB 4-28 v Scotland (Perth) 1987. RAL: HS 18* v Middx (Lord's) 1988. BB 3-22 v Somerset (Bath) 1987.

GREEN, Simon James (Old Swinford Hospital S), b Bloxwich, Staffs 19 Mar 1970. 6'2". RHB, LM. Debut 1988. HS 28 v Lancs (Nuneaton) 1988. NWT: HS 1. RAL: HS 10* v Kent (Birmingham) 1988.

HOLLOWAY, Piran Christopher Laity (Millfield S; Taunton S), b Helston, Cornwall 1 Oct 1970. 5'8". LHB, WK. Debut 1988. HS 16 v Glam (Birmingham) 1988. RAL: HS 13 v Worcs (Worcester) 1988.

HUMPAGE, Geoffrey William (Golden Hillock CS), b Sparkhill, Birmingham 24 Apr 1954. 5'9". RHB, WK, RM. Debut 1974. Cap 1976. Benefit 1987. OFS 1981-82. Wisden 1984. LOI: 3. Tour: SA 1981-82 (SAB). 1000 runs (10); most – 1891 (1984). A.I.Kallicharran. BB 2-13 v Glos (Birmingham) 1980. Awards: NWT 2; BHC 2. NWT: HS 77 v Shropshire (Birmingham) 1984. BHC: HS 100* v Scotland (Birmingham) 1984. BB 2-43 v Worcs (Worcester) 1980. RAL: HS 109* v Glos (Birmingham) 1984. BB 4-53 v Glos (Moreton) 1979.

KALLICHARRAN, Alvin Isaac (Port Mourant CS), b Paidama, British Guiana 21 Mar 1949. Brother of D.I. (Trinidad). 5'4". LHB, OB. Guyana 1966-81. Warwickshire debut 1971. Cap 1972. Benefit 1983. Queensland 1977-78. Transvaal 1981-84. OFS 1984-88 (capt 1984-85). Wisden 1982. **Tests** (WI): 66 (1971-72 to 1980-81, 9 as captain); scored 100* and 101 in first two innings (v NZ); HS 187 v Ind (Bombay) 1979-80; BB 2-16 v NZ (Christchurch) 1979-80. LOI (WI): 31. Tours (WI): Eng 1973, 1976, 1980; Aus 1975-76, 1979-80; SA (WI XI) 1982-83, 1983-84; NZ 1979-80; Ind/SL 1974-75, 1978-79 (capt); Pak 1973-74 (RW), 1974-75, 1980-81. 1000 runs (12+1); most – 2301 (1984). Shared record English 4th-wkt stand of 470 with G.W.Humpage v Lancs (Southport) 1982. HS 243* v Glam (Birmingham) 1983. BB 5-45 Transvaal v W Province (Cape Town) 1983-82. Warwicks BB 4-48 v Derbys (Birmingham) 1978. Awards: NWT 4; BHC 4. **NWT**: HS 206 and BB 6-32 v Oxfordshire (Birmingham) 1984. **BHC**: HS 122* v Northants (Northampton) 1984. **RAL**: HS 102* v Notts (Birmingham) 1981. BB 3-32 v Lancs (Birmingham) 1985.

LLOYD, Timothy Andrew (Oswestry HS; Dorset CHE), b Oswestry, Shropshire 5 Nov 1956. 5'10". LHB, RM/OB. Debut 1977. Cap 1980. Captain 1988-. OFS 1978-80. Shropshire 1975. **Tests**: 1 (1984); HS 10* (rtd hurt) v WI (Birmingham). LOI: 3. Tour: Zim 1984-85 (Eng Co). 1000 runs (7); most – 1673 (1983). HS 208* v Glos (Birmingham) 1983. BB 3-62 v Surrey (Birmingham) 1985. Awards: NWT 2; BHC 2. **NWT**: HS 121 v Cambs (Birmingham) 1988. BB 1-4. **BHC**: HS 137* v Lancs (Birmingham) 1985. **RAL**: HS 90 v Kent (Birmingham) 1980. BB 1-42.

MERRICK, Tyrone Anthony (All Saints S, Antigua), b St John's, Antigua 10 Jun 1963. 6'1". RHB, RFM. Leeward Is 1982-88. Warwicks debut 1987. Cap 1988. Tour (WI B): Zim 1986-87. Hat-trick 1988. HS 74* v Glos (Birmingham) 1987. BB 7-45 (13-115 match) v Lancs (Birmingham) 1987. **NWT**: HS 13 v Cambs (Birmingham) 1988. BB 2-36 v Kent (Canterbury) 1988. **BHC**: HS 13* v Yorks (Birmingham) 1987. BB 4-24 v Leics (Leicester) 1988. **RAL**: HS 59 v Northants (Birmingham) 1987. BB 3-29 v Glos (Bristol) 1987.

MOLES, Andrew James (Finham Park CS; Butts CHE), b Solihull 12 Feb 1961. 5'10". RHB, RM. Debut 1986. Cap 1987. GW 1986-88. 1000 runs (1): 1431 (1987). HS 200* GW v N Transvaal B (Kimberley) 1987-88. Warwicks HS 151 v Kent (Birmingham) 1987. BB 3-21 v OU (Oxford) 1987. Awards: NWT 1; BHC 1. **NWT**: HS 127 v Bucks (Birmingham) 1987. **BHC**: HS 72 v Scotland (Perth) 1987. BB 1-11. **RAL**: HS 85 v Glos (Birmingham) 1986. BB 2-24 v Worcs (Worcester) 1987.

MUNTON, Timothy Alan (Sarson HS; King Edward VII Upper S), b Melton Mowbray, Leics 30 Jul 1965. 6'5". RHB, RMF. Debut 1985. HS 38 v Yorks (Scarborough) 1987. BB 6-21 v Worcs (Birmingham) 1988. **NWT**: HS 0*. BB 2-22 v Bucks (Birmingham) 1987. **BHC**: HS 6*. BB 2-25 v Minor C (Walsall) 1986. **RAL**: HS 7*. BB 3-32 v Glam (Swansea) 1987.

PIERSON, Adrian Roger Kirshaw (Kent C, Canterbury; Hatfield Polytechnic), b Enfield, Middx 21 Jul 1963. 6'4". RHB, OB. Debut 1985. HS 42* v Northants (Northampton) 1986. BB 3-33 v Worcs (Birmingham) 1988. Award: BHC 1. **NWT**: HS 1*. **BHC**: HS 11 v Minor C (Walsall) 1986. BB 3-34 v Lancs (Birmingham) 1988. **RAL**: HS 21* v Hants (Birmingham) 1987. BB 3-21 v Leics (Birmingham) 1988.

RATCLIFFE, Jason David (Sharman's Cross SS; Solihull SFC), b Solihull 19 Jun 1969. Son of D.P. (Warwicks 1957-58). 6'4". RHB, RM. Debut 1988. HS 16 v Sussex (Hove) 1988 (on debut).

REEVE, Dermot Alexander (King George V S, Kowloon), b Kowloon, Hong Kong 2 Apr 1963. 6'0". RHB, RMF. Sussex 1983-87 (cap 1986). Warwickshire debut 1988. Hong Kong 1982 (ICC Trophy). HS 119 Sussex v Surrey (Guildford) 1984. Warwicks HS 103 v Northants (Northampton) 1988. BB 7-37 Sussex v Lancs (Lytham) 1987. Warwicks BB 4-50 v Yorks (Birmingham) 1988. Awards: NWT 2. **NWT:** HS 26* Sussex v Glos (Hove) 1987. BB 4-20 Sussex v Lancs (Lord's) 1986. **BHC:** HS 30* and BB 4-42 Sussex v Kent (Canterbury) 1987. **RAL:** HS 69 v Notts (Birmingham) 1988. BB 5-23 v Essex (Birmingham) 1988.

SMALL, Gladstone Cleophas (Moseley S; Hall Green TC), b St George, Barbados 18 Oct 1961. 5'11". RHB, RFM. Debut 1979-80 (DHR XI in NZ). Warwickshire debut 1980. Cap 1982. S Australia 1985-86. **Tests:** 5 (1986 to 1988); HS 21* and BB 5-48 v Aus (Melbourne) 1986-87. LOI: 25. Tours: Aus 1986-87; NZ 1979-80 (DHR); Pak 1981-82 (Int XI). HS 70 v Lancs (Manchester) 1988. BB 7-15 v Notts (Birmingham) 1988. **NWT:** HS 33 v Surrey (Lord's) 1982. BB 3-22 v Glam (Cardiff) 1982. **BHC:** HS 19* v Yorks (Birmingham) 1981. BB 3-41 v Leics (Leicester) 1984. **RAL:** HS 40* v Essex (Ilford) 1984. BB 5-29 v Surrey (Birmingham) 1980.

SMITH, Neil Michael Knight (Warwick S), b Birmingham 27 Jul 1967. Son of M.J.K.Smith (Leics, Warwicks and England). 6'0". RHB, OB. Debut 1987. HS 23 v Notts (Worksop) 1987, also 23 and BB 2-73 v Lancs (Southport) 1987. **RAL:** HS 22 and BB 1-30 v Sussex (Hove) 1987.

SMITH, Paul Andrew (Heaton GS), b Jesmond, Newcastle upon Tyne 15 Apr 1964. Son of K.D. sr (Leics 1950-51) and brother of K.D. jr (Warwicks 1973-85). 6'2". RHB, RFM. Debut 1982. Cap 1986. 1000 runs (2); most 1508 (1986). HS 119 v Worcs (Birmingham) 1986. BB 4-25 v Lancs (Birmingham) 1985. **NWT:** HS 79 v Durham (Birmingham) 1986. BB 3-10 v Shropshire (Birmingham) 1984. **BHC:** HS 43 v Derbys (Derby) 1988. BB 2-23 v Lancs (Manchester) 1987. **RAL:** HS 56 v Notts (Birmingham) 1987. BB 4-23 v Notts (Birmingham) 1983.

THORNE, David Anthony (Coventry S; Keble C, OU), b Coventry 12 Dec 1964. 5'11". RHB, LM. Warwickshire debut 1983. Oxford U 1984-86 (blue 1984-85-86; captain 1986). HS 124 OU v Zim (Oxford) 1985. Warwicks HS 76 v Worcs (Worcester) 1988. BB 5-39 OU v CU (Lord's) 1984. Warwicks BB 1-21. **NWT:** HS 21 v Essex (Birmingham) 1986. **BHC:** HS 36* Comb Us v Middx (Lord's) 1986. BB 1-67. **RAL:** HS 59* v Derbys (Derby) 1988. BB 3-48 v Kent (Canterbury) 1985.

NEWCOMERS

CHAGAR, Onkar (Boldmere SS, Sutton Coldfield), b Uganda 27 Mar 1970. 5'8". RHB, RM.

EARL, Robert David Oliver (Framlingham C; W London IHE), b Luton, Beds 1 Oct 1967. 6'4". RHB, SLA. Bedfordshire 1986-88.

PIPER, Keith John b Leicester 18 Dec 1969. 5'6". RHB, WK.

STEER, Ian Gary Samuel (St Edmund Campion S), b Aston, Birmingham 17 Aug 1970. 5'7". RHB, RM.

TWOSE, Roger G. b Torquay 17 Apr 1968. MCC staff. **NWT:** HS 56 and BB 1-48 Devon v Notts (Torquay) 1988.

WELCH, G. b Durham 21 Mar 1972. RHB, RM.

WILLIAMSON, Gareth Joel Peter Barkass (Alderbrook S, Solihull), b Stockton-on-Tees, Co Durham 18 Jul 1970. Son of J.G. (Northants 1959-62). 6'1". RHB, RM.

DEPARTURES – see page 152

WARWICKSHIRE 1988

RESULTS SUMMARY

	Place	Won	Lost	Drew	Abandoned
Britannic Assurance Championship	6th	6	8	8	
All First-class Matches		6	8	10	
Refuge Assurance League	10th	6	8		2
NatWest Bank Trophy	2nd Round				
Benson and Hedges Cup	Quarter-Finalist				

BRITANNIC ASSURANCE CHAMPIONSHIP AVERAGES

BATTING AND FIELDING

Cap		M	I	NO	HS	Runs	Avge	100	50	Ct/St
1980	T.A.Lloyd	22	41	2	160*	1439	36.89	4	3	7
1987	Asif Din	21	39	3	131	1208	33.55	1	7	18
1987	A.J.Moles	17	30	2	115	873	31.17	1	4	10
1982	G.C.Small	17	26	5	70	521	24.80	—	3	5
—	D.A.Thorne	14	24	1	76	561	24.39	—	4	17
1986	P.A.Smith	15	27	4	84*	542	23.56	—	3	3
—	D.A.Reeve	16	23	3	103	431	21.55	1	—	11
1972	A.I.Kallicharran	8	14	0	63	301	21.50	—	2	3
1987	G.J.Parsons	8	12	3	52	174	19.33	—	1	1
—	D.A.Banks	6	8	1	47	134	19.14	—	—	4
—	G.A.Tedstone	4	8	0	50	151	18.87	—	1	7/1
—	A.C.Storie	8	16	2	68	233	16.64	—	1	6
1976	G.W.Humpage	15	25	1	80	397	16.54	—	3	52/1
—	S.D.Myles	3	6	0	39	90	15.00	—	—	—
1988	T.A.Merrick	15	21	3	34	256	14.22	—	—	5
—	A.R.K.Pierson	8	12	7	18*	57	11.40	—	—	1
—	A.A.Donald	6	10	3	29	74	10.57	—	—	4
—	T.A.Munton	16	22	7	24*	131	8.73	—	—	2
—	P.C.L.Holloway	3	5	0	16	40	8.00	—	—	8/1
—	J.D.Ratcliffe	2	4	0	16	31	7.75	—	—	2
1983	N.Gifford	17	25	11	23*	104	7.42	—	—	3

Also batted: S.J.Green (1 match) 0, 28.

BOWLING

	O	M	R	W	Avge	Best	5 wI	10 wM
G.C.Small	550.2	146	1380	75	18.40	7-15	8	2
A.A.Donald	167.4	36	507	26	19.50	5-57	1	—
T.A.Merrick	468	104	1416	64	22.12	6-29	5	1
T.A.Munton	425.1	126	1047	46	22.76	6-21	2	—
P.A.Smith	157.3	20	525	22	23.86	3-7	—	—
G.J.Parsons	203	61	513	21	24.42	3-17	—	—
D.A.Reeve	292	71	750	24	31.25	4-50	—	—
N.Gifford	422.1	120	971	31	31.32	3-66	—	—

Also bowled: Asif Din 91-16-326-6; G.W.Humpage 3-0-10-0; T.A.Lloyd 31-1-208-2; S.D.Myles 6-0-28-0, A.R.K.Pierson 148.5-35-431-9; A.C.Storie 6-2-20-0; D.A.Thorne 3-0-11-0.

The First-Class Averages (pp 161-175) give the records of Warwickshire players in all first-class county matches (their other opponents being the Sri Lankans and Cambridge U.), with the exception of:
   G.C.Small 18-26-5-70-521-24.80-0-3-7ct. 654.2-152-1401-76-18.43-7/15-8-2.

WARWICKSHIRE RECORDS

FIRST-CLASS CRICKET

Highest Total	For	657-6d		v Hampshire	Birmingham	1899
	V	887		by Yorkshire	Birmingham	1896
Lowest Total	For	16		v Kent	Tonbridge	1913
	V	15		by Hampshire	Birmingham	1922
Highest Innings	For	305*	F.R.Foster	v Worcs	Dudley	1914
	V	322	I.V.A.Richards	for Somerset	Taunton	1985

Highest Partnerships
Wkt

1st	377*	N.F.Horner/K.Ibadulla		v Surrey	The Oval	1960
2nd	465*	J.A.Jameson/R.B.Kanhai		v Glos	Birmingham	1974
3rd	327	S.P.Kinneir/W.G.Quaife		v Lancashire	Birmingham	1901
4th	470	A.I.Kallicharran/G.W.Humpage		v Lancashire	Southport	1982
5th	268	W.Quaife/W.G.Quaife		v Essex	Leyton	1900
6th	220	H.E.Dollery/J.Buckingham		v Derbyshire	Derby	1938
7th	250	H.E.Dollery/J.S.Ord		v Kent	Maidstone	1953
8th	228	A.J.W.Croom/R.E.S.Wyatt		v Worcs	Dudley	1925
9th	154	G.W.Stephens/A.J.W.Croom		v Derbyshire	Birmingham	1925
10th	128	F.R.Santall/W.Sanders		v Yorkshire	Birmingham	1930

Best Bowling	For	10-41	J.D.Bannister	v Comb Servs	Birmingham	1959
(Innings)	V	10-36	H.Verity	for Yorkshire	Leeds	1931
Best Bowling	For	15-76	S.Hargreave	v Surrey	The Oval	1903
(Match)	V	17-92	A.P.Freeman	for Kent	Folkestone	1932
Most Runs – Season		2,417	M.J.K.Smith	(av 60.42)		1959
Most Runs – Career		35,146	D.L.Amiss	(av 41.64)		1960-1987
Most 100s – Season		9	A.I.Kallicharran			1984
Most 100s – Career		78	D.L.Amiss			1960-1987
Most Wkts – Season		180	W.E.Hollies	(av 15.13)		1946
Most Wkts – Career		2,201	W.E.Hollies	(av 20.45)		1932-1957

LIMITED-OVERS CRICKET

Highest Total	NWT	392-5		v Oxfordshire	Birmingham	1984
	BHC	308-4		v Scotland	Birmingham	1988
	RAL	301-6		v Essex	Colchester	1982
Lowest Total	NWT	109		v Kent	Canterbury	1971
	BHC	96		v Leics	Leicester	1972
	RAL	65		v Kent	Maidstone	1979
Highest Innings	NWT	206	A.I.Kallicharran	v Oxfordshire	Birmingham	1984
	BHC	137*	T.A.Lloyd	v Lancashire	Birmingham	1985
	RAL	123*	J.A.Jameson	v Notts	Nottingham	1973
Best Bowling	NWT	{6-32	K.Ibadulla	v Hampshire	Birmingham	1965
		{6-32	A.I.Kallicharran	v Oxfordshire	Birmingham	1984
	BHC	7-32	R.G.D.Willis	v Yorkshire	Birmingham	1981
	RAL	6-20	N.Gifford	v Northants	Birmingham	1985

WORCESTERSHIRE

Formation of Present Club: 11 March 1865
Colours: Dark Green and Black
Badge: Shield Argent bearing Fess between Three Pears Sable
Championships: (4) 1964, 1965, 1974, 1988
NatWest Trophy/Gillette Cup Finalists: (3) 1963, 1966, 1988
Benson and Hedges Cup Finalists: (2) 1973, 1976
Sunday League Champions: (3) 1971, 1987, 1988
Match Awards: NWT 29; BHC 40

Secretary: Rev M.D.Vockins, County Ground, New Road, Worcester, WR2 4QQ
Captain: P.A.Neale
Scorer: J.W.Sewter
Cricketcall: ☎ 0898 1214 55
Benefit 1989: A.P.Pridgeon

BENT, Paul (Worcester RGS), b Worcester 1 May 1965. 6'0". RHB, OB. Debut 1985. MCC staff. HS 50 v Yorks (Worcester) 1988. **RAL:** HS 36 v Sussex (Worcester) 1988.

BOTHAM, Ian Terence (Buckler's Mead SS, Yeovil), b Heswall, Cheshire 24 Nov 1955. 6'1". RHB, RFM. Somerset 1974-86 (cap 1976; captain 1984-85; benefit 1984). Worcestershire debut/cap 1987. Queensland 1987-88. Wisden 1977. YC 1977. Tests: 94 (1977 to 1987, 12 as captain); HS 208 v India (Oval) 1982; BB 8-34 v Pak (Lord's) 1978. LOI: 95. Tours: Aus 1978-79, 1979-80, 1982-83, 1986-87; WI 1980-81 (capt), 1985-86; NZ 1977-78, 1983-84; Ind 1979-80, 1981-82; Pak 1977-78, 1983-84; SL 1981-82. 1000 runs (4); most – 1530 (1985). 100 wickets (1): 100 (1978). Hit 80 sixes 1985 (f-c record). Shared record Somerset 4th- and 8th-wkt stands of 310 (P.W.Denning) and 172 (I.V.A.Richards) respectively. Hat-trick 1978 (MCC). HS 228 Somerset v Glos (Taunton) 1980. Worcs HS 126* v Somerset (Taunton) 1987. BB 8-34 (Tests). Worcs BB 3-51 v Essex (Worcester) 1987. Awards: NWT 2; BHC 6. **NWT:** HS 101 v Devon (Worcester) 1987. BB 4-20 Somerset v Sussex (Hove) 1983. **BHC:** HS 126* Somerset v Glam (Taunton) 1986. BB 5-41 v Yorks (Worcester) 1988. **RAL:** HS 175* Somerset v Northants (Wellingborough) 1986. BB 5-27 v Glos (Gloucester) 1987.

CURTIS, Timothy Stephen (Worcester RGS; Durham U; Magdalene C, Cambridge), b Chislehurst, Kent 15 Jan 1960. 5'11". RHB, LB. Debut 1979. Cap 1984. Cambridge U 1983 (blue). Tests: 2 (1988), HS 30 v WI (Oval). 1000 runs (5); most 1601 (1987). Shared record Worcs 2nd-wkt stand of 287* with G.A.Hick v Glam (Neath) 1986. HS 153 v Somerset (Worcester) 1986. BB 2-58 CU v Notts (Cambridge) 1983. Awards: NWT 4; BHC 2. **NWT:** HS 120 v Notts (Nottingham) 1988. BB 1-6. **BHC:** HS 78 v Surrey (Oval) 1987. **RAL:** HS 102 v Glam (Worcester) 1986.

DILLEY, Graham Roy (Dartford West SS), b Dartford 18 May 1959. 6'3". LHB, RF. Kent 1977-86 (cap 1980). Worcestershire debut/cap 1987. Natal 1985-86. YC 1980. Tests: 39 (1979-80 to 1988); HS 56 v Aus (Leeds) 1981; BB 6-38 v NZ (Christchurch) 1987-88. LOI: 36. Tours: Aus 1979-80, 1986-87, 1987-88; WI 1980-81; NZ 1983-84, 1987-88; Ind 1979-80, 1981-82; Pak 1983-84, 1987-88; SL 1981-82. 2 hat-tricks (Kent): 1985, 1987. HS 81 Kent v Northants (Northampton) 1979. Worcs HS 36 v Glos (Bristol) 1988. BB 7-63 Natal v Transvaal (Johannesburg) 1985-86. Worcs BB 6-43 v Leics (Worcester) 1987. Awards: NWT 1; BHC 1. **NWT:** HS 25 v Essex (Chelmsford) 1987. BB 5-29 Kent v Scotland 1986 and Worcs v Middx 1988. **BHC:** HS 37* Kent v Hants (Canterbury) 1983. BB 4-14 Kent v Comb

140

Us (Canterbury) 1981. **RAL:** HS 33 Kent v Northants (Northampton) 1982. BB 4-20 Kent v Glos (Canterbury) 1980.

D'OLIVEIRA, Damian Basil (Blessed Edward Oldcorne SS), b Cape Town, SA 19 Oct 1960. Son of B.L. (Worcs and England 1964-80). 5'9". RHB, OB. Debut 1982. Cap 1985. Tour: Zim 1984-85 (Eng Co). 1000 runs (3); most 1244 (1985). HS 146* v Glos (Bristol) 1986. BB 2-17 v Glos (Bristol) 1986. **Awards:** NWT 2; BHC 2. **NWT:** HS 99 v Oxon (Worcester) 1986. BB 2-28 v Notts (Worcester) 1983. **BHC:** HS 66 v Yorks (Leeds) 1986. BB 3-12 v Scotland (Glasgow) 1986. **RAL:** HS 103 v Surrey (Worcester) 1985. BB 3-23 v Derbys (Derby) 1983.

ELLCOCK, Ricardo McDonald (Combermere S, Barbados; Malvern C), b Bridgetown, Barbados 17 Jun 1965. 5'11". RHB, RFM. Debut 1982. Barbados 1983-84. HS 45* v Essex (Worcester) 1984. BB 4-34 v Glam (Worcester) 1984. **NWT:** HS 6. BB 3-49 v Notts (Worcester) 1983. **BHC:** HS 12 and 2-45 v Notts (Nottingham) 1984. **RAL:** HS 5*. BB 4-43 v Kent (Canterbury) 1983.

HICK, Graeme Ashley (Prince Edward HS, Salisbury), b Salisbury, Rhodesia 23 May 1966. 6'3". RHB, OB. Zimbabwe 1983-8?. Worcestershire debut 1984. Cap 1986. Wisden 1986. N Districts 1987-88. Tours (2nd): Eng 1985; SL 1983-84. 1000 runs (4); most 2713 (1988). Youngest to score 2000 (1986). 1019 runs before June 1988. Shares in 4 record Worcs stands: 287* (2nd) with T.S.Curtis; 265 (6th) with S.J.Rhodes; 205 (7th) with P.J.Newport; and 177* (8th) with R.K.Illingworth. HS 405* (Worcs record and 2nd-highest in UK f-c matches) v Somerset (Taunton) 1988. BB 4-31 v Lancs (Manchester) 1987. **Awards:** NWT 2; BHC 4. **NWT:** HS 172* v Devon (Worcester) 1987. BB 4-54 v Hants (Worcester) 1988. **BHC:** HS 103* v Notts and v Northants (Worcester) 1986. BB 2-25 v Lancs (Worcester) 1986. **RAL:** HS 111 v Yorks (Worcester) 1988. BB 4-42 v Sussex (Worcester) 1988.

ILLINGWORTH, Richard Keith (Salts GS), b Bradford 23 Aug 1963. 5'11". RHB, SLA. Debut 1982. Cap 1986. Shared record Worcs 8th-wkt stand of 177* with G.A.Hick v Somerset (Taunton) 1988. HS 120* v Warwicks (Worcester) 1987. BB 7-50 v OU (Oxford) 1985. **NWT:** HS 22 v Northants (Northampton) 1984. BB 4-20 v Devon (Worcester) 1987. **BHC:** HS 17* v Scotland (Glasgow) 1986. BB 4-36 v Yorks (Bradford) 1985. **RAL:** HS 21 v Middx (Worcester) 1982. BB 5-24 v Somerset (Worcester) 1983.

LAMPITT, Stuart Richard (Kingswinford S; Dudley TC), b Wolverhampton 29 Jul 1966. 5'11". RHB, RM. Debut 1985. HS 24 v Hants (Worcester) 1987. BB 2-37 v Middx (Lord's) 1987. **RAL:** HS 12* and BB 2-64 v Glam (Swansea) 1987.

LEATHERDALE, David Anthony (Pudsey Grangefield S), b Bradford, Yorks 26 Nov 1967. 5'10½". RHB, RM. Debut 1988. HS 34* v Kent (Folkestone) 1988. BB 1-12. **NWT:** HS 43 v Hants (Worcester) 1988. **RAL:** HS 62* v Kent (Folkestone) 1988.

LORD, Gordon John (Warwick S; Durham U), b Edgbaston, Birmingham 25 Apr 1961. 5'10". RHB, SLA. Warwickshire 1983-86. Worcestershire debut 1988. HS 199 Warwicks v Yorks (Birmingham) 1985. Worcs HS 101 v Glos (Bristol) 1988. **NWT:** HS 0. **BHC:** HS 15 v Notts (Worcester) 1988. **RAL:** HS 103 Warwicks v Derbys (Birmingham) 1985.

McEWAN, Steven Michael (Worcester RGS), b Worcester 5 May 1962. 6'1". RHB, RFM. Debut 1985. HS 13* v OU (Oxford) 1985. BB 4-43 v Lancs (Worcester) 1988. **RAL:** HS 7*. BB 4-35 v Derbys (Worcester) 1986.

NEALE, Phillip Anthony (Frederick Gough CS; John Leggott SFC; Leeds U), b Scunthorpe, Lincs 5 Jun 1954. 5'11". RHB, RM. Debut 1975. Cap 1978. Captain 1982-. Benefit 1988. Lincolnshire 1972. Wisden 1988. 1000 runs (8); most – 1706

NEALE, P.A. (contd.)
(1984). HS 167 v Sussex (Kidderminster) 1988. BB 1-15. Awards: NWT 1; BHC 2.
NWT: HS 98 v Cumberland (Worcester) 1988. **BHC:** HS 128 v Lancs (Manchester 1980. **RAL:** HS 102 v Northants (Luton) 1982. BB 2-46 v Warwicks (Worcester) 1976.

NEWPORT, Philip John (High Wycombe RGS; Portsmouth Polytechnic), b High Wycombe, Bucks 11 Oct 1962. 6'3". RHB, RFM. Debut 1982. Cap 1986. Boland 1987-88. Buckinghamshire 1981-82. **Tests:** 1 (1988), HS 26 and BB 4-87 v SL (Lord's). Shared record Worcs 7th-wkt stand of 205 with G.A.Hick v Yorks (Worcester) 1988. HS 86 Boland v Transvaal B (Stellenbosch) 1987-88. Worcs HS 77* v Yorks (Worcester) 1988. BB 8-52 v Middx (Lord's) 1988. **NWT:** HS 25 v Northants (Northampton) 1988. BB 3-62 v Hants (Southampton) 1986. **BHC:** HS 15 v Lancs (Worcester) 1986. BB 5-22 v Warwicks (Birmingham) 1987. **RAL:** HS 26* v Leics (Leicester) 1987. BB 3-20 v Somerset (Taunton) 1984.

O'SHAUGHNESSY, Steven Joseph (Harper Green SS, Farnworth), b Bury 9 Sep 1961. 5'10½". RHB, RM. Lancashire 1980-87 (cap 1985). Worcestershire debut 1988. Scored 100 in 35 min to equal world record v Leics (Manchester) 1983. 1000 runs (1): 1167 (1984). HS 159* Lancs v Somerset (Bath) 1984. Worcs HS 44 v Notts (Worcester) 1988. BB 4-66 v Notts (Nottingham) 1982. Worcs BB 2-55 v Leics (Leicester) 1988. Awards: BHC 2. **NWT:** HS 62 Lancs v Surrey 1986 and v Hants 1988. BB 3-28 v Suffolk (Bury St Edmunds) 1985. **BHC:** HS 90 v Worcs (Worcester) 1985. BB 4-17 v Leics (Manchester) 1985. **RAL:** HS 101* v Leics (Leicester) 1984. BB 3-18 v Middx (Manchester) 1984.

PRIDGEON, Alan Paul (Summerhill SS, Kingswinford), b Wall Heath, Staffs 22 Feb 1954. 6'3". RHB, RMF. Debut 1972. Cap 1980. Benefit 1989. HS 67 v Warwicks (Worcester) 1984. BB 7-35 v OU (Oxford) 1976. **NWT:** HS 13* v Somerset (Taunton) 1980. BB 3-7 v Devon (Worcester) 1987. **BHC:** HS 13* v Leics (Worcester) 1982. BB 3-57 v Warwicks 1976 and v Yorks 1986. **RAL:** HS 17 v Kent (Worcester) 1982. BB 6-26 v Surrey (Worcester) 1978.

RADFORD, Neal Victor (Athlone BHS, Johannesburg), b Luanshya, N Rhodesia 7 Jun 1957. Brother of W.R. (OFS). 5'11". RHB, RFM. Transvaal 1978-88. Lancashire 1980-84. Worcestershire debut/cap 1985. Wisden 1985. **Tests:** 3 (1986); HS 12* v NZ (Lord's); BB 2-131 v Ind (Birmingham). LOI: 6. Tour: NZ 1987-88. 100 wickets (2); most – 109 (1987). HS 76* Lancs v Derbys (Blackpool) 1981. Worcs HS 65 v Notts (Worcester) 1988. BB 9-70 v Somerset (Worcester) 1986. **NWT:** HS 37 v Essex (Chelmsford) 1987. BB 3-20 Lancs v Middx 1981 and v Sussex 1986. **BHC:** HS 37* v Notts (Worcester) 1988. BB 4-25 v Northants (Northampton) 1988. **RAL:** HS 48* Lancs v Glam (Cardiff) 1981. BB 5-32 v Warwicks (Worcester) 1987.

RHODES, Steven John (Lapage Middle S; Carlton-Bolling S, Bradford), b Bradford 17 Jun 1964. Son of W.E. (Nottinghamshire 1961-64). 5'7". RHB, WK. Yorkshire 1981-84. Worcestershire debut 1985. Cap 1986. Tour: SL 1985-86 (Eng B). Shared record Worcs 6th-wkt stand of 265 with G.A.Hick v Somerset (Taunton) 1988. HS 108 v Derbys (Derby) 1988. Award: BHC 1. **NWT:** HS 32* v Hants (Southampton) 1986. **BHC:** HS 51* v Warwicks (Birmingham) 1987. **RAL:** HS 46 v Northants (Northampton) 1986.

WESTON, Martin John (Samuel Southall SS), b Worcester 8 Apr 1959. 6'1". RHB, RM. Debut 1979. Cap 1986. 1000 runs (1): 1061 (1984). HS 145* v Northants (Worcester) 1984. BB 4-24 v Warwicks (Birmingham) 1988. **NWT:** HS 45* v Cumberland (Worcester) 1986. BB 4-30 v Suffolk (Worcester) 1984. **BHC:** HS 56 v Scotland (Aberdeen) 1983. BB 2-27 v Yorks (Bradford) 1985. **RAL:** HS 109 v Somerset (Taunton) 1982. BB 4-11 v Hants (Worcester) 1984.

WORCESTERSHIRE 1988

RESULTS SUMMARY

	Place	Won	Lost	Drew	Abandoned
Britannic Assurance Championship	1st	10	3	9	
All First-class Matches		10	3	10	
Refuge Assurance League	1st	12	3		1
NatWest Bank Trophy	Finalist				
Benson and Hedges Cup	Quarter-Final				

BRITANNIC ASSURANCE CHAMPIONSHIP AVERAGES

BATTING AND FIELDING

Cap		M	I	NO	HS	Runs	Avge	100	50	Ct/St
1986	G.A.Hick	22	34	2	405*	2443	76.34	9	4	27
1984	T.S.Curtis	18	31	4	131	1155	42.77	2	6	19
1978	P.A.Neale	21	31	5	167	1036	39.84	4	2	8
—	G.J.Lord	19	32	2	101	862	28.73	1	4	4
1986	M.J.Weston	17	24	5	95*	514	27.05	—	3	14
1986	P.J.Newport	20	24	8	77*	421	26.31	—	1	8
1986	S.J.Rhodes	22	33	10	108	597	25.95	1	1	69/8
1986	R.K.Illingworth	22	22	4	60	404	22.44	—	2	18
1985	N.V.Radford	18	15	6	65	200	22.22	—	1	13
—	P.Bent	3	6	1	50	111	22.20	—	1	—
—	D.A.Leatherdale	10	15	1	34*	255	18.21	—	—	3
1985	D.B.D'Oliveira	8	11	1	37	132	13.20	—	—	6
1987	G.R.Dilley	9	8	1	36	89	12.71	—	—	1
—	R.M.Ellcock	4	4	1	13	27	9.00	—	—	1
—	S.J.O'Shaughnessy	10	17	0	44	133	7.82	—	—	5
1987	I.T.Botham	4	4	0	7	18	4.50	—	—	4
1980	A.P.Pridgeon	10	11	3	11	31	3.87	—	—	3

Also batted: S.M.McEwan (5 matches) 0*, 6 (1 ct).

BOWLING

	O	M	R	W	Avge	Best	5 wI	10 wM
P.J.Newport	544	117	1640	85	19.29	8-52	7	1
G.R.Dilley	251	44	695	34	20.44	5-46	3	—
R.K.Illingworth	578.4	184	1229	56	21.94	5-46	4	2
N.V.Radford	570.5	101	1770	71	24.92	7-73	3	—
M.J.Weston	120	31	316	12	26.33	4-24	—	—
G.A.Hick	204	43	642	21	30.57	4-114	—	—
A.P.Pridgeon	266.3	58	662	21	31.52	3-68	—	—

Also bowled: I.T.Botham 43-11-125-1; T.S.Curtis 14.5-1-74-1; R.M.Ellcock 81.1-8-328-7; D.A.Leatherdale 7-3-20-1; S.M.McEwan 79-7-289-8; P.A.Neale 14-1-62-0; S.J.O'Shaughnessy 34-3-152-4.

The First-Class Averages (pp 161-175) give the records of Worcestershire players in all first-class county matches (their other opponents being the West Indians), with the exception of G.R.Dilley, whose full county figures are as above, and:
The First-Class Averages (pp 161-175)

T.S.Curtis 19-32-4-131-1237-44.17-2-7-19ct. 14.5-1-74-1-74.00-1/53.
G.A.Hick 23-35-2-405*-2615-79.24-10-4-28ct. 204-43-642-21-30.57-4/114.
P.J.Newport 21-24-8-77*-421-26.31-0-1-8ct. 553-118-1680-86-19.53-8/52-7-1.

143

WORCESTERSHIRE RECORDS

FIRST-CLASS CRICKET

Highest Total	For	633		v Warwicks	Worcester	1906
	V	701-4d		by Leics	Worcester	1906
Lowest Total	For	24		v Yorkshire	Huddersfield	1903
	V	30		by Hampshire	Worcester	1903
Highest Innings	For	405*	G.A.Hick	v Somerset	Taunton	1988
	V	331*	J.D.B.Robertson	for Middlesex	Worcester	1949

Highest Partnerships
Wkt

1st	309	F.L.Bowley/H.K.Foster	v Derbyshire	Derby	1901
2nd	287*	T.S.Curtis/G.A.Hick	v Glamorgan	Neath	1986
3rd	314	M.J.Horton/T.W.Graveney	v Somerset	Worcester	1962
4th	281	J.A.Ormrod/Younus Ahmed	v Notts	Nottingham	1979
5th	393	E.G.Arnold/W.B.Burns	v Warwicks	Birmingham	1909
6th	265	G.A.Hick/S.J.Rhodes	v Somerset	Taunton	1988
7th	205	G.A.Hick/P.J.Newport	v Yorkshire	Worcester	1988
8th	177*	G.A.Hick/R.K.Illingworth	v Somerset	Taunton	1988
9th	181	J.A.Cuffe/R.D.Burrows	v Glos	Worcester	1907
10th	119	W.B.Burns/G.A.Wilson	v Somerset	Worcester	1906

Best Bowling	For	9-23	C.F.Root	v Lancashire	Worcester	1931
(Innings)	V	10-51	J.Mercer	for Glamorgan	Worcester	1936
Best Bowling	For	15-87	A.J.Conway	v Glos	Moreton-in-M	1914
(Match)	V	17-212	J.C.Clay	for Glamorgan	Swansea	1937

Most Runs – Season	2,654	H.H.I.Gibbons	(av 52.03)		1934
Most Runs – Career	33,490	D.Kenyon	(av 33.19)		1946-1967
Most 100s – Season	10	G.M.Turner			1970
	10	G.A.Hick			1988
Most 100s – Career	72	G.M.Turner			1967-1982
Most Wkts – Season	207	C.F.Root	(av 17.52)		1925
Most Wkts – Career	2,143	R.T.D.Perks	(av 23.73)		1930-1955

LIMITED-OVERS CRICKET

Highest Total	NWT	404-3		v Devon	Worcester	1987
	BHC	314-5		v Lancashire	Manchester	1980
	RAL	307-4		v Derbyshire	Worcester	1975
Lowest Total	NWT	98		v Durham	Chester-le-S	1968
	BHC	81		v Leics	Worcester	1983
	RAL	86		v Yorkshire	Leeds	1969
Highest Innings	NWT	172*	G.A.Hick	v Devon	Worcester	1987
	BHC	143*	G.M.Turner	v Warwicks	Birmingham	1976
	RAL	147	G.M.Turner	v Sussex	Horsham	1980
Best Bowling	NWT	6-14	J.A.Flavell	v Lancashire	Worcester	1963
	BHC	6-8	N.Gifford	v Minor C (S)	High Wycombe	1979
	RAL	6-26	A.P.Pridgeon	v Surrey	Worcester	1978

YORKSHIRE

Formation of Present Club: 8 January 1863
Substantial Reorganisation: 10 December 1891
Colours: Dark Blue, Light Blue and Gold
Badge: White Rose
Championships (since 1890): (29) 1893, 1896, 1898,
1900, 1901, 1902, 1905, 1908, 1912, 1919, 1922, 1923,
1924, 1925, 1931, 1932, 1933, 1935, 1937, 1938, 1939,
1946, 1959, 1960, 1962, 1963, 1966, 1967, 1968. **Joint:**
(1) 1949
NatWest Trophy/Gillette Cup Winners: (2) 1965, 1969
Benson and Hedges Cup Winners: (1) 1987
Sunday League Champions: (1) 1983
Match Awards: NWT 22; BHC 46

Secretary: J.Lister, Headingley Cricket Ground, Leeds, LS6 3BU
Captain: P.Carrick
Scorer: E.I.Lester (home) and J.T.Potter (away)
Cricketcall: ☎ 0898 1214 44
Benefit 1989: J.D.Love

BAIRSTOW, David Leslie (Hanson GS, Bradford), b Bradford 1 Sep 1951. 5'9½".
RHB, WK, RM. Debut 1970. Cap 1973. Captain 1984-86. Benefit 1982. GW
1976-78 (capt 1977-78). **Tests:** 4 (1979 to 1980-81); HS 59 v Ind (Oval) on debut.
LOI: 21. Tours: Aus 1978-79, 1979-80; WI 1980-81, 1986-87 (Yorks). 1000 runs (3);
most - 1181 (1985). HS 145 v Middx (Scarborough) 1980. BB 3-25 v MCC (Scarborough) 1987. Held 11 catches v Derbys (Scarborough) 1982 to equal world f-c
match record. Awards: NWT 1; BHC 6. **NWT:** HS 92 v Worcs (Leeds) 1982. **BHC:**
HS 103* v Derbys (Derby) 1981. **RAL:** HS 83* v Surrey (Oval) 1986.

BERRY, Philip John (Saltscar CS; Longlands CFE, Redcar), b Saltburn 28 Dec
1966. 6'0". RHB, OB. Debut 1986. HS 23* and B 2-35 v CU (Cambridge) 1988.

BLAKEY, Richard John (Rastrick GS), b Huddersfield 15 Jan 1967. 5'9". RHB,
WK. Debut 1985. Cap 1987. YC 1987. Tour: WI 1986-87 (Yorks). 1000 runs (1):
1361 (1987). HS 204* v Glos (Leeds) 1987. BB 1-68. **NWT:** HS 14 v Wilts
(Trowbridge) 1987. **BHC:** HS 58 v Lancs (Leeds) 1987. **RAL:** HS 40* v Glos
(Cheltenham) 1988.

BOOTH, Paul Antony (Hanley HS), b Huddersfield 5 Sep 1965. 5'10". LHB, SLA.
Debut 1982. HS 33* and BB 5-98 v Lancs (Manchester) 1988. **NWT:** HS 6*. **BHC:**
HS 1. BB 2-28 v Worcs (Bradford) 1985. **RAL:** BB 1-57.

BYAS, David (Scarborough C), b Kilham 26 Aug 1963. 6'4". LHB, RM. Debut
1986. HS 112 v Glos (Cheltenham) 1988. **BHC:** HS 2. **RAL:** HS 69* v Surrey
(Leeds) 1988.

CARRICK, Phillip (Bramley SS; Intake SS; Park Lane CPE), b Armley 16 Jul
1952. 5'11½". RHB, SLA. Debut 1970. Cap 1976. Captain 1987-. Benefit 1985. E
Province 1976-77. N Transvaal 1982-83. Tours: SA 1975-76 (DHR); WI 1986-87
(Yorks - capt); SL 1977-78 (DHR). HS 131* v Northants (Northampton) 1980. BB
8-33 v CU (Cambridge) 1973. Award: BHC 1. **NWT:** HS 54 v Sussex (Leeds) 1986.
BB 3-27 v Northants (Leeds) 1983. **BHC:** HS 53 v Warwicks (Leeds) 1985. BB 3-40
v Warwicks (Birmingham) 1984. **RAL:** HS 43* v Surrey (Oval) 1984. BB 4-13 v
Derbys (Bradford) 1983.

145

FLETCHER, Stuart David (Reins Wood SS), b Keighley 8 Jun 1964. 5'10". RHB, RMF. Debut 1983. Cap 1988. HS 28* v Kent (Tunbridge Wells) 1984. BB 8-58 v Essex (Sheffield) 1988. Award: NWT 1. **NWT:** HS 2*. BB 3-20 v Berks (Finchampstead) 1988. **BHC:** HS 1. BB 4-34 v Scotland (Glasgow) 1987. **RAL:** HS 8. BB 4-11 v Kent (Canterbury) 1988.

HARTLEY, Peter John (Greenhead GS; Bradford C), b Keighley 18 Apr 1960. 6'0". RHB, RMF. Warwickshire 1982. Yorkshire debut 1985. Cap 1987. Tour: WI 1986-87 (Yorks). HS 127* v Lancs (Manchester) 1988. BB 6-68 v Notts (Sheffield) 1986. Award: BHC 1. **NWT:** HS 23 and BB 3-47 v Sussex (Leeds) 1986. **BHC:** HS 29* v Notts (Nottingham) 1986. BB 5-43 v Scotland (Leeds) 1986. **RAL:** HS 35 v Derbys (Chesterfield) 1986. BB 4-27 v Glos (Cheltenham) 1988.

HARTLEY, Stuart Neil (Beckfoot GS, Bingley; Cannington HS, Perth, WA), b Shipley 18 Mar 1956. 6'0". RHB, RM. Debut 1978. Cap 1981. OFS 1981-83. HS 114 v Glos (Bradford) 1982. BB 4-51 v Surrey (Oval) 1985. Award: BHC 1. **NWT:** HS 69 v Somerset (Leeds) 1985. BB 1-41. **BHC:** HS 65* v Warwicks (Birmingham) 1984. BB 4-39 v Scotland (Perth) 1984. **RAL:** HS 83* v Lancs (Scarborough) 1987. BB 3-31 v Notts (Scarborough) 1980.

JARVIS, Paul William (Bydales CS, Marske), b Redcar 29 Jun 1965. 5'10". RHB, RFM. Debut 1981 aged 16yr 75d (youngest Yorkshire player). Cap 1986. **Tests:** 4 (1987-88 and 1988); HS 29* and BB 4-107 v WI (Lord's) 1988. LOI: 5. Tours: WI 1986-87 (Yorks); NZ 1987-88; Pak 1987-88. HS 47 v Essex (Chelmsford) 1986. BB 7-55 v Surrey (Leeds) 1986. **NWT:** HS 16 v Somerset (Leeds) 1985. BB 4-41 v Leics (Leeds) 1987. **BHC:** HS 20 v Worcs (Bradford) 1985. BB 4-43 v Northants (Lord's) 1987. **RAL:** HS 29* v Somerset (Taunton) 1987. BB 4-13 v Worcs (Leeds) 1986.

LOVE, James Derek (Brudenell SS), b Leeds 22 Apr 1955. 6'2½". RHB, RM. Debut 1975. Cap 1980. Benefit 1989. LOI: 3. Tour: WI 1986-87 (Yorks). 1000 runs (2); most - 1203 (1981). HS 170* v Worcs (Worcester) 1979. BB 2-0 v Windward Is (Castries) 1986-87. Awards: BHC 3. **NWT:** HS 67 v Middx (Leeds) 1988. BB 2-39 v Wilts (Trowbridge) 1987. **BHC:** HS 118* v Scotland (Bradford) 1981. **RAL:** HS 118* v Surrey (Leeds) 1987. BB 2-17 v Somerset (Taunton) 1987.

METCALFE, Ashley Anthony (Bradford GS; University C, London), b Horsforth 25 Dec 1963. 5'8". RHB, OB. Debut 1983 scoring 122 v Notts (Bradford). Cap 1986. YC 1986. Tour: WI 1986-87 (Yorks). 1000 runs (3); most - 1803 (1986). HS 216* v Middx (Leeds) 1988. BB 2-18 v Warwicks (Scarborough) 1987. Awards: NWT 1; BHC 4 (all 1987). **NWT:** HS 85 and BB 2-44 v Wilts (Trowbridge) 1987. **BHC:** HS 94* v Warwicks (Birmingham) 1987. **RAL:** HS 115* v Glos (Scarborough) 1984.

MOXON, Martyn Douglas (Holgate GS, Barnsley), b Barnsley 4 May 1960. 6'0". RHB, RM. Debut 1981 scoring 5 and 116 v Essex (Leeds). Cap 1984. GW 1982-84. **Tests:** 9 (1986 to 1988); HS 99 v NZ (Auckland) 1987-88. LOI: 8. Tours: Aus 1987-88; WI 1986-87 (Yorks); NZ 1987-88; Ind 1984-85; SL 1984-85, 1985-86 (Eng B). 1000 runs (4); most - 1485 (1988). HS 191 v Northants (Scarborough) 1988. BB 3-26 D.B.Close's XI v SL (Scarborough) 1984. Awards: NWT 3; BHC 4. **NWT:** HS 82* v Cheshire (Birkenhead) 1985. BB 1-17. **BHC:** HS 106* v Lancs (Manchester) 1986. BB 1-6. **RAL:** HS 86 v Somerset (Bath) 1985. BB 1-9.

PICKLES, Christopher Stephen (Whitcliffe Mount CS), b Mirfield 30 Jan 1966. 6'1". RHB, RM. Debut 1985. HS 31* v Leics (Bradford) 1985. BB 2-31 v Kent (Scarborough) 1985. **BHC:** HS 13* v Scotland (Glasgow) 1987. **RAL:** HS 16* v Glam (Scarborough) 1986. BB 2-19 v Middx (Leeds) 1988.

ROBINSON, Phillip Edward (Greenhead GS, Keighley), b Keighley 3 Aug 1963. 5'9". RHB, LM. Debut 1984. Cap 1988. 1000 runs (1): 1173 (1988). HS 129* v Notts (Sheffield) 1988. **NWT:** HS 66 v Middx (Leeds) 1986. **BHC:** HS 42 v Leics (Leicester) 1985. **RAL:** HS 78* v Leics (Leicester) 1985.

SHARP, Kevin (Abbey Grange HS), b Leeds 6 Apr 1959. 5'9". LHB, OB. Debut 1976. Cap 1982. Tour: WI 1986-87 (Yorks); NZ 1979-80 (DHR). 1000 runs (1): 1445 (1984). HS 181 v Glos (Harrogate) 1986. BB 2-13 v Glam (Bradford) 1984. **NWT:** HS 50 v Leics (Leeds) 1987. BB 4-40 v Wilts (Trowbridge) 1987. **BHC:** HS 105* v Scotland (Leeds) 1986. **RAL:** HS 114 v Essex (Chelmsford) 1985

SHAW, Christopher (Crofton HS), b Hemsworth 17 Feb 1964. 6'1". RHB, RFM. Debut 1984. HS 31 v Notts (Sheffield) 1988. BB 6-64 v Lancs (Leeds) 1987. **NWT:** HS 6*. BB 4-29 v Middx (Leeds) 1988. **BHC:** HS 4*. BB 2-30 v Minor C (Leeds) 1988. **RAL:** HS 26 v Glam (Leeds) 1984. BB 5-41 v Hants (Bournemouth) 1984.

SIDEBOTTOM, Arnold (Broadway GS, Barnsley), b Barnsley 1 Apr 1954. 6'1". RHB, RMF. Debut 1973. Cap 1980. Benefit 1988. OFS 1981-84. **Tests:** 1 (1985); HS 2 and BB 1-65 v Aus (Nottingham). Tours: SA 1981-82 (SAB); WI 1986-87 (Yorks). HS 124 v Glam (Cardiff) 1977. BB 8-72 v Leics (Middlesbrough) 1986. Awards: NWT 1; BHC 2. **NWT:** HS 45 v Hants (Bournemouth) 1977. BB 5-27 v Glam (Leeds) 1987. **BHC:** HS 32 v Notts (Leeds) 1983. BB 5-27 v Worcs (Bradford) 1985. **RAL:** HS 52* v Northants (Middlesbrough) 1982. BB 4-22 v Worcs (Worcester) 1987.

SWALLOW, Ian Geoffrey (Hoyland Kirk CS, Balk), b Barnsley 18 Dec 1962. 5'7½". RHB, OB. Debut 1983. HS 114 v MCC (Scarborough) 1987. BB 7-95 v Notts (Nottingham) 1987. **BHC:** HS 10* v Worcs (Bradford) 1985. BB 1-40. **RAL:** HS 2.

NEWCOMER

KELLETT, Simon Andrew (Whitcliffe Mount S), b Mirfield 16 Oct 1967. 6'2". RHB. Yorkshire 2nd XI debut 1986 (cap 1988).

DEPARTURES

ANDERSON, Paul Napier (Driffield S, Humberside CHE), b Driffield 28 Apr 1966. 6'0". RHB, RM. Yorkshire 1988. HS 0. BB 1-47.

DENNIS, S.J. – see GLAMORGAN

NICHOLSON, Neil George (Whitby CS), b Danby 17 Oct 1963. 5'8". LHB, RM. Yorkshire 1988. HS 16 v CU (Cambridge) 1988.

TOWSE, Anthony David (Headlands S, Bridlington), b Bridlington 22 Apr 1968. 6'3". LHB, RMF. Yorkshire 1988. MCC Yorkshire staff 1987. HS 1 and BB 2-26 v CU (Cambridge) 1988.

YORKSHIRE 1988

RESULTS SUMMARY

	Place	Won	Lost	Drew	Abandoned
Britannic Assurance Championship	13th	4	6	12	
All First-class Matches		5	6	13	
Refuge Assurance League	8th	7	7		2
NatWest Bank Trophy	2nd Round				
Benson and Hedges Cup	4th in Group B				

BRITANNIC ASSURANCE CHAMPIONSHIP AVERAGES

BATTING AND FIELDING

Cap		M	I	NO	HS	Runs	Avge	100	50	Ct/St
1984	M.D.Moxon	18	33	3	191	1297	43.23	2	8	22
1986	A.A.Metcalfe	21	39	5	216*	1268	37.29	2	7	4
1988	P.E.Robinson	22	37	3	129*	1132	33.29	1	8	19
1987	P.J.Hartley	13	17	6	127*	364	33.09	1	—	7
1976	P.Carrick	21	32	7	81	795	31.80	—	2	6
1980	J.D.Love	17	27	2	93*	744	29.76	—	6	11
1980	A.Sidebottom	18	24	5	55	517	27.21	—	2	5
—	D.Byas	12	22	1	112	515	24.52	1	3	8
1973	D.L.Bairstow	14	23	3	94*	416	20.80	—	2	38/1
—	I.G.Swallow	11	19	2	48*	352	20.70	—	—	5
1987	R.J.Blakey	14	21	2	51	347	18.26	—	1	24/2
1982	K.Sharp	11	17	0	57	297	17.47	—	1	9
—	P.A.Booth	4	7	2	33*	82	16.40	—	—	1
—	C.Shaw	21	25	12	31	170	13.07	—	—	2
1988	S.D.Fletcher	16	14	3	18	79	7.18	—	—	7
1986	P.W.Jarvis	5	9	1	13	55	6.87	—	—	1

Also batted (2 matches each): S.J.Dennis (cap 1983) 0, 14*, 0; S.N.Hartley (cap 1982) 22, 12, 26*.

BOWLING

	O	M	R	W	Avge	Best	5 wI	10 wM
P.W.Jarvis	176.1	46	434	31	14.00	6-40	2	1
A.Sidebottom	513.2	135	1303	63	20.68	7-89	3	—
S.D.Fletcher	384.4	59	1252	53	23.62	8-58	2	—
C.Shaw	507.5	110	1522	46	33.08	4-17	—	—
P.Carrick	546	163	1447	42	34.45	5-46	2	—
P.J.Hartley	307.3	32	1219	34	35.85	5-85	1	—

Also bowled: P.A.Booth 109.4-27-281-9; D.Byas 9.2-0-49-0; S.J.Dennis 63-9-196-5; S.N.Hartley 5-1-25-0; J.D.Love 2.3-0-11-1; A.A.Metcalfe 2.5-0-7-0; M.D.Moxon 6-2-15-0; P.E.Robinson 1.2-0-12-0; K.Sharp 1-0-11-0; I.G.Swallow 88-15-311-2.

The First-Class Averages (pp 161-175) give the records of Yorkshire players in all first-class county matches (their other opponents being the Sri Lankans and Cambridge U), with the exception of P.W.Jarvis, whose full county figures are as above, and:

M.D.Moxon 19-35-3-191-1430-44.68-3-8-22ct. 6-2-15-0.

148

YORKSHIRE RECORDS

FIRST-CLASS CRICKET

Highest Total	For	887		v Warwicks	Birmingham	1896
	V	630		by Somerset	Leeds	1901
Lowest Total	For	23		v Hampshire	Middlesbrough	1965
	V	13		by Notts	Nottingham	1901
Highest Innings	For	341	G.H.Hirst	v Leics	Leicester	1905
	V	318*	W.G.Grace	for Glos	Cheltenham	1876

Highest Partnerships
Wkt

1st	555	P.Holmes/H.Sutcliffe	v Essex	Leyton	1932
2nd	346	W.Barber/M.Leyland	v Middlesex	Sheffield	1932
3rd	323*	H.Sutcliffe/M.Leyland	v Glamorgan	Huddersfield	1928
4th	312	D.Denton/G.H.Hirst	v Hampshire	Southampton	1914
5th	340	E.Wainwright/G.H.Hirst	v Surrey	The Oval	1899
6th	276	M.Leyland/E.Robinson	v Glamorgan	Swansea	1926
7th	254	W.Rhodes/D.C.F.Burton	v Hampshire	Dewsbury	1919
8th	292	R.Peel/Lord Hawke	v Warwicks	Birmingham	1896
9th	192	G.H.Hirst/S.Haigh	v Surrey	Bradford	1898
10th	149	G.Boycott/G.B.Stevenson	v Warwicks	Birmingham	1982

Best Bowling	For	10-10	H.Verity	v Notts	Leeds	1932
(Innings)	V	10-37	C.V.Grimmett	for Australians	Sheffield	1930
Best Bowling	For	17-91	H.Verity	v Essex	Leyton	1933
(Match)	V	17-91	H.Dean	for Lancashire	Liverpool	1913
Most Runs – Season		2,883	H.Sutcliffe	(av 80.08)		1932
Most Runs – Career		38,561	H.Sutcliffe	(av 50.20)		1919-1945
Most 100s – Season		12	H.Sutcliffe			1932
Most 100s – Career		112	H.Sutcliffe			1919-1945
Most Wkts – Season		240	W.Rhodes	(av 12.72)		1900
Most Wkts – Career		3,608	W.Rhodes	(av 16.00)		1898-1930

LIMITED-OVERS CRICKET

Highest Total	NWT	317-4		v Surrey	Lord's	1965
	BHC	317-5		v Scotland	Leeds	1986
	RAL	263-8		v Surrey	Bradford	1985
Lowest Total	NWT	76		v Surrey	Harrogate	1970
	BHC	114		v Kent	Canterbury	1978
	RAL	74		v Warwicks	Birmingham	1972
Highest Innings	NWT	146	G.Boycott	v Surrey	Lord's	1965
	BHC	142	G.Boycott	v Worcs	Worcester	1980
	RAL	119	J.H.Hampshire	v Leics	Hull	1971
Best Bowling	NWT	6-15	F.S.Trueman	v Somerset	Taunton	1965
	BHC	6-27	A.G.Nicholson	v Minor C (N)	Middlesbrough	1972
	RAL	7-15	R.A.Hutton	v Worcs	Leeds	1969

BORDER, Allan Robert (N Sydney BHS), b Cremorne, Sydney, Aus 27 Jul 1955. 5'9". LHB, SLA. NSW 1976-80. Queensland 1980-88 (captain 1983-84 to date). Gloucestershire 1977 (1 match). Essex 1986-88 (cap 1986). **Tests** (Aus): 94 (1978-79 to 1987-88, 31 as captain); HS 205 v NZ (Adelaide) 1987-88; BB 3-20 v NZ (Christchurch) 1981-82. LOI (Aus): 172 (record). Tours (Aus)(C=Capt): Eng 1980, 1981, 1985C; WI 1983-84; NZ 1981-82, 1985-86C; Ind 1979-80, 1986-87C; Pak 1979-80, 1982-83; SL 1982-83. 1000 runs (3+7); most – 1393 (1988). HS 205 (Tests). Essex HS 169* v Derbys (Chesterfield) 1988. BB 4-61 Queensland v NSW (Sydney) 1980-81. Essex BB 1-8. Award: BHC 1. **NWT**: HS 46* v Northants (Chelmsford) 1987. BB 1-1. **BHC**: HS 75* v Middx (Lord's) 1988. **RAL**: HS 77 v Sussex (Ilford) 1988. BB 2-21 v Leics (Leicester) 1986.

BROWN, Adrian Desmond (Clacton County HS; Magdalene C, CU), b Clacton on Sea 18 May 1962. 5'10½". RHB, MFG. CU Debut/blue 1986. Essex 1988. Suffolk 1984-85. HS 30 CU v Surrey (Cambridge) 1986. Essex HS 6*. **NWT**: HS 9. **BHC**: HS 10* Comb Us v Surrey (Oval) 1986. **RAL**: HS 1*.

FIELD-BUSS, M.G. see NOTTINGHAMSHIRE

FLETCHER, Keith William Robert (Comberton Village C, Cambs), b Worcester 20 May 1944. 5'9". RHB, LB. Essex 1962-88 (cap 1963; captain 1974-85, 1988; benefit 1973; testimonial 1982). Wisden 1973. OBE 1985. **Tests**: 59 (1968 to 1981-82, 7 as captain); HS 216 v NZ (Auckland) 1974-75; BB 1-6. LOI: 24. Tours: Aus 1970-71, 1974-75, 1976-77; WI 1964-65 (Cav), 1973-74; NZ 1970-71, 1974-75; Ind and SL 1967-68 (Int XI), 1972-73, 1976-77, 1981-82 (captain); Pak 1966-67 (MCC U-25), 1967-68 (Int XI), 1968-69, 1972-73; SL 1968-69, 1969-70. 1000 runs (20); most – 1890 (1968). HS 228* v Sussex (Hastings) 1968. BB 5-41 v Middx (Colchester) 1979. Awards: NWT 2; BHC 8. **NWT**: HS 97 v Kent (Chelmsford) 1982. BB 1-16. **BHC**: HS 101* v Sussex (Hove) 1982. BB 1-25. **RAL**: HS 99* v Notts (Ilford) 1974. BB 1-4.

PONT, Ian Leslie (Sir Anthony Browne's S), b Brentwood 28 Aug 1961. Brother of K.R. Pont (Essex). 6'2½". RHB, RFM. Nottinghamshire 1982. Essex 1985-88. Natal 1985-86. HS 68 v CU (Cambridge) 1988. BB 5-73 v Lancs (Chelmsford) 1987. **NWT**: HS 7*. BB 1-54. **BHC**: HS 13* Minor C v Essex (Slough) 1983. BB 1-42. **RAL**: HS 36 v Yorks (Sheffield) 1988. BB 2-16 v Lancs (Chelmsford) 1987.

ROEBUCK, Paul Gerrard Peter (Millfield S; Emmanuel C, CU), b Bath, Somerset 13 Oct 1963. Younger brother of P.M. (Somerset). 6'0". LHB, RMF. Cambridge U 1983-85 (blue 1984-85). Gloucestershire 1984. Glamorgan 1988. HS 82 CU v Somerset (Taunton) 1985. Glam HS 46 v Hants (Cardiff) 1988. BB 2-44 CU v Kent (Cambridge) 1983. **BHC**: HS 33 Comb Us v Middx (Cambridge) 1985. BB 1-32.

THOMAS, J.G. – see NORTHAMPTONSHIRE.

VAN ZYL, Cornelius Johannes Petrus Gerthardus (**'Corrie'**) (Grey C; U of OFS), b Bloemfontein, SA 1 Oct 1961. 6'2". RHB, RF. OFS 1981-88. Glamorgan 1987-88. HS 49 OFS v Natal B (Bloemfontein) 1984-85. Glam HS 35 v Derbys (Chesterfield) 1987. BB 8-84 OFS v N Transvaal B (Bloemfontein) 1984-85. Glam BB 3-35 v Yorks (Leeds) 1987. **BHC**: HS 5. BB 1-45.

THOMAS, David James (Licensed Victuallers' S, Slough), b Solihull 30 Jun 1959. 6'0". LHB, LFM. Surrey 1977-87; cap 1982. N Transvaal 1980-81. Natal 1983-84. Gloucestershire 1988. HS 119 Surrey v Notts (Oval) 1983. Glos HS 57* v OU

(Oxford) 1988. BB 6-36 Surrey v Somerset (Oval) 1984. Glos BB 2-39 v Northants (Northampton) 1988. Award: NWT 1. **NWT:** HS 65 Surrey v Notts (Oval) 1986. BB 3-16 Surrey v Durham (Oval) 1982. **BHC:** HS 22 Surrey v Sussex (Hove) 1987. BB 3-30 Surrey v Leics (Oval) 1981. **RAL:** HS 72 Surrey v Glamorgan (Swansea) 1983. BB 4-13 Surrey v Sussex (Oval) 1978.

MIDDLESEX – DEPARTURES (continued from p 107)

OLLEY, Martin William Charles (Felsted S), b Romford, Essex 27 Nov 1963. RHB, WK. Northamptonshire 1983. Middlesex 1988. Hertfordshire 1984-88. HS 27* v CU (Cambridge) 1988. **NWT:** HS 20 Herts v Hants (Southampton) 1986.

SLACK, Wilfred Norris (Troumaca Govt S; Wellesbourne SS, High Wycombe) b Troumaca, St Vincent 12 Dec 1954. Died Banjul, The Gambia 15 Jan 1989. 5'11". LHB, RM. Middlesex 1977-88 (cap 1981). Windward Is 1981-83. Buckinghamshire 1976. **Tests:** 3 (1985-86 and 1986); HS 52 v WI (St John's) 1985-86. LOI: 2. Tours: Aus 1986-87; WI 1985-86; Pak 1981-82 (Int XI); SL 1985-86 (Eng B); Zim 1980-81 (Middx). 1000 runs (8); most – 1900 (1985). Shared record Middx 1st-wkt stand of 367* with G.D.Barlow v Kent (Lord's) 1981. HS 248* v Worcs (Lord's) 1981. BB 3-17 v Leics (Uxbridge) 1982. Awards: NWT 2; BHC 1. **NWT:** HS 98 v Cumberland (Uxbridge) 1985. BB 3-37 v Northants (Northampton) 1983. **BHC:** HS 110 v Somerset (Lord's) 1987. **RAL:** HS 101* v Yorks (Lord's) 1986. BB 5-32 v Leics (Lord's) 1983.

NORTHAMPTONSHIRE – DEPARTURES (continued from p 112)

GOULDSTONE, Mark Roger (Newport GS; Braintree CFE), b Bishop's Stortford, Herts 3 Feb 1963. 5'11". RHB, RM. Northamptonshire 1986-88. HS 71 v Essex (Northampton) 1988. **RAL:** HS 11 v Hants (Bournemouth) 1988.

HOFFMAN, Dean Stuart (Moor End CS), b Erdington, Birmingham 13 Jun 1966. 6'2". RHB, RMF. Warwickshire 1985. HS 20* v WI (Northampton) 1988. BB 4-100 Warwicks v Notts (Nuneaton) 1985. Northants BB 1-43. **NWT:** HS 3. BB 2-56 Warwicks v Notts (Nottingham) 1985. **RAL:** HS 2*. BB 2-18 Warwicks v Somerset (Taunton) 1985.

LILLEE, Dennis Keith (Belmont HS), b Subiaco, Perth, Aus 18 Jul 1949. 6'0". RHB, RFM. W Australia 1969-84. Tasmania 1987-88. Northamptonshire 1988. Wisden 1972. **Tests** (Aus): 70 (1970-71 to 1983-84); HS 73* v Eng (Lord's) 1975; BB 7-83 v WI (Melbourne) 1981. LOI (Aus): 63. Tours (Aus): Eng 1972, 1975, 1980, 1981; SA 1975-76 (Int XI); WI 1972-73, 1981-82; NZ 1976-77, 1976-77, 1981-82; Pak 1979-80; SL 1982-83. HS 73* (Tests). Northants HS 22 (4 times) 1988. BB 8-29 Australia v World XI (Perth) 1971-72. Northants BB 6-68 v Glos (Northampton) 1988. **BHC:** HS 7. BB 3-61 v Worcs (Northampton) 1988. **RAL:** HS 6*. BB 3-38 v Warwicks (Birmingham) 1988.

NOTTINGHAMSHIRE – DEPARTURES (continued from p 117)

CALLAGHAN, David John (Grey HS, Port Elizabeth), b Queenstown, SA 1 Feb 1965. 5'10". RHB, RM. E Province 1983-84, 1986-88. GW 1985-86. Nottinghamshire 1988. HS 171 E Province v SA Defence Force (Pt Elizabeth) 1984-85. Notts HS 29 and BB 1-59 v WI (Nottingham) 1988. BB 2-16 E Province v OFS (Pt Elizabeth) 1987-88.

FRASER-DARLING, Callum David (The Edinburgh Academy), b Sheffield, Yorks 30 Sep 1963. 6'5". RHB, RMF. Debut 1984. HS 61 v Northants (Northampton) 1986. BB 5-84 v Northants (Northampton) 1986. **RAL:** HS 11 v Northants (Northampton) 1987. BB 3-23 v Surrey (Nottingham) 1988. Joined Nottingham Police Force.

151

SOMERSET – DEPARTURES (continued from p 122)

DREDGE, Colin Herbert (Oakfield SS) b Frome 4 Aug 1954. 6'5". LHB, RMF. Somerset 1976-88 (cap 1978; benefit 1987). HS: 56* v Yorks (Harrogate) 1977. BB 6-37 v Glos (Bristol) 1981. Award: NWT 1. **NWT**: HS 9. BB 4-23 v Kent (Canterbury) 1978. **BHC**: HS 25 v Essex (Taunton) 1986. BB 4-10 v Hants (Bournemouth) 1980. **RAL**: HS 28* v Glam (Cardiff) 1986. BB 5-35 v Middx (Lord's) 1981.

FELTON, N.A. – see NORTHAMPTONSHIRE.

SCRIVEN, Timothy John Adam (High Wycombe RGS), b High Wycombe, Bucks 15 Dec 1965. 6'3". RHB, SLA. Debut 1988. Buckinghamshire 1986-88. HS 7. BB 1-40. **NWT**: HS 2.

WARWICKSHIRE – DEPARTURES (continued from p 137)

GIFFORD, Norman (Ulverston SS), b Ulverston, Lancs 30 Mar 1940. 5'10½". LHB, SLA. Worcestershire 1960-82 (cap 1961; captain 1971-80; benefit 1974; testimonial 1981). Warwickshire 1983-88 (cap 1983, capt 1985-87). Wisden 1974. MBE 1978. England selector 1982. **Tests**: 15 (1964 to 1973); HS 25* v NZ (Nottingham) 1973; BB 5-55 v Pak (Karachi) 1972-73. LOI: 2. **Tours**: Aus 1971-72 (RW); Rhod/Zim 1961-62 (Int XI), 1964-65 (Worcs), 1972-73 (IW); Ind 1972-73; Pak 1961-62 (Int XI), 1970-71 (RW), 1972-73; SL 1985-86 (Eng B). 100 wickets (4); most – 133 (1961). Hat-trick 1965 (Worcs). HS 89 v Worcs v OU (Oxford) 1963. BB 8-28 Worcs v Yorks (Sheffield) 1968. Awards: NWT 1; BHC 2. **NWT**: HS 38 Worcs v Warwicks (Lord's) 1966. BB 4-7 Worcs v Surrey (Worcester) 1972. **BHC**: HS 33 Worcs v Kent (Lord's) 1973. BB 6-8 Worcs v Minor C (S)(High Wycombe) 1979. **RAL**: HS 32* v Northants (Luton) 1983. BB 6-20 v Northants (Birmingham) 1985. Appointed coach to Sussex.

MYLES, Simon David (King George V School, Hong Kong), b Mansfield, Notts 2 Jun 1966. 5'10". RHB, RM. Sussex 1987. Warwickshire 1988. HS 39 v Leics (Birmingham) 1988. **RAL**: HS 32 v Northants (Birmingham) 1988.

PARSONS, G.J. – see LEICESTERSHIRE

STORIE, Alastair Caleb (St Stithians C, Johannesburg), b Bishopbriggs, Glasgow 25 Jul 1965. 5'9". RHB, RM. Northamptonshire 1985-86. Warwickshire 1987-88. OFS 1987-88. HS 106 Northants v Hampshire (Northampton) 1985 – on debut. Warwicks HS 68 v Notts (Birmingham) 1988. **NWT**: HS 25* v Staffs (Burton) 1987. **BHC**: HS 66 v Scotland (Perth) 1987. **RAL**: HS 55 v Yorks (Birmingham) 1987.

TEDSTONE, Geoffrey Alan (Warwick S; St Paul's C, Cheltenham), b Southport, Lancs 19 Jan 1961. 5'7". RHB, WK. Warwickshire 1982-88. HS 67* v CU (Cambridge) 1983. **NWT**: HS 55* v Glos (Bristol) 1987. **RAL**: HS 31* v Glam (Swansea) 1987. **RAL**: HS 23 v Middx (Birmingham) 1982.

WORCESTERSHIRE – NEWCOMER (continued from p 142)

TOLLEY, Christopher Mark (King Edward VI C, Stourbridge), b Kidderminster 30 Dec 1967. RHB, LMF.

WORCESTERSHIRE – DEPARTURE

VORSTER, Louis Phillipus (Potchefstroom HS; Rand Afrikaans U), b Potchefstroom, SA 2 Nov 1966. 5'9". LHB, OB. Transvaal 1985-88. Worcs 1988. HS 174 Transvaal v W Province (Cape Town) 1987-88. Worcs HS 16* v WI (Worcester) 1988.

152

UNIVERSITY MATCH RESULTS

Played: 143   Wins: Cambridge 54; Oxford 46   Draws: 43.   Abandoned: 1.

This, the oldest surviving first-class fixture, dates from 1827 and, wartime interruptions apart, it has been played annually since 1838. With the exception of five matches played in the area of Oxford (1829, 1843, 1846, 1848 and 1850), all the fixtures have been played at Lord's.

1827	Drawn	1883	Cambridge	1935	Cambridge
1829	Oxford	1884	Oxford	1936	Cambridge
1836	Oxford	1885	Cambridge	1937	Oxford
1838	Oxford	1886	Oxford	1938	Drawn
1839	Cambridge	1887	Oxford	1939	Oxford
1840	Cambridge	1888	Drawn	1946	Oxford
1841	Cambridge	1889	Cambridge	1947	Drawn
1842	Cambridge	1890	Cambridge	1948	Oxford
1843	Cambridge	1891	Cambridge	1949	Cambridge
1844	Drawn	1892	Oxford	1950	Drawn
1845	Cambridge	1893	Cambridge	1951	Oxford
1846	Oxford	1894	Oxford	1952	Drawn
1847	Cambridge	1895	Cambridge	1953	Cambridge
1848	Oxford	1896	Oxford	1954	Drawn
1849	Cambridge	1897	Cambridge	1955	Drawn
1850	Oxford	1898	Oxford	1956	Drawn
1851	Cambridge	1899	Drawn	1957	Cambridge
1852	Oxford	1900	Drawn	1958	Cambridge
1853	Oxford	1901	Drawn	1959	Oxford
1854	Oxford	1902	Cambridge	1960	Drawn
1855	Oxford	1903	Oxford	1961	Drawn
1856	Cambridge	1904	Drawn	1962	Drawn
1857	Oxford	1905	Cambridge	1963	Drawn
1858	Oxford	1906	Cambridge	1964	Drawn
1859	Cambridge	1907	Cambridge	1965	Drawn
1860	Cambridge	1908	Oxford	1966	Drawn
1861	Cambridge	1909	Drawn	1967	Drawn
1862	Cambridge	1910	Oxford	1968	Drawn
1863	Oxford	1911	Oxford	1969	Drawn
1864	Oxford	1912	Cambridge	1970	Drawn
1865	Oxford	1913	Cambridge	1971	Drawn
1866	Oxford	1914	Oxford	1972	Cambridge
1867	Cambridge	1919	Oxford	1973	Drawn
1868	Cambridge	1920	Drawn	1974	Drawn
1869	Cambridge	1921	Cambridge	1975	Drawn
1870	Cambridge	1922	Cambridge	1976	Oxford
1871	Oxford	1923	Oxford	1977	Drawn
1872	Cambridge	1924	Cambridge	1978	Drawn
1873	Oxford	1925	Drawn	1979	Cambridge
1874	Oxford	1926	Cambridge	1980	Drawn
1875	Oxford	1927	Cambridge	1981	Drawn
1876	Cambridge	1928	Drawn	1982	Cambridge
1877	Oxford	1929	Drawn	1983	Drawn
1878	Cambridge	1930	Cambridge	1984	Oxford
1879	Cambridge	1931	Oxford	1985	Drawn
1880	Cambridge	1932	Drawn	1986	Cambridge
1881	Oxford	1933	Drawn	1987	Drawn
1882	Cambridge	1934	Drawn	1988	Abandoned

CAMBRIDGE UNIVERSITY

ATHERTON, M.A. Captain 1988-89. See LANCASHIRE.

ATKINSON, J.C.M. see SOMERSET.

BAIL, Paul Andrew Clayton (Millfield S; Downing C), b Burnham-on-Sea 23 Jun 1965. 5'10". RHB, OB. Somerset 1985-86. CU debut 1986. Blue 1986-87-88. HS 174 CU v OU (Lord's) 1986. BB 1-36.

BATE, Richard (Haberdashers' Aske's S, Elstree; Pembroke C), b Finchley, Middx 27 Dec 1966. 5'9". RHB, RM. Debut 1987. Blue 1988. HS 45 v Glam (Cambridge) 1988.

FENTON, Nigel Charles Windsor (Rugby S; Durham U; Magdalene C), b Bradford, Yorks 22 Jun 1965. 6'5". RHB, RFM. Debut/blue 1988. HS 2. BB 4-64 v Middx (Cambridge) 1988.

GOLDING, Andrew Kenneth (Colchester RGS; St Catharine's C), b Colchester, Essex 5 Oct 1963. 5'9". RHB, SLA. Essex 1983. CU debut 1984. Blue 1986. HS 47 and BB 3-51 v OU (Lord's) 1986.

HART, Richard Joseph (Eltham C; Caius C), b Beckenham, Kent 7 Dec 1967. 5'10½". LHB, SLA. Debut 1987. HS 12 v Essex and v Northants (Cambridge) 1987. BB 4-6 v Yorks (Cambridge) 1988.

HEAP, Russell (Calday Grange GS; Ipswich S; Magdalene C), b Leeds, Yorks 6 Dec 1968. 5'10". RHB. Debut 1988. HS 15 v Essex (Cambridge) 1988.

HEATH, Stephen David (King Edward's S, Birmingham; Trinity C), b Bristol 7 Jul 1967. 6'1". RHB, LB. Debut 1986. Blue 1988. HS 33* v Glam (Cambridge) 1988.

HOOPER, Anthony Mark (Latymer Upper S; St John's C), b Perivale, Middx 5 Sep 1967. 5'7". RHB, RM. Debut/blue 1987. HS 89 v OU (Lord's) 1987.

NOYES, Stephen James (High Wycombe RGS; Bangor U; Homerton C), b High Wycombe, Bucks 17 Sep 1963. 5'11". RHB, SLA. Debut/blue 1988. HS 38 v Surrey (Oval) 1988.

PERRY, Jonathan Nicholas (Ampleforth C; Trinity C), b Frimley, Surrey 29 Dec 1965. 6'1". RHB, RM. Great grandson of J.F.Byrne (Warwicks 1897-1912). Debut 1987. Blue 1987-88. HS 26 v Surrey (Oval) 1988. BB 3-56 Surrey (Cambridge) 1987.

POINTER, Graham Alan (St Dunstan's C; St John's C), b Lewisham, London 2 May 1967. 6'3½". RHB, LMF. Debut 1987. Blue 1987-88. HS 33 v OU (Lord's) 1987. BB 3-31 v Yorks (Cambridge) 1988.

PYMAN, Richard Anthony (Harrow S; Pembroke C), b Changi, Singapore 17 Apr 1968. 5'10". RHB, RM. Debut 1988. HS 4. Eton fives half-blue.

SCOTT, Alastair Martin Gordon (Seaford Head CS; Queens C), b Guildford 31 Mar 1966. 5'10". RHB, LM. Debut 1985. Blue 1985-86-87. Sussex 1986. HS 11* v OU (Lord's) 1987. BB 5-68 v Notts (Cambridge) 1985.

STENNER, Jonathan Maurice Crathorne (Perse S; Magdalene C), b RAF Newton, Notts 18 Jan 1966. 5'11". RHB. Debut 1988. HS 13 v Yorks (Cambridge) 1988.

TREMELLEN, Jonathan Michael (Whitland GS; Bradfield C; St Catharine's C), b Pendine, Carmarthenshire 30 Oct 1965. 6'1". RHB, RM. Debut 1986. Blue 1987-88. HS 39 v OU (Lord's) 1987. BB 1-13.

TURNER, Robert Julian (Millfield S; Magdalene C), b Malvern, Worcs 25 Nov 1967. 6'1½". RHB, WK. Brother of S.J. (Somerset 1984-85). Debut/blue 1988. HS 27 v Warwicks (Cambridge) 1988.

CAMBRIDGE UNIVERSITY 1988

RESULTS SUMMARY

	Played	Won	Lost	Drew	Abandoned
All First-Class Matches	8	0	5	3	1

FIRST-CLASS AVERAGES

BATTING AND FIELDING

	M	I	NO	HS	Runs	Avge	100	50	Ct/St
†M.A.Atherton	8	13	2	151*	665	60.45	2	3	10
†J.C.M.Atkinson	7	12	0	73	257	21.41	—	1	4
†P.A.C.Bail	4	6	0	44	102	17.00	—	—	1
†R.Bate	7	12	2	45	160	16.00	—	—	1
†S.D.Heath	5	8	1	33*	100	14.28	—	—	2
†S.J.Noyes	8	14	1	38	170	13.07	—	—	—
†R.J.Turner	8	14	1	27	155	11.92	—	—	9/2
†G.A.Pointer	7	12	2	18*	114	11.40	—	—	—
†J.M.Tremellen	7	12	0	33	131	10.91	—	—	3
†J.N.Perry	7	9	1	26	73	9.12	—	—	3
A.M.G.Scott	3	5	1	8	9	2.25	—	—	—
R.J.Hart	3	5	1	6	7	1.75	—	—	—
†N.C.W.Fenton	7	9	3	2	4	0.66	—	—	1

Also batted: A.K.Golding (1 match) 18* (2 ct); R.Heap (1 match) 0, 15 (2 ct); A.M.Hooper (2 matches) 3, 2, 0; R.A.Pyman (2 matches) 3, 0, 4 (2 ct); J.M.C.Stenner (1 match) 10, 13.

† Blue 1988

BOWLING

	O	M	R	W	Avge	Best	5 wI	10 wM
N.C.W.Fenton	271.4	65	726	21	34.57	4-64	—	—
A.M.G.Scott	120	26	385	11	35.00	4-66	—	—
J.N.Perry	211	44	643	10	64.30	3-72	—	—
M.A.Atherton	179.2	19	565	7	80.71	2-38	—	—
G.A.Pointer	184.5	24	663	7	94.71	3-31	—	—

Also bowled: J.C.M.Atkinson 17-1-86-1; P.A.C.Bail 14-1-71-1; A.K.Golding 23-11-43-0; R.J.Hart 67-11-231-4; J.M.Tremellen 5-0-13-1.

OXFORD UNIVERSITY

ALMAER, Simon Ashley (Ilford CHS; St Catherine's C), b Wanstead, Essex 12 Jul 1969. 6'0". RHB, RM. Debut/blue 1988. HS 67 v Lancs (Oxford) 1988.

BROWN, Malcolm Edward Osborne (Diocesan C; Cape Town U; Worcester C), Durban, SA 19 Aug 1961. 6'1". RHB, RM. Debut/blue 1988. HS 47 v Lancs (Oxford) 1988.

COPE, James Edward Bailye (St John's S, Leatherhead; Keble C), b Leigh on Sea, Essex 5 May 1966. 6'1". RHB, WK. Debut 1986. Blue 1986-87. HS 8*.

CRAWLEY, Mark Andrew (Manchester GS; Oriel C), b Newton-le-Willows, Lancs 16 Dec 1967. 6'3". RHB, RM. Debut 1987. Blue 1987-88. **Captain 1989.** HS 140 and BB 2-30 OU v CU (Lord's) 1987. Soccer blue.

EDWARDS, Patrick Gervase (Canford S; Christ Church), b Bradford-on-Avon, Wilts 21 Oct 1965. 5'10". RHB, SLA. Debut 1987. Blue 1987-88. HS 9. BB 4-93 v Glos (Oxford) 1987.

GREEN, Neil Howard (Judd S; New C; Wycliffe Hall), b S Norwood, London 8 Oct 1957. 5'9". RHB, OB. Debut 1988. HS 9.

HAGAN, David Andrew (Trinity S, Leamington Spa; St Edmund Hall), b Wide Open Northumberland 25 Jun 1966. 5'9". RHB, OB. Debut 1985. Blue 1986-88. HS 88 v Lancs (Oxford) 1986.

HAMPTON, Anthony **Nicholas** Seymour (Reading S; St John's C), b Burton upon Trent, Derbys 25 Apr 1967. 5'11½". RHB, LM. Debut 1988. HS 12 v Northants (Oxford) 1988.

HENDERSON, Iain Mark (Laxton S, Oundle; Pembroke C), b Glapthorn, Northants 8 Sep 1967. 6'1". RHB, RMF. Debut/blue 1987. HS 21* v Notts (Oxford) 1988. BB 3-48 v Glos (Oxford) 1987.

HEPPEL, Nicolas (Reading S; Queen's C), b Hampton Court, Surrey 12 Dec 1967. 5'11". RHB, SLA. Debut 1988. HS 14* v Glos (Oxford) 1988.

JACK, Trevor Bernard (Aquinas C; W Australia U; Keble C), b Perth, Aus 16 Jul 1960. 6'0". RHB, LB. Debut/blue 1988. HS 29 v Lancs (Oxford) 1988.

KILBORN, Michael John (Farrer HS; U of NSW; St John's C), b Gunnedah, Aus 20 Sep 1962. 6'2". RHB, RM. Debut 1986. Blue 1986-87-88. **Captain 1988.** HS 78 v Notts (Oxford) 1988. BB 3-37 v Hants (Oxford) 1988.

MORRIS, Russell Edward (Dyffryn Conwy S, Llanrwst; Oriel C), b St Asaph, Flintshire, 8 Jun 1967. 5'8". RHB, RM. Debut/blue 1987. HS 34 v Notts (Oxford) 1987. Soccer blue.

NUTTALL, John Daniel (Pocklington S; St Peter's C), b Fulford, Yorks 29 Dec 1967. 6'3". RHB, LM. Debut 1987. Blue 1988. HS 35 v Kent (Oxford) 1988. BB 2-64 v Glos (Oxford) 1988.

POLKINGHORNE, David Andrew (Kearsney C; Natal U; Pembroke C), b Durban, SA 20 Apr 1964. 5'11". RHB, OB. Debut 1988. HS 45* v Hants (Oxford) 1988.

REYNOLDS, Giles Denys (Wellington C; University C), b Wegburg Hospital, Moenchen Gladbach, W Germany 13 Jul 1967. 5'5¾". RHB, WK. Debut/blue 1988. HS 69 v Kent (Oxford) 1988. Eton fives half-blue.

SEARLE, Andrew Monro (Malvern C; Worcester C), b Stamford, Lincs 11 Nov 1968. 6'1". LHB, OB. Debut 1988. HS 2.

SYGROVE, Malcolm Robert (Lutterworth GS; St John's C), b Lutterworth, Leics 17 Feb 1966. 6'0". RHB, RM. Debut 1986. Blue 1988. HS 8*. BB 3-91 v Leics (Oxford) 1988.

WEALE, Simon David (Westminster City S; Keble C), b Knightsbridge, London 16 Sep 1967. 6'2". RHB, SLA. Debut 1986. Blue 1987-88. HS 76 v CU (Lord's) 1987. BB 3-130 v Lancs (Oxford) 1988.

OXFORD UNIVERSITY 1988

RESULTS SUMMARY

	Played	Won	Lost	Drew	Abandoned
All First-class Matches	7	0	2	5	1

FIRST-CLASS AVERAGES

BATTING AND FIELDING

	M	I	NO	HS	Runs	Avge	100	50	Ct/St
†M.A.Crawley	4	7	2	98	177	35.40	—	1	2
†D.A.Hagan	7	13	2	59	306	27.81	—	1	3
†M.J.Kilborn	7	13	0	78	351	27.00	—	2	5
D.A.Polkinghorne	3	4	1	45*	72	24.00	—	—	2
†M.E.O.Brown	3	5	2	47	71	23.66	—	—	—
†S.A.Almaer	6	11	0	67	256	23.27	—	1	2
†T.B.Jack	2	3	0	29	57	19.00	—	—	1
†G.D.Reynolds	6	9	1	69	147	18.37	—	1	6
†S.D.Weale	6	9	0	40	136	15.11	—	—	3
†J.D.Nuttall	5	6	2	35	52	13.00	—	—	2
I.M.Henderson	5	7	1	21*	55	9.16	—	—	1
†P.G.Edwards	5	7	3	9	32	8.00	—	—	1
†M.R.Sygrove	7	8	3	8*	29	5.80	—	—	—
R.E.Morris	4	8	0	21	39	4.87	—	—	1
A.N.S.Hampton	3	6	0	12	22	3.66	—	—	1

Also batted (1 match each): N.H.Green 9 (1 ct); N.Heppel 14* A.M.Searle 2. J.E.B.Cope (1 match) (1 ct) did not bat.

† Blue 1988

BOWLING

	O	M	R	W	Avge	Best	5 wI	10 wM
M.J.Kilborn	41.5	8	185	5	37.00	3-37	—	—
M.R.Sygrove	215.4	34	848	18	47.11	3-91	—	—
J.D.Nuttall	116	20	410	7	58.57	2-64	—	—
P.G.Edwards	171.3	43	560	9	62.22	3-88	—	—
I.M.Henderson	71	10	316	5	63.20	3-104	—	—
S.D.Weale	200	41	681	8	85.12	3-130	—	—

Also bowled: M.A.Crawley 38-7-136-0; D.A.Hagan 3-0-21-0; N.Heppel 14-0-74-0; A.M.Searle 17-2-76-0.

CAMBRIDGE UNIVERSITY RECORDS

FIRST-CLASS CRICKET

Highest Total	For	703-9d	v Sussex	Hove	1890
	V	730-3	by W Indians	Cambridge	1950
Lowest Total	For	30	v Yorkshire	Cambridge	1928
	V	32	by Oxford U	Lord's	1878
Highest Innings	For	254* K.S.Duleepsinhji	v Middlesex	Cambridge	1927
	V	304* E.de C.Weekes	for W Indians	Cambridge	1950

Highest Partnerships
Wkt

1st	349	J.G.Dewes/D.S.Sheppard	v Sussex	Hove	1950
2nd	429*	J.G.Dewes/G.H.G.Doggart	v Essex	Cambridge	1949
3rd	284	E.T.Killick/G.C.Grant	v Essex	Cambridge	1929
4th	275	R.de W.K.Winlaw/J.H.Human	v Essex	Cambridge	1934
5th	220	R.Subba Row/F.C.M.Alexander	v Notts	Nottingham	1953
6th	245	J.L.Bryan/C.T.Ashton	v Surrey	The Oval	1921
7th	289	G.Goonesena/G.W.Cook	v Oxford U	Lord's	1957
8th	145	H.Ashton/A.E.R.Gilligan	v F Foresters	Cambridge	1920
9th	200	G.W.Cook/C.S.Smith	v Lancashire	Liverpool	1957
10th	177	A.E.R.Gilligan/J.H.Naumann	v Sussex	Hove	1919

Best Bowling	For	10-69 S.M.J.Woods	v C.I.T's XI†	Cambridge	1890
(Innings)	V	10-38 S.E.Butler	for Oxford U	Lord's	1871
Best Bowling	For	15-88 S.M.J.Woods	v C.I.T's XI†	Cambridge	1890
(Match)	V	15-95 S.E.Butler	for Oxford U	Lord's	1871

Most Runs – Season	1,581	D.S.Sheppard	(av 79.05)	1952
Most Runs – Career	4,310	J.M.Brearley	(av 38.48)	1961-1968
Most 100s – Season	7	D.S.Sheppard		1952
Most 100s – Career	14	D.S.Sheppard		1950-1952
Most Wkts – Season	80	O.S.Wheatley	(av 17.63)	1958
Most Wkts – Career	208	G.Goonesena	(av 21.82)	1954-1957

UNIVERSITY MATCH RECORDS

Highest Total	432-9d		1936
Lowest Total	39		1858
Highest Innings	211	G.Goonesena	1957
Best Bowling (Innings)	8-44	G.E.Jeffery	1873
Best Bowling (Match)	13-73	A.G.Steel	1878
Hat-Tricks	F.C.Cobden (1870), A.G.Steel (1879), P.H.Morton (1880), J.F.Ireland (1911), R.G.H.Lowe (1926)		
Match Double	No instance		

†C.I.Thornton's XI

OXFORD UNIVERSITY RECORDS

FIRST-CLASS CRICKET

Highest Total	For	651		v Sussex	Hove	1895
	V	679-7d		by Australians	Oxford	1938
Lowest Total	For	12		v MCC	Oxford	1877
	V	24		by MCC	Oxford	1846
Highest Innings	For	281	K.J.Key	v Middlesex	Chiswick Park	1887
	V	338	W.W.Read	for Surrey	The Oval	1888

Highest Partnerships
Wkt

1st	338	T.Bowring/H.Teesdale	v Gentlemen	Oxford	1908
2nd	226	W.G.Keighley/H.A.Pawson	v Cambridge U	Lord's	1947
3rd	273	F.C. de Saram/N.S.M-Innes†	v Glos	Oxford	1934
4th	276	P.G.T.Kingsley/N.M.Ford	v Surrey	The Oval	1930
5th	256*	A.A.Baig/C.A.Fry	v F Foresters	Oxford	1959
6th	270	D.R.Walsh/S.A.Westley	v Warwicks	Oxford	1969
7th	340	K.J.Key/H.Philipson	v Middlesex	Chiswick Park	1887
8th	160	H.Philipson/A.C.M.Croome	v MCC	Lord's	1889
9th	157	H.M.G-Wells‡/C.K.H.Hill-Wood	v Kent	Oxford	1928
10th	149	F.H.Hollins/B.A.Collins	v MCC	Oxford	1901

Best Bowling	For	10-38	S.E.Butler	v Cambridge U	Lord's	1871
(Innings)	V	10-49	W.G.Grace	for MCC	Oxford	1886
Best Bowling	For	15-65	B.J.T.Bosanquet	v Sussex	Oxford	1900
(Match)	V	16-225	J.E.Walsh	for Leics	Oxford	1953

Most Runs – Season	1,307	Nawab of Pataudi, sr	(av 93.35)	1931
Most Runs – Career	3,319	N.S.Mitchell-Innes	(av 47.41)	1934-1937
Most 100s – Season	6	Nawab of Pataudi, sr		1931
Most 100s – Career	{ 9	A.M.Crawley		1927-1930
	{ 9	Nawab of Pataudi, sr		1928-1931
	{ 9	N.S.Mitchell-Innes		1934-1937
	{ 9	M.P.Donnelly		1946-1947
Most Wkts – Season	70	I.A.R.Peebles	(av 18.15)	1930
Most Wkts – Career	182	R.H.B.Bettington	(av 19.38)	1920-1923

UNIVERSITY MATCH RECORDS

Highest Total	503		1900
Lowest Total	32		1878
Highest Innings	238*	Nawab of Pataudi, sr	1931
Best Bowling (Innings)	10-38	S.E.Butler	1871
Best Bowling (Match)	15-95	S.E.Butler	1871
Hat-Trick	No instance		
Match Doubles	{ 160 and 11-66	P.R.le Couteur	1910
	{ 149 and 10-93	G.J.Toogood	1985

†N.S.Mitchell-Innes   ‡H.M.Garland-Wells

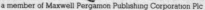

1988 FIRST-CLASS AVERAGES

These averages include performances in all first-class matches played in the British Isles in 1988.

'Cap' denotes the season in which the player was awarded a 1st XI cap by the county he represented in 1988.

Team abbreviations: CU – Cambridge University; D – Derbyshire; E – England; Ex – Essex; Gm – Glamorgan; Gs – Gloucestershire; H – Hampshire; Ire – Ireland; K – Kent; La – Lancashire; Le – Leicestershire; M – Middlesex; Nh – Northamptonshire; Nt – Nottinghamshire; OU – Oxford University; RW – Rest of World XI; Sc – Scotland; SL – Sri Lanka; Sm – Somerset; Sy – Surrey; Sx – Sussex; Wa – Warwickshire; WI – West Indies; Wo – Worcestershire; Y – Yorkshire.

† Left-handed batsman.

BATTING AND FIELDING

	Cap	M	I	NO	HS	Runs	Avge	100	50	Ct/St
†Abrahams, J. (La)	1982	3	4	0	39	58	14.50	—	—	2
Adams, C.J. (D)	—	1	1	0	21	21	21.00	—	—	2
Afford, J.A. (Nt)	—	4	8	3	3	4	0.80	—	—	2
Agnew, J.P. (Le/MCC)	1984	24	29	8	38	271	12.90	—	—	2
†Ahangama, F.S. (SL)	—	5	2	2	3*	3	—	—	—	1
Alderman, T.M. (Gs)	—	20	22	11	43*	135	12.27	—	—	12
Alikhan, R.I. (Sx)	—	10	19	0	98	429	22.57	—	3	8
Alleyne, H.L. (K)	—	4	7	1	9	24	4.00	—	—	1
Alleyne, M.W. (Gs)	—	14	21	1	56	300	15.00	—	1	15
Allott, P.J.W. (La)	1981	19	28	4	31*	308	12.83	—	—	13
Almaer, S.A. (OU)	—	6	11	0	67	256	23.27	—	1	2
†Ambrose, C.E.L. (WI)	—	13	15	3	59	278	23.16	—	1	1
Anderson, P.N. (Y)	—	1	1	0	0	0	0.00	—	—	1
Andrew, S.J.W. (H)	—	11	9	7	12*	41	20.50	—	—	1
Anurasiri, S.D. (SL)	—	3	1	1	4*	4	—	—	—	1
†Arthurton, K.L.T. (WI)	—	10	13	3	121	499	49.90	2	2	8
Asif Din(Wa)	1987	23	41	4	158*	1425	38.51	2	8	18
Atherton, M.A. (CU/La)	—	16	27	4	152*	1121	48.73	4	3	15
Athey, C.W.J. (Gs/E)	1985	13	22	6	168*	1064	66.50	2	6	18
Atkins, P.D. (Sy)	—	6	11	1	114*	357	35.70	1	1—	
Atkinson, J.C.M. (CU)	—	7	12	0	73	257	21.41	—	1	4
†Austin, I.D. (La)	—	6	9	2	64	216	30.85	—	2—	
Ayling, J.R. (H)	—	19	33	4	88*	711	24.51	—	4	5
Aymes, A.N. (H)	—	1	—					—	—	3
†Babington, A.M. (Sx)	—	19	26	8	12	87	4.83	—	—	8
Bail, P.A.C. (CU)	—	4	6	0	44	102	17.00	—	—	1
Bailey, R.J. (Nh/E/MCC)	1985	24	42	2	127*	1448	36.20	3	8	23
Bainbridge, P. (Gs)	1981	23	38	1	169	1334	36.05	4	6	9
Bairstow, D.L. (Y)	1973	18	21	3	94*	416	20.80	—	2	38/1
Bakker, P.J. (H)	—	10	11	8	16	50	16.66	—	—	1
Ball, M.C.J. (Gs)	—	2	1	0	2	2	2.00	—	—	—
Banks, D.A. (Wa)	—	7	9	1	61	195	24.37	—	1	5
†Barnett, A.A. (M)	—	1	1	0	10	10	10.00	—	—	—
Barnett, K.J. (D/E)	1982	19	30	2	239*	1623	57.96	5	8	17
Bartlett, R.J. (Sm/MCC)	—	19	31	3	102*	707	25.25	1	3	13
Barwick, S.R. (Gm)	1987	13	7	2	30	40	8.00	—	—	2
Base, S.J. (D)	—	9	10	3	15	59	8.42	—	—	1
Bastien, S. (Gm)	—	4	6	2	36*	57	14.25	—	—	1
Bate, R. (CU)	—	7	12	2	45	160	16.00	—	—	1

	Cap	M	I	NO	HS	Runs	Avge	100	50	Ct/St
Bee, A. (Sc)	—	1	1	1	11*	11	—	—	—	1
Benjamin, J.E. (Wa)	—	1	—	—	—	—	—	—	—	—
Benjamin, W.K.M. (WI)	—	10	10	4	21*	102	17.00	—	—	6
Benson, J.D.R. (Le)	—	1	1	0	3	3	3.00	—	—	—
†Benson, M.R. (K)	1981	21	37	1	110	1227	34.08	2	8	13
Bent, P. (Wo)	—	3	6	1	50	111	22.20	—	1	—
Berry, P.J. (Y)	—	1	2	1	23*	27	27.00	—	—	1
†Bicknell, D.J. (Sy)	—	11	19	1	62	343	19.05	—	2	3
Bicknell, M.P. (Sy)	—	17	13	3	33	93	9.30	—	—	3
Birch, J.D. (Nt)	1981	24	39	4	114*	776	22.17	1	2	14
Bishop, I.R. (WI)	—	8	6	2	23	56	14.00	—	—	1
Blakey, R.J. (Y)	1987	16	24	4	85*	446	22.30	—	2	26/2
Boiling, J. (Sy)	—	1	2	1	8*	9	9.00	—	—	1
Boon, T.J. (Le)	1986	15	23	1	131	505	22.95	1	2	8
†Booth, P.A. (Y)	—	5	8	2	33*	96	16.00	—	—	1
†Border, A.R. (Ex)	1986	20	32	8	169*	1393	58.04	6	4	27
Bore, M.K. (Nt)	1980	1	2	0	5	5	2.50	—	—	—
Botham, I.T. (Wo)	1987	4	4	0	7	18	4.50	—	—	4
Bowler, P.D. (D)	—	24	42	5	159*	1725	46.62	4	9	13
Brassington, A.J. (Gs)	1978	1	1	0	1	1	1.00	—	—	1/1
Briers, N.E. (Le)	1981	24	41	2	125*	1335	34.23	2	9	14
†Broad, B.C. (Nt/E)	1984	20	34	0	73	872	25.64	—	5	13
Brown, A.D. (Ex)	—	4	5	3	6*	13	6.50	—	—	9/2
Brown, G.E. (Sy)	—	3	2	0	10	10	5.00	—	—	6/1
Brown, K.R. (M)	—	21	34	5	131*	822	28.34	2	2	32
Brown, M.E.O. (OU)	—	3	5	2	47	71	23.66	—	—	—
Brown, S.J. (Nh)	—	4	6	1	25*	34	6.80	—	—	—
Bullen, C.K. (Sy)	—	12	14	2	59*	261	21.75	—	2	8
Bunting, R.A. (Sx)	—	17	21	5	17*	96	6.00	—	—	2
Burns, N.D. (Sm)	1987	23	34	7	133*	708	26.22	1	2	57/2
†Butcher, A.R. (Gm)	1987	23	40	2	166	1282	33.73	1	9	13
Butcher, I.P. (Gs)	—	4	6	0	75	98	16.33	—	1	2
Butcher, R.O. (M)	1979	19	29	3	134	796	30.61	1	4	15
†Byas, D. (Y)	—	14	25	1	112	592	24.66	1	4	12
Cairns, B.L. (RW)	—	1	2	0	19	22	11.00	—	—	—
Cairns, C.L. (Nt)	—	4	5	1	15	31	7.75	—	—	—
Callaghan, D.J. (Nt)	—	1	1	0	29	29	29.00	—	—	1
†Cann, M.J. (Gm)	—	6	7	0	28	78	11.14	—	—	5
Capel, D.J. (Nh/MCC/E)	1986	21	36	5	92	1040	33.54	—	7	5
Carr, J.D. (M)	1987	24	43	6	144	1297	35.05	2	7	21
Carrick, P. (Y)	1976	23	34	7	81	815	30.18	—	2	7
†Childs, J.H. (Ex/E)	1986	20	19	12	25*	73	10.42	—	—	6
Clarke, A.R. (Sx)	—	21	32	8	68	337	14.04	—	1	7
Clarke, S.T. (Sy)	1980	12	10	1	28	141	15.66	—	—	11
Cleal, M.W. (Sm)	—	9	12	1	19	97	8.81	—	—	2
†Clinton, G.S. (Sy)	1980	18	29	5	158	1054	43.91	4	4	8
Cobb, R.A. (Le)	1986	11	20	2	65	432	24.00	—	2	10
Cohen, M.F. (Ire)	—	1	2	0	7	12	6.00	—	—	1
Connor, C.A. (H)	1988	18	22	4	24	135	7.50	—	—	3
Cook, G. (Nh)	1975	18	30	1	203	850	29.31	2	3	11
Cook, N.G.B. (Nh/MCC)	1987	24	27	2	24	181	7.24	—	—	14
†Cooper, K.E. (Nt)	1980	24	34	9	39	282	11.28	—	—	7
Cope, J.E.B. (OU)	—	1	—	—	—	—	—	—	—	1
Cottey, P.A. (Gm)	—	13	23	3	92	603	30.15	—	5	4

162

	Cap	M	I	NO	HS	Runs	Avge	100	50	Ct/St
Cowans, N.G. (M)	1984	20	21	7	27*	119	8.50	—	—	4
Cowdrey, C.S. (K/E)	1979	21	36	7	124*	843	29.06	2	2	33
Cowdrey, G.R. (K)	1988	20	33	4	145	830	28.62	1	4	10
Cowley, N.G. (H)	1978	6	7	3	55	168	42.00	—	1	1
Crawley, M.A. (OU)	—	4	7	2	98	177	35.40	—	1	2
Crowe, M.D. (Sm)	1984	5	9	1	136*	487	60.87	2	2	4
Curran, K.M. (Gs)	1985	19	34	7	142	1005	37.22	2	4	15
Curtis, T.S. (Wo/MCC/E)	1984	22	38	4	131	1337	39.32	2	7	21
Daniel, W.W. (M)	1977	2	2	—	—	—	—	—	—	—
Davis, R.P. (K)	—	19	21	8	23	115	8.84	—	—	12
Davis, W.W. (Nh)	1987	15	18	3	43	306	20.40	—	—	5
DeFreitas, P.A.J. (Le/E)	1986	17	25	1	113	517	21.54	1	3	8
Dennis, S.J. (Y)	1983	4	5	2	36*	50	16.66	—	—	1
Derrick, J. (Gm)	1988	21	28	6	50*	229	10.40	—	1	10
De Silva, P.A. (SL)	—	6	9	3	117*	333	55.50	1	2	3
†Dilley, G.R. (Wo/E)	1987	13	15	2	36	147	11.30	—	—	2
D'Oliveira, D.B. (Wo)	1985	8	11	1	37	132	13.20	—	—	6
Donald, A.A. (Wa)	—	7	10	3	29	74	10.57	—	—	4
Downton, P.R. (M/E)	1981	18	24	5	120	614	32.31	1	2	40/5
†Dredge, C.H. (Sm)	1978	3	6	0	37	82	13.66	—	—	—
Dujon, P.J.L. (WI)	—	12	16	4	141	601	50.08	1	5	31
East, D.E. (Ex)	1982	20	30	2	134	669	23.89	1	2	60/6
Edwards, P.G. (OU)	—	5	7	3	9	32	8.00	—	—	2
Ellcock, R.M. (Wo)	—	5	4	1	13	27	9.00	—	—	1
†Ellison, R.M. (K)	1983	20	27	6	50*	345	16.42	—	1	7
Emburey, J.E. (M/E)	1977	20	27	4	102	673	29.26	1	4	24
Evans, K.P. (Nt)	—	15	24	4	54	406	20.30	—	1	19
Evans, R.J. (Nt)	—	2	2	1	50*	71	71.00	—	1	2
†Fairbrother, N.H. (La)	1985	23	41	4	111	1134	30.64	2	6	9
Falkner, N.J. (Sx)	—	7	14	0	55	232	16.57	—	1	4
Farbrace, P. (K)	—	1	2	0	9	15	7.50	—	—	2
Feltham, M.A. (Sy)	—	22	25	9	74	367	22.93	—	1	10
†Felton, N.A. (Sm)	1986	14	27	2	127	720	28.80	1	4	7
Fenton, N.C.W. (CU)	—	7	9	3	2	4	0.66	—	—	1
Ferris, G.J.F. (Le)	1988	18	20	8	36*	139	11.58	—	—	1
Finney, R.J. (D)	1985	4	5	2	52*	142	47.33	—	1	—
†Fitton, J.D. (La)	—	2	2	1	36	47	47.00	—	—	1
Fletcher, K.W.R. (Ex)	1963	12	14	3	58	303	27.54	—	2	9
Fletcher, S.D. (Y)	1988	17	15	3	18	81	6.75	—	—	7
Folley, I. (La)	1987	19	20	14	30	102	17.00	—	—	6
Fordham, A. (Nh)	—	16	29	6	125*	637	27.69	1	3	13
Foster, D.J. (Sm)	—	13	14	9	20	72	14.40	—	—	—
Foster, N.A. (Ex/E)	1983	16	21	4	34	171	10.05	—	—	8
†Fowler, G. (La/MCC)	1981	21	38	1	172	1134	30.64	2	5	19
Fraser, A.G.J. (M)	—	1	2	1	14	19	19.00	—	—	1
Fraser, A.R.C. (M)	1988	23	28	10	41	223	12.38	—	—	5
Fraser-Darling, C.D. (Nt)	—	1	1	0	18	18	18.00	—	—	2
French, B.N. (Nt)	1980	7	11	1	28	135	13.50	—	—	13
Frost, M. (Sy)	—	4	4	0	7	11	2.75	—	—	—
Garnham, M.A. (Le)	—	1	—	—	—	—	—	—	—	2
Gatting, M.W. (M/E)	1977	20	33	2	210	1469	47.38	3	9	15
†Gifford, N. (Wa)	1983	18	25	11	23*	104	7.42	—	—	3
Golding, A.K. (CU)	—	1	1	1	18*	18	—	—	—	2
Goldsmith, S.C. (D)	—	24	39	4	89	1071	30.60	—	7	16

	Cap	M	I	NO	HS	Runs	Avge	100	50	Ct/St
Gooch, G.A. (Ex/E)	1975	21	37	1	275	2324	64.55	6	15	28
†Gould, I.J. (Sx)	1981	19	31	4	82*	875	32.40	—	6	33
Gouldstone, M.R. (Nh)	—	7	12	1	71	239	21.72	—	2	4
Govan, J.W. (Sc)	—	1	1	0	4	4	4.00	—	—	—
†Gower, D.I. (Le/E)	1977	22	38	4	172	1317	38.73	2	5	16
Graveney, D.A. (Gs)	1976	23	24	9	47	231	15.40	—	—	14
Gray, A.H. (Sy)	1985	1	—	—	—	—	—	—	—	—
†Greatbatch, M.J. (RW)	—	1	2	1	26*	32	32.00	—	—	1
Green, A.M. (Sx)	1985	16	29	2	68	639	23.66	—	4	10
Green, N.H. (OU)	—	1	1	0	9	9	9.00	—	—	1
Green, S.J. (Wa)	—	1	2	0	28	28	14.00	—	—	1
Greene, V.S. (Gs)	—	3	2	0	2	2	1.00	—	—	1
Greenidge, C.G. (WI)	—	11	16	1	111	762	50.80	3	4	6
Greig, I.A. (Sy)	1987	23	28	1	67	529	19.59	—	1	17
Griffith, F.A. (D)	—	5	7	1	37	105	17.50	—	—	2
Hagan, D.A. (OU)	—	7	13	2	59	306	27.81	—	1	3
Haggo, D.J. (Sc)	—	1	1	0	45	45	45.00	—	—	2
Halliday, M. (Ire)	—	1	2	1	29*	55	55.00	—	—	—
Hampton, A.N.S. (OU)	—	3	6	0	12	22	3.66	—	—	—
Harden, R.J. (Sm)	—	6	11	1	78	295	29.50	—	3	3
Hardie, B.R. (Ex)	1974	13	20	3	58	377	22.17	—	2	9
†Hardy, J.J.E. (Sm)	1987	22	39	3	97	927	25.75	—	6	23
Harman, M.D. (K)	—	12	13	6	17*	80	11.42	—	—	8
Harper, R.A. (WI)	—	12	13	5	217*	622	77.75	1	4	22
†Harrison, G.D. (Ire)	—	1	2	0	25	25	12.50	—	—	—
Hart, R.J. (CU)	—	3	5	1	6	7	1.75	—	—	—
Hartley, P.J. (Y)	1987	13	17	6	127*	364	33.09	1	—	7
Hartley, S.N. (Y)	1981	2	3	1	26*	60	30.00	—	—	—
Hayhurst, A.N. (La)	—	14	23	2	107	492	23.42	1	2	2
Haynes, D.L. (WI/RW)	—	15	25	4	158	964	45.90	1	7	6
Heap, R. (CU)	—	1	2	0	15	15	7.50	—	—	2
Heath, S.D. (CU)	—	5	8	1	33*	100	14.28	—	—	2
Hegg, W.K. (La)	—	24	34	5	76	467	16.10	—	1	52/8
Hemmings, E.E. (Nt)	1980	17	25	10	31*	245	16.33	—	—	9
Henderson, I.M. (OU)	—	5	7	1	21*	55	9.16	—	—	1
Heppel, N. (OU)	—	1	1	0	14*	14	—	—	—	—
Hepworth, P.N. (Le)	—	4	6	0	51	132	22.00	—	1	—
Heseltine, P.A.W. (Sx)	—	2	2	0	8	14	7.00	—	—	—
Hick, G.A. (Wo/MCC)	1986	24	37	2	405*	2713	77.51	10	5	28
†Hinks, S.G. (K)	1985	16	27	1	138	764	29.38	1	3	12
Hoffman, D.S. (Nh)	—	1	1	0	20*	20	—	—	—	1
Holding, M.A. (D)	1983	11	12	2	30*	129	12.90	—	—	7
†Holloway, P.C.L. (Wa)	—	3	5	0	16	40	8.00	—	—	8/1
Holmes, G.C. (Gm)	1985	20	32	4	117	999	35.67	4	4	6
†Hookey, S.G. (RW)	—	1	2	0	90	118	59.00	—	1	—
Hooper, A.M. (CU)	—	2	3	0	3	5	1.66	—	—	—
Hooper, C.L. (WI)	—	14	20	1	87	625	32.89	—	5	9
Hopkins, J.A. (Gm)	1977	13	23	1	87	534	24.27	—	4	9
Hughes, D.P. (La)	1970	22	34	4	62	522	17.40	—	3	25
Hughes, S.P. (M)	1981	18	21	5	53	321	20.06	—	1	3
Humpage, G.W. (Wa)	1976	17	26	1	80	411	16.44	—	3	56/1
Hussain, N. (Ex)	—	9	13	3	165*	486	48.60	1	2	5
Hutchinson, I.J.F. (M)	—	3	4	0	25	48	12.00	—	—	—
Ibadulla, K.B.K. (Gs)	—	4	7	3	77	124	31.00	—	1	1

	Cap	M	I	NO	HS	Runs	Avge	100	50	Ct/St
Igglesden, A.P. (K)	—	7	8	2	41	103	17.16	—	—	1
Illingworth, R.K. (Wo)	1986	23	22	4	60	404	22.44	—	2	18
†Ilott, M.C. (Ex)	—	2	1	0	6	6	6.00	—	—	—
Imran Khan (Sx/RW)	1978	5	7	1	55	129	21.50	—	1	—
Jack, T.B. (OU)	—	2	3	0	29	57	19.00	—	—	1
Jackson, P.B. (Ire)	—	1	2	1	2*	2	2.00	—	—	1
†James, K.D. (H)	—	12	22	2	77	320	16.00	—	1	3
Jarvis, K.B.S. (Gs)	—	3	1	1	1*	1		—	—	1
Jarvis, P.W. (Y/E)	1986	7	12	2	29*	97	9.70	—	—	1
Jean-Jacques, M. (D)	—	4	4	0	5	5	1.25	—	—	2
†Jefferies, S.T. (H)	—	14	19	5	60	462	33.00	—	2	4
Jesty, T.E. (La)	—	15	27	3	73	693	28.87	—	3	3
Johnson, P. (Nt)	1986	24	42	3	140	1389	35.61	3	7	12
†Jones, A.N. (Sm)	1987	20	21	8	38	130	10.00	—	—	8
†Kallicharran, A.I. (Wa)	1972	9	15	1	117*	418	29.85	1	2	4
Kelleher, D.J.M. (K)	—	5	7	1	51	150	25.00	—	1	2
Kendrick, N.M. (Sy)	—	1	1	1	8*	8		—	—	1
Ker, J.E. (Sc)	—	1	1	0	5	5	5.00	—	—	—
Kilborn, M.J. (OU)	—	7	13	0	78	351	27.00	—	2	5
Kimber, S.J.S. (Sx)	—	4	7	3	32*	54	13.50	—	—	2
†Knight, R.D.V. (MCC)	—	1	1	0	1	1	1.00	—	—	—
Kuruppu, D.S.B.P. (SL)	—	6	10	1	158	438	48.66	1	2	1/1
Labrooy, G.F. (SL)	—	7	4	1	42	73	24.33	—	—	2
Lamb, A.J. (Nh/E)	1978	16	27	5	155	1163	52.86	5	5	7
Larkins, W. (Nh/MCC)	1976	23	41	2	134	1024	26.25	2	4	23
Lawrence, D.V. (Gs/E)	1985	22	26	3	29	225	9.78	—	—	3
Lawson, G.F. (RW)	—	1	1	0	2	2	2.00	—	—	2
Leatherdale, D.A. (Wo)	—	10	15	1	34*	255	18.21	—	—	3
Lenham, N.J. (Sx)	—	18	32	2	74	733	24.43	—	3	7
Lever, J.K. (Ex)	1970	13	13	1	20	53	4.41	—	—	2
Lewis, C.C. (Le)	—	16	23	4	40	400	21.05	—	—	10
Lewis, D.A. (Ire)	—	1	2	0	17	17	8.50	—	—	—
Lillee, D.K. (Nh/RW)	—	8	11	2	22	120	13.33	—	—	3
Lilley, A.W. (Ex)	1986	21	33	3	80*	803	26.76	—	5	16
Lloyd, G.D. (La)	—	1	2	0	22	22	11.00	—	—	1
†Lloyd, T.A. (Wa)	1980	24	43	3	160*	1448	36.20	4	3	7
†Lloyds, J.W. (Gs)	1985	16	24	3	102*	433	20.61	1	1	20
Logie, A.L. (WI)	—	13	18	4	95*	586	41.85	—	3	9
†Lord, G.J. (Wo)	—	20	33	2	101	862	27.80	1	4	4
Love, J.D. (Y)	1980	18	28	2	93*	751	28.88	—	6	12
Lynch, M.A. (Sy)	1982	21	29	4	103*	996	39.84	2	4	17
McEwan, S.M. (Wo)	—	6	2	1	6	6	6.00	—	—	1
McGurk, G.B.J. (Sc)	—	1	1	0	63	63	63.00	—	1	3
MacLaurin, N.R.C. (M)	—	1	2	0	35	37	18.50	—	—	—
Madugalle, R.S. (SL)	—	8	11	2	97	403	44.77	—	3	4
†Madurasinghe, A.W.R. (SL)	—	6	7	2	30	75	15.00	—	—	1
Mahanama, R.S. (SL)	—	5	8	2	46*	179	29.83	—	—	1
Maher, B.J.M. (D)	1987	24	39	6	121*	974	29.51	1	5	60/1
Makinson, D.J. (La)	—	1	—	—	—	—	—	—	—	—
Malcolm, D.E. (D)	—	20	21	5	22	119	7.43	—	—	4
Mallender, N.A. (Sm/MCC)	1987	17	20	7	44	158	12.15	—	—	8
Maninder Singh (RW)	—	1	1	1	2*	2		—	—	1
Marks, V.J. (Sm)	1979	23	31	2	68	719	24.79	—	3	8
Marsh, S.A. (K)	1986	23	35	6	120	713	24.58	2	1	56/5

165

	Cap	M	I	NO	HS	Runs	Avge	100	50	Ct/St
Marshall, M.D. (WI)	—	9	10	1	76	289	32.11	—	2	3
Martindale, D.J.R. (Nt)	—	9	14	1	52*	261	20.07	—	1	3
Maru, R.J. (H)	1986	23	29	5	74	302	12.58	—	1	31
†Matthews, C.D. (La)	—	3	3	0	31	38	12.66	—	—	—
Maynard, M.P. (Gm/MCC/E)	1987	23	42	6	126	1485	41.25	3	11	22
Mays, C.S. (Sy)	—	2	1	1	13*	13	—	—	—	2
Medlycott, K.T. (Sy)	1988	23	29	5	77*	554	23.08	—	4	28
Mendis, G.D. (La)	1986	24	42	4	151	1364	35.89	2	8	10
Mendis, L.R.D. (SL)	—	9	12	2	124	362	36.20	1	2	2
Merrick, T.A. (Wa)	1988	16	21	3	34	256	14.22	—	—	5
Metcalfe, A.A. (Y)	1986	22	40	5	216*	1320	37.71	2	8	5
Metson, C.P. (Gm)	1987	23	30	8	48	351	15.95	—	—	52/8
Middleton, T.C. (H)	—	1	2	0	23	28	14.00	—	—	—
Miller, G. (Ex)	1988	19	21	4	77	377	22.17	—	1	22
†Millns, D.J. (Nt)	—	11	12	5	7	20	2.85	—	—	4
Moles, A.J. (Wa)	1987	18	31	2	115	968	33.37	1	5	12
Monkhouse, S. (Gm)	—	3	1	1	0	0	—	—	—	—
Moores, P. (Sx)	—	14	24	2	97*	395	17.95	—	1	30/3
Morris, H. (Gm)	1986	19	33	3	87	832	27.73	—	6	14
Morris, J.E. (D)	1986	23	37	5	175	1204	37.62	2	6	6
Morris, R.E. (OU)	—	4	8	0	21	39	4.87	—	—	1
Mortensen, O.H. (D)	1986	12	12	8	15	46	11.50	—	—	6
†Morton, W. (Sc)	—	1	1	0	7	7	7.00	—	—	2
Moxon, M.D. (Y/E)	1984	21	39	3	191	1485	41.25	3	8	23
Mudassar Nazar (RW)	—	1	2	0	20	24	12.00	—	—	1
Mullally, A.D. (H)	—	1	—	—	—	—	—	—	—	1
Munton, T.A. (Wa)	—	16	22	7	24*	131	8.73	—	—	2
Murphy, A.J. (La)	—	4	3	0	3	3	1.00	—	—	2
Myles, S.D. (Wa)	—	4	7	0	39	111	15.85	—	—	—
Neale, P.A. (Wo)	1978	21	31	5	167	1036	39.84	4	2	8
Needham, A. (M)	—	8	12	3	66*	293	32.55	—	2	5
Nelson, A.N. (Ire)	—	1	2	0	22	26	13.00	—	—	1
Newell, M. (Nt)	1987	20	37	3	105	740	21.76	1	2	28
Newman, P.G. (D)	1986	16	19	6	39	187	14.38	—	—	1
Newport, P.J. (Wo/E)	1986	22	25	8	77*	447	26.29	—	1	8
Nicholas, M.C.J. (H/MCC)	1982	25	47	3	132*	1301	29.56	2	5	18
†Nicholson, N.G. (Y)	—	2	4	1	16	47	15.66	—	—	3
North, P.D. (Gm)	—	7	7	3	41*	107	26.75	—	—	2
Noyes, S.J. (CU)	—	8	14	1	38	170	13.07	—	—	6
Nuttall, J.D. (OU)	—	5	6	2	35	52	13.00	—	—	2
O'Gorman, T.J.G. (D)	—	5	9	0	78	152	16.88	—	1	5
Olley, M.W.C. (M)	—	4	5	1	27*	69	17.25	—	—	9
Ontong, R.C. (Gm)	1979	17	25	8	120*	734	43.17	1	4	7
O'Shaughnessy, S.J. (Wo)	—	11	18	1	44	142	8.35	—	—	5
Palmer, G.V. (Sm)	—	1	2	0	23	23	11.50	—	—	—
Parker, P.W.G. (Sx)	1979	21	40	5	124	1359	38.82	5	5	17
Parks, R.J. (H)	1982	23	35	8	38*	420	15.55	—	—	63/10
†Parsons, G.J. (Wa)	1987	10	13	4	52	174	19.33	—	1	1
Patterson, B.M.W. (Sc)	—	1	1	0	100	100	100.00	1	—	3
Patterson, B.P. (WI)	—	9	7	2	23*	60	12.00	—	—	1
†Penn, C. (K)	1987	20	31	12	40	436	22.94	—	—	8
Perry, J.N. (CU)	—	7	9	1	26	73	9.12	—	—	3
Peters, N.H. (Sy)	—	12	15	3	25*	85	12.14	—	—	5
Phillip, I.L. (Sc)	—	1	1	0	27	27	27.00	—	—	—

	Cap	M	I	NO	HS	Runs	Avge	100	50	Ct/St
†Pick, R.A. (Nt)	1987	3	4	1	19	31	10.33	—	—	1
Pickles, C.S. (Y)	—	1	2	1	3*	3	3.00	—	—	1
Pienaar, R.F. (K)	1988	21	35	2	144	1228	37.21	3	7	5
Pierson, A.R.K. (Wa)	—	9	12	7	18*	57	11.40	—	—	1
Pigott, A.C.S. (Sx)	1982	20	34	8	56	668	25.69	—	3	16
Pointer, G.A. (CU)	—	7	12	2	18*	114	11.40	—	—	—
Polkinghorne, D.A. (OU)	—	3	4	1	45*	72	24.00	—	—	2
†Pollard, P. (Nt)	—	9	17	1	142	428	26.75	1	1	6
Pont, I.L. (Ex)	—	8	8	2	68	149	24.83	—	1	2
Pook, R.N. (Ex)	—	1	1	0	6	6	6.00	—	—	3
Pooley, M.W. (Gs)	—	8	13	5	38	149	18.62	—	—	4
Potter, L. (Le)	1988	23	34	7	107	885	32.77	1	5	14
Prichard, P.J. (Ex)	1986	24	39	8	97	1202	38.77	—	9	12
Pridgeon, A.P. (Wo)	1980	10	11	3	11	31	3.87	—	—	3
Pringle, D.R. (Ex/E)	1982	19	27	0	128	516	19.11	1	3	5
Pringle, M.W. (Sx)	—	5	7	0	35	104	14.85	—	—	1
Pringle, N.J. (Sm)	—	8	15	4	54	244	22.18	—	1	8
Pyman, R.A. (CU)	—	2	3	0	4	7	2.33	—	—	2
Radford, N.V. (Wo)	1985	18	15	6	65	200	22.22	—	1	13
Rajadurai, B.E.A. (SL)	—	2	—	—	—	—	—	—	—	—
Ramanayake, C.P.H. (SL)	—	4	3	0	18	20	6.66	—	—	—
Ramprakash, M.R. (M)	—	9	13	4	68*	421	46.77	—	3	2
†Ranatunga, A. (SL)	—	8	9	1	84	271	33.87	—	2	3
Randall, D.W. (Nt)	1973	21	37	4	237	1286	38.96	2	9	9
Ratcliffe, J.D. (Wa)	—	2	4	0	16	31	7.75	—	—	2
†Ratnayeke, J.R. (SL)	—	8	10	5	60*	311	62.20	—	2	1
Rea, M.P. (Ire)	—	1	2	0	53	53	26.50	—	1	—
Reeve, D.A. (Wa)	—	16	23	3	103	431	21.55	1	—	11
Reynolds, G.D. (OU)	—	6	9	1	69	147	18.37	—	1	6
Rhodes, S.J. (Wo)	1986	23	33	10	108	597	25.95	1	1	70/8
Richards, C.J. (Sy/E)	1978	20	25	4	102*	874	41.61	1	6	63/1
Richards, I.V.A. (WI)	—	13	16	1	128	624	41.60	1	5	9
Richardson, R.B. (WI)	—	10	14	0	82	279	19.92	—	1	9
Ripley, D. (Nh/MCC)	1987	25	33	6	49	451	16.70	—	—	80/7
Roberts, B. (D)	1986	24	39	4	71	919	26.25	—	7	15
†Robinson, J.D. (Sy)	—	3	5	2	20	55	18.33	—	—	1
Robinson, M.A. (Nh)	—	15	17	7	19*	37	3.70	—	—	3
†Robinson, M.J. (MCC)	—	1	1	0	19	19	19.00	—	—	—
Robinson, P.E. (Y)	1988	24	40	3	129*	1173	31.70	1	8	21
Robinson, R.T. (Nt/E)	1983	21	35	4	134*	1194	38.51	4	4	17
†Roebuck, P.G.P. (Gm)	—	2	4	0	46	60	15.00	—	—	1
Roebuck, P.M. (Sm)	1978	12	19	3	112*	454	28.37	1	1	6
Romaines, P.W. (Gs)	1983	21	39	3	101*	955	26.52	1	6	13
Rose, G.D. (Sm)	1988	20	25	6	69*	385	20.26	—	1	11
Roseberry, M.A. (M)	—	14	21	3	67	386	21.44	—	1	5
†Russell, R.C. (Gs/MCC/E)	1985	24	36	8	94	870	31.07	—	6	57/12
Sabine, D.J. (K)	—	1	2	0	7	8	4.00	—	—	1
Sadiq, Z.A. (Sy)	—	4	6	0	64	135	22.50	—	1	2
Samarasekera, M.A.R. (SL)	—	9	15	2	104	401	30.84	1	2	5
Saxelby, K. (Nt)	1984	13	14	2	17	47	4.27	—	—	4
Scott, A.M.G. (CU)	—	3	5	1	8	9	2.25	—	—	—
Scott, C.W. (Nt)	1988	19	27	6	63*	356	16.95	—	1	49/2
†Scott, R.J. (H)	—	9	16	1	107*	374	24.93	1	2	10
Scriven, T.J.A. (Sm)	—	2	2	0	7	11	5.50	—	—	—

	Cap	M	I	NO	HS	Runs	Avge	100	50	Ct/St
†Searle, A.M. (OU)	—	1	1	0	2	2	2.00	—	—	—
†Seymour, A.C. (Ex)	—	1	1	1	33*	33	—	—	—	—
Sharma, C. (RW)	—	1	1	0	27	27	27.00	—	—	—
Sharma, R. (D)	—	10	14	3	80	315	28.63	—	1	5
†Sharp, K. (Y)	1982	12	19	0	128	428	22.52	1	1	9
Shastri, R.J. (Gm)	1988	12	19	2	157	575	33.82	1	2	5
Shaw, C. (Y)	—	21	25	12	31	170	13.07	—	—	2
Sidebottom, A. (Y)	1980	18	24	5	55	517	27.21	—	2	5
†Silva, S.A.R. (SL)	—	8	14	1	112	338	26.00	1	1	15
Simmons, J. (La)	1971	21	27	9	57*	362	20.11	—	1	11
Simmons, P.V. (WI)	—	1	1	1	53*	53	—	—	1	—
†Slack, W.N. (M)	1981	19	32	5	163*	1228	45.48	3	6	11
Small, G.C. (Wa/MCC/E)	1982	20	29	7	70	554	25.18	—	3	7
Smith, C.L. (H)	1981	22	43	3	124*	1436	35.90	3	8	14
†Smith, D.M. (Sy)	1980	11	18	5	157*	630	48.46	2	1	3
Smith, M.J. (Sc)	—	1	1	0	40	40	40.00	—	—	1
Smith, N.M.K. (Wa)	—	1	1	0	3	3	3.00	—	—	—
Smith, P.A. (Wa)	1986	16	27	4	84*	542	23.56	—	3	3
Smith, R.A. (H/E)	1985	21	42	8	141*	1356	39.88	4	4	15
Snodgrass, D.L. (Sc)	—	1	1	0	2	2	2.00	—	—	—
Speak, N.J. (La)	—	1	2	0	35	45	22.50	—	—	2
Speight, M.P. (Sx)	—	7	13	0	58	258	19.84	—	2	5
Standing, D.K. (Sx)	—	2	3	0	9	13	4.33	—	—	—
Stanley, N.A. (Nh)	—	8	12	2	66	263	26.30	—	3	4
Stenner, J.M.C. (CU)	—	1	2	0	13	13	11.50	—	—	—
Stephenson, F.D. (Nt)	1988	22	35	0	117	1018	29.08	2	7	10
Stephenson, J.P. (Ex)	—	18	31	4	99	791	29.29	—	6	13
Stewart, A.J. (Sy)	1985	22	32	3	133	1006	34.68	2	6	25
Storie, A.C. (Wa)	—	9	17	2	68	255	17.00	—	1	6
Stovold, A.W. (Gs)	1976	21	39	2	136	1296	35.02	2	6	14
Such, P.M. (Le)	—	8	6	2	6	9	2.25	—	—	—
Swallow, I.G. (Y)	—	11	19	2	48*	352	20.70	—	—	5
Swan, R.G. (Sc)	—	1	1	0	77	77	77.00	—	1	1
Sygrove, M.R. (OU)	—	7	8	3	8	29	5.80	—	—	—
Sykes, J.F. (M)	—	9	13	1	88	292	24.33	—	2	3
Tavaré, C.J. (K)	1978	22	36	2	138*	1430	42.05	4	5	29
Taylor, L.B. (Le)	1981	17	16	6	60	111	11.10	—	1	4
Taylor, N.R. (K)	1982	21	37	3	114	925	27.20	2	4	17
Taylor, R.W. (RW)	—	1	1	0	4	4	4.00	—	—	–/1
Tedstone, G.A. (Wa)	—	4	8	0	50	151	18.87	—	1	7/1
Tennant, L. (Le)	—	1	2	1	3	3	3.00	—	—	—
Terry, V.P. (H)	1983	23	43	3	190	1182	29.55	3	5	33
†Thomas, D.J. (Gs)	—	3	4	1	57*	77	25.66	—	1	1
Thomas, J.G. (Gm)	1986	16	26	5	110	515	24.52	2	—	5
Thompson, N.E. (Ire)	—	1	2	0	38	52	26.00	—	—	—
Thorne, D.A. (Wa)	—	15	25	1	76	566	23.58	—	4	17
†Thorpe, G.P. (Sy)	—	3	6	2	100*	158	39.50	1	—	3
Threlfall, P.W. (Sx)	—	1	—	—	—	—	—	—	—	—
†Tillekeratne, H.P. (SL)	—	6	8	1	50*	121	24.20	—	1	4
Topley, T.D. (Ex)	1988	16	22	6	56*	235	14.68	—	1	8
†Towse, A.D. (Y)	—	1	1	0	1	1	1.00	—	—	1
Tremellen, J.M. (CU)	·	7	12	0	33	131	10.91	—	—	3
Tremlett, T.M. (H)	1983	7	10	2	38	111	13.87	—	—	3
Trump, H.R.J. (Sm/MCC)	—	9	11	1	48	62	6.20	—	—	7

168

	Cap	M	I	NO	HS	Runs	Avge	100	50	Ct/St
Tufnell, P.C.R. (M)	—	11	12	4	20	44	5.50	—	—	5
†Turner, D.R. (H)	1970	22	40	6	150*	1204	35.41	2	6	5
Turner, R.J. (CU)	—	8	14	1	27	155	11.92	—	—	9/2
Van Zyl, C.J.P.G. (Gm)	—	4	5	1	11	30	7.50	—	—	1
†Vincent, D.A. (Ire)	—	1	2	0	16	24	12.00	—	—	—
†Vorster, L.P. (Wo)	—	1	1	1	16*	16	—	—	—	—
†Walker, A. (Nh/MCC)	1987	18	20	10	40*	213	21.30	—	—	7
Wallace, P. (Ire)	—	1	2	—		31	7.75	—	—	—
Walsh, C.A. (WI)	—	9	7	3	9*	31	7.75	—	—	—
Ward, D.M. (Sy)	—	25	36	6	126	942	31.40	1	8	21
Ward, T.R. (K)	—	10	17	0	72	362	21.29	—	3	9
Warke, S.J.S. (Ire)	—	1	2	0	42	46	23.00	—	—	—
Warner, A.E. (D)	1987	19	25	6	45	300	15.78	—	—	4
†Wasim Akram (La)	—	10	18	2	116*	496	31.00	1	3	2
Watkin, S.L. (Gm)	—	16	19	7	23	115	9.58	—	—	1
Watkinson, M. (La)	1987	24	39	4	85*	759	21.68	—	6	15
Waugh, M.E. (Ex)	—	3	4	0	86	178	44.50	—	1	2
Waugh, S.R. (Sm)	1988	15	24	6	161	1314	73.00	6	4	20
Weale, S.D. (OU)	—	6	9	0	40	136	15.11	—	—	3
Wells, A.P. (Sx)	1986	23	42	5	120	1286	34.75	1	9	18
Wells, C.M. (Sx/MCC)	1982	24	41	4	109*	908	24.54	1	4	8
Wells, V.J. (K)	—	1	2	0	6	6	3.00	—	—	1
Weston, M.J. (Wo)	1986	18	24	5	95*	514	27.05	—	3	15
Whitaker, J.J. (Le)	1986	23	39	5	145	1223	35.97	3	5	17
Whitticase, P. (Le)	1987	23	32	10	71	469	21.31	—	2	69/4
†Wild, D.J. (Nh)	1986	18	27	1	75	423	16.26	—	2	3
Willey, P. (Le)	1984	24	40	1	130	978	25.07	2	3	12
Williams, D. (WI)	—	8	10	1	51	182	20.22	—	1	11/1
Williams, N.F. (M)	1984	8	11	2	63*	186	20.66	—	1	1
Williams, R.G. (Nh/MCC)	1979	20	34	9	119	842	33.68	1	4	8
Wright, A.J. (Gs)	1987	24	42	1	137	1268	30.92	2	5	14
†Wright, J.G. (D)	1977	11	20	1	154*	815	42.89	1	5	1
Wyatt, J.G. (Sm)	—	15	26	1	69	578	23.12	—	3	9

BOWLING

(See BATTING and FIELDING section for details of caps and teams.)

	Cat	O	M	R	W	Avge	Best	5 wI	10 wM
Abrahams, J.	OB	23	6	65	2	32.50	1-17	—	—
Afford, J.A.	SLA	83	19	270	9	30.00	3-60	—	—
Agnew, J.P.	RFM	783.5	166	2367	93	25.45	7-61	8	1
Ahangama, F.S.	RM	99.2	22	321	12	26.75	4-51	—	—
Alderman, T.M.	RFM	601	135	1711	75	22.81	8-59	3	—
Alikhan, R.I.	OB	7.3	0	26	2	13.00	2-19	—	—
Alleyne, H.L.	RFM	94.3	17	322	12	26.83	5-54	1	—
Alleyne, M.W.	RM	68	13	227	6	37.83	4-48	—	—
Allott, P.J.W.	RFM	590.2	162	1378	67	20.56	6-59	5	—
Ambrose, C.E.L.	RF	329.1	86	733	35	20.94	4-27	—	—
Anderson, P.N.	RM	17.3	4	47	1	47.00	1-47	—	—
Andrew, S.J.W.	RMF	268.5	68	765	31	24.67	5-36	1	—
Anurasiri, S.D.	SLA	62	16	175	2	87.50	2-67	—	—
Arthurton, K.L.T.	SLA	27.1	8	80	3	26.66	2-1	—	—
Asif Din	LB	101	17	387	6	64.50	3-57	—	—

	Cat	O	M	R	W	Avge	Best	5 wI	10 wM
Atherton, M.A.	LB	269.1	42	807	11	73.36	3-32	—	—
Athey, C.W.J.	RM	5	0	20	0	—	—	—	—
Atkinson, J.C.M.	RMF	17	1	86	1	86.00	1-43	—	—
Austin, I.D.	RM	137.1	43	367	15	24.46	5-79	1	—
Ayling, J.R.	RM	432.1	97	1098	47	23.36	4-57	—	—
Babington, A.M.	RFM	554.5	112	1628	49	33.22	4-66	—	—
Bail, P.A.C.	OB	14	1	71	1	71.00	1-36	—	—
Bailey, R.J.	OB	76.1	10	278	7	39.71	3-27	—	—
Bainbridge, P.	RM	324	62	1054	17	62.00	5-33	1	—
Bakker, P.J.	RMF	293.4	86	670	30	22.33	5-54	1	—
Ball, M.C.J.	OB	34	8	90	2	45.00	1-2	—	—
Banks, D.A.	RM	1	1	0	0	—	—	—	—
Barnett, A.A.	SLA	27	9	65	0	—	—	—	—
Barnett, K.J.	LB	161.1	37	414	14	29.57	3-63	—	—
Bartlett, R.J.	OB	30	4	145	4	36.25	1-9	—	—
Barwick, S.R.	RMF	408.5	112	1064	32	33.25	5-37	1	—
Base, S.J.	RMF	195	20	735	22	33.40	4-74	—	—
Bastien, S.	RMF	119.1	35	289	8	36.12	5-90	1	—
Bee, A.	RMF	17.1	2	55	2	27.50	2-20	—	—
Benjamin, J.E.	RMF	17	6	53	0	—	—	—	—
Benjamin, W.K.M.	RFM	183.1	43	467	33	14.15	4-20	—	—
Benson, M.R.	OB	3.3	0	39	0	—	—	—	—
Berry, P.J.	OB	38.2	13	91	3	30.33	2-35	—	—
Bicknell, D.J.	LM	2	0	19	0	—	—	—	—
Bicknell, M.P.	RFM	516.2	136	1511	50	30.22	9-45	1	—
Birch, J.D.	RM	123.2	35	379	7	54.14	2-52	—	—
Bishop, I.R.	RF	142	30	406	21	19.33	6-39	2	—
Boiling, J.	OB	15	3	40	0	—	—	—	—
Booth, P.A.	SLA	135.4	35	361	11	32.81	5-98	1	—
Border, A.R.	SLA	36	9	113	1	113.00	1-20	—	—
Bore, M.K.	LM	9	2	41	0	—	—	—	—
Botham, I.T.	RFM	43	11	125	1	125.00	1-40	—	—
Bowler, P.D.	OB	169.5	28	577	7	82.42	2-63	—	—
Broad, B.C.	RM	4	0	30	0	—	—	—	—
Brown, K.R.		2	2	0	0	—	—	—	—
Brown, S.J.	LFM	102	34	221	9	24.55	3-20	—	—
Bullen, C.K.	OB	107.1	25	316	11	28.72	4-56	—	—
Bunting, R.A.	RFM	400	63	1320	41	32.19	5-44	3	—
Butcher, A.R.	LM	54	10	198	5	39.60	2-28	—	—
Byas, D.	RM	9.2	0	49	0	—	—	—	—
Cairns, B.L.	RMF	3	0	11	4	2.75	4-11	—	—
Cairns, C.L.	RFM	109	16	384	15	25.60	4-70	—	—
Callaghan, D.J.	RM	17	1	59	1	59.00	1-59	—	—
Cann, M.J.	OB	14	2	63	4	15.75	2-20	—	—
Capel, D.J.	RMF	436.1	76	1451	41	35.39	4-40	—	—
Carr, J.D.	RM/OB	84.1	22	196	5	39.20	1-4	—	—
Carrick, P.	SLA	593	179	1551	50	31.02	5-46	2	—
Childs, J.H.	SLA	654.5	208	1582	62	25.51	6-92	4	1
Clarke, A.R.	LB	618	157	1650	44	37.50	5-60	2	—
Clarke, S.T.	RF	396.4	108	913	63	14.49	6-52	4	2
Cleal, M.W.	RMF	168	25	582	20	29.10	4-41	—	—
Clinton, G.S.	RM	0.4	0	16	0	—	—	—	—
Connor, C.A.	RFM	495.3	92	1497	55	27.21	5-70	1	—
Cook, G.	SLA	5	1	7	0	—	—	—	—

170

	Cat	O	M	R	W	Avge	Best	5 wI	10 wM
Cook, N.G.B.	SLA	769.2	264	1635	68	24.04	6-56	2	—
Cooper, K.E.	RFM	816	220	2179	101	21.57	5-41	5	—
Cowans, N.G.	RF	491.5	123	1290	71	18.16	6-49	3	1
Cowdrey, C.S.	RM	391.2	96	1141	39	29.25	5-46	1	—
Cowdrey, G.R.	RM	93.4	18	365	6	60.83	1-5	—	—
Cowley, N.G.	OB	157.1	47	337	11	30.63	3-39	—	—
Crawley, M.A.	RM	38	7	136	0	—	—	—	—
Curran, K.M.	RMF	414.2	86	1385	65	21.30	7-54	4	3
Curtis, T.S.	LB	14.5	1	74	1	74.00	1-53	—	—
Daniel, W.W.	RF	16	2	37	2	18.50	2-16	—	—
Davis, R.P.	SLA	563	177	1409	38	37.07	5-132	1	—
Davis, W.W.	RF	538.2	91	1614	73	22.10	7-52	7	2
DeFreitas, P.A.J.	RFM	557.3	127	1555	64	24.29	5-38	5	—
Dennis, S.J.	LFM	90	19	262	8	32.75	3-35	—	—
Derrick, J.	RM	540.1	138	1511	47	32.14	6-54	1	—
De Silva, P.A.	RM	14	5	42	1	42.00	1-32	—	—
Dilley, G.R.	RF	387.1	70	1098	49	22.40	5-46	4	—
Donald, A.A.	RFM	180.4	40	534	26	20.53	5-57	1	—
Dredge, C.H.	RMF	68.5	20	225	3	75.00	2-133	—	—
Edwards, P.G.	SLA	171.3	43	560	9	62.22	3-88	—	—
Ellcock, R.M.	RFM	94.1	10	379	9	42.11	3-86	—	—
Ellison, R.M.	RMF	603.4	171	1697	71	23.90	7-75	3	—
Emburey, J.E.	OB	671.5	215	1543	58	26.60	6-24	2	—
Evans, K.P.	RMF	258.5	49	829	22	37.68*	3-22	—	—
Evans, R.J.	RM	25	9	63	3	21.00	3-40	—	—
Fairbrother, N.H.	LM	10.1	0	59	0	—	—	—	—
Feltham, M.A.	RM	584.1	135	1679	56	29.98	5-45	1	—
Felton, N.A.		0.5	0	8	0	—	—	—	—
Fenton, N.C.W.	RFM	271.4	65	726	21	34.57	4-64	—	—
Ferris, G.J.F.	RF	452.1	82	1380	62	22.25	5-47	2	—
Finney, R.J.	LM	59	15	168	1	168.00	1-34	—	—
Fitton, J.D.	OB	58	16	120	7	17.14	6-59	1	—
Fletcher, S.D.	RMF	412	66	1308	59	22.16	8-58	2	—
Folley, I.	SLA	614.3	168	1701	57	29.84	6-20	2	—
Foster, D.J.	RFM	299.3	46	1044	28	37.28	4-46	—	—
Foster, N.A.	RFM	598.3	122	1822	80	22.77	6-53	5	2
Fraser, A.G.J.	RFM	28	6	82	1	82.00	1-57	—	—
Fraser, A.R.C.	RFM	697.1	195	1550	80	19.37	6-68	6	2
Fraser-Darling, C.D.	RMF	12	4	30	0	—	—	—	—
Frost, M.	RMF	99.5	23	326	10	32.60	4-56	—	—
Gatting, M.W.	RM	96	21	287	4	71.75	1-23	—	—
Gifford, N.	SLA	425.1	121	976	31	31.48	3-66	—	—
Golding, A.K.	SLA	23	11	43	0	—	—	—	—
Goldsmith, S.C.	RM	43	8	125	0	—	—	—	—
Gooch, G.A.	RM	152	39	401	10	40.10	2-29	—	—
Gould, I.J.		21	2	84	2	42.00	2-48	—	—
Govan, J.W.	OB	56.5	25	92	9	10.22	5-54	1	—
Graveney, D.A.	SLA	612.2	179	1353	53	25.52	8-127	2	1
Gray, A.H.	RF	26	13	38	2	19.00	1-17	—	—
Green, A.M.	OB	151.5	40	392	10	39.20	6-82	1	—
Greene, V.S.	RMF	69	19	180	8	22.50	5-53	1	—
Greig, I.A.	RMF	402.3	83	1143	49	23.32	6-34	2	—
Griffith, F.A.	RM	99.3	20	347	10	34.70	4-47	—	—
Hagan, D.A.	OB	3	0	21	0	—	—	—	—

	Cat	O	M	R	W	Avge	Best	5 wI	10 wM
Halliday, M.	OB	30	1	97	3	32.33	3-97	—	—
Harden, R.J.	LM	16	1	61	0	—	—	—	—
Hardy, J.J.E.		0.3	0	12	0	—	—	—	—
Harman, M.D.	OB	266.4	86	593	25	23.72	5-55	2	—
Harper, R.A.	OB	227.3	70	521	21	24.80	4-10	—	—
Harrison, G.D.	RFM	12	0	41	0	—	—	—	—
Hart, R.J.	SLA	67	11	231	4	57.75	4-66	—	—
Hartley, P.J.	RMF	307.3	32	1219	34	35.85	5-85	1	—
Hartley, S.N.	RM	5	1	25	0	—	—	—	—
Hayhurst, A.N.	RM	181.3	41	553	17	32.52	4-45	—	—
Hemmings, E.E.	OB	508.5	139	1312	42	31.23	4-50	—	—
Henderson, I.M.	RMF	71	10	316	5	63.20	3-104	—	—
Heppel, N.	SLA	14	0	74	0	—	—	—	—
Heseltine, P.A.W.	OB	28	5	106	1	106.00	1-102	—	—
Hick, G.A.	OB	204	43	642	21	30.57	4-114	—	—
Hinks, S.G.	RM	2	0	28	0	—	—	—	—
Hoffman, D.S.	RMF	32	6	97	2	48.50	1-43	—	—
Holding, M.A.	RF	279.1	49	827	24	34.45	4-74	—	—
Holmes, G.C.	RM	121.2	15	445	11	40.45	5-38	1	—
Hooper, C.L.	OB	106.1	16	303	9	33.66	3-61	—	—
Hopkins, J.A.		5	1	46	0	—	—	—	—
Hughes, S.P.	RFM	441.3	84	1258	27	46.59	4-39	—	—
Humpage, G.W.	RM	3	0	10	0	—	—	—	—
Hussain, N.	LB	9	0	47	0	—	—	—	—
Ibadulla, K.B.K.	OB	34.2	6	143	3	47.66	3-43	—	—
Igglesden, A.P.	RFM	234.3	46	805	37	21.75	6-34	3	1
Illingworth, R.K.	SLA	597.4	189	1274	58	21.96	5-46	4	2
Ilott, M.C.	LMF	49	15	111	3	37.00	2-23	—	—
Imran Khan	RF	122.3	27	310	13	23.84	5-50	1	—
James, K.D.	LMF	298.5	73	763	35	21.80	5-25	2	—
Jarvis, K.B.S.	RFM	47	7	165	1	165.00	1-32	—	—
Jarvis, P.W.	RFM	233.2	52	651	37	17.59	6-40	2	1
Jean-Jacques, M.	RMF	101.1	16	328	9	36.44	3-49	—	—
Jefferies, S.T.	LFM	355.1	82	1216	34	35.76	8-97	2	—
Jesty, T.E.	RM	25	10	56	0	—	—	—	—
Johnson, P.	RM	2	1	1	0	—	—	—	—
Jones, A.N.	RFM	512	86	1658	55	30.14	7-30	1	—
Kelleher, D.J.M.	RMF	94	23	229	9	25.44	4-24	—	—
Kendrick, N.M.	SLA	28.5	7	97	1	97.00	1-92	—	—
Ker, J.E.	RM	18	3	48	2	24.00	2-36	—	—
Kilborn, M.J.	RM	41.5	8	185	5	37.00	3-37	—	—
Kimber, S.J.S.	RMF	83	19	272	7	38.85	3-44	—	—
Labrooy, G.F.	RMF	203.5	30	665	20	33.25	6-61	1	—
Lamb, A.J.	RM	4	0	19	0	—	—	—	—
Larkins, W.	RM	35	18	65	3	21.66	1-0	—	—
Lawrence, D.V.	RF	647.2	103	2296	84	27.33	7-47	4	—
Lawson, G.F.	RF	17	4	50	3	16.66	3-34	—	—
Leatherdale, D.A.	RM	7	3	20	1	20.00	1-12	—	—
Lenham, N.J.	RMF	28.5	3	101	3	33.66	3-57	—	—
Lever, J.K.	LFM	422.4	90	1120	43	26.04	4-61	—	—
Lewis, C.C.	RMF	391.4	83	1210	42	28.80	6-22	2	1
Lillee, D.K.	RFM	245	45	778	21	37.04	6-68	1	—
Lilley, A.W.	RM	11	0	119	0	—	—	—	—
Lloyd, T.A.	RM/OB	31	1	208	2	104.00	2-107	—	—

	Cat	O	M	R	W	Avge	Best	5 wI	10 wM
Lloyds, J.W.	OB	239.3	42	757	13	58.23	2-22	—	—
Love, J.D.	RM	2.3	0	11	1	11.00	1-11	—	—
Lynch, M.A.	OB	29.2	8	88	4	22.00	3-10	—	—
McEwan, S.M.	RFM	86	7	310	8	38.75	4-43	—	—
MacLaurin, N.R.C.	RM	1	0	4	0	—	—	—	—
Madurasinghe, A.W.R.	OB	144.4	35	376	6	62.66	3-50	—	—
Makinson, D.J.	LFM	27	14	50	1	50.00	1-28	—	—
Malcolm, D.E.	RF	488.1	93	1676	56	29.92	6-68	2	—
Mallender, N.A.	RFM	433.1	111	1037	50	20.74	5-12	1	—
Maninder Singh	SLA	20	2	76	4	19.00	3-52	—	—
Marks, V.J.	OB	862.5	222	2214	76	29.13	7-118	5	1
Marshall, M.D.	RF	245.4	56	553	42	13.16	7-22	3	1
Maru, R.J.	SLA	701	201	1792	50	35.84	5-69	1	—
Matthews, C.D.	LFM	77.2	18	225	7	32.14	4-47	—	—
Maynard, M.P.	RM	18	4	55	0	—	—	—	—
Mays, C.S.	OB	25	2	102	1	102.00	1-36	—	—
Medlycott, K.T.	SLA	593.1	159	1660	69	24.05	8-52	6	3
Mendis, G.D.	RM	12	1	44	0	—	—	—	—
Merrick, T.A.	RFM	475.3	105	1437	65	22.10	6-29	5	1
Metcalfe, A.A.	OB	2.5	0	7	0	—	—	—	—
Middleton, T.C.	SLA	1	0	9	0	—	—	—	—
Miller, G.	OB	434.1	106	1177	39	30.17	5-76	1	—
Millns, D.J.	RMF	179	22	683	19	35.94	3-37	—	—
Monkhouse, S.	LFM	67	17	155	5	31.00	3-37	—	—
Moores, P.		1	0	6	0	—	—	—	—
Morris, H.	RM	4.3	0	58	0	—	—	—	—
Morris, J.E.	RM	5.1	0	19	0	—	—	—	—
Mortensen, O.H.	RFM	233.3	73	464	34	13.64	6-35	4	—
Morton, W.	SLA	40	15	79	4	19.75	3-35	—	—
Moxon, M.D.	RM	6	2	15	0	—	—	—	—
Mudassar Nazar	RM	8	3	33	0	—	—	—	—
Mullally, A.D.	LFM	20	5	52	0	—	—	—	—
Munton, T.A.	RMF	425.1	126	1047	46	22.76	6-21	2	—
Murphy, A.J.	RMF	100.5	18	318	6	53.00	3-45	—	—
Myles, S.D.	RM	18	2	65	0	—	—	—	—
Neale, P.A.	RM	14	1	62	0	—	—	—	—
Needham, A.	OB	113.4	19	399	8	49.87	5-125	1	—
Nelson, A.N.	RFM	32	8	100	4	25.00	4-100	—	—
Newell, M.	LB	17.4	4	63	3	21.00	2-38	—	—
Newman, P.G.	RFM	339.5	81	950	35	27.14	8-29	1	—
Newport, P.J.	RFM	600.3	129	1844	93	19.82	8-52	7	1
Nicholas, M.C.J.	RM	34	3	115	1	115.00	1-58	—	—
North, P.D.	SLA	112.5	32	329	7	47.00	3-24	—	—
Nuttall, J.D.	LM	116	20	410	7	58.57	2-64	—	—
Ontong, R.C.	OB	395.1	94	1128	26	43.38	4-38	—	—
O'Shaughnessy, S.J.	RM	36	3	161	4	40.25	2-55	—	—
Palmer, G.V.	RMF	18.2	2	54	1	54.00	1-26	—	—
Parker, P.W.G.	RM	1	0	1	1	1.00	1-1	—	—
Parsons, G.J.	RMF	228	69	553	29	19.06	7-16	1	—
Patterson, B.P.	RF	196	33	632	25	25.28	5-39	1	—
Penn, C.	RFM	646.1	144	1989	81	24.55	7-70	6	—
Perry, J.N.	RM	211	44	643	10	64.30	3-72	—	—
Peters, N.H.	RFM	278.2	50	954	34	28.05	6-31	1	1
Pick, R.A.	RMF	74	14	334	9	37.11	3-37	—	—

173

	Cat	O	M	R	W	Avge	5 Best wI	10 wM
Pickles, C.S.	RM	16.2	5	58	0	—	—	—
Pienaar, R.F.	RMF	404.2	99	1162	36	32.27	5-27 1	—
Pierson, A.R.K.	OB	148.5	35	431	9	47.88	3-33 —	—
Pigott, A.C.S.	RFM	627	108	2078	74	28.08	6-100 2	—
Pointer, G.A.	LMF	184.5	24	663	7	94.71	3-31 —	—
Pollard, P.	RM	1.5	0	5	0	—	—	—
Pont, I.L.	RFM	220	30	795	24	33.12	5-103 1	—
Pooley, M.W.	RM	128.4	30	384	13	29.53	4-80 —	—
Potter, L.	SLA	98.4	26	293	8	36.62	2-24 —	—
Prichard, P.J.		1	0	7	0	—	—	—
Pridgeon, A.P.	RMF	266.3	58	662	21	31.52	3-68 —	—
Pringle, D.R.	RMF	515.2	119	1492	57	26.17	6-39 4	—
Pringle, M.W.	RMF	131	23	458	8	57.25	2-51 —	—
Pringle, N.J.	RMF	13	1	40	1	40.00	1-25 —	—
Radford, N.V.	RFM	570.5	101	1770	71	24.92	7-73 3	—
Rajadurai, B.E.A.	LB	20	3	65	1	65.00	1-28 —	—
Ramanake, C.P.H.	RM	87.2	11	315	7	45.00	2-36 —	—
Ramprakash, M.R.	RM	9	1	53	0	—	—	—
Ranatunga, A.	RM	50.4	11	153	2	76.50	1-6 —	—
Ratnayeke, J.R.	RMF	231.5	36	687	15	45.80	3-47 —	—
Reeve, D.A.	RMF	292	71	750	24	31.25	4-50 —	—
Richards, C.J.	OB	4	1	26	0	—	—	—
Richards, I.V.A.	OB	45.4	10	122	3	40.66	2-1 —	—
Richardson, R.B.	RM/OB	4	0	22	0	—	—	—
Roberts, B.	RM	103	22	307	9	34.11	2-17 —	—
Robinson, J.D.	RM	22	4	105	3	35.00	2-41 —	—
Robinson, M.A.	RFM	402.4	85	1055	46	22.93	4-19 —	—
Robinson, P.E.	LM	1.2	0	12	0	—	—	—
Robinson, R.T.	RM	4	0	38	0	—	—	—
Roebuck, P.M.	LB	28.4	2	106	1	106.00	1-26 —	—
Romaines, P.W.		0.1	0	6	0	—	—	—
Rose, G.D.	RM	504.5	116	1526	57	26.77	6-47 1	—
Roseberry, M.A.	RM	11.4	1	61	2	30.50	1-1 —	—
Russell, R.C.		1	0	12	0	—	—	—
Sabine, D.J.	RM	10	4	29	0	—	—	—
Samarasekera, M.A.R.	RMF	127.4	14	406	10	40.60	3-31 —	—
Saxelby, K.	RMF	245.2	42	837	17	49.23	3-21 —	—
Scott, A.M.G.	LM	120	26	385	11	35.00	4-66 —	—
Scott, C.W.		1	0	10	0	—	—	—
Scott, R.J.	RM	19.3	3	66	0	—	—	—
Scriven, T.J.A.	SLA	96	25	237	3	79.00	1-40 —	—
Searle, A.M.	OB	17	2	76	0	—	—	—
Sharma, C.	RFM	8	1	27	0	—	—	—
Sharma, R.	RM/OB	218.2	49	593	7	84.71	1-0 —	—
Sharp, K.	OB	1	0	11	0	—	—	—
Shastri, R.J.	SLA	304.2	91	709	20	35.45	7-49 1	1
Shaw, C.	RFM	507.5	110	1522	46	33.08	4-17 —	—
Sidebottom, A.	RMF	513.2	135	1303	63	20.68	7-89 3	—
Simmons, J.	OB	629	159	1548	63	24.57	5-53 2	—
Slack, W.N.	RM	2	1	14	0	—	—	—
Small, G.C.	RFM	628.1	170	1605	80	20.06	7-15 8	2
Smith, C.L.	OB	49	0	171	5	34.20	5-69 1	—
Smith, C.L.	OB	49	1	171	5	34.20	5-69 1	—
Smith, M.J.	RM	23	3	51	2	25.50	2-30 —	—

174

	Cat	O	M	R	W	Avge	Best	5 wI	10 wM
Smith, N.M.K.	OB	5	2	20	0	—	—	—	—
Smith, P.A.	RFM	164.3	20	540	23	23.47	3-7	—	—
Smith, R.A.	LB	6.1	1	35	0	—	—	—	—
Snodgrass, D.L.	RFM	4	2	7	0	—	—	—	—
Speight, M.P.		0.3	0	2	1	2.00	1-2	—	—
Stephenson, F.D.	RFM	819.1	196	2289	125	18.31	7-56	10	3
Stephenson, J.P.	RM	71.2	16	212	5	42.40	2-66	—	—
Stewart, A.J.		14.1	3	45	1	45.00	1-18	—	—
Storie, A.C.	RM	7	3	20	0	—	—	—	—
Such, P.M.	OB	123.5	22	340	10	34.00	4-81	—	—
Swallow, I.G.	OB	88	15	311	2	155.50	1-2	—	—
Sygrove, M.R.	RM	215.4	34	848	18	47.11	3-91	—	—
Sykes, J.F.	OB	60	9	205	1	205.00	1-51	—	—
Taylor, L.B.	RFM	324.3	70	967	35	27.62	6-49	1	—
Taylor, N.R.	OB	8	4	7	1	7.00	1-6	—	—
Tennant, L.	RMF	7	2	19	1	19.00	1-0	—	—
Thomas, D.J.	LFM	53.4	9	174	7	24.85	2-39	—	—
Thomas, J.G.	RF	422.2	62	1531	48	31.89	6-68	2	—
Thompson, N.E.	RM	17	2	59	1	59.00	1-59	—	—
Thorne, D.A.	LM	3	0	11	0	—	—	—	—
Thorpe, G.P.	RM	30	3	77	4	19.25	2-33	—	—
Threlfall, P.W.	RMF	12	3	31	0	—	—	—	—
Tillekeratne, H.P.	OB	9	1	35	1	35.00	1-14	—	—
Topley, T.D.	RMF	538.3	87	1663	65	25.58	7-75	4	1
Towse, A.D.	RMF	20	7	50	3	16.66	2-26	—	—
Tremellen, J.M.	RM	5	0	13	1	13.00	1-13	—	—
Tremlett, T.M.	RMF	125.3	35	326	14	23.28	4-19	—	—
Trump, H.R.J.	OB	270	74	696	24	29.00	4-17	—	—
Tufnell, P.C.R.	SLA	433.2	120	1058	25	42.32	4-88	—	—
Turner, D.R.	RM	0.2	0	8	0	—	—	—	—
Van Zyl, C.J.P.G.	RF	114.1	30	339	3	113.00	1-20	—	—
Walker, A.	RFM	465.5	98	1380	54	25.55	5-64	1	—
Wallace, P.	LFM	25	5	91	2	45.50	2-91	—	—
Walsh, C.A.	RF	232.2	55	622	18	34.55	5-49	1	—
Ward, D.M.	OB	6	1	31	0	—	—	—	—
Ward, T.R.	RM	4	1	4	0	—	—	—	—
Warner, A.E.	RFM	445	104	1151	44	26.15	4-22	—	—
Wasim Akram	LFM	291.4	76	666	31	21.48	7-53	2	—
Watkin, S.L.	RMF	527.3	129	1423	46	30.93	8-59	2	—
Watkinson, M.	RMF	647.3	153	1779	52	34.21	6-43	2	—
Waugh, M.E.	RM	12	0	75	0	—	—	—	—
Waugh, S.R.	RMF	23	5	60	3	20.00	2-33	—	—
Weale, S.D.	SLA	200	41	681	8	85.12	3-130	—	—
Wells, A.P.	RM	14	2	54	1	54.00	1-43	—	—
Wells, C.M.	RM	534.4	119	1469	43	34.16	4-43	—	—
Wells, V.J.		14	4	51	1	51.00	1-51	—	—
Weston, M.J.	RM	124	31	320	12	26.66	4-24	—	—
Wild, D.J.	RM	187.5	37	563	18	31.27	4-18	—	—
Willey, P.	OB	341	106	803	19	42.26	4-153	—	—
Williams, N.F.	RFM	178.3	33	511	30	17.03	6-42	2	—
Williams, R.G.	OB	331	72	980	33	29.69	5-86	1	—
Wyatt, J.G.	RM	10	4	34	1	34.00	1-24	—	—

LEADING CURRENT PLAYERS

The leading career records of players currently registered for first-class county cricket. All figures are to the end of the 1988 English season.

BATTING (Qualification: 100 innings)			BOWLING (Qualification: 100 wickets)		
	Runs	Avge		Wkts	Avge
G.A.Hick	9681	59.03	M.D.Marshall	1210	17.89
I.V.A.Richards	30591	49.90	S.T.Clarke	920	19.38
A.J.Lamb	21756	47.19	F.D.Stephenson	235	20.63
M.W.Gatting	21060	46.80	C.A.Walsh	559	22.83
S.R.Waugh	3894	46.35	M.A.Holding	740	23.11
A.I.Kallicharran	31819	44.50	O.H.Mortensen	252	23.13
G.A.Gooch	26745	43.98	N.G.Cowans	475	23.50
S.J.Cook	9258	42.08	A.P.Igglesden	131	23.61
A.J.Moles	4499	41.65	T.M.Tremlett	423	23.66
C.L.Smith	13359	41.48	T.M.Alderman	711	23.72
R.T.Robinson	13548	40.68	T.A.Merrick	220	23.78
R.J.Bailey	7346	40.14	N.A.Foster	578	24.11
D.I.Gower	19889	40.09	J.K.Lever	1696	24.18
R.J.Shastri	7104	39.91	K.M.Curran	181	24.28
M.P.Maynard	4311	39.55	A.Sidebottom	523	24.38
R.A.Smith	7333	39.42	L.B.Taylor	557	24.67
J.J.Whitaker	6713	39.25	P.J.W.Allott	578	24.75
M.R.Benson	10754	38.54	A.A.Donald	158	24.81
M.D.Moxon	9373	38.41	S.J.Base	111	24.96
C.J.Tavaré	18539	37.60	W.K.M.Benjamin	171	25.09
D.W.Randall	23255	37.44	T.D.Topley	173	25.21
T.S.Curtis	8610	37.27	J.E.Emburey	1092	25.22
G.Fowler	11800	36.99	N.V.Radford	667	25.37
A.J.Stewart	6029	36.76	G.J.F.Ferris	244	25.40
N.H.Fairbrother	6922	36.62	T.A.Munton	117	25.46
K.J.Barnett	12850	36.60	A.R.C.Fraser	143	25.65
P.M.Roebuck	14186	36.56	P.A.J.DeFreitas	280	25.75
G.W.Humpage	16429	36.26	M.P.Bicknell	119	26.11
P.A.Neale	14942	36.26	K.E.Cooper	591	26.15

WICKET-KEEPING				FIELDING	
	Total	Ct	St		Ct
D.L.Bairstow	1063	926	137	G.Cook	410
C.J.Richards	675	603	72	I.V.A.Richards	385
G.W.Humpage	668	600	68	G.A.Gooch	380
B.N.French	659	598	61	J.Simmons	336
P.R.Downton	653	574	79	C.J.Tavaré	328
I.J.Gould	576	509	67	B.R.Hardie	313
R.J.Parks	563	501	62	A.I.Kallicharran	310
D.E.East	531	478	53	J.E.Emburey	306
R.C.Russell	372	310	62	I.T.Botham	303
S.J.Rhodes	273	245	28	D.W.Randall	301

FIRST-CLASS CAREER RECORDS

Compiled by Geoffrey Saulez

The following career records are for all players who appeared in first-class cricket during the 1988 season, and are complete to the end of that season. Some players who did not appear for their counties in 1988, but may do so in 1989, are also included.

BATTING AND FIELDING

'1000' denotes instances of 1000 or more runs in a season. Where such aggregates have been achieved outside the United Kingdom, they are shown after a 'plus' sign.

	M	I	NO	HS	Runs	Avge	100	1000	Ct/St
Abrahams, J.	252	390	52	201*	10059	29.76	14	4	162
Adams, C.J.	1	1	0	21	21	21.00	—	—	1
Afford, J.A.	36	31	16	16	48	3.20	—	—	10
Agnew, J.P.	172	175	36	90	1582	11.38	—	—	31
Ahangama, F.S.	10	6	3	11	16	5.33	—	—	2
Alderman, T.M.	181	201	88	52*	1010	8.93	—	—	148
Alikhan, R.I.	60	103	8	98	2350	24.73	—	—	34
Alleyne, H.L.	75	84	19	72	648	9.96	—	—	16
Alleyne, M.W.	45	69	13	116*	1321	23.58	1	—	27/1
Allott, P.J.W.	206	223	54	88	2963	17.53	—	—	93
Almaer, S.A.	6	11	0	67	256	23.27	—	—	2
Ambrose, C.E.L.	22	28	7	59	364	17.33	—	—	3
Anderson, P.N.	1	1	0	0	0	0.00	—	—	1
Andrew, S.J.W.	51	27	18	12*	84	9.33	—	—	11
Anurasiri, S.D.	19	14	4	8	31	3.10	—	—	6
Arthurton, K.L.T.	23	34	5	132	1498	51.65	6	—	14
Asif Din	141	227	35	158*	5837	30.40	5	2	80
Atherton, M.A.	37	62	8	152*	2314	42.85	6	2	22
Athey, C.W.J.	293	490	47	184	14978	33.81	31	7	281/2
Atkins, P.D.	6	11	1	114*	357	35.70	1	—	—
Atkinson, J.C.M.	17	23	3	79	495	24.75	—	—	4
Austin, I.D.	8	10	2	64	253	31.62	—	—	—
Ayling, J.R.	19	33	4	88*	711	24.51	—	—	5
Aymes, A.N.	2	1	0	58	58	58.00	—	—	4
Babington, A.M.	39	44	17	16	146	5.40	—	—	15
Bail, P.A.C.	29	49	2	174	1016	21.61	1	—	7
Bailey, R.J.	134	218	35	224*	7346	40.14	15	5	90
Bainbridge, P.	215	363	54	169	10291	33.30	18	7	102
Bairstow, D.L.	442	624	116	145	13455	26.48	9	3	926/13
Bakker, P.J.	16	14	9	16	56	11.20	—	—	1
Ball, M.C.J.	2	1	0	2	2	2.00	—	—	—
Banks, D.A.	26	38	4	100	886	26.05	1	—	14
Barnett, A.A.	1	1	0	10	10	10.00	—	—	—
Barnett, K.J.	241	384	33	239*	12850	36.60	25	6	153
Bartlett, R.J.	26	41	5	117*	1014	28.16	2	—	17
Barwick, S.R.	116	108	42	30	562	8.51	—	—	24
Base, S.J.	38	46	14	38	292	9.12	—	—	9
Bastien, S.	4	6	2	36*	57	14.25	—	—	1
Bate, R.	10	16	2	45	225	16.07	—	—	2
Beardshall, M.	8	8	3	25	47	9.40	—	—	2
Bee, A.	1	1	1	11*	11	—	—	—	1

177

	M	I	NO	HS	Runs	Avge	100	1000	Ct/St
Benjamin, J.E.	1	—	—	—	—	—	—	—	—
Benjamin, W.K.M.	61	71	22	95*	1060	21.63	—	—	26
Benson, J.D.R.	1	1	0	3	3	3.00	—	—	—
Benson, M.R.	175	300	21	162	10754	38.54	24	7	90
Bent, P.	4	7	1	50	125	20.83	—	—	—
Berry, P.J.	5	3	2	23*	31	31.00	—	—	5
Bicknell, D.J.	23	39	4	105	943	26.94	1	—	8
Bicknell, M.P.	40	37	12	33	222	8.88	—	—	12
Birch, J.D.	250	374	59	125	8673	27.53	6	2	182
Bishop, I.R.	18	21	13	23	133	16.62	—	—	4
Blakey, R.J.	59	93	11	204*	2563	31.25	4	1	71/2
Boiling, J.	1	2	1	8*	9	9.00	—	—	—
Boon, T.J.	117	185	25	144	4900	30.62	6	3	54
Booth, P.A.	21	26	6	33*	178	8.90	—	—	5
Border, A.R.	247	409	62	205	18810	54.20	58	3+7	240
Bore, M.K.	159	158	52	37*	874	8.24	—	—	51
Botham, I.T.	329	509	37	228	16422	34.79	33	4	303
Bowler, P.D.	34	56	6	159*	1989	39.78	5	1	15
Brassington, A.J.	128	156	46	35	882	8.01	—	—	216/49
Briers, N.E.	239	374	37	201*	10063	29.86	14	5	100
Broad, B.C.	228	400	28	171	13344	35.87	25	6	125
Brown, A.D.	13	16	4	30	99	8.25	—	—	24/4
Brown, G.E.	10	11	8	13*	59	19.66	—	—	19/2
Brown, M.E.O.	3	5	2	47	71	23.66	—	—	—
Brown, S.J.	9	11	4	25*	59	8.42	—	—	3
Bullen, C.K.	27	31	5	65	573	22.03	—	—	24
Bunting, R.A.	17	21	5	17*	96	6.00	—	—	2
Burns, N.D.	52	77	14	133*	1521	24.14	2	—	111/10
Butcher, A.R.	328	557	47	216*	17025	33.38	33	9	150
Butcher, I.P.	98	159	9	139	4530	30.20	9	2	79
Butcher, R.O.	264	404	39	197	11419	31.28	16	4	274/1
Byas, D.	15	26	1	112	592	23.68	1	—	13
Cairns, B.L.	148	226	25	110	4165	20.72	1	—	89
Cairns, C.L.	4	5	1	15	31	7.75	—	—	—
Callaghan, D.J.	30	49	3	171	1577	34.28	2	—	24
Cann, M.J.	9	10	3	28	118	16.85	—	—	6
Capel, D.J.	167	244	40	134	5736	28.11	4	1	72
Carr, J.D.	94	150	18	156	4629	35.06	9	2	62
Carrick, P.	360	456	83	131*	8327	22.32	3	—	174
Childs, J.H.	235	219	105	34*	952	8.35	—	—	80
Clarke, A.R.	21	32	8	68	337	14.04	—	—	7
Clarke, S.T.	230	254	43	100*	3167	15.00	1	—	138
Cleal, M.W.	9	12	1	19	97	8.81	—	—	2
Clinton, G.S.	228	378	46	192	10956	33.00	19	6	83
Cobb, R.A.	113	178	15	91	4072	24.98	—	1	65
Cohen, M.F.	6	10	0	29	98	9.80	—	—	3
Connor, C.A.	91	76	27	36	337	6.87	—	—	29
Cook, G.	431	745	61	203	21816	31.89	33	11	410/3
Cook, N.G.B.	261	267	66	75	2426	12.06	—	—	150
Cook, S.J.	141	247	27	201*	9258	42.08	22	0+2	85
Cooper, K.E.	228	226	55	46	1661	9.71	—	—	69
Cope, J.E.B.	12	12	5	8*	28	4.00	—	—	13/1
Cottey, P.A.	24	38	5	92	788	23.87	—	—	8
Cowans, N.G.	159	158	36	66	1091	8.94	—	—	49

	M	I	NO	HS	Runs	Avge	100	1000	Ct/St
Cowdrey, C.S.	256	387	57	159	10127	30.68	16	3	259
Cowdrey, G.R.	50	77	8	145	1723	24.97	1	—	30
Cowley, N.G.	256	356	58	109*	6705	22.50	2	1	96
Crawley, M.A.	11	17	3	140	440	31.42	1	—	4
Crowe, M.D.	165	274	42	242*	13151	56.68	46	2+3	170
Curran, K.M.	114	175	31	142	4959	34.43	9	3	70
Curtis, T.S.	157	267	36	153	8610	37.27	12	5	83
Daniel, W.W.	266	241	106	53*	1551	11.48	—	—	63
Davis, R.P.	27	31	13	23	158	8.77	—	—	18
Davis, W.W.	146	181	52	77	1791	13.88	—	—	50
DeFreitas, P.A.J.	85	111	10	113	1964	19.44	2	—	29
Dennis, S.J.	72	71	27	53*	456	10.36	—	—	20
Derrick, J.	86	114	33	78*	1759	21.71	—	—	32
De Silva, P.A.	38	57	7	122	1875	37.50	5	—	20
Dilley, G.R.	195	212	71	81	1926	13.65	—	—	68
D'Oliveira, D.B.	134	215	16	146*	5436	27.31	6	3	99
Donald, A.A.	44	55	23	37*	348	10.87	—	—	12
Downton, P.R.	270	341	69	126*	6922	25.44	5	1	574/79
Dredge, C.H.	194	224	68	56*	2182	13.98	—	—	84
Dujon, P.J.L.	142	207	33	151*	7193	41.33	18	—	309/16
East, D.E.	188	252	32	134	4551	20.68	4	—	478/53
Edwards, P.G.	12	14	7	9	55	7.85	—	—	5
Ellcock, R.M.	34	40	11	45*	371	12.79	—	—	5
Ellison, R.M.	138	192	45	108	3429	23.32	1	—	52
Emburey, J.E.	353	435	90	133	7874	22.82	3	—	306
Evans, K.P.	26	35	4	54	514	16.58	—	—	25
Evans, R.J.	3	4	1	50*	75	25.00	—	—	3
Fairbrother, N.H.	140	220	30	164*	7028	36.98	13	5	83
Falkner, N.J.	23	38	3	102	966	27.60	2	—	14
Farbrace, P.	6	9	3	75*	149	24.83	—	—	13
Feltham, M.A.	59	68	22	76	974	21.17	—	—	22
Felton, N.A.	108	180	7	173*	4987	28.82	8	2	46
Fenton, N.C.W.	7	9	3	2	4	0.66	—	—	1
Ferris, G.J.F.	78	82	36	36*	511	11.10	—	—	10
Field-Buss, M.G.	2	4	1	34*	56	18.66	—	—	—
Finney, R.J.	114	168	29	82	2856	20.54	—	—	26
Fitton, J.D.	3	3	1	36	50	25.00	—	—	—
Fletcher, K.W.R.	730	1167	170	228*	37665	37.77	63	20	644
Fletcher, S.D.	72	56	22	28*	294	8.64	—	—	16
Folley, I.	130	152	48	69	1353	13.00	—	—	57
Fordham, A.	18	32	6	125*	663	25.50	1	—	13
Foster, D.J.	19	18	10	20	97	12.12	—	—	3
Foster, N.A.	146	175	40	74*	2415	17.88	—	—	64
Fowler, G.	201	337	17	226	11833	36.97	27	7	103/5
Fraser, A.G.J.	5	5	3	19*	51	25.50	—	—	—
Fraser, A.R.C.	54	58	16	41	467	11.11	—	—	5
Fraser-Darling, C.D.	11	12	2	61	242	24.20	—	—	11
French, B.N.	259	334	65	98	5023	18.67	—	—	598/61
Frost, M.	4	4	0	7	11	2.75	—	—	1
Gard, T.	110	124	25	51*	1349	13.62	—	—	176/39
Garnham, M.A.	76	104	18	100	2083	24.22	1	—	162/23
Gatting, M.W.	341	526	76	258	21060	46.80	50	10+1	295
Gifford, N.	710	805	264	89	7047	13.02	—	—	319
Golding, A.K.	17	27	6	47	403	19.19	—	—	6

	M	I	NO	HS	Runs	Avge	100	1000	Ct/St
Goldsmith, S.C.	26	43	4	89	1120	28.71	—	1	17
Gooch, G.A.	389	660	52	275	26745	43.98	66	12+1	380
Gould, I.J.	267	354	57	128	7651	25.76	3	—	509/67
Gouldstone, M.R.	8	13	1	71	274	22.83	—	—	4
Govan, J.W.	2	2	1	5*	9	9.00	—	—	1
Gower, D.I.	341	546	50	215	19889	40.09	40	8	209/1
Graveney, D.A.	353	451	129	119	5836	18.12	2	—	185
Gray, A.H.	77	80	14	54*	782	11.84	—	—	29
Greatbatch, M.J.	44	80	11	149	2392	39.86	6	—	34
Green, A.M.	159	284	19	179	7734	28.96	9	3	82
Green, N.H.	1	1	0	9	9	9.00	—	—	1
Green, S.J.	1	2	0	28	28	14.00	—	—	—
Greene, V.S.	23	27	8	62*	302	15.89	—	—	10
Greenfield, K.	2	4	0	18	34	8.50	—	—	2
Greenidge, C.G.	481	817	69	273*	34440	46.04	83	15+1	487
Greig, I.A.	187	245	30	147*	5419	25.20	5	—	122
Griffith, F.A.	5	7	1	37	105	17.50	—	—	2
Hagan, D.A.	24	43	4	88	870	22.30	—	—	12
Haggo, D.J.	2	3	0	45	54	18.00	—	—	3/1
Halliday, M.	13	14	5	47	199	22.11	—	—	5
Hampton, A.N.S.	3	6	0	12	22	3.66	—	—	—
Harden, R.J.	67	108	15	108	2731	29.36	3	1	37
Hardie, B.R.	349	564	70	162	16583	33.56	23	11	313
Hardy, J.J.E.	99	162	15	119	4389	29.85	2	1	61
Harman, M.D.	21	26	10	41	201	12.56	—	—	16
Harper, R.A.	149	189	31	234	5031	31.84	8	—	187
Harrison, G.D.	6	10	1	86	286	31.77	—	—	—
Hart, R.J.	9	14	2	12	53	4.41	—	—	1
Hartley, P.J.	66	76	21	127*	1354	24.61	1	—	24
Hartley, S.N.	142	215	28	114	4667	24.95	4	—	54
Hayhurst, A.N.	32	46	3	107	892	20.74	1	—	9
Haynes, D.L.	180	302	33	184	11507	42.77	20	0+2	105/1
Heap, R.	1	2	0	15	15	7.50	—	—	2
Heath, S.D.	10	17	2	33*	170	11.33	—	—	2
Hegg, W.K.	41	59	9	130	858	17.16	1	—	80/12
Hemmings, E.E.	413	537	124	127*	8152	19.73	1	—	178
Henderson, I.M.	11	14	2	21*	88	7.33	—	—	3
Heppel, N.	1	1	0	14*	14	—	—	—	—
Hepworth, P.N.	4	6	0	51	132	22.00	—	—	—
Heseltine, P.A.W.	20	20	3	26	186	10.94	—	—	3
Hick, G.A.	115	180	16	405*	9681	59.03	34	4	112
Hinks, S.G.	102	174	9	138	4678	28.35	6	1	74
Hoffman, D.S.	18	16	5	20*	59	5.36	—	—	4
Holding, M.A.	207	263	38	80	3439	15.28	—	—	106
Holloway, P.C.L.	3	5	0	16	40	8.00	—	—	8/1
Holmes, G.C.	173	281	42	117	6591	27.57	8	3	73
Hookey, S.G.	2	4	0	90	178	44.50	—	—	—
Hooper, A.M.	5	7	0	89	117	16.71	—	—	—
Hooper, C.L.	44	61	5	126	1868	33.35	2	—	40
Hopkins, J.A.	305	535	32	230	13742	27.32	18	7	213/1
Hughes, D.P.	403	535	94	153	9643	21.86	8	2	290
Hughes, S.P.	136	142	49	53	1166	12.53	—	—	34
Humpage, G.W.	315	518	65	254	16429	36.26	28	10	600/68
Hussain, N.	11	16	3	165*	518	39.84	1	—	7

	M	I	NO	HS	Runs	Avge	100	1000	Ct/St
Hutchinson, I.J.F.	3	4	0	25	48	12.00	—	—	—
Ibadulla, K.B.K.	17	25	6	107	440	23.15	1	—	7
Igglesden, A.P.	31	34	8	41	263	10.11	—	—	9
Illingworth, R.K.	138	147	44	120*	2018	19.59	1	—	66
Ilott, M.C.	2	1	0	6	6	6.00	—	—	—
Imran Khan	360	551	91	170	16534	35.94	27	4	113
Jack, T.B.	2	3	0	29	57	19.00	—	—	1
Jackson, P.B.	8	11	3	46	143	17.87	—	—	13/3
James, K.D.	70	84	20	142*	1820	28.43	3	—	22
James, S.P.	9	13	1	106	246	20.50	1	—	4
Jarvis, K.B.S.	245	183	82	19	337	3.33	—	—	56
Jarvis, P.W.	88	98	34	47	923	14.42	—	—	30
Jean-Jacques, M.	29	36	7	73	405	13.96	—	—	9
Jefferies, S.T.	118	157	30	93	3348	26.36	—	—	43
Jesty, T.E.	450	714	92	248	19962	32.09	34	9	253/1
Johnson, P.	126	201	20	140	6178	34.13	13	3	85/1
Jones, A.N.	92	88	36	38	528	10.15	—	—	26
Kallicharran, A.I.	482	798	83	243*	31819	44.50	85	12+1	310
Kelleher, D.J.M.	17	19	2	51	231	13.58	—	—	3
Kendrick, N.M.	1	1	1	8*	1		—	—	1
Ker, J.E.	12	16	7	50	189	21.00	—	—	3
Kilborn, M.J.	22	37	3	78	864	25.41	—	—	17
Kimber, S.J.S.	16	19	7	54	266	22.16	—	—	5
Knight, R.D.V.	386	670	60	165*	19541	32.03	31	13	293
Kuruppu, D.S.B.P.	21	35	3	201*	1007	31.46	2	—	17/3
Labrooy, G.F.	12	10	3	42	121	17.28	—	—	4
Lamb, A.J.	327	548	87	294	21756	47.19	55	8	245
Lampitt, S.R.	15	16	4	24	122	10.16	—	—	6
Larkins, W.	352	607	37	252	19266	33.80	42	10	201
Lawrence, D.V.	123	136	26	65*	1040	9.45	—	—	26
Lawson, G.F.	130	163	32	63	1894	14.45	—	—	54
Leatherdale, D.A.	10	15	1	34*	255	18.21	—	—	3
Lenham, N.J.	52	83	12	104*	1907	25.85	1	—	20
Lever, J.K.	520	531	192	91	3622	10.68	—	—	184
Lewis, C.C.	20	27	4	42	453	19.69	—	—	11
Lewis, D.A.	1	2	0	17	17	8.50	—	—	—
Lillee, D.K.	198	241	70	73*	2377	13.90	—	—	67
Lilley, A.W.	103	162	13	102	3881	26.04	2	—	56
Lloyd, G.D.	1	2	0	22	22	11.00	—	—	1
Lloyd, T.A.	230	411	38	208*	13396	35.91	25	7	116
Lloyds, J.W.	196	300	43	132*	8005	31.14	10	2	173
Logie, A.L.	105	161	15	171	4936	33.80	10	—	61/1
Lord, G.J.	50	78	6	199	1723	23.93	2	—	13
Love, J.D.	240	376	57	170*	10063	31.54	13	2	119
Lynch, M.A.	237	385	44	152	11960	35.07	28	6	216
McEwan, S.M.	29	14	8	13*	45	7.50	—	—	9
McGurk, G.B.J.	1	1	0	63	63	63.00	—	—	3
Maclaurin, N.R.C.	1	2	0	35	37	18.50	—	—	—
Madugalle, R.S.	71	105	14	142*	3014	33.12	2	—	39
Madurasinghe, A.W.R.	6	7	2	30	75	15.00	—	—	2
Mahanama, R.S.	22	35	7	91	938	33.50	—	—	5
Maher, B.J.M.	104	159	29	126	3061	23.54	4	—	223/12
Makinson, D.J.	35	39	17	58*	486	22.09	—	—	10
Malcolm, D.E.	50	53	14	29*	239	6.12	—	—	11

	M	I	NO	HS	Runs	Avge	100	1000	Ct/St
Mallender, N.A.	203	230	75	88	2174	14.02	—	—	77
Maninder Singh	92	87	40	61*	421	8.95	—	—	40
Marks, V.J.	322	468	78	134	11597	29.73	5	2	136
Marsh, S.A.	81	112	22	120	2161	24.01	2	—	169/13
Marshall, M.D.	275	342	42	116*	6945	23.15	4	—	107
Martindale, D.J.R.	30	45	6	104*	885	22.69	2	—	12
Maru, R.J.	122	108	30	74	1130	14.48	—	—	119
Matthews, C.D.	36	44	3	65	798	19.46	—	—	10
Maynard, M.P.	75	124	15	160	4311	39.55	8	3	66
Mays, C.S.	12	9	4	13*	39	7.80	—	—	5
Medlycott, K.T.	70	83	18	153	1624	24.98	2	—	50
Mendis, G.D.	279	487	46	209*	15835	35.90	30	9	110/1
Mendis, L.R.D.	107	174	16	194	5604	35.46	11	—	42/1
Merrick, T.A.	56	74	14	74*	909	15.15	—	—	25
Metcalfe, A.A.	89	152	10	216*	4914	34.60	12	3	30
Metson, C.P.	72	98	24	96	1270	17.16	—	—	149/16
Middleton, T.C.	11	19	3	68*	366	22.87	—	—	8
Miller, G.	359	520	83	130	11448	26.19	2	—	295
Millns, D.J.	11	12	5	7*	20	2.85	—	—	4
Moles, A.J.	67	119	11	200*	4499	41.65	13	1	51
Monkhouse, S.	11	12	5	15	30	4.28	—	—	2
Moores, P.	44	63	7	97*	995	17.76	—	—	68/9
Morris, H.	111	185	21	143	5037	30.71	6	2	52
Morris, J.E.	119	194	12	191	6335	34.80	13	3	40
Morris, R.E.	10	17	2	34	137	9.13	—	—	2
Mortensen, O.H.	86	99	53	74*	461	10.02	—	—	26
Morton, W.	13	12	2	13*	57	5.70	—	—	11
Moxon, M.D.	155	262	18	191	9373	38.41	21	4	124
Mudassar Nazar	208	338	32	241	13564	44.32	41	0+4	134
Mullally, A.D.	2	1	1	2*	2	—	—	—	1
Munton, T.A.	52	53	18	38	305	8.71	—	—	6
Murphy, A.J.	17	19	7	6	25	2.08	—	—	6
Myles, S.D.	6	10	1	39	130	14.44	—	—	1
Neale, P.A.	294	482	70	167	14942	36.26	26	8	110
Needham, A.	109	156	23	138	3077	23.13	4	1	50
Nelson, A.N.	1	2	0	22	26	13.00	—	—	1
Newell, M.	70	121	20	203*	3074	30.43	5	1	68/1
Newman, P.G.	119	145	29	115	1843	15.88	1	—	25
Newport, P.J.	112	124	41	86	2173	26.18	—	—	35
Nicholas, M.C.J.	228	378	45	206*	10781	32.37	22	6	145
Nicholson, N.G.	2	4	1	16	47	15.66	—	—	3
North, P.D.	18	20	7	41*	168	12.92	—	—	4
Noyes, S.J.	8	14	1	38	170	13.07	—	—	—
Nuttall, J.D.	6	7	2	35	55	11.00	—	—	2
O'Gorman, T.J.G.	7	13	1	78	171	14.25	—	—	7
Olley, M.W.C.	5	6	1	27*	77	15.40	—	—	12
Ontong, R.C.	351	582	85	204*	14842	29.86	20	5	175
O'Shaughnessy, S.J.	111	179	28	159*	3709	24.56	5	1	57
Palmer, G.V.	54	70	11	78	903	15.30	—	—	30
Parker, P.W.G.	285	486	68	215	14588	34.89	36	8	199
Parks, R.J.	205	224	57	89	3132	18.75	—	—	501/62
Parsons, G.J.	191	242	52	76	3647	19.19	—	—	56
Patterson, B.M.W.	1	1	0	100	100	100.00	1	—	3
Patterson, B.P.	97	95	37	29	363	6.25	—	—	19

	M	I	NO	HS	Runs	Avge	100	1000	Ct/St
Penn, C.	72	87	24	115	1265	20.07	1	—	39
Perry, J.N.	11	12	1	26	104	9.45	—	—	4
Peters, N.H.	12	15	8	25*	85	12.14	—	—	5
Philip, I.L.	3	4	0	145	175	43.75	1	—	3
Pick, R.A.	70	69	19	63	821	16.42	—	—	14
Pickles, C.S.	7	5	2	31*	55	18.33	—	—	4
Pienaar, R.F.	104	173	10	153	5007	30.71	7	1	43
Pierson, A.R.K.	25	29	16	42*	189	14.53	—	—	7
Pigott, A.C.S.	156	185	41	104*	2934	20.37	1	—	74
Pointer, G.A.	15	23	5	33	218	12.11	—	—	1
Polkinghorne, D.A.	3	4	1	45*	72	24.00	—	—	2
Pollard, P.	14	24	1	142	560	24.34	1	—	10
Pont, I.L.	28	35	10	68	404	16.16	—	—	5
Pook, R.N.	1	1	0	6	6	6.00	—	—	3
Pooley, M.W.	8	13	5	38	149	18.62	—	—	4
Potter, L.	118	187	22	165*	4589	27.81	5	—	99
Prichard, P.J.	102	162	20	147*	4645	32.71	2	2	59
Pridgeon, A.P.	235	216	83	67	1164	8.75	—	—	81
Pringle, D.R.	203	299	55	128	6556	26.86	8	—	111
Pringle, M.W.	15	22	4	50*	289	16.05	—	—	4
Pringle, N.J.	20	35	5	79	612	20.40	—	—	9
Pyman, R.A.	2	3	0	4	7	2.33	—	—	2
Radford, N.V.	181	183	46	76*	2269	16.56	—	—	93
Rajadurai, B.E.A.	2	—					—	—	—
Ramanayake, C.P.H.	12	12	1	25	96	8.72	—	—	2
Ramprakash, M.R.	17	27	7	71	742	37.10	—	—	8
Ranatunga, A.	57	85	8	135*	2900	37.66	4	—	29
Randall, D.W.	402	683	62	237	23255	37.44	41	11	301
Ratcliffe, J.D.	2	4	0	16	31	7.75	—	—	2
Ratnayeke, J.R.	56	82	23	93	1531	25.94	—	—	11
Rea, M.P.	3	6	0	53	110	18.33	—	—	—
Reeve, D.A.	107	124	34	119	2192	24.35	2	—	62
Reynolds, G.D.	6	9	1	69	147	18.37	—	—	6
Rhodes, S.J.	109	137	45	108	2521	27.40	1	—	245/28
Richards, C.J.	286	371	87	172*	8012	28.21	8	1	603/72
Richards, I.V.A.	420	656	43	322	30591	49.90	98	12+3	385/1
Richardson, R.B.	92	148	10	185	5102	36.97	14	—	90
Ripley, D.	91	107	23	134*	1590	18.92	2	—	179/36
Roberts, B.	157	252	23	184	7184	31.37	10	2	118/1
Roberts, M.L.	4	3	0	8	14	4.66	—	—	4/1
Robinson, J.D.	3	5	2	20	55	18.33	—	—	1
Robinson, M.A.	22	23	9	19*	41	2.92	—	—	4
Robinson, M.J.	1	1	0	19	19	19.00	—	—	—
Robinson, P.E.	67	106	13	129*	3192	34.32	2	1	45
Robinson, R.T.	221	379	46	207	13548	40.68	31	6	122
Roebuck, P.G.P.	22	38	8	82	771	25.70	—	—	8
Roebuck, P.M.	278	458	70	221*	14186	36.56	25	7	143
Romaines, P.W.	157	282	21	186	7570	29.00	13	3	63
Rose, G.D.	45	56	11	95	948	21.06	—	—	21
Roseberry, M.A.	29	43	7	70*	830	23.05	—	—	13
Russell, R.C.	152	197	48	94	3663	24.58	—	—	310/62
Sabine, D.J.	1	2	0	7	8	4.00	—	—	1
Sadiq, Z.A.	4	6	0	64	135	22.50	—	—	2

	M	I	NO	HS	Runs	Avge	100	1000	Ct/St
Samarasekera, M.A.R.	19	29	2	110	835	30.92	2	—	10
Saxelby, K.	121	120	36	59*	989	11.77	—	—	24
Scott, A.M.G.	28	31	15	11*	67	4.18	—	—	10
Scott, C.W.	50	59	13	78	1016	22.08	—	—	116/7
Scott, R.J.	9	16	1	107*	374	24.93	1	—	10
Scriven, T.J.A.	2	2	0	7	11	5.50	—	—	—
Searle, A.M.	1	1	0	2	2	2.00	—	—	—
Seymour, A.C.	1	1	1	33*	33	—	—	—	—
Sharma, A.	56	62	20	72*	1268	30.19	—	—	27
Sharma, R.	49	70	15	111	1441	26.20	1	—	44
Sharp, K.	198	329	29	181	9132	30.44	14	1	97
Shastri, R.J.	147	211	33	200*	7104	39.91	16	0+1	82
Shaw, C.	61	58	27	31	340	10.96	—	—	9
Sidebottom, A.	205	234	56	124	4042	22.70	1	—	51
Silva, S.A.R.	29	51	5	161*	1371	29.80	4	—	67/3
Simmons, J.	443	553	141	112	9360	22.71	6	—	337
Simmons, P.V.	46	80	3	118	2393	31.07	3	—	47
Slack, W.N.	237	398	40	248*	13950	38.96	25	8	174
Small, G.C.	188	240	57	70	2731	14.92	—	—	53
Smith, C.L.	212	368	46	217	13359	41.48	35	7	138
Smith, D.M.	230	357	71	189*	10165	35.54	19	4	142
Smith, G.	7	7	1	29*	54	9.00	—	—	2
Smith, I.	27	30	5	45	315	12.60	—	—	8
Smith, M.J.	2	3	1	79	119	59.50	—	—	2
Smith, N.M.K.	3	5	1	23	59	14.75	—	—	1
Smith, O.C.K.	1	2	0	14	15	7.50	—	—	—
Smith, P.A.	128	213	24	119	5252	27.78	2	2	38
Smith, R.A.	135	228	42	209*	7333	39.42	15	3	87
Snodgrass, D.L.	4	4	0	49	69	17.25	—	—	5
Speak, N.J.	2	4	0	35	49	12.25	—	—	2
Speight, M.P.	12	15	0	58	279	18.60	—	—	11
Standing, D.K.	43	70	10	65	1130	18.83	—	—	17
Stanley, N.A.	8	12	2	66	263	26.30	—	—	4
Stanworth, J.	34	38	11	50*	236	8.74	—	—	49/8
Stenner, J.M.C.	1	2	0	13	23	11.50	—	—	—
Stephenson, F.D.	53	82	5	165	1991	25.85	3	1	29
Stephenson, J.P.	46	80	8	99	1897	27.31	—	—	30
Stewart, A.J.	119	183	19	166	6029	36.76	10	4	125/3
Storie, A.C.	45	75	12	106	1350	21.42	1	—	29
Stovold, A.W.	345	613	35	212*	17417	30.13	20	8	284/45
Such, P.M.	82	73	28	16	109	2.42	—	—	37
Swallow, I.G.	48	62	16	114	1009	21.93	1	—	23
Swan, R.G.	9	14	1	77	338	26.00	—	—	6
Sygrove, M.R.	8	10	3	8*	37	5.28	—	—	—
Sykes, J.F.	27	34	6	126	655	23.39	1	—	15
Tavaré, C.J.	328	552	59	168*	18539	37.60	35	12	328
Taylor, L.B.	203	181	78	60	1001	9.71	—	—	48
Taylor, N.R.	177	301	39	155*	8834	33.71	20	5	101
Taylor, R.W.	639	880	167	100	12065	16.92	1	—	1473/176
Tedstone, G.A.	32	45	7	67*	641	16.86	—	—	49/10
Tennant, L.	4	4	2	12*	16	8.00	—	—	1
Terry, V.P.	151	251	28	190	7694	34.50	16	5	156
Thomas, D.J.	150	193	41	119	3044	20.02	2	—	50
Thomas, J.G.	138	187	35	110	2550	16.77	2	—	53

184

	M	I	NO	HS	Runs	Avge	100	1000	Ct/St
Thompson, N.E.	1	2	0	38	52	26.00	—	—	—
Thorne, D.A.	64	103	15	124	2389	27.14	2	—	49
Thorpe, G.P.	3	6	2	100*	158	39.50	1	—	3
Threlfall, P.W.	1	—	—	—	—	—	—	—	—
Tillekeratne, H.P.	16	23	9	128*	686	49.00	2	—	13
Topley, T.D.	48	62	16	66	761	16.54	—	—	24
Towse, A.D.	1	1	0	1	1	1.00	—	—	1
Tremellen, J.M.	12	20	3	39	269	15.82	—	—	4
Tremlett, T.M.	192	236	59	102*	3609	20.38	1	—	72
Trump, H.R.J.	9	11	1	48	62	6.20	—	—	—
Tufnell, P.C.R.	26	27	9	20	97	5.38	—	—	11
Turner, D.R.	416	679	70	184*	18641	30.60	28	9	189
Turner, R.J.	8	14	1	27	155	11.92	—	—	9/2
van Zyl, C.J.P.G.	55	75	15	49	744	12.40	—	—	16
Vincent, D.A.	1	2	0	16	24	12.00	—	—	—
Vorster, L.P.	24	37	6	174	1304	42.06	1	—	17
Wakefield, M.	1	1	0	4	4	4.00	—	—	1
Walker, A.	86	78	40	41*	543	14.28	—	—	32
Wallace, P.	1	2	0	0	0	0.00	—	—	—
Walsh, C.A.	143	163	42	52	1281	10.58	—	—	43
Ward, D.M.	41	62	10	143	1499	28.82	2	—	31
Ward, T.R.	12	21	1	72	422	21.10	—	—	9
Warke, S.J.S.	7	12	1	144*	532	48.36	1	—	4
Warner, A.E.	100	140	27	91	2131	18.85	—	—	26
Wasim Akram	55	67	14	116*	1188	22.41	1	—	21
Watkin, S.L.	17	19	7	23	115	9.58	—	—	1
Watkinson, M.	117	170	23	106	3465	23.57	1	—	61
Waugh, M.E.	25	40	6	116	1503	44.20	4	—	31
Waugh, S.R.	66	101	17	170	3894	46.35	11	1	80
Weale, S.D.	15	20	0	76	368	18.40	—	—	3
Wells, A.P.	140	225	37	161*	5856	31.14	8	3	76
Wells, C.M.	214	339	53	203	9580	33.49	18	5	67
Wells, V.J.	1	2	0	6	6	3.00	—	—	1
Weston, M.J.	129	207	16	145*	4716	24.69	3	1	62
Whitaker, J.J.	131	199	28	200*	6713	39.25	16	5	84
Whitticase, P.	78	98	23	71	1558	20.77	—	—	186/7
Wild, D.J.	106	148	21	144	3315	26.10	4	—	33
Willey, P.	502	823	108	227	21981	30.74	42	8	208
Williams, D.	37	51	7	51	780	17.72	—	—	67/12
Williams, N.F.	114	122	30	67	1823	19.81	—	—	26
Williams, R.G.	252	399	56	175*	10832	31.58	17	6	89
Wright, A.J.	114	199	13	161	4899	26.33	4	2	67
Wright, J.G.	314	546	37	192	20849	40.96	47	6+2	172
Wyatt, J.G.	66	111	5	145	2743	25.87	3	—	27

BOWLING

'100wS' denotes instances of 100 or more wickets in a season.

	Runs	Wkts	Avge	Best	5wI	10wM	100wS
Abrahams, J.	2811	56	50.19	3-27	—	—	—
Afford, J.A.	2787	89	31.31	6-81	4	1	—
Agnew, J.P.	14967	537	27.87	9-70	29	5	1
Ahangama, F.S.	828	35	23.65	5-52	1	—	—
Alderman, T.M.	16868	711	23.72	8-46	39	7	—
Alikhan, R.I.	124	3	41.33	2-19	—	—	—
Alleyne, H.L.	6330	238	26.59	8-43	9	2	—
Alleyne, M.W.	951	17	55.94	4-48	—	—	—
Allott, P.J.W.	14310	578	24.75	8-48	29	—	—
Ambrose, C.E.L.	1780	81	21.97	7-61	3	1	—
Anderson, P.N.	47	1	47.00	1-47	—	—	—
Andrew, S.J.W.	3728	134	27.82	7-92	4	—	—
Anurasiri, S.D.	1280	24	53.33	5-38	1	—	—
Arthurton, K.L.T.	144	8	18.00	3-14	—	—	—
Asif Din	2899	50	57.98	5-100	1	—	—
Atherton, M.A.	1351	20	67.55	3-32	—	—	—
Athey, C.W.J.	1706	37	46.10	3-3	—	—	—
Atkinson, J.C.M.	468	5	93.60	2-80	—	—	—
Austin, I.D.	431	18	23.94	5-79	1	—	—
Ayling, J.R.	1098	47	23.36	4-57	—	—	—
Babington, A.M.	2874	85	33.81	4-18	—	—	—
Bail, P.A.C.	103	1	103.00	1-36	—	—	—
Bailey, R.J.	462	14	33.00	3-27	—	—	—
Bainbridge, P.	8708	237	36.74	8-53	7	—	—
Bairstow, D.L.	308	9	34.22	3-25	—	—	—
Bakker, P.J.	1139	48	23.72	7-31	2	—	—
Ball, M.C.J.	90	2	45.00	1-2	—	—	—
Banks, D.A.	17	0			—	—	—
Barnett, A.A.	65	0			—	—	—
Barnett, K.J.	3367	75	44.89	6-115	1	—	—
Bartlett, R.J.	145	4	36.25	1-9	—	—	—
Barwick, S.R.	8148	241	33.80	8-42	6	—	—
Base, S.J.	2771	111	24.96	6-28	4	—	—
Bastien, S.	289	8	36.12	5-90	1	—	—
Beardshall, M.	572	12	47.66	4-68	—	—	—
Bee, A.	55	2	27.50	2-20	—	—	—
Benjamin, J.E.	53	0			—	—	—
Benjamin, W.K.M.	4291	171	25.09	6-33	8	1	—
Benson, M.R.	312	3	104.00	2-55	—	—	—
Berry, P.J.	229	5	45.80	2-35	—	—	—
Bicknell, D.J.	19	0			—	—	—
Bicknell, M.P.	3108	119	26.11	9-45	3	—	—
Birch, J.D.	2446	50	48.92	6-64	1	—	—
Bishop, I.R.	1260	51	24.70	6-39	2	—	—
Boiling, J.	40	0			—	—	—
Blakey, R.J.	68	1	68.00	1-68	—	—	—
Boon, T.J.	249	5	49.80	3-40	—	—	—

	Runs	Wkts	Avge	Best	5wI	10wM	100wS
Booth, P.A.	1470	34	43.23	5-98	1	—	—
Border, A.R.	2332	61	38.22	4-61	—	—	—
Bore, M.K.	11243	372	30.22	8-89	9	—	—
Botham, I.T.	26980	1005	26.84	8-34	53	7	1
Bowler, P.D.	674	7	96.28	2-63	—	—	—
Brassington, A.J.	10	0	—	—	—	—	—
Briers, N.E.	988	32	30.87	4-29	—	—	—
Broad, B.C.	1036	16	64.75	2-14	—	—	—
Brown, K.R.	64	3	21.33	2-7	—	—	—
Brown, S.J.	437	18	24.27	3-20	—	—	—
Bullen, C.K.	984	34	28.94	6-119	1	—	—
Bunting, R.A.	1320	41	32.19	5-44	3	—	—
Butcher, A.R.	5058	134	37.74	6-48	1	—	—
Butcher, I.P.	28	1	28.00	1-2	—	—	—
Butcher, R.O.	180	4	45.00	2-37	—	—	—
Byas, D.	64	0	—	—	—	—	—
Cairns, B.L.	12544	473	26.52	8-46	24	5	—
Cairns, C.L.	384	15	25.60	4-70	—	—	—
Callaghan, D.J.	508	17	29.88	2-16	—	—	—
Cann, M.J.	173	5	34.60	2-20	—	—	—
Capel, D.J.	8872	267	33.22	7-46	9	—	—
Carr, J.D.	2588	56	46.21	6-61	3	—	—
Carrick, P.	25705	860	29.88	8-33	38	5	—
Childs, J.H.	18255	614	29.73	9-56	32	7	—
Clarke, A.R.	1650	44	37.50	5-60	2	—	—
Clarke, S.T.	17831	920	19.38	8-62	58	10	—
Cleal, M.W.	582	20	29.10	4-41	—	—	—
Clinton, G.S.	201	4	50.25	2-8	—	—	—
Cobb, R.A.	46	0	—	—	—	—	—
Connor, C.A.	7590	233	32.57	7-37	3	—	—
Cook, G.	791	15	52.73	3-47	—	—	—
Cook, N.G.B.	19755	687	28.75	7-63	25	3	—
Cook, S.J.	34	1	34.00	1-15	—	—	—
Cooper, K.E.	15459	591	26.15	8-44	20	—	1
Cowans, N.G.	11164	475	23.50	6-31	21	1	—
Cowdrey, C.S.	6890	182	37.85	5-46	2	—	—
Cowdrey, G.R.	457	8	57.12	1-5	—	—	—
Cowley, N.G.	13877	423	32.80	6-48	5	—	—
Crawley, M.A.	652	6	108.66	2-30	—	—	—
Crowe, M.D.	3685	116	31.76	5-18	4	—	—
Curran, K.M.	4396	181	24.28	7-54	6	3	—
Curtis, T.S.	362	7	51.71	2-58	—	—	—
Daniel, W.W.	19490	867	22.47	9-61	31	7	—
Davis, R.P.	2003	54	37.09	5-132	1	—	—
Davis, W.W.	14002	504	27.78	7-52	26	7	—
DeFreitas, P.A.J.	7211	280	25.75	7-44	17	1	—
Dennis, S.J.	6061	194	31.24	5-35	5	—	—
Derrick, J.	4650	125	37.20	6-54	2	—	—
De Silva, P.A.	226	3	75.33	1-16	—	—	—
Dilley, G.R.	14229	527	27.00	7-63	26	2	—
D'Oliveira, D.B.	923	23	40.13	2-17	—	—	—
Donald, A.A.	3921	158	24.81	8-37	7	1	—
Downton, P.R.	5	0	—	—	—	—	—

	Runs	Wkts	Avge	Best	5wI	10wM	100wS
Dredge, C.H.	13338	443	30.10	6-37	12	—	—
Dujon, P.J.L.	44	1	44.00	1-43	—	—	—
East, D.E.	17	0	—	—	—	—	—
Edwards, P.G.	1060	23	46.08	4-93	—	—	—
Ellcock, R.M.	2576	77	33.45	4-34	—	—	—
Ellison, R.M.	9018	341	26.44	7-75	12	2	—
Emburey, J.E.	27551	1092	25.22	7-36	53	8	1
Evans, K.P.	1391	31	44.87	3-22	—	—	—
Evans, R.J.	73	3	24.33	3-40	—	—	—
Fairbrother, N.H.	323	4	80.75	2-91	—	—	—
Falkner, N.J.	9	1	9.00	1-3	—	—	—
Feltham, M.A.	4792	156	30.71	5-45	4	—	—
Felton, N.A.	15	0	—	—	—	—	—
Fenton, N.C.W.	726	21	34.57	4-64	—	—	—
Ferris, G.J.F.	6199	244	25.40	7-42	9	1	—
Finney, R.J.	6297	202	31.17	7-54	8	—	—
Fitton, J.D.	143	8	17.87	6-59	1	—	—
Fletcher, K.W.R.	2296	51	45.01	5-41	1	—	—
Fletcher, S.D.	5394	170	31.72	8-58	3	—	—
Folley, I.	8343	276	30.22	7-15	10	1	—
Foster, D.J.	1563	41	38.12	4-46	—	—	—
Foster, N.A.	13940	578	24.11	8-107	34	6	1
Fowler, G	171	7	24.42	2-34	—	—	—
Fraser, A.G.J.	247	9	27.44	3-46	—	—	—
Fraser, A.R.C.	3669	143	25.65	6-68	6	2	—
Fraser-Darling, C.D.	876	17	51.52	5-84	1	—	—
French, B.N.	22	0	—	—	—	—	—
Frost, M.	326	10	32.60	4-56	—	—	—
Gard, T	8	0	—	—	—	—	—
Gatting, M.W.	4026	145	27.76	5-34	2	—	—
Gifford, N.	48731	2068	23.56	8-28	93	14	4
Golding, A.K.	1647	18	91.50	3-51	—	—	—
Goldsmith, S.C.	162	1	162.00	1-37	—	—	—
Gooch, G.A.	6868	210	32.70	7-14	3	—	—
Gould, I.J.	305	4	76.25	2-48	—	—	—
Govan, J.W.	203	14	14.50	5-54	1	—	—
Gower, D.I.	223	4	55.75	3-47	—	—	—
Graveney, D.A.	21471	749	28.66	8-85	31	5	—
Gray, A.H.	6460	301	21.46	8-40	16	3	—
Greatbatch, M.J.	2	0	—	—	—	—	—
Green, A.M.	2081	46	45.23	6-82	1	—	—
Greene, V.S.	1788	76	23.52	7-96	3	—	—
Greenidge, C.G.	472	17	27.76	5-49	1	—	—
Greig, I.A.	11143	385	28.94	7-43	10	2	—
Griffith, F.A.	347	10	34.70	4-47	—	—	—
Hagan, D.A.	31	0	—	—	—	—	—
Halliday, M.	829	34	24.38	5-39	1	—	—
Harden, R.J.	434	10	43.40	2-7	—	—	—
Hardie, B.R.	238	3	79.33	2-39	—	—	—
Hardy, J.J.E.	20	0	—	—	—	—	—
Harman, M.D.	1111	33	33.66	5-55	2	—	—
Harper, R.A.	11257	416	27.06	6-57	17	2	—
Harrison, G.D.	192	3	64.00	2-30	—	—	—

	Runs	Wkts	Avge	Best	5wI	10wM	100wS
Hart, R.J.	708	13	54.46	4-66	—	—	—
Hartley, P.J.	5500	156	35.25	6-68	4	—	—
Hartley, S.N.	2182	48	45.45	4-51	—	—	—
Hayhurst, A.N.	1436	43	33.39	4-27	—	—	—
Haynes, D.L.	59	3	19.66	1-2	—	—	—
Heath, S.D.	39	0	—	—	—	—	—
Hemmings, E.E.	34882	1201	29.04	10-175	59	14	—
Henderson, I.M.	753	12	62.75	3-48	—	—	—
Heppel, N.	74	0	—	—	—	—	—
Heseltine, P.A.W.	1069	22	48.59	3-33	—	—	—
Hick, G.A.	2982	69	43.21	4-31	—	—	—
Hinks, S.G.	289	44	72.25	1-10	—	—	—
Hoffman, D.S.	1257	31	40.54	4-100	—	—	—
Holding, M.A.	17102	740	23.11	8-92	38	4	—
Holmes, G.C.	3636	80	45.45	5-38	2	—	—
Hooper, C.L.	1912	65	29.41	5-35	3	—	—
Hopkins, J.A.	148	0	—	—	—	—	—
Hughes, D.P.	18392	614	29.95	7-24	20	2	—
Hughes, S.P.	9998	327	30.57	7-35	8	—	—
Humpage, G.W.	462	10	46.20	2-13	—	—	—
Hussain, N.	47	0	—	—	—	—	—
Ibadulla, K.B.K.	601	16	37.56	5-22	1	—	—
Igglesden, A.P.	3093	131	23.61	6-34	8	2	—
Illingworth, R.K.	9585	279	34.35	7-50	10	3	—
Ilott, M.C.	111	3	37.00	2-23	—	—	—
Imran Khan	27444	1255	21.86	8-34	70	13	—
James, K.D.	3797	126	30.13	6-22	6	—	—
Jarvis, K.B.S.	18928	635	29.80	8-97	19	3	—
Jarvis, P.W.	7611	283	26.89	7-55	14	3	—
Jean-Jacques, M.	1995	58	34.39	8-77	1	1	—
Jefferies, S.T.	11103	410	27.08	10-59	16	3	—
Jesty, T.E.	16005	584	27.40	7-75	19	—	—
Johnson, P.	353	3	117.66	1-9	—	—	—
Jones, A.N.	6411	213	30.09	7-30	6	1	—
Kallicharran, A.I.	3975	82	48.47	5-45	1	—	—
Kelleher, D.J.M.	1107	43	25.74	6-109	2	—	—
Kendrick, N.M.	97	1	97.00	1-92	—	—	—
Ker, J.E.	482	19	25.36	4-54	—	—	—
Kilborn, M.J.	208	5	41.60	3.37	—	—	—
Kimber, S.J.S.	1191	31	38.41	4-76	—	—	—
Knight, R.D.V.	13256	369	35.92	6-44	4	—	—
Labrooy, G.F.	1202	35	34.34	7-71	2	—	—
Lamb, A.J.	164	6	27.33	1-1	—	—	—
Lampitt, S.R.	295	3	98.33	2-37	—	—	—
Larkins, W.	1760	42	41.90	5-59	1	—	—
Lawrence, D.V.	11007	331	33.25	7-47	14	—	—
Lawson, G.F.	11578	460	25.16	8-112	21	2	—
Leatherdale, D.A.	20	1	20.00	1-12	—	—	—
Lenham, N.J.	510	12	42.50	4-85	—	—	—
Lever, J.K.	41016	1696	24.18	8-37	84	12	4
Lewis, C.C.	1377	47	29.29	6-22	2	1	—
Lillee, D.K.	20695	882	23.46	8-29	50	13	—
Lilley, A.W.	505	7	72.14	3-116	—	—	—
Lloyd, T.A.	1189	15	79.26	3-62	—	—	—

189

	Runs	Wkts	Avge	Best	5wI	10wM	100wS
Lloyds, J.W.	9138	252	36.26	7-88	11	1	—
Logie, A.L.	128	3	42.66	1-2	—	—	—
Lord, G.J.	61	0			—	—	—
Love, J.D.	815	10	81.50	2-0	—	—	—
Lynch, M.A.	1116	24	46.50	3-6	—	—	—
McEwan, S.M.	1881	49	38.38	4-43	—	—	—
Maclaurin, N.R.C.	4	0			—	—	—
Madugalle, R.S.	158	2	79.00	1-18	—	—	—
Madurasinghe, A.W.R.	376	6	62.66	3-50	—	—	—
Maher, B.J.M.	151	3	50.33	2-69	—	—	—
Makinson, D.J.	2486	70	35.51	5-60	1	—	—
Malcolm, D.E.	4095	129	31.74	6-68	3	—	—
Mallender, N.A.	14604	516	28.30	7-27	11	1	—
Maninder Singh	9174	373	24.59	8-48	27	9	—
Marks, V.J.	26339	812	32.43	8-17	39	5	—
Marshall, M.D.	21655	1210	17.89	8-71	70	10	2
Martindale, D.J.M.	8	0			—	—	—
Maru, R.J.	9542	312	30.58	7-79	10	—	—
Matthews, C.D.	3859	155	24.89	8-101	8	—	—
Maynard, M.P.	161	4	40.25	3-21	—	—	—
Mays, C.S.	1009	16	63.06	3-77	—	—	—
Medlycott, K.T.	4691	159	29.50	8-52	10	4	—
Mendis, G.D.	153	1	153.00	1-65	—	—	—
Mendis, L.R.D.	52	1	52.00	1-4	—	—	—
Merrick, T.A.	5233	220	23.78	7-45	13	2	—
Metcalfe, A.A.	154	3	51.33	2-18	—	—	—
Middleton, T.C.	48	1	48.00	1-13	—	—	—
Miller, G	23082	843	27.38	8-70	38	7	—
Millns, D.J.	683	19	35.94	3-37	—	—	—
Moles, A.J.	1190	27	44.07	3-21	—	—	—
Monkhouse, S.	576	18	32.00	3-37	—	—	—
Moores, P.	6	0			—	—	—
Morris, H.	228	2	114.00	1-6	—	—	—
Morris, J.E.	453	3	151.00	1-13	—	—	—
Morris, R.E.	11	0			—	—	—
Mortensen, O.H.	5831	252	23.13	6-27	11	1	—
Morton, W.	1003	29	34.58	4-40	—	—	—
Moxon, M.D.	1100	18	61.11	3-26	—	—	—
Mudassar Nazar	4961	141	35.18	6-32	2	—	—
Mullally, A.D.	124	2	62.00	1-17	—	—	—
Munton, T.A.	2979	117	25.46	6-21	4	—	—
Murphy, A.J.	1268	33	38.42	4-115	—	—	—
Myles, S.D.	93	0			—	—	—
Neale, P.A.	275	1	275.00	1-15	—	—	—
Needham, A.	5373	124	43.33	6-30	6	—	—
Nelson, A.N.	100	4	25.00	4-100	—	—	—
Newell, M.	203	6	33.83	2-38	—	—	—
Newman, P.G.	8722	285	30.60	8-29	5	—	—
Newport, P.J.	8536	319	26.75	8-52	16	2	—
Nicholas, M.C.J.	2159	49	44.06	5-45	1	—	—
North, P.D.	780	19	41.05	4-43	—	—	—
Nuttall, J.D.	458	8	57.25	2-64	—	—	—
Ontong, R.C.	24973	817	30.56	8-67	32	4	—
O'Shaughnessy, S.J.	4108	114	36.03	4-66	—	—	—

	Runs	Wkts	Avge	Best	5wI	10wM	100wS
Palmer, G.V.	4107	92	44.64	5-38	1	—	—
Parker, P.W.G.	582	11	52.90	2-21	—	—	—
Parks, R.J.	166	0	—	—	—	—	—
Parsons, G.J.	13468	444	30.33	9-72	11	1	—
Patterson, B.P.	7977	290	27.50	7-24	15	2	—
Penn, C.	5265	174	30.25	7-70	9	—	—
Perry, J.N,	836	18	46.44	3-56	—	—	—
Peters, N.H.	954	34	28.05	6-31	1	1	—
Pick, R.A.	5479	156	35.12	6-68	3	1	—
Pickles, C.S.	443	6	73.83	2-31	—	—	—
Pienaar, R.F.	4431	140	31.65	5-24	3	—	—
Pierson, A.R.K.	1312	24	54.66	3-33	—	—	—
Pigott, A.C.S.	11880	417	28.48	7-74	18	1	—
Pointer, G.A.	1231	17	72.41	3-31	—	—	—
Pollard, P.	5	0	—	—	—	—	—
Pont, I.L.	2505	70	35.78	5-73	3	—	—
Pooley, M.W.	384	13	29.53	4-80	—	—	—
Potter, L.	2625	76	34.53	4-52	—	—	—
Prichard, P.J.	12	0	—	—	—	—	—
Pridgeon, A.P.	17218	526	32.73	7-35	10	1	—
Pringle, D.R.	13438	493	27.25	7-32	16	1	—
Pringle, M.W.	1153	32	36.03	6-33	1	—	—
Pringle, N.J.	429	5	85.80	2-35	—	—	—
Radford, N.V.	16924	667	25.37	9-70	34	6	2
Rajadurai, B.E.A.	65	1	65.00	1-28	—	—	—
Ramanayake, C.P.H.	832	23	36.17	3-91	—	—	—
Ramprakash, M.R.	54	0	—	—	—	—	—
Ranatunga, A.	1400	31	45.16	3-66	—	—	—
Randall, D.W.	383	12	31.91	3-15	—	—	—
Ratnayeke, J.R.	4294	121	35.48	8-83	5	—	—
Reeve, D.A.	7478	263	28.43	7-37	5	—	—
Richards, C.J.	224	5	44.80	2-42	—	—	—
Richards, I.V.A.	8218	193	42.58	5-88	1	—	—
Richardson, R.B.	136	5	27.20	5-40	1	—	—
Ripley, D.	89	2	44.50	2-89	—	—	—
Roberts, B.	2863	86	33.29	5-68	1	—	—
Robinson, J.D.	105	3	35.00	2-41	—	—	—
Robinson, M.A.	1556	59	26.37	4-19	—	—	—
Robinson, P.E.	139	0	—	—	—	—	—
Robinson, R.T.	165	2	82.50	1-22	—	—	—
Roebuck, P.G.P.	269	6	44.83	2-44	—	—	—
Roebuck, P.M.	2349	44	53.38	6-50	1	—	—
Romaines, P.W.	217	3	72.33	3-42	—	—	—
Rose, G.D.	2921	111	26.31	6-41	3	—	—
Roseberry, M.A.	86	2	43.00	1-1	—	—	—
Russell, R.C.	19	0	—	—	—	—	—
Sabine, D.J.	29	0	—	—	—	—	—
Samarasekera, M.A.R.	767	19	40.36	3-31	—	—	—
Saxelby, K.	8628	275	31.37	6-49	6	1	—
Scott, A.M.G.	2822	72	39.19	5-68	2	—	—
Scott, C.W.	10	0	—	—	—	—	—
Scott, R.J.	66	0	—	—	—	—	—
Scriven, T.J.A.	237	3	79.00	1-40	—	—	—
Searle, A.M.	76	0	—	—	—	—	—

	Runs	Wkts	Avge	Best	5wI	10wM	100wS
Sharma, C.	5094	182	27.98	7-83	11	1	—
Sharma, R.	1640	33	49.69	6-80	1	—	—
Sharp, K.	802	12	66.83	2-13	—	—	—
Shastri, R.J.	11844	371	31.92	9-101	14	3	—
Shaw, C.	4101	123	33.34	6-64	3	—	—
Sidebottom, A.	12752	523	24.38	8-72	18	2	—
Simmons, J.	27735	1030	26.92	7-59	41	6	—
Simmons, P.V.	558	8	69.75	2-53	—	—	—
Slack, W.N.	688	21	32.76	3-17	—	—	—
Small, G.C.	15139	546	27.72	7-15	24	2	—
Smith, C.L.	2453	43	57.04	5-69	1	—	—
Smith, D.M.	1520	30	50.66	3-40	—	—	—
Smith, G.	440	15	29.33	6-72	1	—	—
Smith, I.	1022	21	48.66	3-65	—	—	—
Smith, M.J.	51	2	25.50	2-30	—	—	—
Smith, N.M.K.	172	4	43.00	2-73	—	—	—
Smith, P.A.	5428	130	41.75	4-25	—	—	—
Smith, R.A.	443	9	49.22	2-11	—	—	—
Snodgrass, D.L.	139	5	27.80	2-26	—	—	—
Speight, M.P.	2	1	2.00	1-2	—	—	—
Standing, D.K.	725	6	120.83	2-28	—	—	—
Stephenson, F.D.	4850	235	20.63	7-56	16	4	1
Stephenson, J.P.	311	6	51.83	2-66	—	—	—
Stewart, A.J.	143	1	143.00	1-18	—	—	—
Storie, A.C.	71	0	—	—	—	—	—
Stovold, A.W.	218	4	54.50	1-0	—	—	—
Such, P.M.	5755	192	29.97	6-123	6	—	—
Swallow, I.G.	2542	48	52.95	7-95	1	—	—
Swan, R.G.	0	0	—	—	—	—	—
Sygrove, M.R.	933	20	46.65	3-91	—	—	—
Sykes, J.F.	1110	26	42.69	4-49	—	—	—
Tavare, C.J.	525	5	105.00	1-3	—	—	—
Taylor, L.B.	13743	557	24.67	7-28	18	1	—
Taylor, N.R.	795	15	53.00	2-20	—	—	—
Taylor, R.W.	75	1	75.00	1-23	—	—	—
Tennant, L.	110	3	36.66	1-0	—	—	—
Terry, V.P.	39	0	—	—	—	—	—
Thomas, D.J.	11415	336	33.97	6-36	7	1	—
Thomas, J.G.	11297	359	31.46	6-68	10	1	—
Thompson, N.E.	59	1	59.00	1-59	—	—	—
Thorne, D.A.	2065	41	50.36	5-39	1	—	—
Thorpe, G.P.	77	4	19.25	2-33	—	—	—
Threlfall, P.W.	31	0	—	—	—	—	—
Tillekeratne, H.P.	100	2	50.00	1-14	—	—	—
Topley, T.D.	4363	173	25.21	7-75	9	2	—
Towse, A.D.	50	3	16.66	2-26	—	—	—
Tremellen, J.M.	224	2	112.00	1-13	—	—	—
Tremlett, T.M.	10010	423	23.66	6-53	11	—	—
Trump, H.R.J.	696	24	29.00	4-17	—	—	—
Tufnell, P.C.R.	2521	63	40.01	6-60	1	—	—
Turner, D.R.	346	9	38.44	2-7	—	—	—
van Zyl, C.J.P.G.	4390	204	21.51	8-84	9	2	—
Vorster, L.P.	31	0	—	—	—	—	—

	Runs	Wkts	Avge	Best	5wI	10wM	100wS
Wakefield, M.	30	1	30.00	1-30	—	—	—
Walker, A.	6187	207	29.88	6-50	2	—	—
Wallace, P.	91	2	45.50	2-91	—	—	—
Walsh, C.A.	12763	559	22.83	9-72	34	6	1
Ward, D.M.	31	0	—	—	—	—	—
Ward, T.R.	4	0	—	—	—	—	—
Warner, A.E.	6337	192	33.00	5-27	2	—	—
Wasim Akram	4143	154	26.90	7-50	9	1	—
Watkin, S.L.	1505	48	31.35	8-59	2	—	—
Watkinson, M.	8017	239	33.54	7-25	11	—	—
Waugh, M.E.	730	20	36.50	4-130	—	—	—
Waugh, S.R.	2628	88	29.86	5-50	2	—	—
Weale, S.D.	1208	14	86.28	3-130	—	—	—
Wells, A.P.	322	5	64.40	3-67	—	—	—
Wells, C.M.	9855	298	33.07	6-34	4	—	—
Wells, V.J.	51	1	51.00	1-51	—	—	—
Weston, M.J.	2559	65	39.36	4-24	—	—	—
Whitaker, J.J.	168	1	168.00	1-41	—	—	—
Wild, D.J.	2836	65	43.63	4-4	—	—	—
Willey, P.	20883	691	30.22	7-37	25	3	—
Williams, N.F.	8674	298	29.10	7-55	6	1	—
Williams, R.G.	11132	335	33.22	7-73	9	—	—
Wright, A.J.	14	0	—	—	—	—	—
Wright, J.G.	282	2	141.00	1-4	—	—	—
Wyatt, J.G.	97	3	32.33	1-0	—	—	—

TEST CAREER RECORDS

(To the end of the 1988 season)

ENGLAND

BATTING AND FIELDING

	Tests	I	NO	HS	Runs	Avge	100	50	Ct/St
Agnew, J.P.	3	4	3	5	10	10.00	—	—	—
Allott, P.J.W.	13	18	3	52*	213	14.20	—	1	4
Athey, C.W.J.	23	41	1	123	919	22.97	1	4	13
Bailey, R.J.	1	2	0	43	46	23.00	—	—	—
Bairstow, D.L.	4	7	1	59	125	20.83	—	1	12/1
Barnett, K.J.	1	2	0	66	66	33.00	—	1	1
Benson, M.R.	1	2	0	30	51	25.50	—	—	—
Botham, I.T.	94	150	5	208	5057	34.87	14	22	109
Broad, B.C.	23	40	2	162	1579	41.55	6	6	8
Butcher, A.R.	1	2	0	20	34	17.00	—	—	—
Butcher, R.O.	3	5	0	32	71	14.20	—	—	3
Capel, D.J.	10	16	0	98	272	17.00	—	2	4
Childs, J.H.	2	4	4	2*	2	—	—	—	1
Cook, G.	7	13	0	66	203	15.61	—	2	9
Cook, N.G.B.	12	20	1	26	134	7.05	—	—	5
Cowans, N.G.	19	29	7	36	175	7.95	—	—	9
Cowdrey, C.S.	6	8	1	38	101	14.42	—	—	5
Curtis, T.S.	2	4	0	30	69	17.25	—	—	2

	Tests	I	NO	HS	Runs	Avge	100	50	Ct/St
DeFreitas, P.A.J.	12	17	1	40	182	11.37	—	—	4
Dilley, G.R.	39	55	18	56	479	12.94	—	2	10
Downton, P.R.	30	48	8	74	785	19.62	—	4	70/5
Ellison, R.M.	11	16	1	41	202	13.46	—	—	2
Emburey, J.E.	57	84	17	75	1409	21.02	—	7	33
Fairbrother, N.H.	4	4	0	3	5	1.25	—	—	3
Foster, N.A.	25	37	5	39	342	10.68	—	—	6
Fowler, G.	21	37	0	201	1307	35.32	3	8	10
French, B.N.	16	21	4	59	308	18.11	—	1	38/1
Gatting, M.W.	67	115	14	207	3848	38.09	9	18	51
Gooch, G.A.	68	123	4	196	4541	38.15	8	27	69
Gower, D.I.	100	172	13	215	7000	44.02	14	35	68
Greig, I.A.	2	4	0	14	26	6.50	—	—	—
Hemmings, E.E.	8	12	3	95	207	23.00	—	1	4
Jarvis, P.W.	4	6	2	29*	76	19.00	—	—	—
Lamb, A.J.	56	98	9	137*	2969	33.35	8	12	53
Larkins, W.	6	11	0	34	176	16.00	—	—	3
Lawrence, D.V.	1	1	0	4	4	4.00	—	—	—
Lever, J.K.	21	31	5	53	306	11.76	—	1	11
Lloyd, T.A.	11	1	10*	10			—	—	—
Marks, V.J.	6	10	1	83	249	27.66	—	3	—
Maynard, M.P.	1	2	0	10	13	6.50	—	—	—
Miller, G.	34	51	4	98*	1213	25.80	—	7	17
Moxon, M.D.	9	15	1	99	437	31.21	—	3	10
Newport, P.J.	1	1	0	26	26	26.00	—	—	—
Parker, P.W.G.	1	2	0	13	13	6.50	—	—	—
Pigott, A.C.S.	1	2	1	8*	12	12.00	—	—	—
Pringle, D.R.	19	33	3	63	479	15.96	—	1	7
Radford, N.V.	3	4	1	12*	21	7.00	—	—	—
Randall, D.W.	47	79	5	174	2470	33.37	7	12	31
Richards, C.J.	8	13	0	133	285	21.92	1	—	20/1
Robinson, R.T.	28	47	5	175	1589	37.83	4	6	7
Russell, R.C.	1	1	0	94	94	94.00	—	1	3
Sidebottom, A.	1	1	0	2	2	2.00	—	—	—
Small, G.C.	5	7	3	21*	61	15.25	—	—	1
Smith, C.L.	8	14	1	91	392	30.15	—	2	5
Smith, D.M.	2	4	0	47	80	20.00	—	—	—
Smith, R.A.	3	6	1	57	145	29.00	—	1	2
Tavaré, C.J.	30	55	2	149	1753	33.07	2	12	20
Taylor, L.B.	2	1	1	1*	1		—	—	1
Terry, V.P.	2	3	0	8	16	5.33	—	—	2
Thomas, J.G.	5	10	4	31*	83	13.83	—	—	—
Whitaker, J.J.	1	1	0	11	11	11.00	—	—	1
Willey, P.	26	50	6	102*	1184	26.90	2	5	3

BOWLING

	Balls	Runs	Wkts	Avge	Best	5wI	10wM
Agnew, J.P.	552	373	4	93.25	2-51	—	—
Allott, P.J.W.	2225	1084	26	41.69	6-61	1	—
Botham, I.T.	20801	10392	373	27.86	8-34	27	4
Broad, B.C.	6	4	0	—	—	—	—
Butcher, A.R.	12	9	0	—	—	—	—
Capel, D.J.	1112	527	10	52.70	2-13	—	—
Childs, J.H.	516	183	3	61.00	1-13	—	—
Cook, G.	42	27	0	—	—	—	—
Cook, N.G.B.	3551	1407	47	29.93	6-65	4	1
Cowans, N.G.	3452	2003	51	39.27	6-77	2	—
Cowdrey, C.S.	399	309	4	77.25	2-65	—	—
DeFreitas, P.A.J.	2338	1080	23	46.95	5-86	1	—
Dilley, G.R.	7682	3789	133	28.48	6-38	6	—
Ellison, R.M.	2264	1048	35	29.94	6-77	3	1
Emburey, J.E.	13315	4763	130	36.63	7-78	6	—
Fairbrother, N.H.	12	9	0	—	—	—	—
Foster, N.A.	5079	2376	76	31.26	8-107	5	1
Fowler, G.	18	11	0	—	—	—	—
Gatting, M.W.	752	317	4	79.25	1-14	—	—
Gooch, G.A.	1431	550	13	42.30	2-12	—	—
Gower, D.I.	36	20	1	20.00	1-1	—	—
Greig, I.A.	188	114	4	28.50	4-53	—	—
Hemmings, E.E.	2332	876	16	54.75	3-53	—	—
Jarvis, P.W.	931	418	12	34.83	4-107	—	—
Lamb, A.J.	30	23	1	23.00	1-6	—	—
Lawrence, D.V.	216	111	3	37.00	2-74	—	—
Lever, J.K.	4433	1951	73	26.72	7-46	3	1
Marks, V.J.	1082	484	11	44.00	3-78	—	—
Miller, G.	5149	1859	60	30.98	5-44	1	—
Moxon, M.D.	48	30	0	—	—	—	—
Newport, P.J.	285	164	7	23.42	4-87	—	—
Pigott, A.C.S.	102	75	2	37.50	2-75	—	—
Pringle, D.R.	3232	1501	43	34.90	5-95	2	—
Radford, N.V.	678	351	4	87.75	2-131	—	—
Randall, D.W.	16	3	0	—	—	—	—
Robinson, R.T.	6	0	0	—	—	—	—
Sidebottom, A.	112	65	1	65.00	1-65	—	—
Small, G.C.	1083	454	20	22.70	5-48	2	—
Smith, C.L.	102	39	3	13.00	2-31	—	—
Tavaré, C.J.	30	11	0	—	—	—	—
Taylor, L.B.	381	178	4	44.50	2-34	—	—
Thomas, J.G.	774	504	10	50.40	4-70	—	—
Willey, P.	1091	456	7	65.14	2-73	—	—

AUSTRALIA

BATTING AND FIELDING

	Tests	I	NO	HS	Runs	Avge	100	50	Ct/St
Alderman, T.M.	22	33	15	23	113	6.27	—	—	17
Boon, D.C.	28	50	3	184*	1896	40.34	6	9	18
Border, A.R.	94	164	27	205	7343	53.59	22	34	102
Dodemaide, A.I.C.	3	4	2	50	81	40.50	—	1	1
Dyer, G.C.	6	6	0	60	131	21.83	—	1	22/2
Gilbert, D.R.	9	12	4	15	57	7.12	—	—	—
Hughes, M.G.	7	9	0	16	44	4.88	—	—	4
Jones, D.M.	15	27	3	210	1181	49.20	3	5	7
Lawson, G.F.	37	60	10	57*	756	15.12	—	3	8
McDermott, C.J.	22	29	2	36	277	10.25	—	—	5
Marsh, G.R.	19	34	2	118	1210	37.81	3	5	12
Matthews, C.D.	2	3	0	11	21	7.00	—	—	1
Matthews, G.R.J.	21	34	6	130	1031	36.82	3	4	13
May, T.B.A.	1	1	1	14*	14	—	—	—	—
O'Donnell, S.P.	6	10	3	48	206	29.42	—	—	4
Phillips, W.B.	27	48	2	159	1485	32.28	2	7	52
Reid, B.A.	15	18	9	13	58	6.44	—	—	1
Ritchie, G.M.	30	53	5	146	1690	35.20	3	7	14
Sleep, P.R.	11	17	0	90	401	23.58	—	3	3
Taylor, P.L.	3	4	0	42	91	22.75	—	—	1
Veletta, M.R.J.	5	6	0	39	127	21.16	—	—	9
Waugh, S.R.	18	27	4	79*	676	29.39	—	6	18
Wellham, D.M.	6	11	0	103	257	23.36	1	—	5
Whitney, M.R.	3	6	2	4	6	1.50	—	—	—
Wood, G.M.	53	101	5	172	3109	32.38	8	13	38
Zoehrer, T.J.	10	14	2	52*	246	20.50	—	1	18/1

BOWLING

	Balls	Runs	Wkts	Avge	Best	5wI	10wM
Alderman, T.M.	5373	2597	79	32.87	6-128	5	—
Boon, D.C.	12	5	0	—	—	—	—
Border, A.R.	1781	699	16	43.68	3-20	—	—
Dodemaide, A.I.C.	757	302	15	20.13	6-58	1	—
Gilbert, D.R.	1647	843	16	52.68	3-48	—	—
Hughes, M.G.	1491	792	21	37.71	5-67	1	—
Jones, D.M.	90	29	1	29.00	1-5	—	—
Lawson, G.F.	8705	4420	145	30.48	8-112	10	2
McDermott, C.J.	4565	2484	73	34.02	8-141	3	—
Matthews, C.D.	421	233	6	38.83	3-95	—	—
Matthews, G.R.J.	3500	1707	39	43.76	5-103	2	1
May, T.B.A.	504	202	4	50.50	3-68	—	—
O'Donnell, S.P.	940	504	6	84.00	3-37	—	—
Reid, B.A.	3301	1482	48	30.87	4-53	—	—
Ritchie, G.M.	6	10	0	—	—	—	—
Sleep, P.R.	2419	1153	22	52.40	5-72	1	—
Taylor, P.L.	546	241	12	20.08	6-78	1	—
Waugh, S.R.	1940	885	28	31.60	5-69	1	—
Whitney, M.R.	789	383	9	42.55	4-92	—	—

WEST INDIES

BATTING AND FIELDING

	Tests	I	NO	HS	Runs	Avge	100	50	Ct/St
Ambrose, C.E.L.	8	12	4	43	122	15.25	—	—	—
Arthurton, K.L.T.	1	1	0	27	27	27.00	—	—	—
Benjamin, W.K.M.	7	9	1	40*	117	14.62	—	—	3
Best, C.A.	3	4	1	35	78	26.00	—	—	4
Butts, C.G.	7	8	1	38	108	15.42	—	—	2
Davis, W.W.	15	17	4	77	202	15.53	—	1	10
Dujon, P.J.L.	55	76	9	139	2607	38.91	5	14	174/5
Garner, J.	58	68	14	60	672	12.44	—	1	42
Gomes, H.A.	60	91	11	143	3171	39.63	9	13	18
Gray, A.H.	5	8	2	12*	48	8.00	—	—	6
Greenidge, C.G.	87	146	14	223	6186	46.86	15	31	83
Harper, R.A.	23	29	3	74	503	19.34	—	3	34
Haynes, D.L.	76	129	15	184	4523	39.67	9	28	47
Holding, M.A.	60	76	10	73	910	13.78	—	6	22
Hooper, C.L.	11	17	1	100*	469	29.31	1	2	5
Logie, A.L.	28	41	4	130	1295	35.00	2	7	28
Marshall, M.D.	58	72	7	92	1278	19.66	—	8	24
Patterson, B.P.	13	15	8	21*	56	8.00	—	—	2
Payne, T.R.O.	1	1	0	5	5	5.00	—	—	5
Richards, I.V.A.	99	147	9	291	7268	52.66	22	33	99
Richardson, R.B.	36	59	6	185	2173	41.00	6	8	50
Simmons, P.V.	2	4	0	16	49	12.25	—	—	1
Walsh, C.A.	25	30	11	18*	189	9.94	—	—	4

BOWLING

	Balls	Runs	Wkts	Avge	Best	5wI	10wM
Ambrose, C.E.L.	1905	810	29	27.93	4-53	—	—
Benjamin, W.K.M.	1182	537	26	20.65	4-52	—	—
Butts, C.G.	1554	596	10	59.60	4-73	—	—
Davis, W.W.	2773	1472	45	32.71	4-19	—	—
Garner, J.	13169	5433	259	20.97	6-56	7	—
Gomes, H.A.	2401	930	15	62.00	2-20	—	—
Gray, A.H.	888	377	22	17.13	4-39	—	—
Greenidge, C.G.	26	4	0	—	—	—	—
Harper, R.A.	3243	1166	45	25.91	6-57	1	—
Haynes, D.L.	18	8	1	8.00	1-2	—	—
Holding, M.A.	12680	5898	249	23.68	8-92	13	2
Hooper, C.L.	655	323	5	64.60	2-42	—	—
Logie, A.L.	7	4	0	—	—	—	—
Marshall, M.D.	13047	5921	290	20.41	7-22	18	3
Patterson, B.P.	2203	1354	47	28.80	5-24	2	—
Richards, I.V.A.	3826	1383	28	49.39	2-17	—	—
Richardson, R.B.	42	9	0	—	—	—	—
Walsh, C.A.	4816	2190	87	25.17	5-54	3	—

NEW ZEALAND

BATTING AND FIELDING

	Tests	I	NO	HS	Runs	Avge	100	50	Ct/St
Blain, T.E.	1	1	0	37	37	37.00	—	—	—
Boock, S.L.	29	40	8	37	199	6.21	—	—	14
Bracewell, J.G.	30	45	10	110	809	23.11	1	3	24
Chatfield, E.J.	38	46	30	21*	160	10.00	—	—	6
Crowe, J.J.	35	59	4	128	1441	26.20	3	6	38
Crowe, M.D.	42	70	6	188	2774	43.34	9	9	46
Franklin, T.J.	5	8	0	62	134	16.75	—	1	1
Gillespie, S.R.	1	1	0	28	28	28.00	—	—	—
Gray, E.J.	9	14	0	50	245	17.50	—	1	5
Greatbatch, M.J.	2	3	1	107*	186	93.00	1	1	—
Hadlee, R.J.	74	118	17	151*	2770	27.42	2	13	36
Horne, P.A.	3	5	0	27	59	11.80	—	—	1
Jones, A.H.	5	9	1	150	423	52.87	1	2	6
Morrison, D.K.	6	6	1	14*	16	3.20	—	—	2
Patel, D.N.	6	12	0	62	265	22.08	—	1	2
Robertson, G.K.	1	1	0	12	12	12.00	—	—	—
Rutherford, K.R.	14	23	3	107*	331	16.55	1	2	6
Smith, I.D.S.	43	59	13	113*	1037	22.54	1	2	120/7
Snedden, M.C.	16	18	3	32	196	13.06	—	—	3
Stirling, D.A.	6	9	2	26	108	15.42	—	—	1
Vance, R.H.	1	1	0	47	47	47.00	—	—	—
Watson, W.	2	2	1	8*	9	9.00	—	—	2
Wright, J.G.	58	103	4	141	3343	33.76	7	14	26

BOWLING

	Balls	Runs	Wkts	Avge	Best	5wI	10wM
Boock, S.L.	6178	2335	73	31.98	7-87	4	—
Bracewell, J.G.	6033	2464	72	34.22	6-32	2	1
Chatfield, E.J.	9016	3457	115	30.06	6-73	3	1
Crowe, J.J.	18	9	0	—	—	—	—
Crowe, M.D.	1239	607	13	46.69	2-25	—	—
Gillespie, S.R.	162	79	1	79.00	1-79	—	—
Gray, E.J.	1770	719	14	51.35	3-73	—	—
Hadlee, R.J.	19135	8378	373	22.46	9-52	32	8
Morrison, D.K.	1092	623	16	38.93	5-69	1	—
Patel, D.N.	187	103	0	—	—	—	—
Robertson, G.K.	144	91	1	91.00	1-91	—	—
Rutherford, K.R.	112	65	1	65.00	1-38	—	—
Smith, I.D.S.	18	5	0	—	—	—	—
Snedden, M.C.	2853	1344	36	37.33	5-68	1	—
Stirling, D.A.	902	601	13	46.23	4-88	—	—
Watson, W.	437	196	4	49.00	2-51	—	—
Wright, J.G.	30	5	0	—	—	—	—

INDIA

BATTING AND FIELDING

	Tests	I	NO	HS	Runs	Avge	100	50	Ct/St
Amarnath, M.	69	113	10	138	4378	42.50	11	24	47
Arshad Ayub.	4	7	2	57	133	26.60	—	1	—
Arun, B.	2	2	1	2*	4	4.00	—	—	2
Arun Lal.	9	16	0	93	513	32.06	—	6	6
Azharuddin, M.	24	36	3	199	1646	49.87	6	5	20
Binny, R.M.H.	27	41	5	83*	830	23.05	—	5	11
Hirwani, N.D.	1	1	0	1	1	1.00	—	—	—
Kapil Dev	92	133	12	163	3889	32.14	6	21	48
Kulkarni, R.R.	3	2	0	2	2	1.00	—	—	1
Lamba, R.	4	5	0	53	102	20.40	—	1	5
Maninder Singh.	31	35	12	15	88	3.82	—	—	9
Manjrekar, S.V.	1	2	1	10*	15	15.00	—	—	—
More, K.S.	17	22	5	49	397	23.35	—	—	29/11
Pandit, C.S.	3	5	1	39	140	35.00	—	—	4/1
Prabhakar, M.	2	4	1	35*	86	28.66	—	—	—
Raman, W.V.	1	2	0	83	92	46.00	—	1	1
Sharma, A.K.	1	2	0	30	53	26.50	—	—	1
Sharma, C.	19	21	7	54	310	22.14	—	1	5
Sharma, G.	4	3	1	10*	11	5.50	—	—	1
Shastri, R.J.	58	86	12	142	2568	34.70	7	9	27
Sidhu, N.S.	2	3	0	20	39	13.00	—	—	1
Srikkanth, K.	32	51	1	123	1590	31.80	2	9	26
Vengsarkar, D.B.	98	158	22	166	6256	46.00	17	30	65
Yadav, N.S.	35	40	12	43	403	14.39	—	—	10

BOWLING

	Balls	Runs	Wkts	Avge	Best	5wI	10wM
Amarnath, M.	3676	1782	32	55.68	4-63	—	—
Arshad Ayub	936	400	6	66.66	4-72	—	—
Arun, B.	252	116	4	29.00	3-76	—	—
Arun Lal	16	7	0	—	—	—	—
Azharuddin, M.	6	8	0	—	—	—	—
Binny, R.M.H.	2870	1534	47	32.63	6-56	2	—
Hirwani, N.D.	203	136	16	8.50	8-61	2	1
Kapil Dev	19225	9454	319	29.63	9-83	19	2
Kulkarni, R.R.	366	227	5	45.40	3-85	—	—
Maninder Singh	7318	2878	79	36.43	7-27	3	2
Prabhakar, M.	174	102	1	102.00	1-68	—	—
Raman, W.V.	6	7	1	7.00	1-7	—	—
Sharma, A.K.	24	9	0	—	—	—	—
Sharma, C.	2930	1797	53	33.90	6-58	4	1
Sharma, G.	1085	353	9	39.22	4-88	—	—
Shastri, R.J.	13051	4911	127	38.66	5-75	2	—
Sidhu, N.S.	6	9	0	—	—	—	—
Srikkanth, K.	150	68	0	—	—	—	—
Vengsarkar, D.B.	47	36	0	—	—	—	—
Yadav, N.S.	8349	3580	102	35.09	5-76	3	—

PAKISTAN

BATTING AND FIELDING

	Tests	I	NO	HS	Runs	Avge	100	50	Ct/St
Aamer Malik	3	4	1	98*	137	45.66	—	1	7/1
Abdul Qadir	54	64	7	61	916	16.07	—	3	15
Ashraf Ali	8	8	3	65	229	45.80	—	—	17/5
Asif Mujtaba	3	5	0	12	39	7.80	—	—	3
Ijaz Ahmed	10	11	0	69	285	25.90	—	2	7
Ijaz Faqih	5	8	1	105	183	26.14	1	—	—
Imran Khan	73	106	18	135*	2860	32.50	4	11	25
Iqbal Qasim	47	53	14	56	481	12.33	—	1	39
Javed Miandad	92	141	18	280*	6621	53.82	17	35	79/1
Mansoor Akhtar	18	27	3	111	636	26.50	1	3	7
Manzoor Elahi	4	6	1	52	109	21.80	—	1	5
Mohsin Kamal	7	7	5	13*	31	15.50	—	—	2
Mudassar Nazar	71	109	8	231	3991	39.51	10	17	44
Ramiz Raja	22	36	3	122	1030	31.21	2	5	16
Rizwan-uz-Zaman	9	17	1	60	312	19.50	—	3	2
Salim Jaffer	5	7	2	9	22	4.40	—	—	1
Salim Malik	47	65	11	119*	2140	39.62	6	11	42
Salim Yousuf	19	26	4	91*	698	31.72	—	3	55/6
Shoaib Mohammad	17	25	2	101	661	28.73	1	4	7
Tausif Ahmed	24	25	14	23*	167	15.18	—	—	8
Wasim Akram	25	31	6	66	410	16.40	—	2	8
Zakir Khan	1	1	1	0*	0	—	—	—	—
Zulqarnain	3	4	0	13	24	6.00	—	—	8/2

BOWLING

	Balls	Runs	Wkts	Avge	Best	5wI	10wM
Aamer Malik	60	46	0	—	—	—	—
Abdul Qadir	14425	6483	205	31.62	9-56	14	5
Asif Mujtaba	18	2	0	—	—	—	—
Ijaz Faqih	534	299	4	74.75	1-38	—	—
Imran Khan	17137	7319	334	21.91	8-58	23	6
Iqbal Qasim	12396	4629	159	29.11	7-49	7	2
Javed Miandad	1470	682	17	40.11	3-74	—	—
Manzoor Elahi	156	84	2	42.00	1-8	—	—
Mohsin Kamal	1024	597	17	35.11	4-127	—	—
Mudassar Nazar	5469	2358	58	40.65	6-32	1	—
Rizwan-uz-Zaman	132	46	4	11.50	3-26	—	—
Salim Jaffer	899	418	10	41.80	3-79	—	—
Salim Malik	212	92	4	23.00	1-3	—	—
Shoaib Mohammad	126	62	3	20.66	2-8	—	—
Tausif Ahmed	5524	2177	75	29.02	6-45	3	—
Wasim Akram	4974	2098	76	27.60	6-91	4	1
Zakir Khan	270	150	3	50.00	3-80	—	—

SRI LANKA

BATTING AND FIELDING

	Tests	I	NO	HS	Runs	Avge	100	50	Ct/St
Ahangama, F.S.	3	3	1	11*	11	5.50	—	—	1
Amalean, K.N.	2	3	2	7*	9	9.00	—	—	1
Anurasiri, S.D.	4	5	2	8	13	4.33	—	—	—
De Alwis, R.G.	11	19	0	28	152	8.00	—	—	21/2
De Silva, P.A.	15	28	2	122	660	25.38	2	1	8
Dias, R.L.	20	36	1	109	1285	36.71	3	8	6
Gurusinha, A.P.	7	12	2	116*	351	35.10	1	—	3
Jurangpathy, B.R.	2	4	0	1	1	0.25	—	—	2
Kaluperama, S.M.S.	4	8	0	23	88	11.00	—	—	6
Kuruppu, D.B.S.P.	3	5	1	201*	294	73.50	1	—	1
Kuruppuarachchi, A.K.	2	2	2	0*	0	—	—	—	—
Labrooy, G.F.	3	5	2	42	64	21.33	—	—	1
Madugalle, R.S.	21	39	4	103	1029	29.40	1	7	9
Madurasinghe, A.W.R.	96	41	0	—	—	—	—	—	—
Mahanama, R.S.	4	7	0	41	148	21.14	—	—	1
Mendis, L.R.D.	24	43	1	124	1329	31.64	4	8	9
Ramanayake, C.P.	2	4	0	9	11	2.75	—	—	1
Ranatunga, A.	24	43	2	135*	1537	37.48	2	12	11
Ratnayake, R.J.	14	23	4	56	272	14.31	—	1	5
Ratnayeke, J.R.	20	35	6	93	667	23.00	—	3	1
Samarasekera, M.A.R.	1	2	0	57	57	28.50	—	1	2
Silva, S.A.R.	9	16	2	111	353	25.21	2	—	33/1
Warnaweera, K.P.J.	1	2	0	3	3	1.50	—	—	—
Weerasinghe, C.D.U.S.	1	1	0	3	3	3.00	—	—	—
Wijesuriya, R.G.C.E.	4	7	2	8	22	4.40	—	—	1

BOWLING

	Balls	Runs	Wkts	Avge	Best	5wI	10wM
Agnew, J.P.	552	373	4	93.25	2-51	—	—
Ahangama, F.S.	801	348	18	19.33	5-52	1	—
Amalean, K.N.	244	156	7	22.28	4-97	—	—
Anurasiri, S.D.	486	159	5	31.80	4-71	—	—
De Silva, P.A.	36	24	0	—	—	—	—
Dias, R.L.	24	17	0	—	—	—	—
Gurusinha, A.P.	107	84	2	42.00	2-25	—	—
Jurangpathy, B.R.	150	93	1	93.00	1-69	—	—
Kaluperuma, S.M.S.	240	124	2	62.00	2-17	-	—
Kuruppuarachchi, A.K.	272	149	8	18.62	5-44	1	—
Labrooy, G.F.	720	415	7	59.28	4-119	—	—
Madugalle, R.S.	84	38	0	—	—	—	—
Madurasinghe, A.W.R.	96	41	0	—	—	—	—
Ramanayake, C.P.	266	144	2	72.00	2-86	—	—
Ranatunga, A.	1441	614	11	55.81	2-17	—	—
Ratnayake, R.J.	2825	1512	41	36.87	6-85	2	—
Ratnayeke, J.R.	3576	1830	55	33.27	8-83	4	—
Samarasekera, M.A.R.	192	104	3	34.66	2-38	—	—
Warnaweera, K.P.J.	51	26	1	26.00	1-26	—	—
Weerasinghe, C.D.U.S.	114	36	0	—	—	—	—
Wijesuriya, R.G.C.E.	586	294	1	294.00	1-68	—	—

LIMITED-OVERS INTERNATIONAL
CAREER RECORDS

These Limited-Overs International career records for players contracted to play county cricket in 1989 are complete to 18 January 1989 inclusive (Benson & Hedges World Series Finals) and are compiled by **Victor Isaacs**.

BATTING AND FIELDING

	M	I	NO	HS	Runs	Avge	100	50	Ct/St
Agnew, J.P.	3	1	1	2*	2	—	—	—	1
Alderman, T.M.	33	13	4	9*	27	3.00	—	—	14
Allott, P.J.W.	13	6	1	8	15	3.00	—	—	2
Ambrose, C.E.L.	19	12	23	87	17.40		—	8	
Athey, C.W.J.	31	30	3	142*	848	31.40	2	4	16
Bailey, R.J.	3	3	2	43*	95	95.00	—	—	1
Bairstow, D.L.	21	20	6	23*	206	14.71	—	—	17/4
Benjamin, W.K.M.	38	22	3	31	92	4.84	—	—	4
Benson, M.R.	1	1	0	24	24	24.00	—	—	—
Bishop, I.R.	12	6	5	33*	43	43.00	—	—	—
Border, A.R.	184	172	23	127*	4589	30.79	3	30	80
Botham, I.T.	95	86	11	72	1693	22.57	—	7	30
Broad, B.C.	34	34	0	106	1361	40.02	1	11	10
Butcher, A.R.	1	1	0	14	14	14.00	—	—	—
Butcher, R.O.	3	3	0	52	58	19.33	—	1	—
Capel, D.J.	11	11	2	50*	221	24.55	—	1	5
Clarke, S.T.	10	8	2	20	60	10.00	—	—	4
Cook, G	6	6	0	32	106	17.66	—	—	2
Cook, N.G.B.	2	—	—	—	—	—	—	—	1
Cowans, N.G.	23	8	3	4*	13	2.60	—	—	5
Cowdrey, C.S.	3	3	1	46*	51	25.50	—	—	—
Curran, K.M.	11	11	0	73	287	26.09	—	2	1
Davis, W.W.	35	5	3	10	28	14.00	—	—	9
DeFreitas, P.A.J.	38	26	10	33	289	18.06	—	—	8
Dilley, G.R.	36	18	8	31*	114	11.40	—	—	4
Dodemaide, A.I.C.	12	8	5	30	84	28.00	—	—	4
Downton, P.R.	28	20	5	44*	242	16.13	—	—	26/3
Ellison, R.M.	14	12	4	24	86	10.75	—	—	2
Emburey, J.E.	55	42	10	34	4671	14.40	—	—	18
Fairbrother, N.H.	11	11	2	54	232	25.77	—	2	5
Foster, N.A.	45	24	11	24	145	11.15	—	—	12
Fowler, G	26	26	3	81*	744	31.00	—	4	4/2
French, B.N.	13	8	3	9*	34	6.80	—	—	13/3
Gatting, M.W.	82	79	17	115*	1991	32.11	1	9	22
Gooch, G.A.	67	66	3	142	2615	41.50	6	15	24
Gould, I.J.	18	14	2	42	155	12.91	—	—	15/3
Gower, D.I.	102	99	8	158	2905	31.92	7	10	39
Hemmings, E.E.	13	3	1	4*	8	4.00	—	—	4
Humpage, G.W.	3	2	0	6	11	5.50	—	—	3
Jarvis, P.W.	5	2	1	5*	5	5.00	—	—	—
Jesty, T.E.	10	10	4	52*	127	21.16	—	1	5
Kallicharran, A.I.	31	28	4	78	826	34.41	—	6	8
Lamb, A.J.	80	78	14	118	2724	42.56	3	16	21
Larkins, W.	6	6	0	34	84	14.00	—	—	2
Lever, J.K.	22	11	4	27*	56	8.00	—	—	6

	M	I	NO	HS	Runs	Avge	100	50	Ct/St
Lloyd, T.A.	3	3	0	49	101	33.66	—	—	—
Love, J.D.	3	3	0	43	61	20.33	—	—	1
Lynch, M.A.	3	3	0	6	8	2.66	—	—	1
Marks, V.J.	34	24	3	44	285	13.57	—	—	8
Marshall, M.D.	100	55	15	66	667	16.67	—	2	10
Moxon, M.D.	8	8	0	70	174	21.75	—	1	5
Patterson, B.P.	31	6	5	13*	22	22.00	—	—	4
Pringle, D.R.	20	16	6	49*	284	28.40	—	—	7
Radford, N.V.	6	3	2	0*	0	0.00	—	—	2
Randall, D.W.	49	45	5	88	1067	26.67	—	5	25
Richards, C.J.	22	16	3	50	154	11.84	—	1	16/1
Richards, I.V.A.	160	145	22	189*	6146	49.96	11	44	79
Robinson, R.T.	26	26	0	83	597	22.96	—	3	6
Russel, R.C.	2	1	1	2*	2	—	—	—	3
Shastri, R.J.	105	84	16	102	2152	31.64	2	14	31
Small, G.C.	25	10	5	8*	33	6.60	—	—	—
Smith, C.L.	4	4	0	70	109	27.25	—	1	—
Smith, D.M.	1	1	1	10*	10	—	—	—	—
Smith, R.A.	1	1	0	9	9	9.00	—	—	—
Tavaré, C.J.	29	28	2	83*	720	27.69	—	4	7
Taylor, L.B.	2	1	1	1*	1	—	—	—	—
Thomas, J.G.	3	3	2	1*	1	1.00	—	—	—
Walsh, C.A.	67	21	9	18	79	6.58	—	—	9
Wasim Akram	71	48	9	48*	390	10.00	—	—	15
Waugh, M.E.	7	6	0	42	131	21.83	—	—	2
Waugh, S.R.	70	63	18	83*	1598	35.51	—	8	19
Wells, C.M.	2	2	0	17	22	11.00	—	—	—
Whitaker, J.J.	2	2	1	44*	48	48.00	—	—	1
Willey, P.	26	24	1	64	538	23.39	—	5	4

BOWLING

	Balls	Runs	Wkts	Avge	4w	Best
Agnew, J.P.	126	120	3	40.00	—	3-38
Alderman, T.M.	1752	1074	42	25.57	1	5-17
Allott, P.J.W.	819	552	15	36.80	—	3-41
Ambrose, C.E.L.	1025	634	41	15.46	5	5-17
Athey, C.W.J.	6	10	0		—	—
Bailey, R.J.	36	25	0		—	—
Benjamin, W.K.M.	1981	1382	37	37.35	—	3-21
Bishop, I.R.	656	446	21	21.23	2	5-27
Border, A.R.	1494	1173	39	30.07	—	3-21
Botham, I.T.	5076	3398	116	29.29	1	4-56
Broad, B.C.	6	6	0		—	—
Capel, D.J.	582	433	11	39.36	—	3-38
Clarke, S.T.	524	245	13	18.84	—	3-22
Cook, N.G.B.	84	52	3	17.33	—	2-18
Cowans, N.G.	1282	913	23	39.69	—	3-44
Cowdrey, C.S.	52	55	2	27.50	—	1-3
Curran, K.M.	506	398	9	44.22	—	3-65
Davis, W.W.	1923	1302	39	33.38	1	7-51
DeFreitas, P.A.J.	2138	1280	47	27.23	1	4-35
Dilley, G.R.	2043	1291	48	26.89	3	4-23
Dodemaide, A.I.C.	655	360	20	18.00	1	5-21
Ellison, R.M.	696	510	12	42.50	—	3-42
Emburey, J.E.	3083	2087	69	30.24	2	4-37

	Balls	Runs	Wkts	Avge	4w	Best
Foster, N.A.	2435	1706	52	32.80	—	3-20
Gatting, M.W.	368	320	10	32.00	—	3-32
Gooch, G.A.	1243	966	23	42.00	—	2-12
Gower, D.I.	5	14	0	—	—	—
Hemmings, E.E.	714	538	6	31.16	1	4-52
Jarvis, P.W.	287	187	6	31.00	1	4-33
Jesty, T.E.	108	93	1	93.00	—	1-23
Kallicharran, A.I.	105	64	3	21.33	—	2-10
Lamb, A.J.	6	3	0	—	—	—
Larkins, W.	12	21	0	—	—	—
Lever, J.K.	1152	713	24	29.70	1	4-29
Marks, V.J.	1772	1076	44	24.45	2	5-20
Marshall, M.D.	5315	2980	127	23.46	4	4-23
Patterson, B.P.	1617	1230	54	22.77	2	6-29
Pringle, D.R.	1130	852	20	42.60	—	3-21
Radford, N.V.	348	230	2	115.00	—	1-32
Randall, D.W.	2	2	1	2.00	—	1-2
Richards, I.V.A.	4741	3510	95	36.94	1	5-41
Shastri, R.J.	4952	3400	101	33.66	2	4-38
Small, G.C.	1422	941	27	34.85	1	4-34
Smith, C.L.	36	28	2	14.00	—	2-8
Tavaré, C.J.	12	3	0	—	—	—
Taylor, L.B.	84	47	0	—	—	—
Thomas, J.G.	156	144	3	48.00	—	2-59
Walsh, C.A.	3561	2280	76	30.00	4	5-1
Wasim Akram	3534	2317	92	25.18	3	5-21
Waugh, S.R.	3139	2341	79	29.63	2	4-33
Willey, P.	1031	659	13	50.69	—	3-33

CAREER RECORDS OF PROSPECTIVE AUSTRALIAN TOURISTS NOT INLUDED ABOVE

BATTING AND FIELDING

	M	I	NO	HS	Runs	Avge	100	50	Ct/St
Boon, D.C.	71	69	0	122	2455	35.57	2	15	21
Healy, I.A.	12	7	2	23*	54	10.80	—	—	10/2
Hughes, M.G.	9	4	1	13	25	8.33	—	—	1
Jones, D.M.	74	73	14	121	2633	44.62	3	18	22
Marsh, G.R.	68	68	3	126*	2442	37.56	6	9	20
McDermott, C.J.	64	44	9	37	324	9.25	—	—	16
O'Donnell, S.P.	51	40	10	74*	627	20.90	—	4	18
Taylor, P.L.	35	21	11	27*	154	15.40	—	—	17
Wood, G.M.	83	77	11	114*	2219	33.62	3	11	17

BOWLING

	Balls	Runs	Wkts	Avge	4w	Best
Boon, D.C.	28	41	0	—	—	—
Hughes, M.G.	414	309	14	22.07	1	4-44
Jones, D.M.	61	41	1	41.00	—	1-4
Marsh, G.R.	6	4	0	—	—	—
McDermott, C.J.	3501	2585	90	28.72	3	5-44
O'Donnell, S.P.	2563	1863	59	31.57	3	4-19
Taylor, P.L.	1729	1254	44	28.50	1	4-38

CRICKET RECORDS
FIRST-CLASS MATCHES

UPDATED TO THE END OF THE 1988 SEASON

TEAM RECORDS
Highest Innings Totals

1107	Victoria v New South Wales	Melbourne	1926-27
1059	Victoria v Tasmania	Melbourne	1922-23
951-7d	Sind v Baluchistan	Karachi	1973-74
918	New South Wales v South Australia	Sydney	1900-01
912-8d	Holkar v Mysore	Indore	1945-46
910-6d	Railways v Dera Ismail Khan	Lahore	1964-65
903-7d	England v Australia	The Oval	1938
887	Yorkshire v Warwickshire	Birmingham	1896
849	England v West Indies	Kingston	1929-30

There have been 23 instances of a team scoring 800 runs or more in an innings, the most recent being by North Zone (800 + 68 penalty runs) v West Zone at Bhilai in the final of the 1987-88 Duleep trophy.

Highest Second Innings Total

770	New South Wales v South Australia	Adelaide	1920-21

Highest Fourth Innings Total

654-5	England v South Africa	Durban	1938-39

Highest Match Aggregate

2376	Maharashtra v Bombay	Poona	1948-49

Record Margin of Victory

Innings and 851 runs	Railways v Dera Ismail Khan	Lahore	1964-65

Most Runs in a Day

721	Australians v Essex	Southend	1948

Most Hundreds in an Innings

6	Holkar v Mysore	Indore	1945-46
5	New South Wales v South Australia	Sydney	1900-01
5	Australia v West Indies	Kingston	1954-55

Lowest Innings Totals

12	†Oxford University v MCC and Ground	Oxford	1877
12	Northamptonshire v Gloucestershire	Gloucester	1907
13	Auckland v Canterbury	Auckland	1877-78
13	Nottinghamshire v Yorkshire	Nottingham	1901
14	Surrey v Essex	Chelmsford	1983
15	MCC v Surrey	Lord's	1839

15	†Victoria v MCC	Melbourne	1903-04
15	†Northamptonshire v Yorkshire	Northampton	1908
15	Hampshire v Warwickshire	Birmingham	1922

† Batted one man short

There have been 26 instances of a team being dismissed for under 20, the most recent being by Surrey in 1983 (above).

Lowest Match Aggregate by One Team

| 34 (16 and 18) | Border v Natal East | London | 1959-60 |

Lowest Completed Match Aggregate by Both Teams

| 105 | MCC v Australians | Lord's | 1878 |

Fewest Runs in an Uninterrupted Day's Play

| 95 | Australia (80) v Pakistan (15-2) | Karachi | 1956-57 |

Tied Matches

Before 1948 a match was considered to be tied if the scores were level after the fourth innings, even if the side batting last had wickets in hand when play ended. Law 22 was amended in 1948 and since then a match has been tied only when the scores are level after the fourth innings has been completed. There have been 46 tied first-class matches, five of which would not have qualified under the current law. The most recent are:

| Australia (574-7d/170-5d) v India (397/347) | Madras | 1986-87 |
| Derbyshire (340/226-5d) v Gloucestershire (288/278) | Bristol | 1987 |

BATTING RECORDS

Highest Individual Innings

499	Hanif Mohammad	Karachi v Bahawalpur	Karachi	1958-59
452*	D.G.Bradman	New South Wales v Queensland	Sydney	1929-30
443*	B.B.Nimbalkar	Maharashtra v Kathiawar	Poona	1948-49
437	W.H.Ponsford	Victoria v Queensland	Melbourne	1927-28
429	W.H.Ponsford	Victoria v Tasmania	Melbourne	1922-23
428	Aftab Baloch	Sind v Baluchistan	Karachi	1973-74
424	A.C.MacLaren	Lancashire v Somerset	Taunton	1895
405*	G.A.Hick	Worcestershire v Somerset	Taunton	1988
385	B.Sutcliffe	Otago v Canterbury	Christchurch	1952-53
383	C.W.Gregory	New South Wales v Queensland	Brisbane	1906-07
369	D.G.Bradman	South Australia v Tasmania	Adelaide	1935-36
365*	C.Hill	South Australia v NSW	Adelaide	1900-01
365*	G.St A.Sobers	West Indies v Pakistan	Kingston	1957-58
364	L.Hutton	England v Australia	The Oval	1938
359*	V.M.Merchant	Bombay v Maharashtra	Bombay	1943-44
359	R.B.Simpson	New South Wales v Queensland	Brisbane	1963-64
357*	R.Abel	Surrey v Somerset	The Oval	1899
357	D.G.Bradman	South Australia v Victoria	Melbourne	1935-36
356	B.A.Richards	S Australia v W Australia	Perth	1970-71
355	B.Sutcliffe	Otago v Auckland	Dunedin	1949-50
352	W.H.Ponsford	Victoria v New South Wales	Melbourne	1926-27
350	Rashid Israr	Habib Bank v National Bank	Lahore	1976-77

There have been 99 triple hundreds in first-class cricket, the most recent being 405* by G.A.Hick on 5/6 May 1988 as above. The most recent overseas is 320 by R.Lamba for North Zone v West Zone at Bhilai in 1987-88.

Most Hundreds in Successive Innings

6	C.B.Fry	Sussex and Rest of England		1901
6	D.G.Bradman	South Australia and D.G.Bradman's XI		1938-39
6	M.J.Procter	Rhodesia		1970-71
5	E.de C.Weekes	West Indians (in New Zealand)		1955-56

Two Double Hundreds in a Match

244	202*	A.E.Fagg	Kent v Essex	Colchester	1938

Double Hundred and Hundred in a Match Most Times

4	Zaheer Abbas	Gloucestershire	1976-81

Two Hundreds in a Match Most Times

8	Zaheer Abbas	Gloucestershire and PIA	1976-82
7	W.R.Hammond	Gloucestershire, England and MCC	1927-45

Most Hundreds in a Season

18	D.C.S.Compton	1947
16	J.B.Hobbs	1925
15	W.R.Hammond	1938

Most Hundreds in a Career

(The season in which his 100th hundred was scored is given in brackets)

197	J.B.Hobbs (1923)		117	D.G.Bradman (1947-48)
170	E.H.Hendren (1928-29)		108	Zaheer Abbas (1982-83)
167	W.R.Hammond (1935)		107	A.Sandham (1935)
153	C.P.Mead (1927)		107	M.C.Cowdrey (1973)
151	G.Boycott (1977)		104	T.W.Hayward (1913)
149	H.Sutcliffe (1932)		103	J.H.Edrich (1977)
145	F.E.Woolley (1929)		103	G.M.Turner (1982)
129	L.Hutton (1951)		102	E.Tyldesley (1934)
126	W.G.Grace (1895)		102	L.E.G.Ames (1950)
123	D.C.S.Compton (1952)		102	D.L.Amiss (1986)
122	T.W.Graveney (1964)			

Most Runs in a Month

1294	(avge 92.42)	L.Hutton	Yorkshire	June 1949

Most Runs in a Season

Runs			I	NO	HS	Avge	100	Season
3816	D.C.S.Compton	Middlesex	50	8	246	90.85	18	1947
3539	W.J.Edrich	Middlesex	52	8	267	80.43	12	1947
3518	T.W.Hayward	Surrey	61	8	219	66.37	13	1906

The feat of scoring 3000 runs in a season has been achieved on 28 occasions, the most recent instance being by W.E.Alley (3019) in 1961. The highest aggregate in a season since 1969, when the number of County Championship matches was substantially reduced, is 2713 by G.A.Hick in 1988.

1000 Runs in a Season Most Times

28   W.G.Grace (Gloucestershire), F.E.Woolley (Kent)

Highest Batting Average in a Season

(Qualification: 12 innings)

Avge			I	NO	HS	Runs	100	Season
115.66	D.G.Bradman	Australians	26	5	278	2429	13	1938
102.53	G.Boycott	Yorkshire	20	5	175*	1538	6	1979
102.00	W.A.Johnston	Australians	17	16	28*	102	–	1953
100.12	G.Boycott	Yorkshire	30	5	233	2503	13	1971

Fastest Hundred

35 min	P.G.H.Fender	Surrey v Northamptonshire	Northampton	1920
35 min	S.J.O'Shaughnessy	Lancashire v Leicestershire	Manchester	1983

Fastest Double Hundred

113 min	R.J.Shastri	Bombay v Baroda	Bombay	1984-85

Fastest Triple Hundred

181 min	D.C.S.Compton	MCC v NE Transvaal	Benoni	1948-49

Most Sixes in an Innings

15	J.R.Reid	Wellington v N Districts	Wellington	1962-63
13	Majid Khan	Pakistanis v Glamorgan	Swansea	1967
13	C.G.Greenidge	D.H.Robins' XI v Pakistanis	Eastbourne	1974
13	C.G.Greenidge	Hampshire v Sussex	Southampton	1975
13	G.W.Humpage	Warwickshire v Lancashire	Southport	1982
13	R.J.Shastri	Bombay v Baroda	Bombay	1984-85

Most Sixes in a Match

17	W.J.Stewart	Warwickshire v Lancashire	Blackpool	1959

Most Sixes in a Season

80	I.T.Botham	Somerset and England		1985

Most Boundaries in an Innings

68	P.A.Perrin	Essex v Derbyshire	Chesterfield	1904

Most Runs off One Over

36	G.St A.Sobers	Nottinghamshire v Glamorgan	Swansea	1968
36	R.J.Shastri	Bombay v Baroda	Bombay	1984-85

Both batsman hit all six balls of an over (bowled by M.A.Nash and Tilak Raj respectively) for six.

Most Runs in a Day

345	C.G.Macartney	Australians v Nottinghamshire	Nottingham	1921

There have been 17 instances of a batsman scoring 300 or more runs in a day, the most recent being by K.R.Rutherford (317) for the New Zealanders v D.B.Close's XI at Scarborough in 1986.

Highest Partnerships

First Wicket

561	Waheed Mirza/Mansoor Akhtar, Karachi W v Quetta; Karachi	1976-77
555	P.Holmes/H.Sutcliffe, Yorkshire v Essex; Leyton	1932
554	J.T.Brown/J.Tunnicliffe, Yorkshire v Derbys; Chesterfield	1898

Second Wicket

465*	J.A.Jameson/R.B.Kanhai, Warwickshire v Glos; Birmingham	1974
455	K.V.Bhandarkar/B.B.Nimbalkar, Maha'tra v Kathiawar; Poona	1948-49
451	D.G.Bradman/W.H.Ponsford, Australia v England; The Oval	1934

Third Wicket

456	Khalid Irtiza/Aslam Ali, United Bank v Multan; Karachi	1975-76
451	Mudassar Nazar/Javed Miandad, Pakistan v India; Hyderabad	1982-83
445	P.E.Whitelaw/W.N.Carson, Auckland v Otago; Dunedin	1936-37
434	J.B.Stollmeyer/G.E.Gomez, Trinidad v Br Guiana; Port-of-Spain	1946-47
424*	W.J.Edrich/D.C.S.Compton, Middlesex v Somerset; Lord's	1948

Fourth Wicket

577	V.S.Hazare/Gul Mahomed, Baroda v Holkar; Baroda	1946-47
574*	C.L.Walcott/F.M.M.Worrell, Barbados v Trinidad; Port-of-Spain	1945-46
502*	F.M.M.Worrell/J.D.C.Goddard, Barbados v Trinidad; Bridgetown	1943-44
470	A.I.Kallicharran/G.W.Humpage, Warwickshire v Lancs; Southport	1982

Fifth Wicket

405	S.G.Barnes/D.G.Bradman, Australia v England; Sydney	1946-47
397	W.Bardsley/C.Kelleway, NSW v S Australia; Sydney	1920-21
393	E.G.Arnold/W.B.Burns, Worcs v Warwickshire; Birmingham	1909

Sixth Wicket

487*	G.A.Headley/C.C.Passailaigue, Jamaica v Tennyson's; Kingston	1931-32
428	W.W.Armstrong/M.A.Noble, Australians v Sussex; Hove	1902
411	R.M.Poore/E.G.Wynyard, Hampshire v Somerset; Taunton	1899

Seventh Wicket

347	D.St E.Atkinson/C.C.Depeiza, W Indies v Australia; Bridgetown	1954-55
344	K.S.Ranjitsinhji/W.Newham, Sussex v Essex; Leyton	1902
340	K.J.Key/H.Philipson, Oxford U v Middlesex; Chiswick Park	1887

Eighth Wicket

433	A.Sims/V.T.Trumper, Australians v C'bury; Christchurch	1913-14
292	R.Peel/Lord Hawke, Yorkshire v Warwicks; Birmingham	1896
270	V.T.Trumper/E.P.Barbour, NSW v Victoria; Sydney	1912-13

Ninth Wicket

283	J.Chapman/A.Warren, Derbys v Warwicks; Blackwell	1910
251	J.W.H.T.Douglas/S.N.Hare, Essex v Derbyshire; Leyton	1921
245	V.S.Hazare/N.D.Nagarwalla, Maharashtra v Baroda; Poona	1939-40

Tenth Wicket

307	A.F.Kippax/J.E.H.Hooker, NSW v Victoria; Melbourne	1928-29
249	C.T.Sarwate/S.N.Bannerjee, Indians v Surrey; The Oval	1946
235	F.E.Woolley/A.Fielder, Kent v Worcs; Stourbridge	1909

Most Runs in a Career

	Career	I	NO	HS	Runs	Avge	100
J.B.Hobbs	1905-34	1315	106	316*	**61237**	50.65	197
F.E.Woolley	1906-38	1532	85	305*	**58969**	40.75	145
E.H.Hendren	1907-38	1300	166	301*	**57611**	50.80	170
C.P.Mead	1905-36	1340	185	280*	**55061**	47.67	153
W.G.Grace	1865-1908	1493	105	344	**54896**	39.55	126
W.R.Hammond	1920-51	1005	104	336*	**50551**	56.10	167
H.Sutcliffe	1919-45	1088	123	313	**50138**	51.95	149
G.Boycott	1962-86	1014	162	261*	**48426**	56.83	151
T.W.Graveney	1948-71/72	1223	159	258	**47793**	44.91	122
T.W.Hayward	1893-1914	1138	96	315*	**43551**	41.79	104
D.L.Amiss	1960-87	1139	126	262*	**43423**	42.86	102
M.C.Cowdrey	1950-76	1130	134	307	**42719**	42.89	107
A.Sandham	1911-1937/38	1000	79	325	**41284**	44.82	107
L.Hutton	1934-60	814	91	364	**40140**	55.51	129
M.J.K.Smith	1951-75	1091	139	204	**39832**	41.84	69
W.Rhodes	1898-1930	1528	237	267*	**39802**	30.83	58
J.H.Edrich	1956-78	979	104	310*	**39790**	45.47	103
R.E.S.Wyatt	1923-57	1141	157	232	**39405**	40.04	85
D.C.S.Compton	1936-64	839	88	300	**38942**	51.85	123
E.Tyldesley	1909-36	961	106	256*	**38874**	45.46	102
J.T.Tyldesley	1895-1923	994	62	295*	**37897**	40.60	86
K.W.R.Fletcher	1962-88	1167	170	228*	**37665**	37.77	63
J.W.Hearne	1909-36	1025	116	285*	**37252**	40.98	96
L.E.G.Ames	1926-51	951	95	295	**37248**	43.51	102
D.Kenyon	1946-67	1159	59	259	**37002**	33.63	74
W.J.Edrich	1934-58	964	92	267*	**36965**	42.39	86
J.M.Parks	1949-76	1227	172	205*	**36673**	34.76	51
D.Denton	1894-1920	1163	70	221	**36479**	33.37	69
G.H.Hirst	1891-1929	1215	151	341	**36323**	34.13	60
A.Jones	1957-83	1168	72	204*	**36049**	32.89	56
W.G.Quaife	1894-1928	1203	185	255*	**36012**	35.37	72
R.E.Marshall	1945/46-72	1053	59	228*	**35725**	35.94	68
G.Gunn	1902-32	1061	82	220	**35208**	35.96	62

BOWLING RECORDS

All Ten Wickets in an Innings

This feat has been achieved on 71 occasions at first-class level.
Three Times: A.P.Freeman (1929, 1930, 1931)
Twice: V.E.Walker (1859, 1865); H.Verity (1931, 1932); J.C.Laker (1956)

Instances since 1945:

W.E.Hollies	Warwickshire v Notts	Birmingham	1946
J.M.Sims	East v West	Kingston on Thames	1948
J.K.R.Graveney	Gloucestershire v Derbyshire	Chesterfield	1949
T.E.Bailey	Essex v Lancashire	Clacton	1949
R.Berry	Lancashire v Worcestershire	Blackpool	1953
S.P.Gupte	President's XI v Combined XI	Bombay	1954-55
J.C.Laker	Surrey v Australians	The Oval	1956
K.Smales	Nottinghamshire v Glos	Stroud	1956
G.A.R.Lock	Surrey v Kent	Blackheath	1956
J.C.Laker	England v Australia	Manchester	1956

P.M.Chatterjee	Bengal v Assam	Jorhat	1956-57
J.D.Bannister	Warwicks v Combined Services	Birmingham	1959
A.J.G.Pearson	Cambridge U v Leicestershire	Loughborough	1961
N.I.Thomson	Sussex v Warwickshire	Worthing	1964
P.J.Allan	Queensland v Victoria	Melbourne	1965-66
I.J.Brayshaw	Western Australia v Victoria	Perth	1967-68
Shahid Mahmood	Karachi Whites v Khairpur	Karachi	1969-70
E.E.Hemmings	International XI v W Indians	Kingston	1982-83
P.Sunderam	Rajasthan v Vidarbha	Jodhpur	1985-86
S.T.Jefferies	Western Province v OFS	Cape Town	1987-88

Most Wickets in a Match

| 19 | J.C.Laker | England v Australia | Manchester | 1956 |

Most Wickets in a Season

Wkts		Season	Matches	Overs	Mdns	Runs	Avge
304	A.P.Freeman	1928	37	1976.1	423	5489	18.05
298	A.P.Freeman	1933	33	2039	651	4549	15.26

The feat of taking 250 wickets in a season has been achieved on 12 occasions, the last instance been by A.P.Freeman in 1933. 200 or more wickets in a season have been taken on 59 occasions, the last being by G.A.R.Lock (212 wickets, average 12.02) in 1957.

The highest aggregates of wickets taken in a season since the reduction of the County Championship matches in 1969 are as follows:

Wkts		Season	Matches	Overs	Mdns	Runs	Avge
134	M.D.Marshall	1982	22	822	225	2108	15.73
131	L.R.Gibbs	1971	23	1024.1	295	2475	18.89
125	F.D.Stephenson	1988	22	819.1	196	2289	18.31
121	R.D.Jackman	1980	23	746.2	220	1864	15.40

Since 1969 there have been 44 instances of bowlers taking 100 wickets in a season.

Most Hat-Tricks in a Career

7	D.V.P.Wright
6	T.W.J.Goddard, C.W.L.Parker
5	S.Haigh, V.W.C.Jupp, A.E.G.Rhodes, F.A.Tarrant

Most Wickets in a Career

	Career	Runs	Wkts	Avge	100w
W.Rhodes	1898-1930	69993	4187	16.71	23
A.P.Freeman	1914-36	69577	3776	18.42	17
C.W.L.Parker	1903-35	63817	3278	19.46	16
J.T.Hearne	1888-1923	54352	3061	17.75	15
T.W.J.Goddard	1922-52	59116	2979	19.84	16
W.G.Grace	1865-1908	51545	2876	17.92	10
A.S.Kennedy	1907-36	61034	2874	21.23	15
D.Shackleton	1948-69	53303	2857	18.65	20
G.A.R.Lock	1946-70/71	54709	2844	19.23	14
F.J.Titmus	1949-82	63313	2830	22.37	16
M.W.Tate	1912-37	50571	2784	18.16	13+1
G.H.Hirst	1891-1929	51282	2739	18.72	15
C.Blythe	1899-1914	42136	2506	16.81	14

	Career	Runs	Wkts	Avge	100w
D.L.Underwood	1963-87	49993	**2465**	20.28	10
W.E.Astill	1906-39	57783	**2431**	23.76	9
J.C.White	1909-37	43759	**2356**	18.57	14
W.E.Hollies	1932-57	48656	**2323**	20.94	14
F.S.Trueman	1949-69	42154	**2304**	18.29	12
J.B.Statham	1950-68	36995	**2260**	16.36	13
R.T.D.Perks	1930-55	53770	**2233**	24.07	16
J.Briggs	1879-1900	35430	**2221**	15.95	12
D.J.Shepherd	1950-72	47302	**2218**	21.32	12
E.G.Dennett	1903-26	42571	**2147**	19.82	12
T.Richardson	1892-1905	38794	**2104**	18.43	10
T.E.Bailey	1945-67	48170	**2082**	23.13	9
R.Illingworth	1951-83	42023	**2072**	20.28	10
F.E.Woolley	1906-38	41066	**2068**	19.85	8
N.Gifford	1960-88	48731	**2068**	23.56	4
G.Geary	1912-38	41339	**2063**	20.03	11
D.V.P.Wright	1932-57	49307	**2056**	23.98	10
J.A.Newman	1906-30	51111	**2032**	25.15	9
A.Shaw	1864-97	24579	**2027**†	12.12	9
S.Haigh	1895-1913	32091	**2012**	15.94	11

† Excluding one wicket for which no analysis is available

ALL-ROUND RECORDS

The 'Double'

3000 runs and 100 wickets: J.H.Parks (1937)
2000 runs and 200 wickets: G.H.Hirst (1906)
2000 runs and 100 wickets: F.E.Woolley (4), J.W.Hearne (3), W.G.Grace (2), G.H.Hirst (2), W.Rhodes (2), T.E.Bailey, D.E.Davies, G.L.Jessop, V.W.C. Jupp, James Langridge, F.A.Tarrant, C.L.Townsend, L.F.Townsend
1000 runs and 200 wickets: M.W.Tate (3), A.E.Trott (2), A.S.Kennedy
Most Doubles: W.Rhodes (16), G.H.Hirst (14), V.W.C.Jupp (10)
Double in debut season: D.B.Close (1949) – aged 18, he is the youngest to achieve this feat

The feat of scoring 1000 runs and taking 100 wickets in a season has been achieved on 305 occasions, R.J.Hadlee (1984) and F.D.Stephenson (1988) being the only players to perform this feat since the reduction of Championship matches in 1969.

WICKET-KEEPING RECORDS

Most Dismissals in an Innings

8 (8ct)	A.T.W.Grout	Queensland v W Australia	Brisbane	1959-60
8 (8ct)	D.E.East	Essex v Somerset	Taunton	1985

Most Dismissals in a Match

12 (8ct, 4st)	E.Pooley	Surrey v Sussex	The Oval	1868
12 (9ct, 3st)	D.Tallon	Queensland v NSW	Sydney	1938-39
12 (9ct, 3st)	H.B.Taber	NSW v South Australia	Adelaide	1968-69

Most Catches in a Match

11	A.Long	Surrey v Sussex	Hove	1964
11	R.W.Marsh	W Australia v Victoria	Perth	1975-76
11	D.L.Bairstow	Yorkshire v Derbyshire	Scarborough	1982

Most Dismissals in a Season

128 (79ct, 49st)   L.E.G.Ames   1929

Most Dismissals in a Career

	Career	*Dismissals*	*Ct*	*St*
R.W.Taylor	1960-88	**1649**	1473	176
J.T.Murray	1952-75	**1527**	1270	257
H.Strudwick	1902-27	**1497**	1242	255
A.P.E.Knott	1964-85	**1344**	1211	133
F.H.Huish	1895-1914	**1310**	933	377
B.Taylor	1949-73	**1294**	1083	211
D.Hunter	1889-1909	**1253**	906	347
H.R.Butt	1890-1912	**1228**	953	275
J.H.Board	1891-1914/15	**1207**	852	355
H.Elliott	1920-47	**1206**	904	302
J.M.Parks	1949-76	**1181**	1088	93
R.Booth	1951-70	**1126**	948	178
L.E.G.Ames	1926-51	**1121**	703	418
G.Duckworth	1923-47	**1096**	753	343
H.W.Stephenson	1948-64	**1082**	748	334
J.G.Binks	1955-75	**1071**	895	176
T.G.Evans	1939-69	**1066**	816	250
D.L.Bairstow	1970-88	**1063**	926	137
A.Long	1960-80	**1046**	922	124
G.O.Dawkes	1937-61	**1043**	895	148
R.W.Tolchard	1965-83	**1037**	912	125
W.L.Cornford	1921-47	**1017**	675	342

FIELDING RECORDS

Most Catches in an Innings

7	M.J.Stewart	Surrey v Northants	Northampton	1957
7	A.S.Brown	Gloucs v Notts	Nottingham	1966

Most Catches in a Match

10	W.R.Hammond	Gloucestershire v Surrey	Cheltenham	1928

Most Catches in as Season

78	W.R.Hammond	(1928)	77	M.J.Stewart	(1957)

Most Catches in a Career

1018	F.E.Woolley	(1906-38)	784	J.G.Langridge	(1928-55)
887	W.G.Grace	(1865-1908)	764	W.Rhodes	(1898-1930)
831	G.A.R.Lock	(1946-70/71)	758	C.A.Milton	(1948-74)
819	W.R.Hammond	(1920-51)	754	E.H.Hendren	(1907-38)
813	D.B.Close	(1949-86)			

213

TEST CRICKET RECORDS

(Updated to the end of the 1988 season)

TEAM RECORDS
HIGHEST INNINGS TOTALS

903-7d	England v Australia	The Oval	1938
849	England v West Indies	Kingston	1929-30
790-3d	West Indies v Pakistan	Kingston	1957-58
758-8d	Australia v West Indies	Kingston	1954-55
729-6d	Australia v England	Lord's	1930
708	Pakistan v England	The Oval	1987
701	Australia v England	The Oval	1934
695	Australia v England	The Oval	1930
687-8d	West Indies v England	The Oval	1976
681-8d	West Indies v England	Port-of-Spain	1953-54
676-7	India v Sri Lanka	Kanpur	1986-87
674-6	Pakistan v India	Faisalabad	1984-85
674	Australia v India	Adelaide	1947-48
668	Australia v West Indies	Bridgetown	1954-55
659-8d	Australia v England	Sydney	1946-47
658-8d	England v Australia	Nottingham	1938
657-8d	Pakistan v West Indies	Bridgetown	1957-58
656-8d	Australia v England	Manchester	1964
654-5	England v South Africa	Durban	1938-39
652-7d	England v India	Madras	1984-85
652-8d	West Indies v England	Lord's	1973
652	Pakistan v India	Faisalabad	1982-83
650-6d	Australia v West Indies	Bridgetown	1964-65

The highest innings for other countries are:

622-9d	South Africa v Australia	Durban	1969-70
553-7d	New Zealand v Australia	Brisbane	1985-86
491-7d	Sri Lanka v England	Lord's	1984

LOWEST INNINGS TOTALS

26	New Zealand v England	Auckland	1954-55
30	South Africa v England	Port Elizabeth	1895-96
30	South Africa v England	Birmingham	1924
35	South Africa v England	Cape Town	1898-99
36	Australia v England	Birmingham	1902
36	South Africa v Australia	Melbourne	1931-32
42	Australia v England	Sydney	1887-88
42	New Zealand v Australia	Wellington	1945-46
42	India v England	Lord's	1974
43	South Africa v England	Cape Town	1888-89
44	Australia v England	The Oval	1896
45	England v Australia	Sydney	1886-87
45	South Africa v Australia	Melbourne	1931-32
47	South Africa v England	Cape Town	1888-89
47	New Zealand v England	Lord's	1958

53	West Indies v Pakistan	Faisalabad	1986-87
62	Pakistan v Australia	Perth	1981-82
93	Sri Lanka v New Zealand	Wellington	1982-83

BATTING RECORDS
HIGHEST INDIVIDUAL INNINGS

365*	G.St A.Sobers	WI v P	Kingston	1957-58
364	L.Hutton	E v A	The Oval	1938
337	Hanif Mohammad	P v WI	Bridgetown	1957-58
336*	W.R.Hammond	E v NZ	Auckland	1932-33
334	D.G.Bradman	A v E	Leeds	1930
325	A.Sandham	E v WI	Kingston	1929-30
311	R.B.Simpson	A v E	Manchester	1964
310*	J.H.Edrich	E v NZ	Leeds	1965
307	R.M.Cowper	A v E	Melbourne	1965-66
304	D.G.Bradman	A v E	Leeds	1934
302	L.G.Rowe	WI v E	Bridgetown	1973-74
299*	D.G.Bradman	A v SA	Adelaide	1931-32
291	I.V.A.Richards	WI v E	The Oval	1976
287	R.E.Foster	E v A	Sydney	1903-04
285*	P.B.H.May	E v WI	Birmingham	1957
280*	Javed Miandad	P v I	Hyderabad	1982-83
278	D.C.S.Compton	E v P	Nottingham	1954
274	R.G.Pollock	SA v A	Durban	1969-70
274	Zaheer Abbas	P v E	Birmingham	1971
270*	G.A.Headley	WI v E	Kingston	1934-35
270	D.G.Bradman	A v E	Melbourne	1936-37
268	G.N.Yallop	A v P	Melbourne	1983-84
266	W.H.Ponsford	A v E	The Oval	1934
262*	D.L.Amiss	E v WI	Kingston	1973-74
261	F.M.M.Worrell	WI v E	Nottingham	1950
260	C.C.Hunte	WI v P	Kingston	1957-58
260	Javed Miandad	P v E	The Oval	1987
259	G.M.Turner	NZ v WI	Georgetown	1971-72
258	T.W.Graveney	E v WI	Nottingham	1957
258	S.M.Nurse	WI v NZ	Christchurch	1968-69
256	R.B.Kanhai	WI v I	Calcutta	1958-59
256	K.F.Barrington	E v A	Manchester	1964
255*	D.J.McGlew	SA v NZ	Wellington	1952-53
254	D.G.Bradman	A v E	Lord's	1930
251	W.R.Hammond	E v A	Sydney	1928-29
250	K.D.Walters	A v NZ	Christchurch	1976-77
250	S.F.A.F.Bacchus	WI v I	Kanpur	1978-79

The highest individual innings for other countries are:

| 236* | S.M.Gavaskar | I v WI | Madras | 1983-84 |
| 201* | D.S.B.P.Kuruppu | SL v NZ | Colombo (CCC) | 1986-87 |

MOST RUNS IN A SERIES

Runs			Series	M	I	NO	HS	Avge	100	50
974	D.G.Bradman	A v E	1930	5	7	0	334	139.14	4	—
905	W.R.Hammond	E v A	1928-29	5	9	1	251	113.12	4	—
834	R.N.Harvey	A v SA	1952-53	5	9	0	205	92.66	4	3
829	I.V.A.Richards	WI v E	1976	4	7	0	291	118.42	3	2

Runs		Series	M	I	NO	HS	Avge	100	50
827	C.L.Walcott	WI v A	1954-55	5	10	0	155	82.70	5	2
824	G.St A.Sobers	WI v P	1957-58	5	8	2	365*	137.33	3	3
810	D.G.Bradman	A v E	1936-37	5	9	0	270	90.00	3	1
806	D.G.Bradman	A v SA	1931-32	5	5	1	299*	201.50	4	—
779	E.de C.Weekes	WI v I	1948-49	5	7	0	194	111.28	4	2
774	S.M.Gavaskar	I v WI	1970-71	4	8	3	220	154.80	4	3
761	Mudassar Nazar	P v I	1982-83	6	8	2	231	126.83	4	1
758	D.G.Bradman	A v E	1934	5	8	0	304	94.75	2	1
753	D.C.S.Compton	E v SA	1947	5	8	0	208	94.12	4	2

RECORD WICKET PARTNERSHIPS

1st	413	V.Mankad/Pankaj Roy	I v NZ	Madras	1955-56
2nd	451	W.H.Ponsford/D.G.Bradman	A v E	The Oval	1934
3rd	451	Mudassar Nazar/Javed Miandad	P v I	Hyderabad	1982-83
4th	411	P.B.H.May/M.C.Cowdrey	E v WI	Birmingham	1957
5th	405	S.G.Barnes/D.G.Bradman	A v E	Sydney	1946-47
6th	346	J.H.W.Fingleton/D.G.Bradman	A v E	Melbourne	1936-37
7th	347	D.St E.Atkinson/C.C.Depeiza	WI v A	Bridgetown	1954-55
8th	246	L.E.G.Ames/G.O.B.Allen	E v NZ	Lord's	1931
9th	190	Asif Iqbal/Intikhab Alam	P v E	The Oval	1967
10th	151	B.F.Hastings/R.O.Collinge	NZ v P	Auckland	1972-73

WICKET PARTNERSHIPS OF OVER 300

451	2nd	W.H.Ponsford/D.G.Bradman	A v E	The Oval	1934
451	3rd	Mudassar Nazar/Javed Miandad	P v I	Hyderabad	1982-83
446	3rd	C.C.Hunte/G.St A.Sobers	WI v P	Kingston	1957-58
413	1st	V.Mankad/Pankaj Roy	I v NZ	Madras	1955-56
411	4th	P.B.H.May/M.C.Cowdrey	E v WI	Birmingham	1957
405	5th	S.G.Barnes/D.G.Bradman	A v E	Sydney	1946-47
399	4th	G.St A.Sobers/F.M.M.Worrell	WI v E	Bridgetown	1959-60
397	3rd	Qasim Omar/Javed Miandad	P v SL	Faisalabad	1985-86
388	4th	W.H.Ponsford/D.G.Bradman	A v E	Leeds	1934
387	1st	G.M.Turner/T.W.Jarvis	NZ v WI	Georgetown	1971-72
382	2nd	L.Hutton/M.Leyland	E v A	The Oval	1938
382	1st	W.M.Lawry/R.B.Simpson	A v WI	Bridgetown	1964-65
370	3rd	W.J.Edrich/D.C.S.Compton	E v SA	Lord's	1947
369	2nd	J.H.Edrich/K.F.Barrington	E v NZ	Leeds	1965
359	1st	L.Hutton/C.Washbrook	E v SA	Jo'burg	1948-49
351	2nd	G.A.Gooch/D.I.Gower	E v A	The Oval	1985
350	4th	Mushtaq Mohammad/Asif Iqbal	P v NZ	Dunedin	1972-73
347	7th	D.St E.Atkinson/C.C.Depeiza	WI v A	Bridgetown	1954-55
346	6th	J.H.W.Fingleton/D.G.Bradman	A v E	Melbourne	1936-37
344*	2nd	S.M.Gavaskar/D.B.Vengsarkar	I v WI	Calcutta	1978-79
341	3rd	E.J.Barlow/R.G.Pollock	SA v A	Adelaide	1963-64
338	3rd	E.de C.Weekes/F.M.M.Worrell	WI v E	Pt-of-Spain	1953-54
336	4th	W.M.Lawry/K.D.Walters	A v WI	Sydney	1968-69
331	2nd	R.T.Robinson/D.I.Gower	E v A	Birmingham	1985
323	1st	J.B.Hobbs/W.Rhodes	E v A	Melbourne	1911-12
319	3rd	A.Melville/A.D.Nourse	SA v E	Nottingham	1947
316†	3rd	G.R.Viswanath/Yashpal Sharma	I v E	Madras	1981-82
308	7th	Waqar Hassan/Imtiaz Ahmed	P v NZ	Lahore	1955-56
308	3rd	R.B.Richardson/I.V.A.Richards	WI v A	St John's	1983-84
303	3rd	I.V.A.Richards/A.I.Kallicharran	WI v E	Nottingham	1976
301	2nd	A.R.Morris/D.G.Bradman	A v E	Leeds	1948

†415 runs were added for this wicket in two separate partnerships. D.B.Vengsarkar
retired hurt and was replaced by Yashpal Sharma after 99 runs had been added.

216

4000 RUNS IN TESTS

Runs			M	I	NO	HS	Avge	100	50
10122	S.M.Gavaskar	I	125	214	16	236*	51.12	34	45
8114	G.Boycott	E	108	193	23	246*	47.72	22	42
8032	G.St A.Sobers	WI	93	160	21	365*	57.78	26	30
7624	M.C.Cowdrey	E	114	188	15	182	44.06	22	38
7515	C.H.Lloyd	WI	110	175	14	242*	46.67	19	39
7343	A.R.Border	A	94	164	27	205	53.59	22	34
7268	I.V.A.Richards	WI	99	147	9	291	52.66	22	33
7249	W.R.Hammond	E	85	140	16	336*	58.45	22	24
7110	G.S.Chappell	A	87	151	19	247*	53.86	24	31
7000	D.I.Gower	E	100	172	13	215	44.02	14	35
6996	D.G.Bradman	A	52	80	10	334	99.94	29	13
6971	L.Hutton	E	79	138	15	364	56.67	19	33
6806	K.F.Barrington	E	82	131	15	256	58.67	20	35
6621	Javed Miandad	P	92	141	18	280*	53.82	17	35
6256	D.B.Vengsarkar	I	98	158	22	166	46.00	17	30
6227	R.B.Kanhai	WI	79	137	6	256	47.53	15	28
6186	C.G.Greenidge	WI	87	146	14	223	46.86	15	31
6149	R.N.Harvey	A	79	137	10	205	48.41	21	24
6080	G.R.Viswanath	I	91	155	10	222	41.93	14	35
5807	D.C.S.Compton	E	78	131	15	278	50.06	17	28
5410	J.B.Hobbs	E	61	102	7	211	56.94	15	28
5357	K.D.Walters	A	74	125	14	250	48.26	15	33
5345	I.M.Chappell	A	75	136	10	196	42.42	14	26
5234	W.M.Lawry	A	67	123	12	210	47.15	13	27
5138	J.H.Edrich	E	77	127	9	310*	43.54	12	24
5062	Zaheer Abbas	P	78	124	11	274	44.79	12	20
5057	I.T.Botham	E	94	150	5	208	34.87	14	22
4882	T.W.Graveney	E	79	123	13	258	44.38	11	20
4869	R.B.Simpson	A	62	111	7	311	46.81	10	27
4737	I.R.Redpath	A	66	120	11	171	43.45	8	31
4555	H.Sutcliffe	E	54	84	9	194	60.73	16	23
4341	G.A.Gooch	E	68	123	4	196	38.15	8	27
4537	P.B.H.May	E	66	106	9	285*	46.77	13	22
4523	D.L.Haynes	WI	76	129	15	184	39.67	9	28
4502	E.R.Dexter	E	62	102	8	205	47.89	9	27
4455	E.de C.Weekes	WI	48	81	5	207	58.61	15	19
4415	K.J.Hughes	A	70	124	6	213	37.41	9	22
4399	A.I.Kallicharran	WI	66	109	10	187	44.43	12	21
4389	A.P.E.Knott	E	95	149	15	135	32.75	5	30
4378	M.Amarnath	I	69	113	10	138	42.50	11	24
4334	R.C.Fredericks	WI	59	109	7	169	42.49	8	26

MOST HUNDREDS

34	S.M.Gavaskar	I	22	M.C.Cowdrey	E
29	D.G.Bradman	A	22	W.R.Hammond	E
26	G.St A.Sobers	WI	22	I.V.A.Richards	WI
24	G.S.Chappell	A	21	R.N.Harvey	A
22	A.R.Border	A	20	K.F.Barrington	E
22	G.Boycott	E			

BOWLING RECORDS
MOST WICKETS IN AN INNINGS

10-53	J.C.Laker	E v A	Manchester	1956
9-28	G.A.Lohmann	E v SA	Johannesburg	1895-96
9-37	J.C.Laker	E v A	Manchester	1956
9-52	R.J.Hadlee	NZ v A	Brisbane	1985-86
9-56	Abdul Qadir	P v E	Lahore	1987-88
9-69	J.M.Patel	I v A	Kanpur	1959-60
9-83	Kapil Dev	I v WI	Ahmedabad	1983-84
9-86	Sarfraz Nawaz	P v A	Melbourne	1978-79
9-95	J.M.Noreiga	WI v I	Port-of-Spain	1970-71
9-102	S.P.Gupte	I v WI	Kanpur	1958-59
9-103	S.F.Barnes	E v SA	Johannesburg	1913-14
9-113	H.J.Tayfield	SA v E	Johannesburg	1956-57
9-121	A.A.Mailey	A v E	Melbourne	1920-21

MOST WICKETS IN A TEST

19-90	J.C.Laker	E v A	Manchester	1956
17-159	S.F.Barnes	E v SA	Johannesburg	1913-14
16-136	N.D.Hirwani	I v WI	Madras	1987-88
16-137	R.A.L.Massie	A v E	Lord's	1972
15-28	J.Briggs	E v SA	Cape Town	1888-89
15-45	G.A.Lohmann	E v SA	Port Elizabeth	1895-96
15-99	C.Blythe	E v SA	Leeds	1907
15-104	H.Verity	E v A	Lord's	1934
15-123	R.J.Hadlee	NZ v A	Brisbane	1985-86
15-124	W.Rhodes	E v A	Melbourne	1903-04

MOST WICKETS IN A SERIES

Wkts			Series	M	Balls	Runs	Avge	5 wI	10 wM
49	S.F.Barnes	E v SA	1913-14	4	1356	536	10.93	7	3
46	J.C.Laker	E v A	1956	5	1703	442	9.60	4	2
44	C.V.Grimmett	A v SA	1935-36	5	2077	642	14.59	5	3
42	T.M.Alderman	A v E	1981	6	1950	893	21.26	4	—
41	R.M.Hogg	A v E	1978-79	6	1740	527	12.85	5	2
40	Imran Khan	P v I	1982-83	6	1339	558	13.95	4	2
39	A.V.Bedser	E v A	1953	5	1591	682	17.48	5	1
39	D.K.Lillee	A v E	1981	6	1870	870	22.30	2	1
38	M.W.Tate	E v A	1924-25	5	2528	881	23.18	5	1
37	W.J.Whitty	A v SA	1910-11	5	1395	632	17.08	2	—
37	H.J.Tayfield	SA v E	1956-57	5	2280	636	17.18	4	1
36	A.E.E.Vogler	SA v E	1909-10	5	1349	783	21.75	4	1
36	A.A.Mailey	A v E	1920-21	5	1465	946	26.27	4	2
35	G.A.Lohmann	E v SA	1895-96	3	520	203	5.80	4	2
35	B.S.Chandrasekhar	I v E	1972-73	5	1747	662	18.91	4	—
35	M.D.Marshall	WI v E	1988	5	1219	443	12.65	3	1

200 WICKETS IN TESTS

Wkts			M	Balls	Runs	Avge	5wI	10wM
373	I.T.Botham	E	94	20801	10392	27.86	27	4
373	R.J.Hadlee	NZ	74	19135	8378	22.46	32	8
355	D.K.Lillee	A	70	18467	8493	23.92	23	7
334	Imran Khan	P	73	17137	7319	21.91	23	6
325	R.G.D.Willis	E	90	17357	8190	25.20	16	—
319	Kapil Dev	I	92	19225	9454	29.63	19	2
309	L.R.Gibbs	WI	79	27115	8989	29.09	18	2
307	F.S.Trueman	E	67	15178	6625	21.57	17	3
297	D.L.Underwood	E	86	21862	7674	25.83	17	6
290	M.D.Marshall	WI	58	12047	5921	10.41	18	3
266	B.S.Bedi	I	67	21364	7637	28.71	14	1
259	J.Garner	WI	58	13169	5433	20.97	7	—
252	J.B.Statham	E	70	16056	6261	24.84	9	1
249	M.A.Holding	WI	60	12680	5898	23.68	13	2
248	R.Benaud	A	63	19108	6704	27.03	16	1
246	G.D.McKenzie	A	60	17681	7328	29.78	16	3
242	B.S.Chandrasekhar	I	58	15963	7199	29.74	16	2
236	A.V.Bedser	E	51	15918	5876	24.89	15	5
235	G.St A.Sobers	WI	93	21599	7999	34.03	6	—
228	R.R.Lindwall	A	61	13650	5251	23.03	12	—
216	C.V.Grimmett	A	37	14513	5231	24.21	21	7
205	Abdul Qadir	P	54	14425	6483	31.62	14	5
202	A.M.E.Roberts	WI	47	11136	5174	25.61	11	2
202	J.A.Snow	E	49	12021	5387	26.66	8	1
200	J.R.Thomson	A	51	10535	5601	28.00	8	—

HAT-TRICKS

F.R.Spofforth	Australia v England	Melbourne	1878-79
W.Bates	England v Australia	Melbourne	1882-83
J.Briggs	England v Australia	Sydney	1891-92
G.A.Lohmann	England v South Africa	Port Elizabeth	1895-96
J.T.Hearne	England v Australia	Leeds	1899
H.Trumble	Australia v England	Melbourne	1901-02
H.Trumble	Australia v England	Melbourne	1903-04
T.J.Matthews (2)*	Australia v South Africa	Manchester	1912
M.J.C.Allom†	England v New Zealand	Christchurch	1929-30
T.W.J.Goddard	England v South Africa	Johannesburg	1938-39
P.J.Loader	England v West Indies	Leeds	1957
L.F.Kline	Australia v South Africa	Cape Town	1957-58
W.W.Hall	West Indies v Pakistan	Lahore	1958-59
G.M.Griffin	South Africa v England	Lord's	1960
L.R.Gibbs	West Indies v Australia	Adelaide	1960-61
P.J.Petherick	New Zealand v Pakistan	Lahore	1976-77

In each innings.   † Four wickets in five balls.

219

WICKET-KEEPING RECORDS

MOST DISMISSALS IN AN INNINGS

7	Wasim Bari	Pakistan v New Zealand	Auckland	1978-79
7	R.W.Taylor	England v India	Bombay	1979-80
6	A.T.W.Grout	Australia v South Africa	Johannesburg	1957-58
6	D.T.Lindsay	South Africa v Australia	Johannesburg	1966-67
6	J.T.Murray	England v India	Lord's	1967
6†	S.M.H.Kirmani	India v New Zealand	Christchurch	1975-76
6	R.W.Marsh	Australia v England	Brisbane	1982-83
6	S.A.R.Silva	Sri Lanka v India	Colombo (SSC)	1985-86

† Including one stumping

MOST STUMPINGS IN AN INNINGS

5	K.S.More	India v West Indies	Madras	1987-88

MOST DISMISSALS IN A TEST

10	R.W.Taylor	England v India	Bombay	1979-80
9†	G.R.A.Langley	Australia v England	Lord's	1956
9	D.A.Murray	West Indies v Australia	Melbourne	1981-82
9	R.W.Marsh	Australia v England	Brisbane	1982-83
9	S.A.R.Silva	Sri Lanka v India	Colombo (SSC)	1985-86
9†	S.A.R.Silva	Sri Lanka v India	Colombo (SO)	1985-86

† Including one stumping

MOST DISMISSALS IN A SERIES

28	R.W.Marsh	Australia v England	1982-83
26 (inc 3st)	J.H.B.Waite	South Africa v New Zealand	1961-62
26	R.W.Marsh	Australia v West Indies (6 Tests)	1975-76
24 (inc 2st)	D.L.Murray	West Indies v England	1963
24	D.T.Lindsay	South Africa v Australia	1966-67
24 (inc 3st)	A.P.E.Knott	England v Australia (6 Tests)	1970-71

100 DISMISSALS IN TESTS

Total			Tests	Ct	St
355	R.W.Marsh	Australia	96	343	12
269	A.P.E.Knott	England	95	250	19
228	Wasim Bari	Pakistan	81	201	27
219	T.G.Evans	England	91	173	46
198	S.M.H.Kirmani	India	88	160	38
189	D.L.Murray	West Indies	62	181	8
187	A.T.W.Grout	Australia	51	163	24
179†	P.J.L.Dujon	West Indies	55	174	5
174	R.W.Taylor	England	57	167	7
141	J.H.B.Waite	South Africa	50	124	17
130	W.A.S.Oldfield	Australia	54	78	52
127	I.D.S.Smith	New Zealand	43	120	7
114†	J.M.Parks	England	46	103	11

† Including two catches taken in the field

FIELDING RECORDS
(Excluding Wicket-Keepers)

MOST CATCHES IN AN INNINGS

5	V.Y.Richardson	Australia v South Africa	Durban	1935-36
5	Yajurvindra Singh	India v England	Bangalore	1976-77

MOST CATCHES IN A TEST

7	G.S.Chappell	Australia v England	Perth	1974-75
7	Yajurvindra Singh	India v England	Bangalore	1976-77

MOST CATCHES IN A SERIES

15	J.M.Gregory	Australia v England	1920-21

100 CATCHES IN TESTS

Total			Tests
122	G.S.Chappell	Australia	87
120	M.C.Cowdrey	England	114
110	R.B.Simpson	Australia	62
110	W.R.Hammond	England	85
109	G.St A.Sobers	West Indies	93
109	I.T.Botham	England	94
108	S.M.Gavaskar	India	125
105	I.M.Chappell	Australia	75
102	A.R.Border	Australia	94

MOST TEST APPEARANCES

England	M.C.Cowdrey	114
Australia	R.W.Marsh	96
South Africa	J.H.B.Waite	50
West Indies	C.H.Lloyd	110
New Zealand	R.J.Hadlee	74
India	S.M.Gavaskar	125
Pakistan	Javed Miandad	92
Sri Lanka	{ L.R.D.Mendis	24
	{ A.Ranatunga	24

MOST CONSECUTIVE TEST APPEARANCES

106	S.M.Gavaskar	India	Bombay Jan 1975 to Madras Feb 1987

MOST MATCHES BETWEEN APPEARANCES

104	Younis Ahmed	Pakistan	Lahore Nov 1969 to Jaipur Feb 1987

SUMMARY OF ALL TEST MATCHES

To end of 1988 season in England

		Tests	Won by								Tied	Drawn
			E	A	SA	WI	NZ	I	P	SL		
England	v Australia	263	88	97	—	—	—	—	—	—	—	78
	v South Africa	102	46	—	18	—	—	—	—	—	—	38
	v West Indies	95	21	—	—	39	—	—	—	—	—	35
	v New Zealand	63	30	—	—	—	4	—	—	—	—	29
	v India	75	30	—	—	—	—	11	—	—	—	34
	v Pakistan	47	13	—	—	—	—	—	5	—	—	29
	v Sri Lanka	3	2	—	—	—	—	—	—	0	—	1
Australia	v South Africa	53	—	29	11	—	—	—	—	—	—	13
	v West Indies	62	—	27	—	19	—	—	—	—	1	15
	v New Zealand	24	—	10	—	—	5	—	—	—	—	9
	v India	45	—	20	—	—	—	8	—	—	1	16
	v Pakistan	28	—	11	—	—	—	—	8	—	—	9
	v Sri Lanka	2	—	2	—	—	—	—	—	0	—	0
South Africa	v New Zealand	17	—	—	9	—	2	—	—	—	—	6
West Indies	v New Zealand	24	—	—	—	8	4	—	—	—	—	12
	v India	58	—	—	—	6	—	6	—	—	—	29
	v Pakistan	25	—	—	—	9	—	—	6	—	—	10
New Zealand	v India	25	—	—	—	—	4	10	—	—	—	11
	v Pakistan	27	—	—	—	—	3	—	10	—	—	14
	v Sri Lanka	6	—	—	—	—	4	—	—	0	—	2
India	v Pakistan	40	—	—	—	—	—	4	7	—	—	29
	v Sri Lanka	7	—	—	—	—	—	2	—	1	—	4
Pakistan	v Sri Lanka	9	—	—	—	—	—	—	5	1	—	3
		1103	230	196	38	98	26	41	41	2	2	429

	Tests	Won	Lost	Drawn	Tied	Toss Won
England	651	230	174	247	—	323
Australia	477	196	139	140	2	240
South Africa	172	38	77	57	—	80
West Indies	264	98	64	101	1	141
New Zealand	189	26	77	86	—	93
India	250	41	85	123	1	123
Pakistan	176	41	41	94	—	90
Sri Lanka	27	2	15	10	—	13

LIMITED-OVERS INTERNATIONALS

RESULTS SUMMARY

Updated to 18 January 1989 inclusive.

		Matches	E	A	I	NZ	P	SL	WI	C	EA	Z	Tied	NR
England	v Australia	43	22	20										1
	v India	19	12		7									
	v New Zealand	27	13			11								3
	v Pakistan	27	18				9							
	v Sri Lanka	7	6					1						
	v West Indies	32	14						18					
	v Canada	1	1											
	v East Africa	1	1											
Australia	v India	30		16	11									3
	v New Zealand	39		25		12								2
	v Pakistan	25		11			12							2
	v Sri Lanka	14		9				3						2
	v West Indies	52		16					35				1	
	v Canada	1		1										
	v Zimbabwe	4		3								1		
India	v New Zealand	26			15	11								
	v Pakistan	27			10		16							1
	v Sri Lanka	18			13			3						1
	v West Indies	24			5				19					
	v East Africa	1			1									
	v Zimbabwe	4			4									
New Zealand	v Pakistan	14				7	6							1
	v Sri Lanka	14				7		6						1
	v West Indies	19				7			11					1
	v East Africa	1				1								
	v Zimbabwe	2				2								
Pakistan	v Sri Lanka	20					15	4						1
	v West Indies	44					10		34					
	v Canada	1					1							
Sri Lanka	v West Indies	10							10					
West Indies	v Zimbabwe	2							2					
		548	87	101	66	60	69	16	129	0	0	1	1	18

	Matches	Won	Lost	Tied	NR
England	157	87	66	0	4
Australia	208	101	96	1	10
India	149	66	78	0	5
New Zealand	141	60	74	0	7
Pakistan	158	69	84	0	5
Sri Lanka	88	16	68	0	4
West Indies	177	129	46	1	1
Canada	3	0	3	0	0
East Africa	3	0	3	0	0
Zimbabwe	12	1	11	0	0
	1096	529	529	2	36

LIMITED-OVERS INTERNATIONALS RECORDS

Compiled by Victor Isaacs to 18 January 1989 inclusive.

TEAM RECORDS

Highest Innings Totals

360-4 (50 overs)	West Indies v Sri Lanka	Karachi	1987-88
338-5 (60 overs)	Pakistan v Sri Lanka	Swansea	1983
334-4 (60 overs)	England v India	Lord's	1975
333-9 (60 overs)	England v Sri Lanka	Taunton	1983
333-8 (45 overs)	West Indies v India	Jamshedpur	1983-84
330-6 (60 overs)	Pakistan v Sri Lanka	Nottingham	1975

Highest Total Batting Second

297-6 (48.5 overs)	New Zealand v England	Adelaide	1982-83

Highest Match Aggregate

626-14 (120 overs)	Pakistan v Sri Lanka	Swansea	1983

Lowest Innings Totals
(*Excluding abbreviated matches*)

45 (40.3 overs)	Canada v England	Manchester	1979
55 (28.3 overs)	Sri Lanka v West Indies	Sharjah	1986-87
63 (25.5 overs)	India v Australia	Sydney	1980-81
64 (35.5 overs)	New Zealand v Pakistan	Sharjah	1985-86
70 (25.2 overs)	Australia v England	Birmingham	1977
70 (26.3 overs)	Australia v New Zealand	Adelaide	1985-86

Lowest Match Aggregate

91-12 (54.2 overs)	England v Canada	Manchester	1979

Largest Margins of Victory

232 runs	Australia beat Sri Lanka	Adelaide	1984-85
206 runs	New Zealand beat Australia	Adelaide	1985-86
202 runs	England beat India	Lord's	1975
10 wickets	India beat East Africa	Leeds	1975
10 wickets	New Zealand beat India	Melbourne	1980-81
10 wickets	West Indies beat Zimbabwe	Birmingham	1983
10 wickets	India beat Sri Lanka	Sharjah	1983-84
10 wickets	West Indies beat New Zealand	Port-of-Spain	1984-85
10 wickets	Pakistan beat New Zealand	Sharjah	1985-86
10 wickets	West Indies beat New Zealand	Christchurch	1986-87

Tied Matches

Australia	222-9	West Indies	222-5	Melbourne	1983-84
India	212-6	Pakistan	212-7	Hyderabad	1986-87

(*Match awarded to India for losing fewer wickets*)

Pakistan	229-7	Australia	229-8	Lahore	1988-89

(*Match awarded to Pakistan for losing fewer wickets*)

Smallest Margins of Victory

(Excluding abbreviated matches)

1 run	New Zealand beat Pakistan	Sialkot	1976-77
1 run	New Zealand beat Australia	Sydney	1980-81
1 run	Australia beat India	Madras	1987-88
1 wicket	England beat West Indies	Leeds	1973
1 wicket	West Indies beat Pakistan	Birmingham	1975
1 wicket	New Zealand beat West Indies	Christchurch	1979-80
1 wicket	West Indies beat Pakistan	Adelaide	1983-84
1 wicket	Pakistan beat New Zealand	Multan	1984-85
1 wicket	Pakistan beat India	Sharjah	1985-86
1 wicket	Pakistan beat Australia	Perth	1986-87
1 wicket	England beat Pakistan	Birmingham	1987
1 wicket	Pakistan beat West Indies	Lahore	1987-88

BATTING RECORDS

Highest Individual Innings

180*	I.V.A. Richards	West Indies v England	Manchester	1984
181	I.V.A. Richards	West Indies v Sri Lanka	Karachi	1987-88
175*	Kapil Dev	India v Zimbabwe	Tunbridge Wells	1983
171*	G.M. Turner	New Zealand v East Africa	Birmingham	1975
158	D.I. Gower	England v New Zealand	Brisbane	1982-83
153*	I.V.A. Richards	West Indies v Australia	Melbourne	1979-80

Hundred On Debut

103	D.L. Amiss	England v Australia	Manchester	1972
148	D.L. Haynes	West Indies v Australia	St John's	1977-78

Highest Partnership for Each Wicket

1st	212	G.R. Marsh/D.C. Boon	A v I	Jaipur	1986-87
2nd	221	C.G. Greenidge/I.V.A. Richards	WI v I	Jamshedpur	1983-84
3rd	224*	D.M. Jones/A.R. Border	A v SL	Adelaide	1984-85
4th	173	D.M. Jones/S.R. Waugh	A v P	Perth	1986-87
5th	152	I.V.A. Richards/C.H. Lloyd	WI v SL	Brisbane	1984-85
6th	144	Imran Khan/Shahid Mahboob	P v SL	Leeds	1983
7th	115	P.J.L. Dujon/M.D. Marshall	WI v P	Gujranwala	1986-87
8th	117	D.L. Houghton/I.P. Butchart	Z v NZ	Hyderabad (P)	1987-88
9th	126*	Kapil Dev/S.M.H. Kirmani	I v Z	Tunbridge Wells	1983
10th	106*	I.V.A. Richards/M.A. Holding	WI v E	Manchester	1984

Most Runs in a Career

		I	NO	HS	Runs	Avge	100	50
I.V.A. Richards	WI	145	22	189*	6146	49.96	11	44
D.L. Haynes	WI	153	18	148	5631	41.71	12	30
Javed Miandad	P	139	31	119*	5043	46.69	6	37
A.R. Border	A	172	23	127*	4589	30.79	3	30
C.G. Greenidge	WI	109	11	133*	4511	46.03	10	27
D.B. Vengsarkar	I	104	19	105	3110	36.58	1	21
S.M. Gavaskar	I	102	14	103*	3092	35.13	1	27
J.G. Wright	NZ	113	1	101	3078	27.48	1	17
D.I. Gower	E	99	8	158	2905	31.92	7	10
A.J. Lamb	E	78	14	118	2724	42.56	3	16
G.A. Gooch	E	66	3	142	2615	41.50	6	15
Zaheer Abbas	P	60	6	123	2572	47.62	7	13

BOWLING RECORDS

Most Wickets in an Innings

7-51	W.W. Davis	West Indies v Australia	Leeds	1983
6-14	G.J. Gilmour	Australia v England	Leeds	1975
6-14	Imran Khan	Pakistan v India	Sharjah	1984-85
6-15	C.E.H. Croft	West Indies v England	Kingston	1980-81
6-39	K.H. MacLeay	Australia v England	Nottingham	1983

Hat-Tricks

Jalaluddin	Pakistan v Australia	Hyderabad	1982-83
B.A. Reid	Australia v New Zealand	Sydney	1985-86
C. Sharma	India v New Zealand	Nagpur	1987-88

Most Wickets in a Career

		Balls	Runs	Wkts	Avge	Best	4w
Kapil Dev	I	6720	4165	157*	26.52	5-43	2
J. Garner	WI	5330	2752	146	18.84	5-31	5
R.J. Hadlee	NZ	5759	3145	144	21.84	5-25	5
M.A. Holding	WI	5473	3034	142	21.36	5-26	6
E.J. Chatfield	NZ	6005	3584	140	25.60	5-34	4
Imran Khan	P	4866	3081	130	23.70	6-14	4
M.D. Marshall	WI	5315	2980	127	23.46	4-23	4
I.T. Botham	E	5076	3398	116	29.29	4-56	1
Abdul Qadir	P	3959	2610	106	24.62	5-44	6
Mudassar Nazar	P	4585	3255	106	30.70	5-28	2
D.K. Lillee	A	3593	2145	103	20.82	4-26	1
M.C. Snedden	NZ	3880	2881	100	28.81	4-34	1

WICKET-KEEPING RECORDS

Most Dismissals in an Innings

5 (all ct)	R.G. de Alwis	SL v A	Colombo	1982-83
5 (all ct)	S.M.H. Kirmani	I v ZIM	Leicester	1983
5 (all ct)	R.W. Marsh	A v E	Leeds	1981
5 (3 ct, 2 st)	S. Viswanath	I v E	Sydney	1984-85

Most Dismissals in a Career

P.J.L. Dujon	West Indies	164 (146 ct, 12 st) in 133 matches

FIELDING RECORDS

Most Catches in an Innings

4	Salim Malik	P v NZ	Sialkot	1984-85
4	S.M. Gavaskar	I v P	Sharjah	1984-85

Most Catches in a Career

A.R. Border	Australia	80 in 184 matches
I.V.A. Richards	West Indies	79 in 160 matches

ALL ROUND RECORDS
1000 Runs and 100 Dismissals

I.T. Botham	England	1693 runs	116 wickets
P.J.L. Dujon	West Indies	1303 runs	164 dismissals (146 ct, 18 st)
R.J. Hadlee	New Zealand	1601 runs	144 wickets
Imran Khan	Pakistan	2133 runs	130 wickets
Kapil Dev	India	2720 runs	157 wickets
R.W. Marsh	Australia	1220 runs	123 dismissals (119 ct, 4 st)
Mudassar Nazar	Pakistan	2534 runs	106 wickets

TEXACO TROPHY 1972-88

(Including the Prudential Trophy)

Highest Total	320-8	England v Australia	Birmingham	1980
Lowest Total	70	Australia v England	Birmingham	1977
Highest Aggregate	593	Eng (320-8) v Aus (273-5)	Birmingham	1980
Largest Victories	9 wkts	England beat India	Leeds	1982
	9 wkts	India beat England	The Oval	1986
	132 runs	England beat Pakistan	Manchester	1978
Narrowest Victories	1 wkt	England beat West Indies	Leeds	1973
	1 wkt	England beat Pakistan	Birmingham	1987
	2 runs	Australia beat England	Birmingham	1981
Highest Score	I.V.A. Richards	189*	WI v E	Manchester	1984
Hundreds (20)	D.L. Amiss (3)	103	E v A	Manchester	1972
		100	E v NZ	Swansea	1973
		108	E v A	The Oval	1977
	C.W.J. Athey	142*	E v NZ	Manchester	1986
	G.S. Chappell	125*	A v E	Manchester	1977
	R.C. Fredericks	105	WI v E	The Oval	1973
	G.A. Gooch (3)	108	E v A	Birmingham	1980
		115	E v A	Birmingham	1985
		117*	E v A	Lord's	1985
	D.I. Gower (2)	114*	E v P	The Oval	1978
		102	E v A	Lord's	1985
	Javed Miandad	113	E v P	The Oval	1987
	A.J. Lamb	118	E v P	Nottingham	1982
	D. Lloyd	116*	E v P	Nottingham	1974
	Majid Khan	109	P v E	Nottingham	1974
	C.T. Radley	117*	E v NZ	Manchester	1978
	I.V.A. Richards (2)	119*	WI v E	Scarborough	1976
		189*	WI v E	Manchester	1984
	G.M. Wood (2)	108	A v E	Leeds	1981
		114*	A v E	Lord's	1985
Fastest Hundred	88 balls – Majid Khan		P v E	Nottingham	1974
Fastest Fifties	35 balls – R.O. Butcher		E v A	Birmingham	1980
	35 balls – Kapil Dev		I v E	Leeds	1982

Highest Partnership for each Wicket

1st	193	G.A.Gooch/C.W.J.Athey	E v NZ	Manchester	1986
2nd	202	G.A.Gooch/D.I.Gower	E v A	Lord's	1985
3rd	159	A.J.Lamb/D.I.Gower	E v I	The Oval	1982
4th	116	G.A.Gooch/I.T.Botham	E v A	Manchester	1985
5th	113	M.D.Crowe/J.J.Crowe	NZ v E	Manchester	1986
6th	104	R.J.Shastri/Kapil Dev	I v E	Manchester	1986
7th	77	A.W.Greig/A.P.E.Knott	E v A	Lord's	1972
8th	68	B.E.Congdon/B.L.Cairns	NZ v E	Scarborough	1978
9th	47	A.J.Lamb/N.A.Foster	E v WI	Manchester	1984
10th	106*	I.V.A.Richards/M.A.Holding	WI v E	Manchester	1984

Best Bowling	5-18	G.J.Cosier	A v E	Birmingham	1977
	5-20	G.S.Chappell	A v E	Birmingham	1977
	5-28	B.L.Cairns	NZ v E	Scarborough	1978
	5-31	M.Hendrick	E v A	The Oval	1980
	5-50	V.A.Holder	WI v E	Birmingham	1976

Most Economical Bowling

11-5-11-0	C.A.Walsh	WI v E	Lord's	1988

Most Expensive Bowling

11-0-84-0	B.L.Cairns	NZ v E	Manchester	1978

Most Wicket-Keeping Dismissals

5 (5ct)	R.W.Marsh	A v E	Leeds	1981

Most Catches in the Field

3	A.W.Greig, B.S.Bedi, Kapil Dev, M.Azharuddin

RESULTS SUMMARY 1972-1988

	Played	Won	Lost	No Result
England	49	30	18	1
West Indies	13	7	6	—
Australia	14	6	8	—
Pakistan	9	3	6	—
India	6	1	5	—
New Zealand	6	1	4	1
Sri Lanka	1	—	1	—

ENGLAND v AUSTRALIA
1876-77 to 1987-88

		Captains					
Season	England	Australia	P	E	A	D
1876-77	James Lillywhite	D.W. Gregory	2	1	1	0
1878-79	Lord Harris	D.W. Gregory	1	0	1	0
1880	Lord Harris	W.L. Murdoch	1	1	0	0
1881-82	A. Shaw	W.L. Murdoch	4	0	2	2
1882	A.N. Hornby	W.L. Murdoch	1	0	1	0
1882-83	Hon. Ivo Bligh	W.L. Murdoch	4	2	2	0
1884	Lord Harris[1]	W.L. Murdoch	3	1	0	2
1884-85	A. Shrewsbury	T. Horan[2]	5	3	2	0
1886	A.G. Steel	H.J.H. Scott	3	3	0	0
1886-87	A. Shrewsbury	P.S. McDonnell	2	2	0	0
1887-88	W.W. Read	P.S. McDonnell	1	1	0	0
1888	W.G. Grace[3]	P.S. McDonnell	3	2	1	0
1890†	W.G. Grace	W.L. Murdoch	2	2	0	0
1891-92	W.G. Grace	J. McC. Blackham	3	1	2	0
1893	W.G. Grace[4]	J. McC. Blackham	3	1	0	2
1894-95	A.E. Stoddart	G. Giffen[5]	5	3	2	0
1896	W.G. Grace	G.H.S. Trott	3	2	1	0
1897-98	A.E. Stoddart[6]	G.H.S. Trott	5	1	4	0
1899	A.C. MacLaren[7]	J. Darling	5	0	1	4
1901-02	A.C. MacLaren	J. Darling[8]	5	1	4	0
1902	A.C. MacLaren	J. Darling	5	1	2	2
1903-04	P.F. Warner	M.A. Noble	5	3	2	0
1905	Hon. F.S. Jackson	J. Darling	5	2	0	3
1907-08	A.O. Jones[9]	M.A. Noble	5	1	4	0
1909	A.C. MacLaren	M.A. Noble	5	1	2	2
1911-12	J.W.H.T. Douglas	C. Hill	5	4	1	0
1912	C.B. Fry	S.E. Gregory	3	1	0	2
1920-21	J.W.H.T. Douglas	W.W. Armstrong	5	0	5	0
1921	Hon. L.H. Tennyson[10]	W.W. Armstrong	5	0	3	2
1924-25	A.E.R. Gilligan	H.L. Collins	5	1	4	0
1926	A.W. Carr[11]	H.L. Collins[12]	5	1	0	4
1928-29	A.P.F. Chapman[13]	J. Ryder	5	4	1	0
1930	A.P.F. Chapman[14]	W.M. Woodfull	5	1	2	2
1932-33	D.R. Jardine	W.M. Woodfull	5	4	1	0
1934	R.E.S. Wyatt[15]	W.M. Woodfull	5	1	2	2
1936-37	G.O. Allen	D.G. Bradman	5	2	3	0
1938†	W.R. Hammond	D.G. Bradman	4	1	1	2
1946-47	W.R. Hammond[16]	D.G. Bradman	5	0	3	2
1948	N.W.D. Yardley	D.G. Bradman	5	0	4	1
1950-51	F.R. Brown	A.L. Hassett	5	1	4	0
1953	L. Hutton	A.L. Hassett	5	1	0	4
1954-55	L. Hutton	I.W. Johnson[17]	5	3	1	1
1956	P.B.H. May	I.W. Johnson	5	2	1	2
1958-59	P.B.H. May	R. Benaud	5	0	4	1
1961	P.B.H. May[18]	R. Benaud[19]	5	1	2	2
1962-63	E.R. Dexter	R. Benaud	5	1	1	3
1964	E.R. Dexter	R.B. Simpson	5	0	1	4
1965-66	M.J.K. Smith	R.B. Simpson[20]	5	1	1	3
1968	M.C. Cowdrey[21]	W.M. Lawry[22]	5	1	1	3
1970-71	R. Illingworth	W.M. Lawry[23]	6	2	0	4
1972	R. Illingworth	I.M. Chappell	5	2	2	1

Season	England	Captains	Australia	P	E	A	D
1974-75	M.H. Denness[24]	I.M. Chappell		6	1	4	1
1975	A.W. Greig[25]	I.M. Chappell		4	0	1	3
1976-77	A.W. Greig	G.S. Chappell		1	0	1	0
1977	J.M. Brearley	G.S. Chappell		5	3	0	2
1978-79	J.M. Brearley	G.N. Yallop		6	5	1	0
1979-80	J.M. Brearley	G.S. Chappell		3	0	3	0
1980	I.T. Botham	G.S. Chappell		1	0	0	1
1981	J.M. Brearley[26]	K.J. Hughes		6	3	1	2
1982-83	R.G.D. Willis	G.S. Chappell		5	1	2	2
1985	D.I. Gower	A.R. Border		6	3	1	2
1986-87	M.W. Gatting	A.R. Border		5	2	1	2
1987-88	M.W. Gatting	A.R. Border		1	0	0	1
	The Oval			29	13	5	11
	Manchester			24	7	4	13
	Lord's			28	5	10	13
	Nottingham			15	3	4	8
	Leeds			19	6	5	8
	Birmingham			7	3	1	3
	Sheffield			1	0	1	0
	Melbourne			48	18	23	7
	Sydney			48	20	23	5
	Adelaide			24	7	13	4
	Brisbane			14	5	6	3
	Perth			6	1	2	3
	In England			123	37	30	56
	In Australia			140	51	67	22
	Totals			263	88	97	78

The following deputised for the official captain or were appointed for only a minor proportion of the series: [1]A.N. Hornby (1st). [2]W.L. Murdoch (1st), H.H. Massie (3rd), J.M. Blackham (4th). [3]A.G. Steel (1st). [4]A.E. Stoddart (1st). [5]J.M. Blackham (1st). [6]A.C. MacLaren (1st, 2nd, 5th). [7]W.G. Grace (1st). [8]H. Trumble (4th, 5th). [9]F.L. Fane (1st, 2nd, 3rd). [10]J.W.T. Douglas (1st, 2nd). [11]A.P.F. Chapman (5th). [12]W. Bardsley (3rd, 4th). [13]J.C. White (5th). [14]R.E.S. Wyatt (5th). [15]C.F. Walters (1st). [16]N.W.D. Yardley (5th). [17]A.R. Morris (2nd). [18]M.C. Cowdrey (1st, 2nd). [19]R.N. Harvey (2nd). [20]B.C. Booth (1st, 3rd). [21]T.W. Graveney (4th). [22]B.N. Jarman (4th). [23]I.M. Chappell (7th). [24]J.H. Edrich (4th). [25]M.H. Denness (1st). [26]I.T. Botham (1st, 2nd).

HIGHEST INNINGS TOTALS

England	in England	903-7d	The Oval	1938
	in Australia	636	Sydney	1928-29
Australia	in England	729-6d	Lord's	1930
	in Australia	659-8d	Sydney	1946-47

LOWEST INNINGS TOTALS

England	in England	52	The Oval	1948
	in Australia	45	Sydney	1886-87
Australia	in England	36	Birmingham	1902
	in Australia	42	Sydney	1887-88

HIGHEST INDIVIDUAL INNINGS

England	in England	364	L. Hutton	The Oval	1938
	in Australia	287	R.E. Foster	Sydney	1903-04
Australia	in England	334	D.G. Bradman	Leeds	1930
	in Australia	307	R.M. Cowper	Melbourne	1965-66

HIGHEST AGGREGATE OF RUNS IN A SERIES

England	in England	732 (av 81.33)	D.I. Gower	1985
	in Australia	905 (av 113.12)	W.R. Hammond	1928-29
Australia	in England	974 (av 139.14)	D.G. Bradman	1930
	in Australia	810 (av 90.00)	D.G. Bradman	1936-37

RECORD WICKET PARTNERSHIPS – ENGLAND

1st	323	J.B. Hobbs (178), W. Rhodes (179)	Melbourne	1911-12
2nd	382	L. Hutton (364), M. Leyland (187)	The Oval	1938
3rd	262	W.R. Hammond (177), D.R. Jardine (98)	Adelaide	1928-29
4th	222	W.R. Hammond (240), E. Paynter (99)	Lord's	1938
5th	206	E. Paynter (216*), D.C.S. Compton (102)	Nottingham	1938
6th	{215	L. Hutton (364), J. Hardstaff, jr (169*)	The Oval	1938
	{215	G. Boycott (107), A.P.E. Knott (135)	Nottingham	1977
7th	143	F.E. Woolley (133*), J. Vine (36)	Sydney	1911-12
8th	124	E.H. Hendren (169), H. Larwood (70)	Brisbane[1]	1928-29
9th	151	W.H. Scotton (90), W.W. Read (117)	The Oval	1884
10th	130	R.E. Foster (287), W. Rhodes (40*)	Sydney	1903-04

RECORD WICKET PARTNERSHIPS – AUSTRALIA

1st	244	R.B. Simpson (225), W.M. Lawry (119)	Adelaide	1965-66
2nd	451	W.H. Ponsford (266), D.G. Bradman (244)	The Oval	1934
3rd	276	D.G. Bradman (187), A.L. Hassett (128)	Brisbane[2]	1946-47
4th	388	W.H. Ponsford (181), D.G. Bradman (304)	Leeds	1934
5th	405	S.G. Barnes (234), D.G. Bradman (234)	Sydney	1946-47
6th	346	J.H.W. Fingleton (136), D.G. Bradman (270)	Melbourne	1936-37
7th	165	C. Hill (188), H. Trumble (46)	Melbourne	1897-98
8th	243	R.J. Hartigan (113), C. Hill (160)	Adelaide	1907-08
9th	154	S.E. Gregory (201), J.M. Blackman (74)	Sydney	1894-95
10th	127	J.M. Taylor (108), A.A. Mailey (46*)	Sydney	1924-25

BEST INNINGS BOWLING ANALYSIS

England	in England	10-53 J.C. Laker	Manchester	1956
	in Australia	8-35 G.A. Lohmann	Sydney	1886-87
Australia	in England	8-31 F. Laver	Manchester	1909
	in Australia	9-121 A.A. Mailey	Melbourne	1920-21

BEST MATCH BOWLING ANALYSIS

England	in England	19-90 J.C. Laker	Manchester	1956
	in Australia	15-124 W. Rhodes	Melbourne	1903-04
Australia	in England	16-137 R.A.L. Massie	Lord's	1972
	in Australia	13-77 M.A. Noble	Melbourne	1901-02

HIGHEST AGGREGATE OF WICKETS IN A SERIES

England	in England	46 (av 9.60)	J.C. Laker	1956
	in Australia	38 (av 23.18)	M.W. Tate	1924-25
Australia	in England	42 (av 21.26)	T.M. Alderman	1981
	in Australia	41 (av 12.85)	R.M. Hogg	1978-79

MOST RUNS

	Tests	I	NO	HS	Runs	Avge
D.G. Bradman (A)	37	63	7	334	**5028**	89.78
J.B. Hobbs (E)	41	71	4	187	**3636**	54.26
G. Boycott (E)	38	71	9	191	**2945**	47.50
W.R. Hammond (E)	33	58	3	251	**2852**	51.85
H. Sutcliffe (E)	27	46	5	194	**2741**	66.85
C. Hill (A)	41	76	1	188	**2660**	35.46
J.H. Edrich (E)	32	57	3	175	**2644**	48.96
G.S. Chappell (A)	35	65	8	144	**2619**	45.94
D.I. Gower (E)	31	56	3	215	**2479**	46.77
M.C. Cowdrey (E)	43	75	4	113	**2433**	34.26
L. Hutton (E)	27	49	6	364	**2428**	56.46
R.N. Harvey (A)	37	68	5	167	**2416**	38.34
A.R. Border (A)	30	57	14	196	**2392**	55.62
V.T. Trumper (A)	40	74	5	185*	**2263**	32.79
W.M. Lawry (A)	29	51	5	166	**2233**	48.54
S.E. Gregory (A)	52	92	7	201	**2193**	25.80
W.W. Armstrong (A)	42	71	9	158	**2172**	35.03
I.M. Chappell (A)	30	56	4	192	**2138**	41.11
K.F. Barrington (E)	23	39	6	256	**2111**	63.96
A.R. Morris (A)	24	43	2	206	**2080**	50.73

D.G. Bradman holds the unique record of scoring 2000 runs in both countries in this series (2674 runs in England and 2354 in Australia). J.B. Hobbs is the only other batsman to score 2000 runs in either country (2493 runs in Australia).

MOST WICKETS

	Tests	Balls	Runs	Wkts	Ave	BB	5wI
D.K. Lillee (A)	29	8516	3507	**167**	21.00	7-89	11
I.T. Botham (E)	33	7999	3852	**145**	26.56	6-78	9
H. Trumble (A)	31	7895	2945	**141**	20.88	8-65	9
R.G.D. Willis (E)	35	7294	3346	**128**	26.14	8-43	7
M.A. Noble (A)	39	6845	2860	**115**	24.86	7-17	9
R.R. Lindwall (A)	29	6728	2559	**114**	22.44	7-63	6
W. Rhodes (E)	41	5791	2616	**109**	24.00	8-68	6
S.F. Barnes (E)	20	5749	2288	**106**	21.58	7-60	12
C.V. Grimmett (A)	22	9224	3439	**106**	32.44	6-37	11
D.L. Underwood (E)	29	8000	2770	**105**	26.38	7-50	4
A.V. Bedser (E)	21	7065	2859	**104**	27.49	7-44	7
G. Giffen (A)	31	6325	2791	**103**	27.09	7-117	7
W.J. O'Reilly (A)	19	7864	2587	**102**	25.36	7-54	8
R. Peel (E)	20	5216	1715	**102**	16.81	7-31	6
C.T.B. Turner (A)	17	5195	1670	**101**	16.53	7-43	11
J.R. Thomson (A)	21	4951	2418	**100**	24.18	6-46	5

MOST WICKET-KEEPING DISMISSALS

	Tests	Ct	St	Total
R.W. Marsh (A)	42	141	7	**148**
A.P.E. Knott (E)	34	97	8	**105**
W.A.S. Oldfield (A)	38	59	31	**90**
A.F.A. Lilley (E)	32	65	19	**84**
A.T.W. Grout (A)	22	69	7	**76**
T.G. Evans (E)	31	63	12	**75**

FIRST-CLASS UMPIRES 1989

BALDERSTONE, John **Christopher** (Paddock Council S, Huddersfield), b Longwood, Huddersfield, Yorks 16 Nov 1940. 6'0½". RHB, SLA. Yorkshire 1961-69. Leicestershire 1971-86 (cap 1973; testimonial 1984). **Tests:** 2 (1976); HS 35 v WI (Leeds) 1976; BB 1-80. Tour: Zim 1980-81 (Leics). 1000 runs (11); most – 1482 (1982). Hat-trick 1976. HS 181* Leics v Glos (Leicester) 1984. BB 6-25 Leics v Hants (Southampton) 1978. F-c career: 390 matches; 19,034 runs @ 34.11, 32 hundreds; 310 wickets @ 26.32; 210 ct. Soccer for Huddersfield Town, Carlisle United, Doncaster Rovers and Queen of the South. Appointed 1988.

BIRD, Harold Dennis ('Dickie'**) (Raley SM, Barnsley), b Barnsley, Yorks 19 Apr 1933. RHB, RM. Yorkshire 1956-59. Leicestershire 1960-64 (cap 1960). MBE 1986. 1000 runs (1): 1028 (1960). HS 181* Yorks v Glamorgan (Bradford) 1959. F-c career: 93 matches; 3314 runs @ 20.71, 2 hundreds. Appointed 1970. Umpired 39 Tests (1973 to 1988). Officiated in 1987 Reliance World Cup in India and Pakistan. Completed 100 'internationals' (Tests and LOI) 1988.

BOND, John David (**'Jack'**) (Bolton S), b Kearsley, Lancashire, 6 May 1932. RHB, LB. Lancashire 1955-72 (cap 1955; captain 1968-72; coach 1973; manager 1980-86; benefit 1970). Nottinghamshire 1974 (captain/coach 1974). 1000 (2); most – 2125 (1963). HS 157 Lancs v Hants (Manchester) 1962. Test selector 1974. F-c career: 362 matches; 12,125 runs @ 25.90, 14 hundreds; 222 ct. Appointed 1988.

CONSTANT, David John, b Bradford-on-Avon, Wiltshire 9 Nov 1941. LHB, SLA. Kent 1961-63. Leicestershire 1965-68. HS 80 Leics v Glos (Bristol) 1966. F-c career: 61 matches; 1517 runs @ 19.20; 1 wicket @ 36.00. Appointed 1969. Umpired 36 Tests (1971 to 1988). Represented Gloucestershire at bowls 1984-86.

DUDLESTON, Barry (Stockport S), b Bebington, Cheshire 16 Jul 1945. RHB, SLA. Leicestershire 1966-80 (cap 1969; benefit 1980). Gloucestershire 1981-83. Rhodesia 1976-80. 1000 (8); most – 1374 (1970). HS 202 Leics v Derbyshire (Leicester) 1979. BB 4-6 Leics v Surrey (Leicester) 1972. F-c career: 295 matches; 14,747 runs @ 32.48, 32 hundreds; 47 wickets @ 29.04. Appointed 1984.

EELE, Peter James (Taunton S), b Taunton, Somerset 27 Jan 1935. LHB, WK. Somerset 1958-65 (cap 1964). Devon 1966-70. HS 103* v Pakistan Eaglets (Taunton) 1963. F-c career: 54 matches; 612 runs @ 12.24, 1 hundred; 106 dismissals (87 ct, 19 st). F-c umpire 1981-84. Reappointed 1989.

EVANS, David Gwilliam Lloyd, b Lambeth, London 27 Jul 1933. RHB, WK. Glamorgan 1956-69 (cap 1959; benefit 1969). HS 46* v Oxford U (Oxford) 1961. F-c career: 270 matches; 2875 runs @ 10.53; 558 dismissals (502 ct, 56 st). Appointed 1971. Umpired 9 Tests (1981 to 1985).

HAMPSHIRE, John Harry (Oakwood THS, Rotherham), b Thurnscoe, Yorkshire 10 Feb 1941. RHB, LB. Son of John (Yorks 1937); brother of A.W. (Yorks 1975). Yorkshire 1961-81 (cap 1963; benefit 1976; captain 1979-80). Derbyshire 1982-84 (cap 1982). Tasmania 1967-69, 1977-79. **Tests: 8 (1969 to 75); 403 runs @ 26.86, HS 107 v WI (Lord's) 1969 on debut (only England player to score hundred at Lord's on debut in Tests). Tours: Aus 1970-71; SA 1972-73 (DHR), 1974-75 (DHR); WI 1964-65 (Cavs); NZ 1970-71; Pak 1967-68 (Cwlth XI); SL 1969-70; Zim 1980-81 (Leics XI). 1000 runs (15); most – 1596 (1978). HS 183* Yorks v Sussex (Hove) 1971. BB 7-52 Yorks v Glamorgan (Cardiff) 1963. F-c career: 577 matches; 28,059 runs @ 34.55, 43 hundreds; 30 wickets @ 54.56; 445 ct. Appointed 1985.

HARRIS, John Henry, b Taunton 13 Feb 1936. LHB, RFM. Somerset 1952-59. Suffolk 1960-62. Devon 1975. HS 41 v Worcs (Taunton) 1957. BB 3-29 v Worcs (Bristol) 1959. F-c career: 15 matches; 154 runs @ 11.00; 19 wickets @ 32.57. Appointed 1983.

HASSAN, Basharat (City HS, Nairobi), b Nairobi, Kenya 24 March 1944. 5'10½". RHB, RM, WK. Debut 1963-64 (East African XI). Nottinghamshire 1966-85 (cap 1970; benefit 1978). 1000 runs (5); most – 1395 (1970). HS 182* v Glos (Nottingham) 1977. BB 3-33 v Lancs (Manchester) 1976. F-c career: 332 matches; 14,394 runs @ 29.07, 15 hundreds; 6 wickets @ 67.83; 309 dismissals (308 ct, 1 st). Appointed 1989.

*****HOLDER, John** Wakefield (Combermere S, Barbados), b St George, Barbados 19 Mar 1945. RHB, RFM. Hampshire 1968-72. Hat-trick 1972. HS 33 v Sussex (Hove) 1971. BB 7-79 v Glos (Gloucestershire) 1972. F-c career: 47 matches; 374 runs @ 10.68; 139 wickets @ 24.56. Appointed 1983. Umpired 1 Test (1988).

JONES, Allan Arthur (St John's C, Horsham), b Horley, Surrey 9 Dec 1947. RHB RFM. Sussex 1966-69. Somerset 1970-75 (cap 1972). Northern Transvaal 1972-73. Middlesex 1976-79 (cap 1976). Orange Free State 1976-77. Glamorgan 1980-81. HS 33 Middlesex v Kent (Canterbury) 1978. BB 9-51 Somerset v Sussex (Hove) 1972. F-c career: 214 matches; 799 runs @ 5.39; 549 wickets @ 28.07. Appointed 1985.

JULIAN, Raymond (Wigston SM), b Cosby, Leics 23 Aug 1936. RHB, WK. Leicestershire 1953-71 (cap 1961). HS 51 v Worcs (Worcester) 1962. F-c career: 192 matches; 2581 runs @ 9.73; 421 dismissals (382 ct, 39 st). Appointed 1972.

KITCHEN, Mervyn John (Backwell SM, Nailsea), b Nailsea, Somerset 1 Aug 1940. LHB, RM. Somerset 1960-79 (cap 1966; testimonial 1973). Tour: Rhodesia 1972-73 (Int Wand). 1000 runs (7); most – 1730 (1968). HS 189 v Pakistanis (Taunton) 1967. BB 1-4. F-c career: 354 matches; 15,230 runs @ 26.25, 17 hundreds; 2 wickets @ 54.50. Appointed 1982.

LEADBEATER, Barrie (Harehills SS), b Harehills, Leeds 14 Aug 1943. RHB, RM. Yorkshire 1966-79 (cap 1969; joint benefit with G.A.Cope 1980). Tour: WI 1969-70 (DN). HS 140* v Hants (Portsmouth) 1976. F-c career: 147 matches; 5373 runs @ 25.34, 1 hundred; 1 wicket @ 5.00. Appointed 1981.

LYONS, Kevin James (Lady Mary's HS), b Cardiff 18 Dec 1946. RHB, RM. Glamorgan 1967-77. Tour: WI 1969-70 (Glam). HS 92 v Cambridge U (Cambridge) 1972. F-c career: 62 matches; 1673 runs @ 19.68; 2 wickets @ 126.00. Appointed 1985.

*****MEYER, Barrie** John (Boscombe SS), b Bournemouth 21 Aug 1932. RHB, WK. Gloucestershire 1957-71 (cap 1958; benefit 1971). HS 63 v Indians (Cheltenham) 1959, 63 v Oxford U (Bristol) 1962, and 63 v Sussex (Bristol) 1964. F-c career: 406 matches; 5367 runs @ 14.16; 826 dismissals (707 ct, 119 st). Soccer for Bristol Rovers, Plymouth Argyle, Newport County and Bristol City. Appointed 1973. Umpired 20 Tests (1978 to 1987).

OSLEAR, Donald Osmund, b Cleethorpes, Lincs 3 Mar 1929. No first-class appearances. Appointed 1975. Umpired in 5 Tests (1980 to 1984).

*PALMER, Kenneth Ernest (Southbroom SM, Devizes), b Winchester 22 Apr 1937. RHB, RFM. Brother of Roy (below) and father of G.V. (Somerset 1982-). Somerset 1955-69 (cap 1958; testimonial 1968). Tours: WI 1963-64 (Cavs), Pak 1963-64 (Cwlth XI). **Tests**: 1 (1964-65; while coaching in South Africa); 10 runs; 1 wicket. 1000 runs (1): 1036 (1961). 100 wickets (4); most – 139 (1963). HS 125* v Northants (Northampton) 1961. BB 9-57 v Notts (Nottingham) 1963. F-c career: 314 matches; 7,761 runs @ 20.64, 2 hundreds; 866 wickets @ 21.34. Appointed 1972. Umpired 17 Tests (1978 to 1988).

PALMER, Roy (Southbroom SM), b Devizes, Wiltshire 12 Jul 1942. RHB, RFM. Brother of K.E. (above). Somerset 1965-1970. HS 84 v Leics (Taunton) 1967. BB 6-45 v Middx (Lord's) 1967. F-c career: 74 matches; 1037 runs @ 13.29; 172 wickets @ 31.62. Appointed 1980.

*PLEWS, Nigel Trevor, b Nottingham 5 Sep 1934. Former policeman (Fraud Squad). No first-class appearances. Appointed 1982. Umpired 1 Test (1988).

*SHEPHERD, David Robert (Barnstaple GS; St Luke's C, Exeter), b Bideford, Devon 27 Dec 1940. RHB, RM. Gloucestershire 1965-79 (cap 1969; joint benefit with J. Davey 1978). Scored 108 on debut (v OU). Devon 1959-64. 1000 runs (2); most – 1079 (1970). HS 153 v Middlesex (Bristol) 1968. F-c career: 282 matches; 10,672 runs @ 24.47, 12 hundreds; 2 wickets @ 53.00. Appointed 1981. Umpired 7 Tests (1985 to 1988). Officiated in 1987 Reliance World Cup in India and Pakistan.

THOMPSETT, Donald Stanley, b Uckfield, Sussex 8 Apr 1935. Employed in poultry industry. Chippenham CC. No first-class appearances. Minor Counties List 1979-86. Reserve F-c List 1985-88. Appointed 1989.

WHITE, Robert Arthur (Chiswick GS), b Fulham, London 6 Oct 1936. LHB, OB. Middlesex 1958-65 (cap 1963). Nottinghamshire 1966-80 (cap 1966; benefit 1974). 1000 runs (1): 1355 (1963). HS 116* Notts v Surrey (Oval) 1967. BB 7-41 Notts v Derby (Ilkeston) 1971. F-c career: 413 matches; 12,452 runs @ 23.18, 5 hundreds; 693 wickets @ 30.50. Appointed 1983.

WHITEHEAD, Alan Geoffrey Thomas, b Butleigh, Somerset 28 Oct 1940. LHB, SLA Somerset 1957-61. HS 15 v Hants (Southampton) 1959, and 15 v Leics (Leicester) 1960. BB 6-74 v Sussex (Eastbourne) 1959. F-c career: 38 matches; 137 runs @ 5.70; 67 wickets @ 34.41. Appointed 1970. Umpired 5 Tests (1982 to 1987).

WIGHT, Peter Bernard, b Georgetown, British Guiana 25 Jun 1930. RHB, OB. Brother of G.L. (West Indies), H.A. and N (all British Guiana). British Guiana 1950-51. Somerset 1953-65 (cap 1954; benefit 1963). Canterbury 1963-64. 1000 runs (10); most – 2375 (1960). HS 222* v Kent (Taunton) 1959. BB 6-29 v Derbyshire (Chesterfield) 1957. F-c career: 333 matches 17,773 runs @ 33.09, 28 hundreds; 68 wickets @ 33.26. Appointed 1966.

RESERVE LIST

M.J.HARRIS, V.A.HOLDER, H.J.RHODES and TAYLOR.

* On Test Match and Texaco Trophy Panel for 1988
See page 63 for key to abbreviations.

PRINCIPAL FIXTURES 1989

Including Sunday play

Saturday 15 April

Lord's: MCC v Worcestershire (4 days)
*Fenner's: Cambridge U v Glamorgan
The Parks: Oxford U v Northants

Wednesday 19 April

Fenner's: Cambridge U v Gloucs
The Parks: Oxford U v Surrey

Thursday 20 April

*Britannic Assurance Championship
(4 days)*
Derby: Derbys v Northants
Southampton: Hants v Somerset
Canterbury: Kent v Essex
Leicester: Leics v Glamorgan
Lord's: Middx v Yorks
Trent Bridge: Notts v Worcs
Edgbaston: Warwicks v Lancs

Sunday 23 April

Refuge Assurance League
Derby: Derbys v Northants
Southampton: Hants v Somerset
Canterbury: Kent v Essex
Leicester: Leics v Glam
Lord's: Middx v Yorks
Trent Bridge: Notts v Worcs
The Oval: Surrey v Gloucs
Edgbaston: Warwicks v Lancs

Tuesday 25 April

Benson & Hedges Cup
Edgbaston: Warwicks v Northants
Old Trafford: Lancs v Leics
Cardiff: Glam v Kent
Hove: Sussex v Essex
Fenner's: Combined U v Surrey
Lord's: Middx v Worcs
Derby: Derbys v Somerset
Jesmond: Minor Counties v Yorks

Thursday 27 April

*Britannic Assurance Championship
(4 days)*
Chelmsford: Essex v Middx
Bristol: Gloucs v Northants
Old Trafford: Lancs v Notts
The Oval: Surrey v Hants
Hove: Sussex v Kent
*Edgaston: Warwicks v Worcs
Other Matches
Fenner's: Cambridge U v Leics
The Parks: Oxford U v Derbys

Friday 28 April

*Britannic Assurance Championship
(4 days)*
*Taunton: Somerset v Glam

Sunday 30 April

Refuge Assurance League
Chelmsford: Essex v Middx
Old Trafford: Lancs v Notts
Leicester: Leics v Derbys
The Oval: Surrey v Hants
Hove: Sussex v Kent

Tuesday 2 May

Benson & Hedges Cup
Leicester: Leics v Warwicks
Perth (North Inch): Scotland v Lancs
Chelmsford: Essex v Hants
Canterbury: Kent v Sussex
Bristol: Gloucs v Middx
The Oval: Surrey v Worcs
Taunton: Somerset v Minor Counties
Trent Bridge: Notts v Derbys

Thursday 4 May

Britannic Assurance Championship
(4 days)
Chelmsford: Essex v Derbys
Cardiff: Glam v Gloucs
Southampton: Hants v Kent
Lord's: Middx v Surrey
Northampton: Northants v Leics
Taunton: Somerset v Sussex
Worcester: Worcs v Lancs
Headingley: Yorks v Notts
Other Match
Fenner's: Cambridge U v Warwicks

Friday 5 May

Tourist match
West Bromwich, Dartmouth: League
Cricket Conference v Australia
(1 day)

Sunday 7 May

Refuge Assurance League
Chelmsford: Essex v Derbys
Cardiff: Glam v Gloucs
Southampton: Hants v Kent
Lord's: Middx v Surrey
Northampton: Northants v Warwicks
Taunton: Somerset v Sussex
Worcester: Worcs v Lancs
Headingley: Yorks v Notts
Tourist Match
Arundel: Lavinia, Duchess of
Norfolk's XI v Australia (1 day)

Tuesday 9 May

Benson & Hedges Cup
Leicester: Leics v Scotland
Northampton: Northants v Lancs
Canterbury: Kent v Essex
Southampton: Hants v Glam
Worcester: Worcs v Gloucs
The Parks: Combined U v Middx
Headingley: Yorks v Somerset
Oxton (Birkenhead): Minor Counties v
Notts
Tourist Match
Hove: Sussex v Australia (1 day)

Thursday 11 May

Benson & Hedges Cup
Northampton: Northants v Leics
Edgbaston: Warwicks v Scotland
Chelmsford: Essex v Glam
Hove: Sussex v Hants
The Oval: Surrey v Gloucs
Worcester: Worcs v Combined U
Trent Bridge: Notts v Yorks
Derby: Derbys v Minor Counties
Tourist Match
Lord's: MCC v Australia (1 day)

Saturday 13 May

Benson & Hedges Cup
Glasgow (Hamilton Crescent):
Scotland v Northants
Old Trafford: Lancs v Warwicks
Southampton: Hants v Kent
*Swansea: Glam v Sussex
Lord's: Middx v Surrey
Bristol: Gloucs v Combined U
Headingley: Yorks v Derbys
Taunton: Somerset v Notts
Tourist Match
*Worcester: Worcs v Australia

Sunday 14 May

Refuge Assurance League
Leek: Derbys v Lancs
Chelmsford: Essex v Hants
Bristol: Gloucs v Middx
Canterbury: Kent v Surrey
Leicester: Leics v Yorks

Tuesday 16 May

Britannic Assurance Championship
(4 days)
Northampton: Northants v Yorks

Wednesday 17 May

Britannic Assurance Championship
Chesterfield: Derbys v Leics
Old Trafford: Lancs v Warwicks
Lord's: Middx v Hants
Hove: Sussex v Surrey
Tourist Match
Taunton: Somerset v Australia
Other Matches
Fenner's: Cambridge U v Kent
The Parks: Oxford U v Notts

Saturday 20 May

Britannic Assurance Championship
Swansea: Glam v Northants
Bristol: Gloucs v Essex
*Dartford: Kent v Derbys
*Trent Bridge: Notts v Hants
Taunton: Somerset v Lancs
Edgbaston: Warwicks v Surrey
Tourist Match
Lord's: Middx v Australia

Sunday 21 May

Refuge Assurance League
Ebbw Vale: Glam v Northants
Bristol: Gloucs v Essex
Taunton: Somerset v Lancs
Hove: Sussex v Leics
Worcester: Worcs v Surrey
Headingley: Yorks v Warwicks

Tuesday 23 May

Tourist Match
Headingley: Yorks v Australia (1 day)

Wednesday 24 May

Britannic Assurance Championship
Leicester: Leics v Kent
The Oval: Surrey v Lancs
Worcester: Worcs v Notts
Headingley: Yorks v Derbys
Other Matches
Fenner's: Cambridge U v Essex
The Parks: Oxford U v Middx

Thursday 25 May

TEXACO TROPHY
Old Trafford: ENGLAND v
   AUSTRALIA (First One-Day
   International)

Saturday 27 May

TEXACO TROPHY
Trent Bridge: ENGLAND v
 . AUSTRALIA (Second One-Day
   International)
Britannic Assurance Championship
Chelmsford: Essex v Somerset
Cardiff: Glam v Notts
Bristol: Gloucs v Worcs
Bournemouth: Hants v Leics

Liverpool: Lancs v Sussex
The Oval: Surrey v Yorks
Edgbaston: Warwicks v Middx

Sunday 28 May

Refuge Assurance League
Chelmsford: Essex v Somerset
Llanelli: Glam v Notts
Bristol: Gloucs v Worcs
Bournemouth: Hants v Leics
Canterbury: Kent v Northants
Old Trafford: Lancs v Sussex
The Oval: Surrey v Yorks
Edgbaston: Warwicks v Middx

Monday 29 May

TEXACO TROPHY
Lord's: ENGLAND v AUSTRALIA
   (Third One-Day International)

Wednesday 31 May

Benson & Hedges Cup
Quarter Finals
Tourist Match
Old Trafford or Edgbaston: Lancs or
   Warwicks v Australia

Saturday 3 June

Britannic Assurance Championship
Tunbridge Wells: Kent v Hants
Northampton: Northants v Surrey
Trent Bridge: Notts v Yorks
Edgbaston: Warwicks v Sussex
Worcester: Worcs v Glam
Tourist Match
*Derby: Derbys v Australia

Sunday 4 June

Refuge Assurance League
Leicester: Leics v Lancs
Lord's: Middx v Hants
Northampton: Northants v Surrey
Trent Bridge: Notts v Somerset
Edgbaston: Warwicks v Sussex
Worcester: Worcs v Glam

Wednesday 7 June

Britannic Assurance Championship
Cardiff: Glam v Somerset
Basingstoke: Hants v Surrey
Tunbridge Wells: Kent v Sussex
Leicester: Leics v Yorks
Lord's: Middx v Notts
Northampton: Northants v Gloucs
Nuneaton (Griff & Coton): Warwicks
   v Derbys
Other Match
The Parks: Oxford U v Lancs

Thursday 8 June

**CORNHILL INSURANCE
   TEST MATCH**
**Headingley: ENGLAND v
   AUSTRALIA (First Test Match)**

Saturday 10 June

Britannic Assurance Championship
Abergavenny: Glam v Middx
Leicester: Leics v Gloucs
Trent Bridge: Notts v Kent
Taunton: Somerset v Yorks
The Oval: Surrey v Essex
Hove: Sussex v Northants
Worcester: Worcs v Derbys
Other Match
The Parks: Oxford U v Hants

Sunday 11 June

Refuge Assurance League
Merthyr Tydfil: Glam v Middx
Basingstoke: Hants v Warwicks
Leicester: Leics v Gloucs
Trent Bridge: Notts v Kent
Taunton: Somerset v Yorks
The Oval: Surrey v Essex
Hove: Sussex v Northants
Worcester: Worcs v Derbys

Wednesday 14 June

Benson & Hedges Cup
Semi Finals
Tourist Match
Edgbaston or Old Trafford: Warwicks
   or Lancs v Australia
Other Matches
Harrogate: Tilcon Trophy (3 days)

Saturday 17 June

Britannic Assurance Championship
Derby: Derbys v Sussex
Chelmsford: Essex v Leics
Old Trafford: Lancs v Glam
Bath: Somerset v Kent
The Oval: Surrey v Middx
Harrogate: Yorks v Gloucs
Tourist Match
*Northampton: Northants v Australia
Other Match
*Fenner's: Cambridge U v Notts

Sunday 18 June

Refuge Assurance League
Derby: Derbys v Sussex
Chelmsford: Essex v Leics
Blackpool: Lancs v Glam
Bath: Somerset v Kent
Edgbaston: Warwicks v Worcs
Headingley: Yorks v Gloucs

Wednesday 21 June

Britannic Assurance Championship
Ilford: Essex v Hants
Southport: Lancs v Northants
Bath: Somerset v Gloucs
Edgbaston: Warwicks v Glam
Sheffield: Yorks v Worcs
Other Match
Hove: Sussex v Cambridge U

Thursday 22 June

**CORNHILL INSURANCE
   TEST MATCH**
**Lord's: ENGLANG v AUSTRALIA
   (Second Test Match)**

Saturday 24 June

Britannic Assurance Championship
Ilford: Essex v Warwicks
Southampton: Hants v Sussex
Old Trafford: Lancs v Kent
Leicester: Leics v Notts
Luton: Northants v Somerset
The Oval: Surrey v Gloucs
Worcester: Worcs v Middx
Headingley: Yorks v Glam

239

Sunday 25 June

Refuge Assurance League
Ilford: Essex v Warwicks
Southampton: Hants v Sussex
Old Trafford: Lancs v Kent
Luton: Northants v Leics
Trent Bridge: Notts v Derbys
Bath: Somerset v Gloucs
Worcester: Worcs v Middx
Hull: Yorks v Glam

Wednesday 28 June

NatWest Bank Trophy
First Round
March: Cambs v Worcs
Chester (Boughton Hall): Cheshire v
Hants
Carlisle: Cumberland v Lancs
Derby: Derbys v Ireland
Darlington: Durham v Middx
Cardiff: Glam v Staffs
Hitchin: Herts v Notts
Canterbury: Kent v Dorset
Jesmond: Northumberland v Surrey
Oxford (Christ Church College): Oxon
v Gloucs
Telford (St George's): Shrops v Leics
Taunton: Somerset v Essex
Bury St Edmunds: Suffolk v Northants
Hove: Sussex v Berks
Edgbaston: Warwicks v Wilts
Headingley: Yorks v Scotland
Tourist Match
The Parks: Oxbridge v Australia
(1 day)

Saturday 1 July

Britannic Assurance Championship
Derby: Derbys v Somerset
Gloucester: Gloucs v Notts
Southampton: Hants v Yorks
Hinckley: Leics v Warwicks
Lord's: Middx v Lancs
Northampton: Northants v Worcs
Horsham: Sussex v Essex
Tourist Match
*Neath: Glam v Australia

Sunday 2 July

Refuge Assurance League
Derby: Derbys v Somerset
Gloucester: Gloucs v Notts
Southampton: Hants v Yorks
Leicester: Leics v Warwicks
Lord's: Middx v Lancs
Tring: Northants v Worcs
Horsham: Sussex v Essex

Wednesday 5 July

Britannic Assurance Championship
Derby: Derbys v Essex
Gloucester: Gloucs v Sussex
Maidstone: Kent v Northants
Leicester: Leics v Lancs
Guildford: Surrey v Notts
Worcester: Worcs v Warwicks
Other Match
Lord's: Oxford U v Cambridge U
(Varsity Match)

Thursday 6 July

**CORNHILL INSURANCE
TEST MATCH**
**Edgbaston: ENGLAND v AUSTRALIA
(Third Test Match)**

Saturday 8 July

Britannic Assurance Championship
Swansea: Glam v Essex
Maidstone: Kent v Gloucs
Lord's: Middx v Derbys
Northampton: Northants v Hants
Trent Bridge: Notts v Warwicks
Guildford: Surrey v Somerset
Kidderminster: Worcs v Leics
Middlesbrough: Yorks v Sussex
Other Match
*Dublin (Clontarf): Ireland v Scotland
(3 days)

Sunday 9 July

Refuge Assurance League
Neath: Glam v Essex
Maidstone: Kent v Gloucs
Lord's: Middx v Derbys
Northampton: Northants v Hants
Trent Bridge: Notts v Warwicks
The Oval: Surrey v Somerset
Worcester: Worcs v Leics
Middlesbrough: Yorks v Sussex

Wednesday 12 July

NatWest Bank Trophy
Second Round
March or Worcester: Cambs or Worcs
   v Derbys or Ireland
Darlington or Uxbridge: Durham or
   Middx v Herts or Notts
Cardiff or Burton (Ind Coope): Glam
   or Staffs v Cheshire or Hants
Canterbury or Bournemouth (Dean
   Park): Kent or Dorset v Warwicks or
   Wilts
Jesmond or The Oval:
   Northumberland or Surrey v Yorks
   or Scotland
Oxford (Christ Church) or Bristol:
   Oxon or Gloucs v Cumberland or
   Lancs
Taunton or Chelmsford: Somerset or
   Essex v Suffolk or Northants
Hove or Finchampstead: Sussex or
   Berks v Shrops or Leics

Saturday 15 July

Benson & Hedges Cup
Lord's: Final
Tourist Match
Glasgow (Hamilton Crescent):
   Scotland v Australia (1 day)

Sunday 16 July

Refuge Assurance League
Bristol: Gloucs v Hants
Canterbury: Kent v Derbys
Old Trafford: Lancs v Northants
Leicester: Leics v Notts
Taunton: Somerset v Glam
The Oval: Surrey v Sussex
Scarborough: Yorks v Worcs

Monday 17 July

Tourist Match
Trowbridge: Minor Counties v
   Australia (1 day)

Wednesday 19 July

Britannic Assurance Championship
Southend: Essex v Kent
Bristol: Gloucs v Glam
Old Trafford: Lancs v Worcs
Leicester: Leics v Northants
Trent Bridge: Notts v Somerset
Headingley: Yorks v Middx
Tourist Match
Southampton: Hants v Australia

Saturday 22 July

Britannic Assurance Championship
Derby: Derbys v Glam
Southend: Essex v Yorks
Portsmouth: Hants v Lancs
Uxbridge: Middx v Kent
Northampton: Northants v Notts
Taunton: Somerset v Leics
Hove: Sussex v Worcs
Tourist Match
*Bristol: Gloucs v Australia

Sunday 23 July

Refuge Assurance League
Heanor: Derbys v Glam
Southend: Essex v Yorks
Portsmouth: Hants v Lancs
Lord's: Middx v Kent
Finedon: Northants v Notts
Taunton: Somerset v Leics
Hove: Sussex v Worcs
Edgbaston: Warwicks v Surrey

Wednesday 26 July

Britannic Assurance Championship
Cardiff: Glam v Leics
Portsmouth: Hants v Gloucs
Uxbridge: Middx v Essex
Northampton: Northants v Derbys
Worksop: Notts v Lancs
Hove: Sussex v Somerset
Edgbaston: Warwicks v Yorks
Worcester: Worcs v Surrey

Thursday 27 July

CORNHILL INSURANCE
   TEST MATCH
Old Trafford: ENGLAND v
   AUSTRALIA (Fourth Test Match)

Saturday 29 July

Britannic Assurance Championship
Derby: Derbys v Surrey
Cardiff: Glam v Hants
Lord's: Middx v Leics
Trent Bridge: Notts v Essex
Edgbaston: Warwicks v Gloucs
Worcester: Worcs v Kent

Sunday 30 July

Refuge Assurance League
Derby: Derbys v Surrey
Cardiff: Glam v Hants
Lord's: Middx v Leics
Northampton: Northants v Somerset
Trent Bridge: Notts v Essex
Edgbaston: Warwicks v Gloucs
Worcester: Worcs v Kent

Wednesday 2 August

NatWest Bank Trophy
Quarter Finals
Tourist Match
Trent Bridge or The Oval: Notts or
   Surrey v Australia

Thursday 3 August

Jesmond: England XI v Rest of the
   World XI (1 day)

Friday 4 August

Jesmond: England XI v Rest of the
   World XI (1 day)

Saturday 5 August

Britannic Assurance Championship
Derby: Derbys v Hants
Colchester: Essex v Worcs
Cheltenham: Gloucs v Lancs
Canterbury: Kent v Warwicks
Weston-super-Mare: Somerset v
   Middx

The Oval: Surrey v Glam
Eastbourne: Sussex v Notts
Sheffield: Yorks v Northants
Tourist Match
*Leicester: Leics v Australia
Other Match
Edgbaston: England Young Cricketers
   v New Zealand Young Cricketers
   (First One-Day Youth International)

Sunday 6 August

Refuge Assurance League
Derby: Derbys v Hants
Colchester: Essex v Worcs
Cheltenham: Gloucs v Lancs
Canterbury: Kent v Warwicks
Weston-super-Mare: Somerset v
   Middx
The Oval: Surrey v Glam
Eastbourne: Sussex v Notts
Sheffield: Yorks v Northants
Other Match
Northampton: England Young
   Cricketers v New Zealand Young
   Cricketers (Second One-Day Youth
   International)

Tuesday 8 August

Lord's: England Young Cricketers v
   New Zealand Young Cricketers
   (Third One-Day Youth
   International)

Wednesday 9 August

Britannic Assurance Championship
Chesterfield: Derbys v Lancs
Colchester: Essex v Northants
Cheltenham: Gloucs v Middx
Bournemouth: Hants v Warwicks
Canterbury: Kent v Surrey
Weston-Super-Mare: Somerset v
   Worcs
Eastbourne: Sussex v Leics

Thursday 10 August

CORNHILL INSURANCE
   TEST MATCH
Trent Bridge: ENGLAND v
   AUSTRALIA (Fifth Test Match)

Saturday 12 August

Britannic Assurance Championship
Swansea: Glam v Sussex
Cheltenham: Gloucs v Derbys
Bournemouth: Hants v Worcs
Lytham: Lancs v Essex
Lord's: Middx v Northants
Edgbaston: Warwicks v Somerset
Scarborough: Yorks v Kent

Sunday 13 August

Refuge Assurance League
Ebbw Vale: Glam v Sussex
Cheltenham: Gloucs v Derbys
Bournemouth: Hants v Worcs
Old Trafford: Lancs v Essex
Lord's: Middx v Northants
The Oval: Surrey v Notts
Edgbaston: Warwicks v Somerset
Scarborough: Yorks v Kent

Monday 14 August

Bain Clarkson Trophy (First Semi
Final) (1 day)

Tuesday 15 August

Bain Clarkson Trophy (Second Semi
Final) (1 day)

Wednesday 16 August

NatWest Bank Trophy
Semi Finals
Tourist Match
Canterbury or Hove: Kent or Sussex v
Australia

Saturday 19 August

Britannic Assurance Championship
Canterbury: Kent v Glam
Old Trafford: Lancs v Yorks
Leicester: Leics v Surrey
Northampton: Northants v Warwicks
Trent Bridge: Notts v Derbys
Taunton: Somerset v Hants
Hastings: Sussex v Middx
Tourist Match
*Chelmsford: Essex v Australia

Sunday 20 August

Refuge Assurance League
Moreton-in-Marsh: Gloucs v
  Northants
Canterbury: Kent v Glam
Old Trafford: Lancs v Yorks
Leicester: Leics v Surrey
Trent Bridge: Notts v Hants
Hastings: Sussex v Middx
Edgbaston: Warwicks v Derbys
Worcester: Worcs v Somerset
Other Match
Scarborough: England Young
  Cricketers v New Zealand Young
  Cricketers (First Youth Test Match)
  (4 days)

Thursday 24 August

**CORNHILL INSURANCE
  TEST MATCH**
**The Oval: ENGLAND v AUSTRALIA
  (Sixth Test Match)**

Thursday 24 August

Britannic Assurance Championship
(4 days)
Chesterfield: Derbys v Yorks
Swansea: Glam v Warwicks
Folkestone: Kent v Leics
Old Trafford: Lancs v Surrey
Northampton: Northants v Essex
Trent Bridge: Notts v Middx
Hove: Sussex v Gloucs
*Worcester: Worcs v Somerset

Sunday 27 August

Refuge Assurance League
Chesterfield: Derbys v Yorks
Aberystwyth: Glam v Warwicks
Folkestone: Kent v Leics
Old Trafford: Lancs v Surrey
Northampton: Northants v Essex
Trent Bridge: Notts v Middx
Hove: Sussex v Gloucs

Tuesday 29 August

Britannic Assurance Championship (4 days)
Chelmsford: Essex v Surrey
Leicester: Leics v Derbys
Hove: Sussex v Hants
Worcester: Worcs v Gloucs
Headingley: Yorks v Warwicks
Other Match
Canterbury: England Young
  Cricketers v New Zealand Young
  Cricketers (Second Youth Test
  Match) (4 days)

Wednesday 30 August

Scarborough: Michael Parkinson
  International XI Match (days)

Saturday 2 September

NatWest Bank Trophy
Lord's: Final
Other Match
Scarborough: Michael Parkinson
  International XI Match (3 days)

Sunday 3 September

Scarborough: Four Counties Knock-
  Out Competition (3 days)
Hove: Seeboard Trophy (3 days)

Monday 4 September

Bain Clarkson Trophy Final (1 day)

Wednesday 6 September

Refuge Assurance Cup
Semi Finals

Thursday 7 September

Scarborough: The White Horse
  Yorkshire Ashes (Yorkshire v The
  Yorkshiremen) (1 day)

Friday 8 September

Britannic Assurance Championship (4 days)
*Derby: Derbys v Notts
*Bristol: Gloucs v Somerset
*Southampton: Hants v Glam
*Leicester: leics v Essex
*Lord's: Middx v Sussex
*The Oval: Surrey v Kent
*Edgbaston: Warwicks v Northants
*Scarborough: Yorks v Lancs
  Other Match
*Old Trafford: England Young
  Cricketers v New Zealand Young
  Cricketers (Third Youth Test
  Match) (4 days)

Wednesday 13 September

Britannic Assurance Championship (4 days)
Pontypridd: Glam v Worcs
Bristol: Gloucs v Hants
Canterbury: Kent v Middx
Old Trafford: Lancs v Derbys
Trent Bridge: Notts v Leics
Taunton: Somerset v Warwicks
The Oval: Surrey v Sussex

Sunday 17 September

Refuge Assurance Cup
Edgbaston: Final

COUNTY BENEFITS AWARDED FOR 1989

Derbyshire	Club Funds
Essex	J.K.Lever (Testimonial)
Glamorgan	R.C.Ontong
Gloucestershire	P.Bainbridge
Hampshire	M.N.S.Taylor (Testimonial)
Kent	C.S.Cowdrey
Lancashire	Old Trafford Pavilion Fund
Leicestershire	L.B.Taylor
Middlesex	R.O.Butcher
Northamptonshire	R.G.Williams
Nottinghamshire	J.D.Birch
Somerset	D.Breakwell/T.Gard
Surrey	G.S.Clinton
Sussex	Club – 150th Anniversary Fund
Warwickshire	none
Worcestershire	A.P.Pridgeon
Yorkshire	J.D.Love

YOUNG CRICKETER OF THE YEAR

Every September since 1950 the Cricket Writer's Club has selected their best young cricketer of the season. In 1986 their ballot resulted in a dead heat for the first time. Only five of their selections have ended their first-class careers without a Test cap.

1950	R.Tattersall	1970	C.M.Old
1951	P.B.H.May	1971	J.Whitehouse
1952	F.S.Trueman	1972	D.R.Owen-Thomas
1953	M.C.Cowdrey	1973	M.Hendrick
1954	P.J.Loader	1974	P.H.Edmonds
1955	K.F.Barrington	1975	A.Kennedy
1956	B.Taylor	1976	G.Miller
1957	M.J.Stewart	1977	I.T.Botham
1958	A.C.D.Ingleby-Mackenzie	1978	D.I.Gower
1959	G.Pullar	1979	P.W.G.Parker
1960	D.A.Allen	1980	G.R.Dilley
1961	P.H.Parfitt	1981	M.W.Gatting
1962	P.J.Sharpe	1982	N.G.Cowans
1963	G.Boycott	1983	N.A.Foster
1964	J.M.Brearley	1984	R.J.Bailey
1965	A.P.E.Knott	1985	D.V.Lawrence
1966	D.L.Underwood	1986	A.A.Metcalfe / J.J.Whitaker
1967	A.W.Greig	1987	R.J.Blakey
1968	R.M.H.Cottam	1988	M.P.Maynard
1969	A.Ward		

MINOR COUNTIES FIXTURES, 1989

APRIL

| Tue 25 | Jesmond | BENSON & HEDGES CUP
Minor Counties v Yorkshire |

MAY

Tue 2	Taunton	Somerset v Minor Counties
Tue 9	Oxton	Minor Counties v Nottinghamshire
Thu 11	Derby	Derbyshire v Minor Counties
		KNOCKOUT, *Qualifying Round*
Sun 21	Swardeston	Norfolk v Bedfordshire
	Framlingham	Suffolk v Cambridgeshire
	Beaconsfield	Buckinghamshire v Hertfordshire
	Christ Church	Oxfordshire v Berkshire
		CHAMPIONSHIP
Sun 28	Sleaford	(E) Lincolnshire v Hertfordshire
	Jesmond	(E) Northumberland v Bedfordshire
	Colwyn Bay	(W) Wales MC v Oxfordshire
Mon 29	Sherborne School	(W) Dorset v Buckinghamshire
Tue 30	Netherfield (Kendal)	(E) Cumberland v Bedfordshire
	Sunderland	(E) Durham v Hertfordshire
Wed 31	Framlingham	(E) Suffolk v Cambridgeshire

JUNE

Sun 4	Stevenage or tba	**KNOCKOUT,** *First Round* Norfolk or Bedfordshire v Suffolk or Cambridgeshire
	Aylesbury or St Albans	Buckinghamshire or Hertfordshire v Oxfordshire or Berkshire
	Old Hill	Staffordshire v Cheshire
	Perkins, Shrewsbury	Shropshire v Wales MC
	Trowbridge	Wiltshire v Devon
	Sherborne School	Dorset v Cornwall
	Grimsby (Ross)	Lincolnshire v Northumberland
	Durham City	Durham v Cumberland
		CHAMPIONSHIP
Tue 6	Ammanford	(W) Wales MC v Buckinghamshire
Sun 11	Henlow	(E) Bedfordshire v Staffordshire
	Kidmore End	(W) Berkshire v Wiltshire
	Tring	(E) Hertfordshire v Cumberland
	Jesmond	(E) Northumberland v Norfolk
Mon 12	Stalybridge	(W) Cheshire v Cornwall
Tue 13	Stockton on Tees	(E) Durham v Norfolk
	Bourne	(E) Lincolnshire v Cumberland
	Trowbridge	(W) Wiltshire v Wales MC
Wed 14	Shifnal	(W) Shropshire v Cornwall

Sun 18		**KNOCKOUT,** *Quarter Finals*	
		CHAMPIONSHIP	
Wed 21	Wisbech	(E)	Cambridgeshire v Lincolnshire
	Neston	(W)	Cheshire v Wales MC
Sun 25	Pressed Steel Fisher	(W)	Oxfordshire v Buckinghamshire
	Truro	(W)	Cornwall v Devon
	Potter's Bar	(E)	Hertfordshire v Staffordshire
	Jesmond	(E)	Northumberland v Lincolnshire
JULY			
Sun 2		**KNOCKOUT,** *Semi Finals*	
		CHAMPIONSHIP	
Sun 2	Bishop's Stortford	*(E)	Hertfordshire v Northumberland
	Burghley Park	*(E)	Lincolnshire v Norfolk
	Beaconsfield	*(W)	Buckinghamshire v Berkshire
Mon 3	Dorchester	(W)	Dorset v Wales MC
Tue 4	Ransomes, Ipswich	(E)	Suffolk v Northumberland
Wed 5	Burton (Ind Coope)	(E)	Staffordshire v Cambridgeshire
Thu 6	Sidmouth	(W)	Devon v Dorset
Sun 9	Gateshead Fell	(E)	Durham v Northumberland
	Hitchin	(E)	Hertfordshire v Bedfordshire
	Christ Church	(W)	Oxfordshire v Berkshire
	Shrewsbury	(W)	Shropshire v Cheshire
Wed 12	Finchampstead	†(W)	Berkshire v Dorset)
Sun 16	Luton	(E)	Bedfordshire v Durham
	Falmouth	(W)	Cornwall v Buckinghamshire
	Banbury XX Club	(W)	Oxfordshire v Cheshire
	Bignall End	(E)	Staffordshire v Lincolnshire
		REPRESENTATIVE MATCH	
Mon 17	Trowbridge	Minor Counties v Australians (1 day)	
		CHAMPIONSHIP	
Mon 17	North Runcton	(E)	Norfolk v Cumberland
Tue 18	Fenner's	(E)	Cambridgeshire v Durham
	Exmouth	(W)	Devon v Buckinghamshire
	Bridgnorth	(W)	Shropshire v Wales MC
	Swindon (BR)	(W)	Wiltshire v Cheshire
Wed 19	Ipswich School	(E)	Suffolk v Cumberland
Sun 23	St Austell	(W)	Cornwall v Berkshire
	Jesmond	(E)	Northumberland v Cambridgeshire
	Morris Motors	(W)	Oxfordshire v Shropshire
Tue 25	Barrow	(E)	Cumberland v Cambridgeshire
	Bovey Tracey	(W)	Devon v Berkshire
	Leek	(E)	Staffordshire v Durham
	Chippenham	(W)	Wiltshire v Shropshire
Sun 30	Southill Park	(E)	Bedfordshire v Suffolk
	Warrington	(W)	Cheshire v Dorset
	Grimsby Town	(E)	Lincolnshire v Durham
	Lakenham	(E)	Norfolk v Hertfordshire
	Stone	(E)	Staffordshire v Northumberland

AUGUST

Tue 1	Newport	(W)	Shropshire v Dorset
Wed 2	Lakenham	(E)	Norfolk v Bedfordshire
	Mildenhall	(E)	Suffolk v Hertfordshire
	Ebbw Vale	(W)	Wales MC v Berkshire
Fri 4	Lakenham	(E)	Norfolk v Suffolk
Sun 6	Bedford Town	(E)	Bedfordshire v Lincolnshire
	Slough	(W)	Buckinghamshire v Cheshire
	Carlisle	(E)	Cumberland v Durham
	Hertford	(E)	Hertfordshire v Cambridgeshire
	Marlborough	(W)	Wiltshire v Dorset
Mon 7	Wadebridge	(W)	Cornwall v Oxfordshire
	Lakenham	(E)	Norfolk v Staffordshire
Tue 8	Reading CC	(W)	Berkshire v Cheshire
Wed 9	Torquay	(W)	Devon v Oxfordshire
	Bury St Edmunds	(E)	Suffolk v Staffordshire
Sun 13	Falkland CC	(W)	Berkshire v Shropshire
	Lincoln Lindum	(E)	Lincolnshire v Suffolk
	Jesmond	(E)	Northumberland v Cumberland
	Devizes	(W)	Wiltshire v Oxfordshire
Mon 14	Usk	(W)	Wales MC v Cornwall
Tue 15	Marlow	(W)	Buckinghamshire v Shropshire
	Hartlepool	(E)	Durham v Suffolk
Wed 16	March	(E)	Cambridgeshire v Norfolk
	Millom	(E)	Cumberland v Staffordshire
	Weymouth	(W)	Dorset v Cornwall
Sat 19	Lord's		**KNOCKOUT FINAL**
			CHAMPIONSHIP
Mon 21	Swansea	(W)	Wales MC v Devon
Tue 22	Helston	(W)	Cornwall v Wiltshire
Wed 23	Weymouth	(W)	Dorset v Oxfordshire
Thu 24	Torquay	(W)	Devon v Wiltshire
Sun 27	Amersham	(W)	Buckinghamshire v Wiltshire
Mon 28	Wellington	(W)	Shropshire v Devon
Tue 29	Fenner's	(E)	Cambridgeshire v Bedfordshire
Wed 30	Toft	(W)	Cheshire v Devon

SEPTEMBER

Sun 10	Worcester	**CHAMPIONSHIP FINAL**

* These matches could be affected by progress in the Knockout.
† This match could be affected by progress in the NatWest Trophy.

1989 SECOND XI FIXTURES

(S)   Second XI Championship (*Three days*)
(BC)   Bain Clarkson Trophy (*One day*)

APRIL

Wed 19	(S)	Old Trafford	Lancashire v Warwickshire
Wed 26	(S)	Southampton	Hampshire v Somerset
	(S)	Canterbury	Kent v Lancashire
	(S)	Trent Bridge	Nottinghamshire v Sussex
	(S)	Coventry & NWCC	Warwickshire v Worcestershire

MAY

Tues 2	(BC)	Derby	Derbyshire v Nottinghamshire
	(BC)	Old Trafford	Lancashire v Northamptonshire
	(BC)	Hove	Sussex v Surrey
Wed 3	(S)	Derby	Derbyshire v Yorkshire
	(S)	Pontardulais	Glamorgan v Somerset
	(S)	Folkestone	Kent v Worcestershire
	(S)	Old Trafford	Lancashire v Northamptonshire
	(S)	Hinckley	Leicestershire v Warwickshire
	(S)	Shireoaks (Steetley)	Nottinghamshire v Gloucestershire
	(S)	Hove	Sussex v Surrey
Mon 8	(BC)	Bristol	Gloucestershire v Worcestershire
	(BC)	Trent Bridge	Nottinghamshire v Derbyshire
Tues 9	(BC)	Bournemouth	Hampshire v Sussex
	(BC)	Uppingham	Leicestershire v Northamptonshire
	(BC)	Potters Bar	Middlesex v Kent
	(BC)	Edgbaston	Warwickshire v Somerset
	(BC)	Scarborough	Yorkshire v Nottinghamshire
Wed 10	(S)	Bristol	Gloucestershire v Derbyshire
	(S)	Bournemouth	Hampshire v Sussex
	(S)	Old Trafford	Lancashire v Surrey
	(S)	Market Harborough	Leicestershire v Northamptonshire
	(S)	Ealing	Middlesex v Kent
	(S)	Knowle & Dorridge	Warwickshire v Somerset
	(S)	Scarborough	Yorkshire v Nottinghamshire
	(S)	Abergavenny	Glamorgan v Worcestershire
Mon 15	(BC)	Edgbaston	Warwickshire v Worcestershire
	(BC)	Elland	Yorkshire v Leicestershire
Tues 16	(BC)	Orsett	Essex v Sussex
	(BC)	Southampton	Hampshire v Kent
	(BC)	Trent Bridge	Nottinghamshire v Northamptonshire
	(BC)	The Oval	Surrey v Middlesex
	(BC)	Edgbaston	Warwickshire v Gloucestershire
Wed 17	(S)	Colchester	Essex v Sussex
	(S)	Cardiff	Glamorgan v Lancashire
	(S)	Southampton	Hampshire v Kent
	(S)	The Oval	Surrey v Leicestershire
	(S)	Studley	Warwickshire v Gloucestershire
	(S)	Worcester	Worcestershire v Middlesex

Mon 22	(BC)	Northampton	Northamptonshire v Derbyshire
	(BC)	Clipstone	Nottinghamshire v Yorkshire
Tues 23	(BC)	Chesterfield	Derbyshire v Lancashire
	(BC)	Ynysygerwn	Glamorgan v Gloucestershire
	(BC)	Harrow	Middlesex v Surrey
	(BC)	Farnsfield	Nottinghamshire v Leicestershire
	(BC)	Hastings	Sussex v Kent
Wed 24	(S)	Chesterfield	Derbyshire v Lancashire
	(S)	BP Llandarcy	Glamorgan v Gloucestershire
	(S)	Harrow	Middlesex v Surrey
	(S)	Northampton	Northamptonshire v Essex
	(S)	Caythorpe	Nottinghamshire v Leicestershire
	(S)	Glastonbury	Somerset v Worcestershire
	(S)	Hastings	Sussex v Kent
Tues 30	(BC)		Essex v Hampshire
	(BC)	Maidstone	Kent v Surrey
	(BC)	Mansfield	Nottinghamshire v Lancashire
	(BC)	Sheffield (Bawtry Road)	Yorkshire v Northamptonshire
Wed 31	(S)	Ilkeston	Derbyshire v Gloucestershire
	(S)	Leigh-on-Sea	Essex v Hampshire
	(S)	Swansea	Glamorgan v Leicestershire
	(S)	Sittingbourne (Gore Court)	Kent v Surrey
	(S)	Newark (Worthington Simpson)	Nottinghamshire v Lancashire
	(S)	Eastbourne	Sussex v Worcestershire
	(S)	Leamington Spa	Warwickshire v Middlesex
	(S)	Elland	Yorkshire v Northamptonshire

JUNE

Tues 6	(BC)	Maldon	Essex v Surrey
	(BC)	Canterbury	Kent v Hampshire
	(BC)	Old Trafford	Lancashire v Leicestershire
	(BC)	Taunton	Somerset v Worcestershire
	(BC)	Hove	Sussex v Middlesex
	(BC)	Solihull (Old Edwardians)	Warwickshire v Glamorgan
Wed 7	(S)	Chesterfield	Derbyshire v Northamptonshire
	(S)	Chelmsford	Essex v Surrey
	(S)	Bristol	Gloucestershire v Somerset
	(S)	Canterbury	Kent v Hampshire
	(S)	Old Trafford	Lancashire v Leicestershire
	(S)	Worksop (Central Avenue)	Nottinghamshire v Yorkshire
	(S)	Arundel Castle	Sussex v Middlesex
	(S)	Stratford-upon-Avon	Warwickshire v Glamorgan
Mon 12	(BC)	Lydney	Gloucestershire v Glamorgan
	(BC)	Ealing	Middlesex v Essex
	(BC)	Oundle School	Northamptonshire v Nottinghamshire
Tues 13	(BC)	Bristol	Gloucestershire v Warwickshire
	(BC)	Peterborough (Baker Perkins)	Northamptonshire v Leicestershire
	(BC)	Oxted	Surrey v Essex
	(BC)	Hull	Yorkshire v Lancashire

Wed 14	(S)	Cardiff	Glamorgan v Derbyshire
	(S)	Stroud	Gloucestershire v Warwickshire
	(S)	Old Northamptonians	Northamptonshire v Leicestershire
	(S)	Yeovil (Westlands)	Somerset v Kent
	(S)	Banstead	Surrey v Essex
	(S)	Ombersley	Worcestershire v Hampshire
	(S)	Scarborough	Yorkshire v Lancashire
Mon 19	(BC)	Guildford	Surrey v Hampshire
	(BC)	Worcester	Worcestershire v Somerset
Tues 20	(BC)	Gorseinon	Glamorgan v Warwickshire
	(BC)	Southampton	Hampshire v Middlesex
	(BC)	Northampton	Northamptonshire v Lancashire
Wed 21	(S)	Swansea	Glamorgan v Warwickshire
	(S)	Bristol	Gloucestershire v Essex
	(S)	Bournemouth	Hampshire v Middlesex
	(S)	Canterbury	Kent v Yorkshire
	(S)	Leicester	Leicestershire v Nottinghamshire
	(S)	Northampton	Northamptonshire v Lancashire
	(S)	Foster's Oval	Surrey v Somerset
	(S)	Kidderminster	Worcestershire v Derbyshire
Mon 26	(BC)	Bristol	Gloucestershire v Somerset
Tues 27	(BC)	Chesterfield	Derbyshire v Yorkshire
	(BC)	Maidstone	Kent v Essex
	(BC)	Middleton	Lancashire v Nottinghamshire
	(BC)	Teddington (Lensbury Club)	Middlesex v Sussex
Wed 28	(S)	Brentwood	Essex v Kent
	(S)	Bristol	Gloucestershire v Hampshire
	(S)	Old Trafford	Lancashire v Nottinghamshire
	(S)	Uppingham	Leicestershire v Glamorgan
	(S)	Teddington (Lensbury Club)	Middlesex v Sussex
	(S)	Wolverton	Northamptonshire v Derbyshire
	(S)	The Oval	Surrey v Yorkshire
	(S)	Worcester	Worcestershire v Warwickshire

JULY

Mon 3	(BC)	Ross-on-Wye	Worcestershire v Gloucestershire
Tues 4	(BC)	Chelmsford	Essex v Middlesex
	(BC)	Old Trafford	Lancashire v Derbyshire
	(BC)	Taunton	Somerset v Warwickshire
	(BC)	The Oval	Surrey v Kent
Wed 5	(S)	Chelmsford	Essex v Middlesex
	(S)	Ammanford	Glamorgan v Hampshire
	(S)	Old Trafford	Lancashire v Derbyshire
	(S)	Worksop College	Nottinghamshire v Northamptonshire
	(S)	Taunton	Somerset v Warwickshire
	(S)	The Oval	Surrey v Kent
	(S)	Hove	Sussex v Leicestershire
	(S)	Leeds	Yorkshire v Worcestershire

Mon 10	(BC)	Derby	Derbyshire v Northamptonshire
	(BC)	Leicester	Leicestershire v Nottinghamshire
	(BC)	Weston-super-Mare	Somerset v Gloucestershire
Tues 11	(BC)	Aveley	Essex v Kent
	(BC)	Southampton	Hampshire v Surrey
	(BC)	Old Trafford	Lancashire v Yorkshire
	(BC)	Leicester	Leicestershire v Derbyshire
	(BC)	Weston-super-Mare	Somerset v Glamorgan
Wed 12	(S)	Derby	Derbyshire v Worcestershire
	(S)	Southampton	Hampshire v Surrey
	(S)	Maidstone	Kent v Essex
	(S)	Old Trafford	Lancashire v Yorkshire
	(S)	Northampton	Northamptonshire v Middlesex
	(S)	Nottingham (John Player)	Nottinghamshire v Glamorgan
	(S)	Bristol (Imperial)	Somerset v Gloucestershire
	(S)	Mitchells & Butlers	Warwickshire v Leicestershire
Mon 17	(BC)	Bournemouth	Hampshire v Essex
	(BC)	Leicester	Leicestershire v Yorkshire
	(BC)	The Oval	Surrey v Sussex
Tues 18	(BC)	Chesterfield	Derbyshire v Leicestershire
	(BC)	Canterbury	Kent v Middlesex
	(BC)	Northampton	Northamptonshire v Yorkshire
	(BC)	Horsham	Sussex v Essex
	(BC)	Worcester	Worcestershire v Glamorgan
Wed 19	(S)	Chesterfield	Derbyshire v Leicestershire
	(S)	Canterbury	Kent v Middlesex
	(S)	Wellingborough School	Northamptonshire v Nottinghamshire
	(S)	Clevedon	Somerset v Yorkshire
	(S)	Horsham	Sussex v Essex
	(S)	Nuneaton (Griff & Coton) CC	Warwickshire v Lancashire
	(S)	Flagge Meadow	Worcestershire v Surrey
Mon 24	(BC)	Chichester	Sussex v Hampshire
Tues 25	(BC)	Swansea	Glamorgan v Somerset
	(BC)	Canterbury	Kent v Sussex
	(BC)	Leicestershire	Leicestershire v Lancashire
	(BC)	South Hampstead	Middlesex v Hampshire
	(BC)	Flagge Meadow	Worcestershire v Warwickshire
	(BC)	Bradford	Yorkshire v Derbyshire
Wed 26	(S)	Heanor	Derbyshire v Nottinghamshire
	(S)	Romford	Essex v Somerset
	(S)	Bristol	Gloucestershire v Glamorgan
	(S)	Canterbury	Kent v Sussex
	(S)	Leicester	Leicestershire v Lancashire
	(S)	Harefield	Middlesex v Hampshire
	(S)	Bedford School	Northamptonshire v Worcestershire
	(S)	Bradford	Yorkshire v Warwickshire

AUGUST

Wed 2	(S)	Ilford	Essex v Nottinghamshire
	(S)	Southampton	Hampshire v Glamorgan
	(S)	Crosby (Northern CC)	Lancashire v Somerset
	(S)	Hinckley	Leicestershire v Derbyshire
	(S)	Watford (Town Ground)	Middlesex v Warwickshire
	(S)	Hastings	Sussex v Northamptonshire
	(S)	Old Hill	Worcestershire v Gloucestershire
	(S)	Todmorden	Yorkshire v Surrey
Wed 9	(S)	Ilkeston	Derbyshire v Glamorgan
	(S)	Dover	Kent v Gloucestershire
	(S)	Leicester	Leicestershire v Worcestershire
	(S)	Northampton	Northamptonshire v Yorkshire
	(S)	Newark (Worthington Simpson)	Nottinghamshire v Essex
	(S)	Taunton	Somerset v Hampshire
	(S)	The Oval	Surrey v Lancashire
	(S)	Walmley	Warwickshire v Sussex
Mon 14	(BC)	Semi-Finals	
Tues 15	(BC)	Semi-Finals	
Wed 16	(S)	Bristol	Gloucestershire v Worcestershire
	(S)	Southampton	Hampshire v Essex
	(S)	Blackpool	Lancashire v Glamorgan
	(S)	Market Harborough	Leicestershire v Sussex
	(S)	Enfield	Middlesex v Northamptonshire
	(S)	Banstead	Surrey v Nottinghamshire
	(S)	Marske-by-Sea	Yorkshire v Somerset
Wed 23	(S)	Southend (Access)	Essex v Northamptonshire
	(S)	Ebbw Vale	Glamorgan v Nottinghamshire
	(S)	Bristol	Gloucestershire v Kent
	(S)	Taunton	Somerset v Lancashire
	(S)	Uxbridge	Middlesex v Leicestershire
	(S)	Guildford	Surrey v Hampshire
	(S)	Harrogate	Yorkshire v Derbyshire
Wed 30	(S)	Southampton	Hampshire v Gloucestershire
	(S)	Old Trafford	Lancashire v Kent
	(S)	Harrow	Middlesex v Essex
	(S)	Taunton	Somerset v Glamorgan
	(S)	Oxted	Surrey v Sussex
	(S)	Edgbaston	Warwickshire v Yorkshire
	(S)	Kidderminster	Worcestershire v Northamptonshire

SEPTEMBER

Mon 4	(BC)	Final	
	(S)	Leicester	Leicestershire v Surrey
Wed 6	(S)	Southend	Essex v Lancashire
	(S)	Hove	Sussex v Hampshire
	(S)	Moseley	Warwickshire v Nottinghamshire
	(S)	Worcester	Worcestershire v Glamorgan
	(S)	York	Yorkshire v Kent
Mon 11	(S)	Shireoaks (Steetley)	Nottinghamshire v Derbyshire
Wed 13	(S)	Wimbledon	Surrey v Middlesex
	(S)	Worcester	Worcestershire v Lancashire

FUTURE TOURS

1989
India to West Indies
Pakistan to New Zealand
Australia to England

1989-90
Sri Lanka and Pakistan to Australia
India to Pakistan

1990
England to West Indies
India to New Zealand and Sri Lanka*
Australia to New Zealand
New Zealand and India to England
New Zealand to Pakistan

1990-91
England to Australia
West Indies to Sri Lanka* and India
Sri Lanka to Pakistan

1991
New Zealand to Australia*
Pakistan to India*
Sri Lanka to New Zealand*
Australia to West Indies
West Indies to England

1991-92
New Zealand and India to Australia*
England to Pakistan*
West Indies to Australia

1992
England to New Zealand*
Sri Lanka to India
Sri Lanka and Pakistan to England*

1992-93
England to India*
West Indies to Australia
India to West Indies

1993
Australia to England*

Tours not confirmed

COUNTY CAPS AWARDED IN 1988

Essex	G.Miller, T.D.Topley
Glamorgan	J.Derrick, R.J.Shastri
Hampshire	C.A.Connor
Kent	G.R.Cowdrey, R.F.Pienaar
Leicestershire	G.J.F.Ferris, L.Potter
Middlesex	A.R.C.Fraser
Nottinghamshire	C.W.Scott, F.D.Stephenson
Somerset	G.D.Rose, S.R.Waugh
Surrey	K.T.Medlycott
Warwickshire	T.A.Merrick
Yorkshire	S.D.Fletcher, P.E.Robinson

No caps were awarded by Derbyshire, Gloucestershire, Lancashire, Northamptonshire, Sussex or Worcestershire.

PLAYFAIR 1988 ERRATA

Page 28   Add R. B. Richardson (2nd inns) **not out 0**
                Amend Fall: WI 2nd 1-3

Page 29   Amend D. L. Haynes (2nd inns) **c and b** Shastri 47

A *Queen Anne Press* Book

© Queen Anne Press 1989

Cover photograph: Jack Russell (Gloucestershire)
                  by Graham Morris

First published in Great Britain in 1989 by
Queen Anne Press, Macdonald & Co (Publishers) Ltd,
66-73 Shoe Lane,
London EC4P 4AB
Maxwell Pergamon Publishing Corporation plc

British Library Cataloguing in Publication Data

Playfair cricket annual. – 1989
  1. Cricket – Serials
  I. Frindall, Bill
  796.35'8'05

ISBN 0-356-17640-1

Reproduced, printed and bound in Great Britain by
Hazell Watson & Viney Limited
Aylesbury Bucks